EFFECTIVE
GENERATIONAL
MINISTRY

EFFECTIVE GENERATIONAL MINISTRY

Biblical and Practical Insights for Transforming Church Communities

Elisabeth A. Nesbit Sbanotto
and Craig L. Blomberg

Baker Academic
a division of Baker Publishing Group
Grand Rapids, Michigan

© 2016 by Elisabeth A. Nesbit Sbanotto and Craig L. Blomberg

Published by Baker Academic
a division of Baker Publishing Group
P.O. Box 6287, Grand Rapids, MI 49516-6287
www.bakeracademic.com

Printed in the United States of America

Library of Congress Cataloging-in-Publication Data

Nesbit Sbanotto, Elisabeth A., 1981–
    Effective generational ministry : biblical and practical insights for transforming church
  communities / Elisabeth A. Nesbit Sbanotto and Craig L. Blomberg.
        pages cm
    Includes bibliographical references and index.
    ISBN 978-0-8010-4948-4 (pbk.)
    1. Church work. 2. Intergenerational relations—Religious aspects—Christianity. I. Title.
BV4470.N47 2015
253—dc23   2015027242

16 17 18 19 20 21 22   7 6 5 4 3 2 1

In keeping with biblical principles of creation stewardship, Baker Publishing Group advocates the responsible use of our natural resources. As a member of the Green Press Initiative, our company uses recycled paper when possible. The text paper of this book is composed in part of post-consumer waste.

(from Elisabeth) to Joan Burgess Wells—my teacher, my supervisor, my mentor, and my friend. You have generously shared yourself, your faith, your tears, and your joys with me, modeling well what it means to have a disproportionate influence on the generations that follow.

and

(from Craig) to Jim Beck—my friend, my encourager, my prayer companion, and my colleague. You have generously shared yourself, your faith, your commitments, and your wisdom with me, modeling well how to integrate biblical theology and psychology in scholarship and in life.

Contents

Preface

Numerous voices in the publishing world these days clamor for collaborative projects. In a world characterized by the explosion of information and access to that information, many projects require multiple authors. At least the finished products are better if more than one person contributes to them. In addition to numerous singly authored books, I (Craig) have been privileged to coauthor and coedit several other books (and a couple of journal articles) with talented and gifted friends and colleagues. Not only has this made better contributions to my field (New Testament studies) possible, but I have benefited from learning about topics and disciplines into which I might not otherwise have ventured so extensively. This book is the latest result of my coauthoring and cross-disciplinary interests.

Elisabeth Nesbit Sbanotto was my student and is now my colleague at Denver Seminary. She is a vivacious, hardworking, bright, and very gifted researcher, professor, consultant, and counselor. As the years go by, I expect her to make a considerable mark in the field of publishing as well. I have learned so much from her already in her four years on faculty with us, and I count her as a dear friend.

Generational similarities and differences have always intrigued me. I never understood the need for the "generation gap" that my peers made famous when we were young adults. I liked my parents and appreciated most of their values! The best small group and Bible study experiences I have had, hands down, have always been intergenerational in makeup. Although I am a Baby Boomer who works with primarily Baby Boomer colleagues, at least those who are full-time professors at Denver Seminary, I attend a church that was established as a city-outreach ministry to Gen-Xers fifteen years ago. Today it has at least as many Millennials as Xers. My two daughters and their clos-est friends are Millennials, and the longer I teach, the higher a percentage of my students fall into that category as well. So I have at least some sustained experience with the topics in which Elisabeth is an expert, and it behooves me to learn as much as I can to complement those experiences with the solid research foundation she brings to the table.

The 1970s and 1980s formed the peak years of the development of the homogeneous church growth movement as a philosophy. Practitioners carried on with some success through the 1990s and early 2000s. But over the last ten years or so, Millennials have been increasingly calling for more intergenera-tional activities. Given half a chance, they like their parents and their parents' peers. Meanwhile, aging Baby Boomers, not least those becoming grandpar-ents, value connections with their children, their children's peers, and with their grandchildren as well. And Xers patiently wait their turn in leadership, hoping to be given the opportunity rather than become the generation that just gets skipped over.

Too many churches and parachurch organizations know too little about the similarities and differences among the three largest generations that make up the American populace today, and they often suffer because of it. That fact more than any other forms the motive for creating this book. We would like to thank the administration and board of trustees of Denver Seminary for continuing to value and promote faculty research and writing in an era when too many Christian institutions value it too little. I am grateful for so many congenial colleagues on our faculty who support those of us who write a little more than some others. I have profoundly appreciated the help of my research assistants Emily Gill and Sara Bibb Evans during the parts of the three academic years during which this work was conceived and carried out. I am particularly beholden to my grader, Darlene Seal, who stayed with me for three years in that capacity and developed such expertise that I rarely needed to go over her work with anything more than the most cursory of spot-checking. These three young women freed up so much time for my actual writing that I can scarcely begin to thank them enough. Elisabeth would like to thank Roy Farley, Kristin Higgins, Lynn Koch, and Jim Hammons at the University of Arkansas for serving as her committee in the design, execution, and completion of her dissertation, and to all who participated in the focus groups themselves. She is grateful to dear friends Amy Anderson, Alycia Homeyer, and Joy Meekins, and to her parents, Gary and Hanna Nesbit, for their unwavering support and encouragement throughout the disserta-tion research process that provided the foundational material for this book. Finally, she is indebted to her mother, Hanna Nesbit, and her "Mormor,"

Lisa Schmidt, for teaching her to be curious about people—always striving to see the good in others and to understand both how and why others see the world the way they do.

Elisabeth and I would like to dedicate this book to two of our senior professors on the Denver Seminary faculty. Joan Burgess Wells taught counseling for eighteen years full-time and several more part-time both before and after that tenure. Jim Beck taught counseling for twenty-two years full-time and several more classes after his retirement. Joan was a special encouragement to Elisabeth as well as a mentor and friend. Jim was a special encouragement to me, as well as a cherished colleague, fellow pray-er, and good friend. It is to these two special individuals that we offer this volume.

Introduction

But those who bemoan the next generation's shortcomings grow more and more bitter, angry, disappointed and cynical. On the other hand, those who bless not only grow old with grace and joy, they have a disproportionate influence on the generation that follows.

Gordon T. Smith[1]

Little did I (Elisabeth) know, sitting in a Bible class in seminary, that nearly ten years later I would be writing a book on the topic of generational differences in ministry with one of my esteemed professors. It was in one of my Bible classes (although I don't remember which course or with which professor specifically) that the seeds for this book were planted. I had grown up in the church with godly parents who discussed theology over dinner like some families discuss local sports teams. I loved it and intentionally chose to attend Denver Seminary for my counseling degree so that I could appease my own interest in theology while still acquiring solid training in my vocational area of interest. But, sitting in that classroom, I remember having the distinct thought, *If Scripture doesn't change, and doctrine doesn't change, why do I feel as if this class helps me have a conversation with my parents but it will not help me answer the questions of my peers?* At the time, I was aware that the work of integration and application was mine to do, but simultaneously I was also keenly aware that the theological questions of my peers were vastly different from those of my parents and their friends. I left that course, and seminary as a whole, with a greater awe and appreciation for Scripture, church

1. Gordon T. Smith, *Courage and Calling* (Downers Grove, IL: InterVarsity, 1999), 71.

history, and doctrine, as well as a deep curiosity and passion for discovering what my peers and those younger than myself needed differently in order to passionately capture the power, awe, and mystery of faith in Jesus. I wanted to figure out why those born after 1981 struggled so deeply to connect with the church and saw the church as intolerant and archaic, and how pastors, ministry leaders, and mentors needed to re-envision evangelism and discipleship in order to reach them.

A few years later I found myself at a secular state university in need of a dissertation topic for my PhD in Counselor Education and Supervision. I needed something that would be relevant in the field of counseling but was also something I was passionate about. I knew that I could not do anything expressly "Christian" in the program I was a part of, and I wondered what the underlying question was beneath the pondering I had had in my Bible class. Counselors love studying and understanding multiculturalism, and after doing some foundational research I began to wonder whether it were possible to look at each generation as a separate culture. I realized that this study was not likely to answer my Bible class question directly, but I wondered whether it could possibly enlighten the backdrop of that question and provide a foundation on which to build. It did. A grounded theory qualitative study utilizing focus groups allowed me to explore whether it were possible to view Baby Boomers, Generation Xers, and Millennials as separate *cultures* based on each cohort having their own unique values, beliefs, and worldviews.[2] My study serves as the foundation upon which this book was written and, throughout this book, provides firsthand narrative from Baby Boomers, Xers, and Millennials about how their generational affiliation has shaped their values, beliefs, and worldview.[3] Any unattributed quotations throughout this book are from the interviews used to complete this study.

Fast forward a couple more years, and I delightedly found myself back at Denver Seminary, but this time in the role of a professor. A few months into the position, I was asked to give an alumni webinar titled "Millennials in Ministry," in which I described the characteristics of each generational cohort and focused on how to use mentoring to reach Millennials.[4] Specifically, I concentrated on how those of older cohorts needed to seek out those in younger ones to intentionally invest in. After that presentation, Craig came

2. The definition of culture used in this study was drawn from the American Counseling Association, *ACA Code of Ethics* (Alexandria, VA: American Counseling Association, 2005), 20.

3. Elisabeth Anne Nesbit, "Generational Affiliation as a Component of Culture: Focus Group Perspectives of Three Generational Cohorts" (PhD diss., University of Arkansas, 2010).

4. A podcast of this presentation can be found at http://www.denverseminary.edu under the alumni tab and is titled "February 2012—Engaging Millennials."

up to me and said, "I'm going to do what you said." I paused, panicked a moment inside, and said, "What did I say?" Craig proceeded to invite me into a mentoring relationship in which we eat lunch together once a month; he shares his wisdom and experiences of over thirty years in theological higher education, and I have a safe place to ask questions, share what I am learning, and bounce ideas around. It is from that relationship and Craig's initiative that I was finally able to embark on a project that let me explore the question I had raised nearly ten years before from my seminary Bible class.

Who Are We Talking About?

The three generations explored in this book span birth years from 1946 through 2001 and include Baby Boomers (1946–1964), Generation Xers (1965–1981), and Millennials (1982–2001).[5] Most generational researchers agree on the boundary lines for Baby Boomers, but some disagree on when Generation X ends and when Millennials begin. We have chosen to use the above boundary lines as they are in keeping with the bulk of the research and follow the guidelines in generational research that demarcate a generation based on duration (at least sixteen years but generally less than twenty-one years) and shared historical life events that take place during key developmental periods of life.[6] Some generational researchers have identified three separate waves within each generational cohort that generally span five to seven years each.[7] This means that someone born in 1946 may have some seemingly stark differences from someone born in 1963, even though they are both Baby Boomers. Although different waves may exist, part of what makes a generation a cohort is that older Xers (born in 1966) are likely to still have more in common with younger Xers (born in 1981) than they are with the majority of Baby Boomers.

People of the Silent Generation (1925–1945) have been foundational members in many of our churches.[8] Earning their name from their steadfastness in life, the Silents made their mark by quietly going about getting done what needed to be done.[9] We have chosen to start our journey with Baby Boomers,

5. These generational breakdowns and descriptions are unique to American society. While some European and Australian research has found similar themes, the research used in this book is limited to American participants because broadening further into Western society introduces other confounding variables.

6. Betty R. Kupperschmidt, "Multigeneration Employees: Strategies for Effective Management," *Health Care Manager* 19, no. 1 (2000): 66.

7. Ibid., 65–76.

8. Also occasionally referred to as "Builders" or the "Veteran" generation.

9. See Neil Howe and William Strauss, *Generations: The History of America's Future, 1584–2069* (Fort Mill, SC: Quill, 1991).

as the Silents are currently only approximately one-third to one-half the size of any other generation in our exploration and because there is significantly less empirical research on Silents than on any of the three other cohorts. Spanning ages seventy to ninety in 2015, many have obviously also passed away. With that being said, we want to acknowledge and give thanks for those in this generation—without them, many of our churches, institutions, and organizations would not have had the foundation upon which Boomers (and later Xers and Millennials) could build. In many ways, the social, political, and cultural growth that Boomers helped to accomplish was only made possible by the steady and solid groundwork laid by Silents.

We divide the book, therefore, into three main sections, one for each cohort—Boomers, Xers, and Millennials. Each section subdivides into three chapters. The first describes common distinctive generational traits. The second assesses those characteristics from a biblical perspective. In every instance, some of the distinctives of the cohort more or less match Christian values, while others work against them. The third chapter in each section makes suggestions for how best to minister among and with that cohort. What will attract them to Christianity and the church, bring them to Christ, help them grow and mature, and maximize their gifts and usefulness within God's kingdom? What, conversely, should be avoided because it proves counterproductive more often than not? Here we have drawn on a wide variety of recommendations of others but only after we ourselves had reflected on the strengths and weaknesses of each generation and made suggestions that do not closely duplicate what we have found elsewhere.

Who Are Your Guides on This Exploration?

Part of the fun and beauty of this book is that each of us represents a different generation and therefore brings different perspectives to the research. I (Elisabeth) am a "cusper"—born in 1981, I am on the *cusp* of the Generation X and Millennial division line. Although a cusper, I identify more as a Gen-Xer in culture as I was the oldest of three girls raised by Boomer parents. This dynamic caused me to identify as "older" and connected me to those chronologically ahead of me. In my research, as I began to learn more about each cohort, I talked with my sisters (born in 1984 and 1990) about where they saw me affiliating myself. Embodying Millennial culture themselves, they both adamantly rejected the idea that I could pass for a Millennial—a conversation I still find humorous in my memory, due to their outrage at even the consideration that I was "one of them." In true Xer form, I grew up identifying myself more as an individual than as part of a collective. I am an adapter or innovator more than an inventor, preferring to identify ways to modify an existing system rather than wanting to design something from scratch. And while I appreciate hierarchy in the workplace, I would much rather be evaluated on my skill than on the duration of time I have spent in any one position.

Craig is a Baby Boomer—born in 1955, smack in the middle of his generational cohort. He also was the older of two children. His younger brother, born in 1962, is a cusper who shares many of the features of Gen-Xers while still ultimately identifying with Baby Boomers. As a result, as Craig was growing up, he had a lot of friends and acquaintances about his age but also a number at the younger end of his cohort. But he also taught high school math for one year straight out of college, attended seminary immediately after that, and went directly on to PhD studies afterward. He got a job teaching New Testament to undergraduate students at age twenty-seven and to masters-level students at thirty-one, so during those years he regularly related mostly to Silents and older Baby Boomers. He believes that, in general, he relates equally well to people of all ages in his cohort and thus does represent them well in the characteristics this book discusses. But those very close to his age will have more shared cultural experiences from their formative years than they will with people on the cusps.

Some Caveats about Culture

In many ways cultural research is an attempt to put together an understanding of the "stereotypical" person within a particular culture or subculture. As we discuss each generation, it will be important to keep in mind that not every person born within that generation's time frame will perfectly fit the given description. Personality, socioeconomic status, religious affiliation in childhood, ages and marital status of guardians, presence or absence of siblings, and geographic location all contribute to the shaping of someone's generational identity or generational culture. Just as you would not assume that all people from New York are exactly the same or that every African American has an identical outlook on life, please do not impose such rigidity onto people based on their generational affiliation. In addition to race or ethnicity and the part of the nation or world with which you most identify, other important factors in molding you into who you are include gender, educational opportunities, chances for travel (especially cross-culturally), the presence or absence of major trauma in your life (especially in your early years), birth order, and the like.

Instead, use what you learn about each generation as a starting point for conceptualization, as a single piece in the puzzle of that which contributes to who each person is. People, including you, are far too complex to be defined by a single attribute or group membership. Let this information be informative and descriptive without being prescriptive. In other words, where the insights of this book are helpful in explaining various individuals' likes and dislikes, hopes and fears, questions, experiences, styles, convictions, and feelings and how best to interact with certain individuals, please apply these insights liberally. But where other life factors or character traits outweigh generational trends, then be astute enough not to overemphasize the principles we delineate here. Yet even then, some of the elements typically underscored in generational research will apply and be helpful in knowing how best to relate to members of those cohorts, especially those that are not your own. Churches and ministries that fail to take into account the distinctions among the generations run the serious risk of being niche congregations only— serving, at best, one generation well. But they will not understand why they cannot attract or retain others from very different cohorts, or from specific phases of those cohorts.

Furthermore, in its early stages, most cultural research is based on samples of convenience. In the big scope of research, generational research is still very young, so that much of the data is based on convenience samples—meaning whomever the researchers can find.[10] A small handful of researchers are starting to embark on larger-scale research projects that have the time (and budget) to attempt more representative and random sampling.[11] The research for this book takes its starting point from my doctoral dissertation but moves beyond it to interact with a wealth of scholarly and popular literature, both Christian and non-Christian, both religious and secular. What makes it particularly distinctive are the biblical evaluations Craig offers for the characteristics of each cohort. And, of course, the specifics of how I summarize the traits of each generation bring some necessary nuancing to the literature, while the suggestions for ministering to and with each cohort that both Craig and I have offered, as I noted above, do not closely overlap with other works available.[12]

10. Howe and Strauss, *Generations*, is considered the first major work addressing generational differences in the United States.
11. For example, David Kinnaman, *You Lost Me* (Grand Rapids: Baker Books, 2011); and Thom S. Rainer and Jess W. Rainer, *The Millennials* (Nashville: B&H, 2011).
12. The most important existing literature dealing with all three of the cohorts we discuss includes Paul Taylor, *The Next America: Boomers, Millennials, and the Looming Generational Showdown* (New York: Public Affairs, 2014); multiple works by Jean M. Twenge, esp. *Generation Me—Revised and Updated: Why Today's Young Americans Are More Confident, Assertive, Entitled—and More Miserable Than Ever Before* (New York: Atria, 2014); and Ron Zemke,

Comments on *Generational* Culture

Every generation takes for granted the good that went before it, reacts against the bad, and responds within its own historical context.[13] It is a pattern that we as individual humans embody and therefore manifest in large-scale culture as well. Think about it: when you were growing up, there were rules or approaches to parenting that your parents implemented that just "worked" for you. As such, when you became a parent (or you think about how you would want to parent someday), those are the things you just assume you too will implement. Things such as curfews, family dinners, or sports participation may be parts of growing up that you see as amiable and beneficial to your development—you take for granted the good in them. But then there are those things you look back on and think, "I will never be the parent who . . . !" From discipline, to cliché sayings, to burdensome expectations, your approach to parenthood seeks to react against or intentionally act differently from what you experienced. Finally, you take in the messages in the larger society about what is "good" parenting—are children supposed to wear helmets when they ride bikes? Are infants supposed to sleep on their backs or their stomachs? While you are taking for granted the good and reacting against the bad, you are also responding to your own historical context. As we will see, this pattern holds true for Boomers, Xers, and Millennials alike, as each generation approaches life with its own collective personality. Because of this phenomenon, we will present the generations in chronological order, allowing for you as the reader to see how the generations react and respond to those that have gone before them.

A final thing to keep in mind is that *lived* experience is very different than *learned* experience.[14] For example, the civil rights movement is an event that is significant to all American people, having drastically shaped the larger society. For many of you Baby Boomers, this was a *lived* experience; you have personal memories of what life was like before, during, and after desegregation. You

Claire Raines, and Bob Filipczak, *Generations at Work: Managing the Clash of Boomers, Gen Xers, and Gen Yers in the Workplace* (New York: American Management Association, 2013).

13. While the phrase "generational culture" is my own, it comes from observing the comments made throughout the focus group discussions for my dissertation research in which participants would often reference a cause-and-effect perspective on their values, beliefs, and life choices connected to how they interpreted those of their parents and their parents' generation. See Nesbit, "Generational Affiliation as a Component of Culture," 18, 100, 133.

14. Although not a direct parallel, this concept overlaps with the educational literature on experience-based learning. For an educational explanation of how experiencing a phenomenon changes the way it is learned and understood, see Lee Andresen, David Boud, and Ruth Cohen, "Experience-Based Learning," in *Understanding Adult Education and Training*, ed. Griff Foley, 2nd ed. (Sydney: Allen & Unwin, 2001), 225–39.

have stories of people you knew and loved who were personally impacted by these events, not to mention your own personal experiences. For everyone who comes after Baby Boomers, desegregation and the 1960s civil rights movement are something we have *learned* about. We have heard stories about what life was like before and after these events, and we may even know people who were impacted by them. But we didn't hear their stories until ten, twenty, or even thirty years after they took place. Whatever these events taught Baby Boomers and however the events shaped them, we did not learn or experience them in the same way. We couldn't have; we weren't there. Regardless of the generational cohort, we must remember that those who come after us cannot understand our history as we do, for we lived it while they learned about it. Similarly, we must also recognize that two people from different generations can live through the same event, but because of their developmental age, they will experience it differently. For example, 9/11 is a lived experience for Baby Boomers, Generation Xers, and Millennials (and was a significant enough event to mark the end of the birth years for the Millennial cohort). The impact of 9/11 on someone who was a forty-five-year-old Baby Boomer, who already had developed their worldview and sense of self, would have been significantly different than the impact it had on one who was a seven-year-old Millennial, who was unable to cognitively and emotionally differentiate between the first time the plane flew into the tower and all the replays they saw on television. Emotionally, such children would have felt as if the event were actually happening over and over again, drastically shaping their internalized sense of safety and security in the world.[15]

And We're Off!

It was my privilege and joy to write the first draft of this introduction, along with the first drafts of chapters 1, 4, 6, 7, and 9, providing a psychological and sociological snapshot of each generation and then providing the practical pastoral applications for working with Xers and Millennials. Craig wrote the first drafts of chapters 2, 3, 5, and 8, and the conclusion, offering a biblical and theological interaction with the defining features of each generation along with practical pastoral applications for working with Boomers. But we each read one another's first drafts, made numerous suggestions for improving the style, and reworked the content. These led to multiple revisions of each

15. Paramjit T. Joshi, Adair F. Parr, and Lisa A. Efron, "TV Coverage of Tragedies: What Is the Impact on Children?," *Indian Pediatrics* 45 (2008), http://www.indianpediatrics.net/aug2008 /aug-629-634.htm.

segment, and each of us has reread the entire book; therefore together we stand by everything that the book asserts. On the other hand, because those revisions have not been so extensive as to blur the identity of the primary author of each segment, we often speak in the first-person singular. The first occurrence of such a convention in each chapter will be followed in parentheses with a reminder of who the "I" refers to.

We hope this little volume is accessible and useful for a wide group of readers, including ordinary churchgoers as well as leadership and clergy. It is unique in that it is based on one piece of extended field research and analyzed via state-of-the-art psychological and sociological methods, while at the same time addressing the everyday needs of the church and of Christians. Indeed, although aimed at a Christian audience, enough of its principles are sufficiently broad and broadly applicable to be of help to people of any or no religious outlook. All this contrasts markedly with the written resources currently available, most of which fall into one of two distinct categories. Either they are written at a popular level for a widespread readership but without the empirical research to give psychological and sociological validity, or they do fine with the technical scholarship specific to a particular domain or attribute but don't make it understandable for a broad cross section of our society. We have attempted to do both in this small book.

We hope you enjoy the journey and find it both enlightening and inspiring. Each generation we look at brings to the table something of significant value and worth, something that the church body desperately needs. Each generation reflects a different part of God's heart and vision for the world and has the potential to draw us all closer in our understanding of who he is and who he has called his people to be. We encourage you to read this book through two lenses. First, read to understand yourself—the strengths and the weaknesses of your cohort. Find camaraderie with your cohort as you reminisce about childhood novelties and bond over common experiences and understandings. But second, and most important, read to appreciate others. Be open to seeing what other generations bring that you don't or can't. Choose to bless those older and younger than you with grace and joy, recognizing that we are all one body with many parts (1 Cor. 12:12).

1

Boomers at Large

Loud, proud, and in charge! From the time of their birth, Baby Boomers have had a significant hand in shaping, influencing, and contributing to the defining elements of American culture. Eager to join together to promote a cause or fight an injustice, Boomers bring an optimism, idealism, and drive to life.[1] As we will see, much of what is commonly understood as "American culture" is actually representative of *Boomer* culture, as this enormous cohort has had that significant of an influence on American society over the past five decades.

The Oldest Child

In the family system that is American culture, the Boomer generation serves as the oldest child. While we are well aware that there have been plenty of generations to come before the Boomers, something happened culturally that allowed Boomers to really take hold of American society and make it their own, almost setting a "launch" or "reset" button that catapulted the culture

---

1. Karen Hart, "Generations in the Workplace: Finding Common Ground," *MLO: Medical Laboratory Observer* 38, no. 10 (October 2006): 26.

forward. Similar to an oldest child within a family, Boomers acted like the firstborn who sets the precedent for family expectations and norms and in many ways represents the magnified values, beliefs, and worldview of their family. They often become the token or model child. Interestingly enough, the description psychologists give of an oldest child succinctly captures the defining characteristics that we see in Boomers as a group: "perfectionist, reliable, conscientious, a list maker, well organized, hard driving, a natural leader, critical, serious, scholarly, logical, doesn't like surprises, a techie."[2]

As we discussed in the introduction, not every individual Boomer will perfectly fit the characteristics of their generational cohort, but as a collective, generational descriptions consistently hold true.[3] As we continue to unfold the values, beliefs, and worldview of Boomers, watch for the valuable and unique elements that make a Boomer a Boomer, while simultaneously letting the individual Boomers in your life say, do, think, feel, and believe in ways that deviate from their cohort. Each person you meet is shaped by both shared and individual identity, bonding over the shared humanness while delighting in individual uniqueness.

Boomers' Place in the World

Born between 1946 and 1964, primarily to World War II–era parents, the Baby Boomer generation boasts a current membership of approximately 83 million members in the United States alone.[4] Formerly the largest generational cohort in American history, the Boomers have had over half a century to make a loud and indelible mark on American culture. Boomers, by and large, are proud to be Boomers and see their generational identity as an integral part of their personal identity.

Getting their name from their place in history, the Boomer generation is identified as beginning with the "boom" in birth rates that occurred immediately following World War II (1946) and ending when the number of annual live births went back down below 3.8 million in 1964.[5] Every generational

2. Kevin Leman, *The Birth Order Book: Why You Are the Way You Are*, 3rd ed. (Grand Rapids: Revell, 2009), 18.

3. Paul M. Arsenault, "Validating Generational Differences: A Legitimate Diversity and Leadership Issue," *Leadership & Organization Development Journal* 25, no. 2 (2004): 124–41; Hart, "Generations in the Workplace," 26–27; Andrea Hershatter and Molly Epstein, "Millennials and the World of Work: An Organization and Management Perspective," *Journal of Business Psychology* 25 (2010): 211–23.

4. Lindsay M. Howden and Julie A. Meyer, "Age and Sex Composition: 2010," *2010 Census Briefs*, May 2011, 2.

5. Info Please, "Live Births and Birthrates, by Year," *Information Please Database*, 2007, http://www.infoplease.com/ipa/A0005067.html.

cohort is shaped by the shared, lived experiences that happen during key developmental times in the lives of its members, and Baby Boomers are no exception. If anything, Baby Boomers provide a quintessential example of how lived, shared experiences can shape a generation. When asked what events shaped their sense of themselves and their place in the world, Boomers listed defining national and international events such as the John F. Kennedy and Martin Luther King Jr. assassinations, the moon landing, the civil rights movement, the Vietnam War, and the *Roe v. Wade* decision.[6] While younger generations also identify these same events as critical times in American history, for Boomers they are significant *lived* experiences rather than simply significant historical events.

Baby Boomers, Media, and Technology

The presence and use of technology, and the perspectives on it, are also unique factors in how each generation sees themselves and their place in the world. For Boomers, technology grew as they grew. Let's take the older Boomers for example. Starting with a radio in their home as young children, they then moved to black-and-white television, to color television, to a top-loading VCR that popped up to receive a VHS tape (complete with a corded remote control), to a front-loading VCR (and cordless remote control), to a DVD player, to a plasma or LCD television with a Blu-Ray player and DVR, and finally to an HD or even 3-D television with a touch screen. To compare a radio to a 3-D touch-screen television is to truly see the technological advances and development that have happened during the life span of the Boomers. A similar comparison could be made with telephones (operator controlled to cellular), typing instruments (from typewriters to iPads with keyboards), music-playing devices (record players to iPods), and on and on.[7] The technological world grew as Boomers grew, and in many ways it represents Boomers' drive toward growth and development. Going back to television in particular, Boomers have a lived experience of the introduction of television into everyday life that enables them to see and feel the unifying and frightening impact that television has had on their sense of self and the world, an impact unique to their cohort.

For Boomers, the introduction of television as a mainstay in the home simultaneously made the world larger and smaller. It became larger by bringing

6. Arsenault, "Validating Generational Differences," 133; Nicky Dries, Roland Pepermans, and Evelien De Kerpel, "Exploring Four Generations' Beliefs about Career: Is 'Satisfied' the New 'Successful'?," *Journal of Managerial Psychology* 23, no. 8 (2008): 910.

7. In fact, by the time this book is published, at least one of these items is likely to be out of date!

the events in New York City or Phnom Penh into the living room of rural Iowa farmers, expanding their sense of awareness and exposure to the broader world. This same act simultaneously made the world smaller, as news no longer came with a delay or simply with a narrative report; it was now relatively immediate, up close, and personal. One Boomer captured well the effects of television on the Boomer worldview by stating,

> *Everybody*, in *all* parts of the country, wherever we lived, watchin' the same TV: "Ah, this is how the people [live], this is what they wear, this is how they talk to each other." You know? I mean, the radio's one thing, but television *and* radio *and* music, and you know, all being exposed to these same things has a homogenizing effect.[8]

Another Boomer spoke of additional unifying effects in that "[media] brought the world to us. Like before, we knew nothing about the world. And now, with, you know, all this technology it's brought the world to us." But Boomers also see the growth of technology as having negative repercussions, fostering fear and distrust. With more news and information sources available to the public, less certainty remained about whom or what could be trusted. As one Boomer put it, "You could trust Walter Cronkite, [now] everything's got a spin-factor to it; you've really got to search to figure out what's really happening, who's really telling you the truth." Because this is a recurring remark by Boomers, we'll come back to the significance of Cronkite later in our discussion.

A Sense of Self in Comparison to Others

When asked to reflect on who as a cohort they see themselves to be, Baby Boomers stated that they saw themselves as "clearly the best generation" or at the least "the generation that was responsible for creating the best" (referring to the children of Boomers). It always makes me (Elisabeth) chuckle when I go to speak to different organizations about generational differences and introduce the Boomers. Almost without fail, someone in the crowd lets out a loud "Woohoo!" complete with arms raised and pointer fingers extended. There is something about being a part of this generation that stirs up a sense of pride and identity not found to the same degree in any of the other generational cohorts. More than either cohort that comes after them, Boomers communicate a sense of feeling connected with their generational identity

8. The values, beliefs, worldviews, and descriptions of Baby Boomers summarized in this chapter, as well as any otherwise undocumented quotations, can be found in Elisabeth A. Nesbit, "Generational Affiliation as a Component of Culture: Focus Group Perspectives of Three Generational Cohorts" (PhD diss., University of Arkansas, 2010), 15–32, 55–75.

and see this collective identity as something positive, powerful, and beneficial within their community.

United We Stand

A collective identity has fared well for Baby Boomers as they have engaged together in civil rights protests, education reform, and various other national-level advocacy movements throughout their lives. They have experienced the power of numbers and the change that can happen when people are united for a shared cause. The combined values of being responsible and accountable for their actions and influence in the world are key underpinnings to the Boomer identity and greatly influence their drive to collectively make change in their world. For this generation, collective activism on a large scale is not only important but foundational to their sense of self. They see themselves as system changers and system builders and deeply believe that persistence, determination, and a united voice will bring about the change they want to see in the world around them. They are the generation of sit-ins, picket signs, and marches on Washington, DC, not out of spite or a critical spirit but out of hope, optimism, and dedication to what they believe America can be.

When asked, Boomers often describe who they were based on how they differed from Generation Xers and Millennials. Specifically, they see themselves as possessing greater traits of accountability, integrity, and responsibility than younger cohorts, having more empathy and understanding for the effects of war, and being more intentional and dedicated to the work they do, whether in a vocation, volunteer position, or parenting. One Boomer captures the generation's sentiment by stating,

> I think it's very, very important that if a person says they're going to do something, they're going to do it. And when I say I'm going to do something, I'm going to do it. And I think, real close to 100 percent of the time I live that, but some of these younger generations that you're also working with I don't think they have that same, even, meaning.

Significant People and Heroes

While Boomers criticize Xers and Millennials, they also speak of feeling sadness for the younger cohorts and for the lack of strong role models available to them within the family, community, or church. In comparison, Boomers have a sense of collective heroes—those individuals within political, military, social, and religious domains that became iconic models of who they aspired to be or represented the values and causes they held dear. Specific examples of Boomer heroes include John F. Kennedy, Martin Luther King Jr., Malcolm X, Gandhi, and Mother Teresa.[9] While Boomers recognize that these leaders may at times have been painted more mythically than they were in reality, they still have a shared, lived experience in which leaders were elevated above the average person. This experience of seeing leaders as slightly more godlike than the average person has allowed leaders to be mythologized to a degree, and in so doing cast a vision for the dream or hope of what Boomers could be. This sense of idealized heroism is unknown to younger cohorts who, when speaking of the heroes or role models given to them by older generations, express a sense of shattered dreams as every role model or hero given to them has been "deconstructed" rather than idealized.

One of the most fascinating pieces of Boomers' shared identity to come out of my research was the shared understanding of who Walter Cronkite was and, more specifically, what he represents to Boomers. Whether talking about heroes, the role of media and technology, or the influences on worldview, Boomers time and again come back to Walter Cronkite. Sure, many will also admit that it was not Cronkite *personally*, but more what he represented in a broader sense that is significant to their sense of identity and place in the world. Nevertheless, Cronkite was a regular point of reference. For Boomers, the day Cronkite went off the air in 1981 was the end of an era, the end of feeling as if you could trust there to be a speaker or definer of truth within the culture. Xers also reference Cronkite's role in providing a foundation for trust and truth, but, except for some older Xers, this reference was less a lived experience and more a historical understanding. Cronkite began his career in the 1930s and anchored the CBS Evening News from 1962 to 1981, eventually becoming identified as "the most trusted man in America."[10] Throughout his time on television, Cronkite delivered the news for nearly every key event throughout Boomers' childhoods and young adulthoods, including the assassinations of Kennedy and King, the Vietnam War, the moon landing, Watergate, and the Iranian hostage crisis. No public figure or concept provides such a unifying identity for Xers and Millennials; both younger cohorts speak of never having known where or whom to turn to for truth, representing again the power of shared, lived experience.

Baby Boomer Values

More than any other cohort, Baby Boomers explain their behavior and pursuits in life as being rooted in core cohort-shared principles or values. These

9. Arsenault, "Validating Generational Differences," 133.
10. Richard Galant, "The Most Trusted Man in America," CNN.com, June 5, 2012, http://www.cnn.com/2012/06/05/opinion/brinkley-walter-cronkite.

principles influence relationships, domains, and seasons of life, truly permeating Boomers' sense of self and their understanding of how the world should work. As with every other generation, core values are both defined and reinforced by lived experiences. For Boomers, their core values and life-guiding principles came out of their experiences of growing up when the American economy was on the rise, there were more jobs than there were people to fill them, and personal and professional growth seemed unhindered by anything other than one's own self-imposed limitations.[11]

Work Ethic and Personal Responsibility

In light of such a developmental environment, it is no wonder that Boomers regularly function from the value and belief that "with enough hard work, people can accomplish anything they want to," and "if you work hard, you get ahead." This perspective represents the Boomers' hope and optimism, rooted in their shared, lived experience that it is possible to start at the bottom of a company, organization, or social status and work your way up. For a Boomer, a work ethic is defined by the ability to undertake this journey to the top, steadfastly pursuing a goal or dream without being significantly deterred. It includes a sense of loyalty and determination, a willingness to go above and beyond the stated requirements, job description, and baseline expectations.[12]

Connected to the value of a work ethic is a sense of personal responsibility and self-sufficiency. These characteristics color every sphere of life for Boomers, whether in work, play, or relationships. Like the oldest child in a family, Boomers go through life carrying the weight of believing they are singlehandedly responsible for the welfare and success of themselves, their family, and whatever work they are involved in. This, on the one hand, has created a generation of people who are driven, responsible, accomplished, and trustworthy.[13] On the other hand, it also has created a generation that struggles to retire or hand off responsibilities to others who may be more qualified, better suited, or simply less busy.[14]

11. Arsenault, "Validating Generational Differences," 129; Valerie I. Sessa, Robert I. Kabacoff, Jennifer Deal, and Heather Brown, "Generational Differences in Leader Values and Leadership Behavior," *Psychologist-Manager Journal* 10, no. 1 (2007): 50.

12. James B. Davis, Suzanne D. Pawlowski, and Andrea Houston, "Work Commitments of Baby Boomers and Gen-Xers in the IT Profession: Generational Differences or Myth?," *Journal of Computer Information Systems* 46, no. 3 (Spring 2006): 44.

13. Ibid.

14. Jim Hater and Sangeeta Agrawal, "Many Baby Boomers Reluctant to Retire: Engaged, Financially Struggling Boomers More Likely to Work Longer," *Gallup Economy*, January 20,

Equality

Three values that are interwoven for Baby Boomers are those of a passion for equality, a hatred of injustice, and a belief in hope and change. Growing up in the middle of the civil rights movement, this cohort is particularly sensitive to issues of racial and gender equality. While each generation that comes after the Boomers likewise values equality, the Boomers' shared, lived experience with the pursuit of this value is strikingly different than anything experienced by Xers and Millennials as cohorts. For Boomers, racial segregation and inequality were real and lived experiences and happened on scales unseen by future cohorts. One Caucasian Boomer shared her experience of growing up in Mississippi in the 1960s with the following story.

> There was a lady named Katie Lee, who was a black lady who used to babysit us. And Katie Lee had to come stay with us while mother went with dad in the, well it wasn't even an ambulance, good-gosh it was a hearse because they didn't even have ambulances! But anyway, it came time to go to bed and I said to Katie Lee, "Well, mom and dad aren't here so why don't you just sleep in their bed." [Katie Lee said,] "Oh! I can't do that!" And I said, "Why not!?" [Katie Lee replied,] "I can't sleep in white folks' bed." And I said, "Where are you gonna sleep?" And she said, "I'm sleepin' on the living room floor." I said, "Then so am I!" And our little sister said, "Well then so am I!" and he [the brother] said, "Well I am too!" And we all just slept on the floor because it was like, you know I wasn't about to go crawl into bed and have Katie Lee who we loved and respected so much, sleep on the floor in our house!

A deep desire to be heard and to give voice to others who feel unheard characterizes a core value of Boomers. Tied into their sense of responsibility, Boomers see it as a personal responsibility, even an obligation, to confront injustice and promote equality, particularly as it pertains to issues of racial discrimination. Their belief in hope and change fuels their drive for activism. One Boomer captured this sentiment well by stating, "And you have to be optimistic to think that the change will have effect, and yet you have to be cautious, and somewhat an alarmist to get someone to get their butts in gear and do something." Instant change is not something Boomers expect; rather they are dedicated to causes and strive toward hope and change.

2014, http://www.gallup.com/poll/166952/baby-boomers-reluctant-retire.aspx. Many of the Baby Boomers I have spoken with talk about this perception, particularly for those who have embedded their identity in their work. They do not trust that those who come after them are capable of doing what they have done or are as invested in the job as they have been.

Materialism

A generational cohort cannot exist without being influenced by the broader culture in which it lives, and Boomers are no different. As Americans, placing a value on materialism permeates nearly every facet of who we are. Sure, people may embrace this value to greater or lesser degrees, but it is part of the collective American identity nonetheless. As we will see, each cohort pursues and expresses this broader value in different ways. For Baby Boomers, materialism comes in an appreciation for big toys (i.e., cars, boats, lake cabins, etc.) and in accumulating wealth.[15] Boomers make a stark distinction between what was their parents' money and what is their money, seeing financial freedom and accumulation as a sign of their ability to live out other values, such as their work ethic and self-sufficiency.

Ironically, many Boomers have coupled valuing financial success with their valuing of responsibility and have applied it to how they parent, often seeing it as their *responsibility* to take care of their children financially well into early adulthood. When asked, many Boomers explain this phenomenon by stating their desire to see their children have a better starting point in life than they had themselves, and they see their ability to provide financially as offering their children a leg up from where they started as young adults. Depending on one's perspective, this is where many Boomers take for granted the good of their upbringing (self-sufficiency producing drive and personal ownership), react against the bad (feeling alone and unable to rely on family for support), and respond within their own historical context (economic and social growth). We will see the impact of this decision by Boomers particularly when we explore the Millennial generation's characteristics.

As we look more deeply into the different spheres of life for Boomers, we will see many of these principles or values being lived out, whether in community, work, home, or the church. Behavior is purposeful; people do what they do for a reason, and that reason is often a drive to express both core values and the core value of a group or individual.

Boomers: Up Close and Personal

So far we have taken more of a big-picture view of the Baby Boomers, exploring the broad and overarching traits and values that characterize this influential generation. Now it's time to focus in and really explore who they

15. Ron Zemke, Claire Raines, and Bob Filipczak, *Generations at Work: Managing the Clash of Boomers, Gen Xers, and Gen Yers in the Workplace* (New York: American Management Association, 2013), 71.

are in more intimate and personal spaces. In particular, who are Boomers within their social communities, workplaces, homes, and churches? How do their core values and principled living influence their presence, involvement, and engagement within these everyday contexts?

Baby Boomers in Community

When asked to explain their worldview, Baby Boomers had an interesting response, one unique from any other cohort I studied—they made distinctions between their view of the world as children and adolescents, and their view of the world now as adults. For Boomers, their sense of community and their place in the world has changed drastically over their life span, whereas Xers and Millennials have maintained a rather consistent worldview perspective. As Boomers grew, "the world got smaller, and life got bigger," which then changed their ability to trust and feel safe in the world.[16]

CITIZENSHIP, PATRIOTISM, AND NATIONALISM

In the largest sense, Boomers feel like they are "citizen[s] of the world," and as such are responsible and accountable for their contribution to this expansive, worldwide community. While this sense of being citizens of the world is acknowledged by Boomers, we will see other cohorts who actively engage this citizenship in more direct and interpersonal ways. For Boomers, an awareness of global connectedness is something they intellectually understand to a greater degree than their parents but not nearly to the degree of Xers, or especially Millennials. Boomers instead focus their sense of interpersonal connectedness and community on a more national to local level, and explain community as "my neighbors, the people right around me." Connecting to values of responsibility, accountability, and self-sufficiency, Boomers understand that "if it's not for you to volunteer in your community, you won't have a community."

A unique part of Boomers' sense of community came in their discussions of patriotism and nationalism. This discussion consistently happened within Boomer focus groups and never once occurred among the younger generations.[17] Despite their deep distrust of government, Boomers express great

16. Any unattributed quotations throughout this book are from the interviews used to complete this study.

17. Using a semistructured interview format, each focus group was permitted the opportunity to address topics significant to their specific group. In the Baby Boomer focus groups, topics of patriotism and nationalism organically emerged from the group discussion but were not mentioned by Generation Xers or Millennials during their focus groups.

patriotism and a sense of pride in and appreciation for military men and women. One Boomer captured the generation's sentiment by saying, "So it was, to me, there was never a question about the importance of the military, the value placed on our veterans. There was just never any question about that; it's just the way we lived. And I think we had such pride in our country and what we stood for."

While Boomers see the lack of support for veterans following the Vietnam War as deeply unpatriotic, they see their protests over the Vietnam War itself as acts of sincere patriotism. One Boomer clarified this by stating, "I believe that it is patriotic to try to tell your country when they're doing something you believe is wrong." Connecting to their values of responsibility and activism, Boomers feel a sense of responsibility and ownership in the shaping of American culture and government. This sense of patriotism that moves Boomers to speak up, protest, and challenge government decisions is undergirded by their values of hope and change. They believe that "we can be victorious over anything we want to, any challenges in this country." One Boomer explained the role these overlapping values have in her life by stating, "I've laughed in the last dozen years; who thought back in 1965 you'd still be on a protest march in Washington, DC? An anti-war march! But, you know, I'm still doin' it, and probably always will. I can't envision my life without having that as a part of it: to be active, to participate in things."

Boomers' sincere love for the United States of America and hope for what it could be also motivates their activism and involvement in government concerns. As one Boomer summarized, "We were very proud of our country, we [have] a good sense of our nationalism, and helping society is very dear to us."

Now let us clarify. Boomers' patriotism and love of the United States do not translate into a love, respect, or appreciation for American *government*. From the early days of this generation's existence, part of their seemingly innate nature was a lived tension between respect for authority and a simultaneous deep distrust of authority. Particularly as it pertains to a distrust of government, Boomers repeatedly go back to the Vietnam War as an example of their anger and distrust with statements such as, "I think what the Vietnam War did, it created a suspicion of the government and the decision that they were making, that maybe they really weren't in our best interest." Much of Boomers' distrust and resentment toward governmental authority comes out of feeling betrayed by government decisions and reflects more a sentiment of having *lost* trust in the government than never having had trust. This feeling again reflects Boomers' view of "then versus now" in how they see the world.

EXPECTATIONS OF AUTHORITY

Ironically to anyone in a younger cohort, Boomers' distrust of government often gets coupled with a belief that America is a Christian nation and that the government should reflect Christian values.[18] Interestingly, there appears to be little consensus as to what kind of "Christian" Boomers are hoping for but simply that government decisions should be made in such a way as to provide the greatest benefit to the Christian segment of the population. From an outsider's perspective, it can often appear as if Boomers believe that we, as Americans, have replaced Israel as God's chosen people and that our government should reflect such a redesignation.[19] Similar to every generation that holds seemingly contradictory values, Boomers' distrust of government seems to come out of their disappointment that our government is not reflecting the Christian values that it "should."

Beyond government authority, Boomers have lost trust in pretty much all authority at various points throughout their development—at least all authority that isn't theirs or that they didn't have a hand in creating! As we will see within the discussions of Boomers at home and in the church, a sense of who is trustworthy and dependable drastically shifted between "then" and "now" in Boomer development. One Boomer described her loss of trust in authority:

Yeah, I distinctly recall the day it kind of dawned on me that there, like, really wasn't anybody in charge. You thought when you were a little kid: somebody was watching this whole deal and they had it figured out. And then you finally realize, you see, like, well God, dad ran out of gas; that's not real bright. And then you see something else, and then you, you know, you hear a rumor about the preacher doing something ugly, and you know what I mean? The more exposure you have to being able to understand what happens with the president and the world leaders and stuff like that, you just like, "Aaahh! There's just nothing going on that's very good."

18. The founding of the Moral Majority by Jerry Falwell in 1979 is seen by many as the movement that brought significant attention to the issue of religion in politics (see "People and Ideas: Jerry Falwell," *God in America*, PBS.org, October 11, 2010, http://www.pbs.org /godinamerica/people/jerry-falwell.html). Daniel K. Williams, *God's Own Party: The Making of the Christian Right* (New York: Oxford University Press, 2010), provides a history of the development of the Christian right in American society.

19. Southern Baptist blogger Laura Coulter addresses this observation and challenges it with a Millennial's view of America as Babylon in "Living in Babylon: How Millennials View the Church and Culture," *Laura Coulter Writes* (blog), July 22, 2014, http://www.lauracoulter writes.com/babylon/. Conrad Cherry, in his book *God's New Israel: Religious Interpretations of American Destiny* (Chapel Hill: University of North Carolina Press, 1998), compiles thirty-one different historical readings that speak to the belief that America has a unique and prized position as God's chosen land.

Now, there is an exception for Boomers' distrust of authority, and this exception is evoked when *they* are the ones in power. Of the three generations we are looking at, Boomers value hierarchy and clear leadership structures more than the younger two cohorts.[20] Additionally, they expect that the respect as well as the distrust that they hold toward authority is also being extended toward them. What many Boomers have trouble understanding is that neither of the younger generations hold the same level of respect for authority that Boomers do, and that Xers and Millennials feel distrust for vastly different reasons.

Baby Boomers at Work

With Baby Boomers' entrance into the workforce, the concept of "workaholism" was also introduced to American society.[21] Today Boomers work an average of fifty-five hours per week.[22] Prior to their arrival, working long days and rarely taking vacation was done for survival, not because identity and sense of self were inextricably linked to career. More than any other generational cohort, Boomers see their identity as being deeply connected with their profession.[23] For example, let's say you go to a neighborhood block party and start making small talk with Joe from down the street. You say to your new acquaintance, "So, Joe, tell me about yourself." If Joe is a Baby Boomer, he will, in all likelihood, answer this question by first telling you what his profession is and will also include the name of the company or organization he works for. He may also include his title and how long he has worked for that particular company or in that particular field. This is a vastly different answer from what you would hear from Joe the Gen-Xer or Joe the Millennial, which we will see in future chapters. For Joe the Baby Boomer, a primary piece of his identity is connected to his work.

20. Dogan Gursoy, Thomas A. Maier, and Christina G. Chi, "Generational Differences: An Examination of Work Values and Generational Gaps in the Hospitality Workforce," *International Journal of Hospitality Management* 27 (2008): 451.

21. Zemke, Raines, and Filipczak, *Generations at Work*, 84.

22. Terri Manning, Bobbie Everett, and Cheryl Roberts, "The Millennial Generation: The Next Generation in College Enrollment" (Charlotte, NC: Central Piedmont Community College, 2007), slide 14.

23. Sue Fleschner, "Counseling across Generations: Bridging the Baby Boomer, Generations X, and Generations Y Gap," in *Compelling Counseling Interventions: Celebrating VISTAS' Fifth Anniversary* (Alexandria, VA: American Counseling Association, 2008), 140; Betty R. Kupperschmidt, "Addressing Multigenerational Conflict: Mutual Respect and Carefronting as Strategy," *Online Journal of Issues in Nursing* 11, no. 2 (2006), http://www.nursingworld.org/MainMenuCategories/ANAMarketplace/ANAPeriodicals/OJIN/TableofContents/Volume112006/No2May06/tpc30_316075.html.

PAY YOUR DUES

Out of their respect for hierarchical structure, the belief that hard work pays off, and the value of self-sufficiency, Boomers go about work from a "pay your dues" perspective.[24] Over the decades they have worked themselves into positions of authority, management, and status and expect the same approach from younger generations. While Boomers may distrust and dislike most authority, when the authority is theirs, they often feel entitled to such positions and privileges. They believe they have "paid their dues," and now it's their turn.

Baby Boomers bring to the workplace a sense of loyalty and dedication to an organization that is truly unique.[25] Stemming from their value of collective identity, Boomers very much identify with the companies, organizations, and groups they choose to be a part of. Boomers entered the workforce when full benefits, retirement, and pensions were assumed. Dedication to a company meant the company in turn would be dedicated to the employee, rewarding thirty or forty years of service with a pension and a gold watch. While this expectation has not remained true throughout their lifetime, it was the starting expectation for many, and a lived memory exists when this expectation was a reality. For younger generations, retirement with a pension is simply a story we hear that happened once upon a time; it is not part of our lived experience. One Boomer shared her journey with the dissolution of this expectation in the following story.

> I retired from IBM, and when I started with IBM, I mean, I still got it. I can go home and find it. I signed an agreement with them and they were going to pay: here's how your pension will be calculated in thirty years, and [here] we're going to pay for your medical care for life, and all that. And as you got into it, starting in the '90s, oh, that's not true anymore, we're going to change our minds, we're not going to do that anymore; we're going to cut like one-third of your pension, we're not going to give you what we've promised you all these friggin' years, twenty-some years, we told you this is what your pension's going to be. Well that's not true anymore.

For many Boomers, their value and expectation of loyalty collide with their respect and distrust of authority as we look at their work experiences.

Boomers came into the workforce at a time when it appeared as if nothing was impossible if one had enough dedication, determination, and drive. Throughout their careers, many Boomers demonstrated the possibilities of

24. Hart, "Generations in the Workplace," 26.
25. Ibid.

such determination and drive as the growing economy created the perfect space for them to start at the bottom of an organization and work into the role of at least vice president, rising above the social class of their parents, relatively early in their adulthood. This pay-your-dues approach to work and leadership is a double-edged sword for Boomers. On the one hand it demonstrates an ability to set a long-term goal and see the steps needed to get there, to work for deferred gratification and to function well within a structured hierarchy. On the other hand this approach can leave little room for out-of-the-box thinking; it can ignore or deny a younger upstart who may truly be more skilled or gifted; and it can reward longevity over genuine ability and skill.

FINANCIAL MOTIVATION

More than the generations after them, Boomers are motivated in work by financial benefits.[26] Time and again I have anecdotally heard this confirmed in the consulting work I do. Usually, the confirmation comes in the form of a Baby Boomer supervisor or manager who is struggling to motivate younger employees and so offers them a financial bonus or some sort of financial reward. To the Boomer's surprise, the younger employee seems unimpressed (and perhaps ungrateful from a Boomer perspective) and instead proceeds to ask for more time off. To the Boomer, incentives and rewards often come in the form of cash, a year-end bonus, or even a promise of long-term *financial* payoff, such as retirement. To a Gen-Xer or Millennial, money just simply does not create the same motivation, incentive, or appeal as it does for many Boomers.[27]

FROM THE TOP DOWN

Another key characteristic of Baby Boomers in the workplace is the way they manage and like to be managed. "It's all good unless you hear otherwise" is a foundational principle of Boomer management. Feedback for most Boomers is meant for annual reviews or for when someone is not performing according to expectation. Beyond that, expressions of affirmation, appreciation, validation, or encouragement are not expected, sought, or abundantly given. Boomers approach their workspace with their values of self-sufficiency and responsibility, and their respect and appreciation for structure and hierarchy deeply influence their expectations and preferences. The generation that most prefers lists, meetings, and micromanaging, Boomers communicate with other

26. Greg Hammill, "Mixing and Managing Generations," *FDU Magazine Online* (Winter/ Spring 2005), table 2: Personal and Lifestyle Characteristics by Generation, http://www.fdu .edu/newspubs/magazine/05ws/generations.htm.
27. Ibid., table 3: Workplace Characteristics.

employees often but usually for the purpose of giving instruction, correction, or providing needed facts.[28] Additionally, Boomers expect information and communication to flow from the top down rather than from the bottom up. If power, respect, and authority are earned by paying your dues, then it is those at the top who have earned the right to be heard.[29] We will see that younger generations bring a great need for positive feedback, encouragement, and more holistic and egalitarian communication that is as much bottom-up as it is top-down.[30]

The Wrestle with Retirement

For many Boomers, their identity-informed dedication to work combined with their value of self-sufficiency has made them rather self-focused and reluctant to retire. The plans they once had for what life after sixty-five would look like have dramatically changed. Many Boomers are finding that they cannot or will not retire, either because the economy over the past decade no longer allows them to retire as planned, or because they are now helping raise grandchildren, or because they find themselves as primary caretakers for aging parents, or simply because they cannot envision who they would be without their work.[31] In the business world, this is particularly evident as I talk with Boomers in middle to upper management. Time and again I hear them express a tension between not wanting to retire for fear of who they will be or of no one else being truly able to carry on the work or legacy they have created thus far, and yet desperately wanting to cash in and reap the benefits of their decades of work and dedication. As a counselor, what I hear about most is the fear of losing identity, but as a management consultant what I hear most about is the fear of who is worthy of continuing the legacy of the Boomers.

This brings us to the flip side of Boomers' dedication to self-sufficiency: Boomers struggle to mentor and plan for the "hand-off" that must happen as one generation looks to move out and another looks to move in. Boomers, in many ways, have been so busy and so focused on their success and goals that they have not planned for what it will look like to pass the baton to future generations. Therefore, in addition to financial pressures keeping them from retiring, a lack of planning for legacy building and an overemphasis on

28. Gursoy, Maier, and Chi, "Generational Differences," 455–56.
29. Ibid., 451.
30. Ibid., 455.
31. Mary Finn Maples and Paul C. Abney, "Baby Boomers Mature and Gerontological Counseling Comes of Age," *Journal of Counseling and Development* 84 (Winter 2006): 4–5; George James, "In Person: A Survival Course for the Sandwich Generation," *New York Times*, January 17, 1990, http://www.nytimes.com/1999/01/17/nyregion/in-person-a-survival-course-for-the-sandwich-generation.html.

self-sufficiency are leaving many Boomers in an identity crisis and panic as they reach retirement age.

TRUE MENTORS, WANNA-BES, AND TALKERS

We will talk more about the value of mentorship when we discuss Millennials, but what is important to note here is that many Boomers have told me they love the idea of mentoring and fully embrace or support this notion. The problem comes when I ask Boomers who they actually mentor and what they think mentoring is. I have seen Boomers take one of three general approaches to these questions: the true mentors, the wanna-bes, and the talkers.[32] The first category is the small group of Boomers who are true mentors, taking the time to individually invest in someone younger, to pass on what they know and how they know it in a way that is personable and applicable to their mentorees. One example is the creation of this book, in which Craig (a senior faculty member) came to me (when I was a first-year faculty member) and asked what my career goals were and who I felt God was calling me to be. In that conversation he heard and saw who I was and offered support, investment, and mentorship by sharing his expertise, experience, and wisdom in a way that was personal and purposeful to who I am and who God is shaping me to be. Such an amazing gift! Another mentor of mine put words to this approach as she talked about her role as a counseling supervisor by saying,

> My job as a supervisor is to help make you a better clinician than either you or I could be on our own. I will share with you who I am and what I have learned and experienced over the years, and you will bring your own giftings, experiences, and training, and together you will leave with more than either of us have on our own. The student should surpass the teacher.[33]

True mentors such as these are able and willing to share not just what they know but also *who they are*, and they do so within the context of understanding their mentorees and who God is shaping those mentorees to be.

The second category of mentors is the wanna-bes. The wanna-bes will say that mentoring is important and will even tell you that they do mentor, but their version of mentoring leaves much to be desired. Instead of coming

32. See Jeff Myers, *Cultivate: Forming the Emerging Generation through Life-on-Life Mentoring* (Dayton, TN: Passing the Baton International, 2010), for a thorough description of good and bad mentoring, along with resources for effectively mentoring younger generations.

33. I am truly indebted to Dr. Joan Burgess Wells for her investment in my life as a clinician, as an educator, and as a person.

alongside a younger person, learning what the mentoree needs and how the mentor might facilitate that growth, the wanna-bes often come in more like a drill sergeant or lecturer. The wanna-bes may have good motives or self-seeking motives in their approach, but either way the effect is one of a top-down, "listen to me" approach. A well-intended wanna-be often shares stories, anecdotes, and "words of wisdom" out of a desire to save the mentoree from the hurts, hurdles, and struggles that the wanna-be has experienced, or to encourage the mentoree to take a similar path that the wanna-be took, assuming that the journey of the mentoree will closely mirror his or her own. A self-seeking wanna-be often shares advice, corrections, and reprimands from a position of authority, believing on some level that age, experience or position has earned him or her the right to "share" such insights with a younger coworker or employee and is therefore a mark of status, power, or superiority. It is important to note that most wanna-bes are well intended and would express a desire to mentor well, but their top-down perspective on mentorship often communicates a patronizing and disrespectful attitude toward the value of the mentoree.

The final category of mentors is the talker. Talkers are the Boomers who *say* mentoring is important and valuable but never actually do anything to personally share and invest in a younger person close to them. The talkers may have good intentions and know that mentoring is important, but they are caught up with more personal or pressing needs that leave them little time to invest in others in this way. Or perhaps their own self-doubt and insecurity keep them from believing that they truly have something to pass on to the next generation. At the same time, the talkers may have more self-seeking intentions, where their value of self-sufficiency and personal accomplishment overrides their desire, value, or ability to look outside themselves and pass on part of their legacy to someone younger. The self-seeking talkers see mentorship as something that could threaten their success or legacy rather than something that could strengthen and carry on all that they have accomplished.

In many ways, the current social norms, expectations, and standards of "work" in the United States were set by Baby Boomers. A generation that fought against "the man" and rebelled against "the system" has succeeded in creating its own system and rising to the top of the power structure. The workplace as most Americans understand it has been designed, created, and dominated by Boomers for more than forty years. As Boomers retire, it will be interesting to see whether they can effectively mentor the younger generations and hand off their legacy, or if the younger generations' values and perspectives will simply step in to fill the void as Boomers leave the workplace.

Baby Boomers at Home

Who is your family? For Baby Boomers the traditional answer of blood relatives is still the most prevailing response. For Boomers, even if they dislike their family, have been hurt by their family, or have moved halfway across the country to get away from their family, there is still an expressed loyalty to blood relatives that is unique among the three generational cohorts.[34] As we will also see in the younger generations, Boomers express a sentiment that family is both blood or marriage-based relatives and the people you "picked up" along the way. But what is unique to Boomers in this is that they start their explanation of family as being based in blood or marriage-based relationships and then move out to chosen family later in their descriptions and conversations.[35] For younger generations, this explanation is often reversed, starting with chosen family and then acknowledging what role (if any) blood or marriage-based family plays. Additionally, Boomers express a sense of responsibility to their families and talk about the sense of belonging and identity they received from their families. One stated, "You had responsibility in your family, . . . you were relied on, . . . you knew your place in the family. You didn't ever have to question that, you were part of it."

GROWING UP BOOMER

In understanding what home means to Boomers, it is important to look at the homes Boomers grew up in and the homes Boomers created. We will start with the homes they were born into. Boomers grew up at a time when the nuclear family was still the national norm, with a two-parent home where Mom stayed home and Dad was the primary breadwinner.[36] Many of them were the children of Depression-era parents and World War II veterans. In 1960, there were only 25.8 divorces for every one hundred marriages, and the average family had 2.3 children.[37] This shared experience for Boomers of what "family" looked like was the last of an era, as the family composition of Generation Xers and Millennials took on very different forms.

34. This phenomenon was repeatedly seen and expressed in the interviews I conducted with Baby Boomers. See Nesbit, "Generational Affiliation as a Component of Culture," 56–75.

35. Ibid., 65.

36. Thom S. Rainer and Jess W. Rainer, *The Millennials: Connecting to America's Largest Generation* (Nashville: B&H, 2011), 10; Manning, Everett, and Roberts, "Millennial Generation," slide 13.

37. This is approximately half the rate of divorce that younger generations grew up under. See "Marriages and Divorces, 1900–2009," *Information Please Database* (2007), http://www.infoplease.com/ipa/A0005044.html; Jennifer Cheeseman Day, "Changing Families, Changing Workforce," *PAA Webinar*, United States Census Bureau, December 13, 2011, slide 7, http://www.populationassociation.org/wp-content/uploads/Changing-Families-Changing-Workforce.pdf.

Many Boomers I interviewed described the parenting style in which they were raised as more authoritarian, detached, and having a lack of emotional connection between parent and child. One Boomer described her family environment by stating, "I knew they loved me, I guess, because they kept me fed, and watered—and sheltered and everything. But there was not much affection at all." Although many described a similar emotional detachment in their homes, the sense of family responsibility and loyalty is captured in one Boomer's statement that "there was never the doubt there that if I needed my parents that they were there. I mean, there was always that. I knew in my heart and I believed it. You know, if something happened to me, my parents were always there. They would be there. Now, kids don't have that."

For many Boomers, a sense of belonging and protection came with being a part of their family, even if it did not come with the relational warmth and attachment that Boomers then tried to bring into the families they created.

The House That Boomers Built

When Boomers became parents, they did what every other generation does: they took for granted the good, reacted against the bad, and responded within their own historical context. In homes parented by Boomers, a very different picture emerges than that which was found during Boomers' childhood. Having grown up in an era focused on personal growth and development, many Boomers chose to delay having children. In many ways they saw children as the pinnacle of their personal accomplishments and wanted to bring children into a better financial situation than that in which they themselves were raised.[38] The children of Boomers are predominantly the younger half of the Gen-Xers and the older half of the Millennials.

Over a span of two decades, the median age for a first marriage in the United States demonstrated Boomers' tendency to delay marriage in comparison to previous generations. In 1956, the median age for marriage was 20.1 for women and 22.5 for men, representative of the Silent generation, and the average family had 3.59 people.[39] In 1970 the median ages for a first marriage started to slowly rise with early Boomers—20.8 for women and 23.2 for men (making their median birth years 1950 for women and 1947 for

---

38. Neil Howe and William Strauss, *Millennials Rising: The Next Great Generation* (New York: Vintage, 2000), 77; Manning, Everett, and Roberts, "The Millennial Generation," slide 26.

39. Gary R. Lee and Krista K. Payne, "Changing Marriage Patterns Since 1970: What's Going On, and Why?," *Journal of Comparative Family Studies* 41, no. 4 (2010): 538; "U.S. Households, Families, and Married Couples, 1890–2006," *Information Please Database* (2007), http://www.infoplease.com/ipa/A0005055.html.

men), and the average family consisted of 3.58 people.[40] In 1990, the median age of first marriages in the United States had jumped for both genders by nearly three years, with women being 23.9 (early Xers, born 1966) and men being 26.1 (late Boomers, born 1964), while the average family dropped in number to 3.17 people.[41]

It was the Boomer parents who introduced their children to bike helmets and rubber playground equipment, who introduced their cars to "Baby on Board" stickers, and who introduced higher education to the concept of "helicopter parents."[42] Boomers, as parents, spoke often of intentionally and consciously pushing against the model they grew up under, wanting their children to experience a relational connection that they themselves felt they missed out on in childhood. Boomers who were raised under more strict and authoritarian parents chose to parent from the position of being their child's friend, actively avoiding saying such things as "because I'm the parent, that's why" to their children. As such, the children of Boomers were often given explanations for every rule and instruction and were also brought into the parenting process in a more collaborative way than Boomers themselves had been parented.

On the other hand, Boomer families fell apart far more often than had their families of origin. For a generation whose focus in life was more likely to be on personal growth and satisfaction, commitments to marriage and family were often seen as hindrances to their personal development, especially if it meant being "unhappy." Astonishingly, in 2010, 35 percent of all Baby Boomers had been divorced, and that number only seems to be rising.[43] For better or worse, Baby Boomers changed the face of the American family by

40. Lee and Payne, "Changing Marriage Patterns," 547; "U.S. Households," *Information Please Database*.

41. Lee and Payne, "Changing Marriage Patterns," 547; "U.S. Households," *Information Please Database*.

42. Neil Howe and William Strauss, *Millennials Go to College* (Great Falls, VA: American Association of Registrars and Admissions Officers and LifeCourse Associates, 2003), 11, define "helicopter parents" as "always hovering—ultra-protective, unwilling to let go, enlisting 'the team' (physician, lawyer, psychiatrist, professional counselors) to assert a variety of special needs and interests" on behalf of their children. It has become commonplace enough that Merriam-Webster includes the term with the following definition: "a parent who is overly involved in the life of his or her child." It is most often used to describe parents' involvement in their child's educational process, but it is becoming more and more common in workplace literature describing the parents of Millennials.

43. Richard Schlesinger, "Why Are So Many Baby Boomers Divorced?," *CBS Evening News*, December 14, 2010, http://www.cbsnews.com/news/why-are-so-many-baby-boomers-divorced/; Susan L. Brown and I-Fen Lin, "The Gray Divorce Revolution: Rising Divorce among Middle-Aged and Older Adults, 1990–2010," *Journals of Gerontology Series B: Psychological Sciences and Social Sciences* 67, no. 6 (2012): 731–41.

promoting the importance of personal growth and camaraderie in marriage while also promoting an attitude of selfishness and self-interest above all else.

Baby Boomers in Church

Within American culture, the topic of religion and/or spirituality is still relevant and of high value, even if formal affiliation is waning. Every generational cohort I interviewed wanted to discuss this topic and how their views and values surrounding it differ from the generations around them. It is interesting to note how differently each generation defines the topics of religion and spirituality and how passionate they are about how they came to that understanding. Baby Boomers are no different in this passion.

I Hate You, Don't Leave Me

In each generation there are differing opinions on important topics such as politics and religion. The Boomers find themselves split between two seemingly opposed positions pertaining to religion but united in their passion and general intentionality about the topic. On the one hand, you have the Boomers who vocally and definitively pushed against the religion of their youth and organized religion as they saw it in the broader American culture, defining for themselves a personal spirituality that was often grounded in principles of humanism and self-growth. This group of Boomers tended to live out more of the distrust of authority and organizations and placed a strong value on self-sufficiency. On the other hand, you will also find a group of Boomers who more prominently lived out the value of collective identity and strongly identified themselves with a religious tradition or even a specific denomination. For this second subset of Boomers, denominational affiliation and church membership are of more importance, something that is rarely seen and often adamantly avoided by younger generations.[44]

Respect coupled with distrust not only captures Boomers' sentiment about governmental authority but also succinctly captures their perspective on religion. For the subset of Boomers who rejected organized religion, many referenced fallen religious leaders or what they perceived to be inconsistent teachings as their reasons for distrust. For those who stayed involved or found a new way to get involved in organized religion, the value of respect for authority and pay-your-dues leadership often helps to soften, but not remove, the distrust.

More than any other cohort I talked with, Boomers spoke about having been involved with or significantly influenced by organized religion at some

---

44. Peter Menconi, *The Intergenerational Church: Understanding Congregations from WWII to WWW.com* (Littleton, CO: Mt. Sage Publishing, 2010), 84.

point in their lives. For many Boomers, more traditional forms of Christianity provided a baseline of beliefs that was used as a springboard for the exploration of other religions and forms of spirituality. Where younger cohorts spoke of having knowledge or interest in other religions, picking and choosing pieces they liked and rarely wanting to affiliate themselves with a formalized label or organized religious identity, Boomers spoke more of actively engaging and exploring different religions in their full or formalized form. While Boomers attach to organized religion more readily than younger generations, they still pick and choose more than the generations who went before them.[45] The first generation to truly embrace and express the idea that one could be spiritual without being religious, the Boomers brought religion into the public domain and started to challenge the idea that topics of religion were taboo in social settings.[46]

In their distrust of authority, Boomers pushed against the institutional religions of their childhood and sought the "freedom to make the choice to find the religion and decide for themselves." Wade Roof reports that "nearly two-thirds of all boomers reared in a religious tradition dropped out of their churches and synagogues during their teens or early twenties."[47] The Boomers I interviewed reflected this same trend, having pushed against the primarily Christian religious beliefs of their parents and going on to explore or participate in other forms of spirituality. Many I interviewed also spoke of returning to those same beliefs in mid-life, either for the sake of their children or because they discovered a new form of their previous faith, often by way of a different denomination. Even for those who spoke of returning to organized religion, there was still a sense of hurt and disappointment in the loss of trust they had once had for such authority. One Boomer reflected this hurt and confusion in speaking of her Catholic background by saying, "They started changing the rules of their religion; I think you're going to see people questioning their beliefs. . . . This church has been telling me this all along, how can they just now change their mind?"

PUTTING PIECES TOGETHER

In my conversations with Boomers, time and again they brought discussions about religion and spirituality back to morality and "traditional values," such as "kindness," "being compassionate," having "a clear sense of right and wrong," and "good manners." They talked about how they still hold to the values and principles they learned through organized religion in their childhood

45. Ibid., 83.
46. Ibid.
47. Wade Clark Roof, *A Generation of Seekers* (San Francisco: HarperSanFrancisco, 1993), 154.

but also of a struggle with where or how to apply those values. Specifically, one Boomer explained how as he aged he was becoming "convinced that the old values were right, but," he added, "I don't know how we can apply them and get to them exactly."

For many Baby Boomers, religion is still a topic and an experience that is in flux and under exploration. Boomers bring their love of personal growth and self-improvement to this domain of their life, and as a cohort are not stagnant or disengaged in this journey. Regardless of specific beliefs held, nearly every Boomer I interviewed spoke of the significance that religion and/or spirituality holds in their life, even if they were uncertain as to the specific role it plays.

Where Career and Church Collide

For many Baby Boomers, life is compartmentalized: family, work, and church all function as separate domains of life, and integration can be quite challenging. While it could be argued that hierarchies have been established since the beginning of Israel's history to distinguish "sacred" work from "secular" work, Boomers live out this dichotomy more boldly than either Xers or Millennials in today's society.[48] For a generation of people that ties their worth and identity to what they do, Boomers who hold positions in full-time ministry have their identity all the more wrapped up in their work. On the flip side, those who pursue careers in fields such as accounting or carpentry are often left to feel as if their career is somehow less holy or sacred. This falsehood, on both sides of the fence, amplifies Boomers' struggles with retirement and their sense of self-worth. It also complicates their feelings toward the church, as vocational ministry has become intricately interwoven with personal worth.

Conclusion

The oldest child, and to date the loudest voice in American culture, the Baby Boomers have shaped American culture in significant and undeniable ways. The value placed on collective identity, coupled with a drive toward self-sufficiency, has launched Boomers into positions of power and influence, both individually and as a cohort. Leaders in business, politics, the community,

---

48. Understandably, in the Old Testament, the role of priest was a set-apart profession within Israel, and yet God still saw and recognized the work of mason and craftsman as a spiritual job that was simultaneously an act of worship. See Richard Foster, *Streams of Living Water: Celebrating Great Traditions of Christian Faith* (San Francisco: HarperSanFrancisco, 2001), 249. In the New Testament, Paul also challenges this dichotomy in his metaphor of the body (1 Cor. 12:12–31) and through his own tent-making (Acts 18:3).

their families, and religious institutions, Boomers today find themselves in influential positions where they can and must choose the final legacy they will leave for future generations.

Boomers bring to the community a strong sense of collective identity and a lived history that has seen collectivism move societal mountains. A major force in the defining of American culture, Boomers now face their older years and the reality that they will not live forever. In the workplace, Boomers have created empires, mastered managerial processes, and implemented systems of efficiency and productivity. As younger cohorts have entered the workforce, Boomers are now being confronted with the ways in which their hierarchical leadership, which expects the younger generations to pay their dues, impacts those who were raised within a more egalitarian environment.

In their families, Boomers have placed great value on the role of women, have elevated companionship and happiness in marriage, and have fostered personal growth and development. Simultaneously, they have left us with scars from divorce, self-seeking pleasure, and materialism at the expense of relationships. In their churches, Boomers have had the privilege of being the primary audience for multiple decades. Now, as Boomers reach retirement and begin to pass on the torch of leadership to younger generations, what legacy will they choose to leave behind? Where will Boomers bless the younger generations? Where will they bemoan the younger generations? How will they choose to influence those who follow?

2

Boomers in Light of the Bible

I (Craig) recognize myself in Elisabeth's description of Baby Boomers. As the popular play on words puts it, "I resemble those remarks!" That may make it harder for me to be appropriately critical of unbiblical characteristics of Baby Boomers than I am regarding Generation X and Millennials. On the other hand, I might overcompensate and be harder on myself and on my peers. Readers will have to decide for themselves.

Leadership

Whether or not Boomers were uniquely born or trained to be leaders, they are now at the age in which they are indeed "in charge." Therefore, the metaphor of "firstborn" is an apt one. In the Old Testament, firstborn sons benefited from the principle of a double portion of their father's inheritance (Deut. 21:15–17).[1] But there were plenty of instances where privileges among God's people were surprisingly given to a younger son, so we dare never absolutize that principle. Isaac, not Ishmael, inherited the line of promise (Gen.

1. There are debates about the meaning of the Hebrew expression here, but all are agreed that "by law the firstborn receives a more generous portion of the inheritance in ancient Israel." Duane L. Christensen, *Deuteronomy 21:10–34:12* (Nashville: Nelson, 2002), 480.

17:19–21). So did Jacob, rather than his (ever so slightly) older twin brother, Esau (25:29–34). The most prominent son of Jacob in the Genesis narrative was his second youngest, Joseph (chaps. 37–50), while God promised that the messianic line would go through the descendants of the fourth of the twelve sons, Judah (49:10). Perhaps most famously of all, David was the last and youngest of Jesse's sons, overlooked entirely when Samuel first asked Jesse to assemble his family to see which son God would anoint to be king (1 Sam. 16:1–13). In the New Testament, the only passage that even hints at the possible continuance of the rights of primogeniture is 1 Timothy 2:13, referring to Adam being created before Eve as a reason for the woman not holding the authoritative teaching role in church.[2] Yet even with the vexed question of gender roles in church and family (see below, "Self-Identity and Values"), if the man retains any unique role, it is one of responsibility rather than privilege.[3] In short, if Boomers resemble the firstborn, it is nothing of which to be overly proud by biblical standards!

Broadening from the role of the firstborn to the role of the leader more generally, Jesus turns many expectations upside down with his emphasis on servant leadership. Most famous and important of all is Mark 10:42–45 (and parallels).

> Jesus called [the Twelve] together and said, "You know that those who are regarded as rulers of the Gentiles lord it over them, and their high officials exercise authority over them. Not so with you. Instead, whoever wants to become great among you must be your servant, and whoever wants to be first must be slave of all. For even the Son of Man did not come to be served, but to serve, and to give his life as a ransom for many."

Baby Boomers have written a lot about servant leadership but have not always practiced it as much as they have touted it.[4] Sometimes the corporate world can be particularly ruthless in its top-down management style. But, ironically, as secular businesses have increasingly recognized how counterproductive

2. I understand "teaching" and "exercising authority" in v. 12 to form a hendiadys (two parallel words where one functions adjectivally to modify the other). See Craig L. Blomberg, "Women in Ministry: A Complementarian Perspective," in *Two Views of Women in Ministry*, ed. James R. Beck, rev. ed. (Grand Rapids: Zondervan, 2005), 168–70.

3. Paul begins with what sounds like culturally traditional instructions to wives but then adds completely countercultural "expectations about the husband's authority so that his power is used entirely for his wife's benefit, even if loving her in this way should involve laying down his life for her." Frank Thielman, *Ephesians* (Grand Rapids: Baker Academic, 2010), 392.

4. Of many possible examples, see Efraín Agosto, *Servant Leadership: Jesus and Paul* (St. Louis: Chalice, 2005); Bill Hybels, *Descending into Greatness* (Grand Rapids: Zondervan, 1993); and Leith Anderson, *Leadership That Works* (Minneapolis: Bethany, 1999).

such approaches are to their own interests, churches and other Christian organizations have at times wound up being more hierarchical and heavy-handed
than their non-Christian counterparts.[5] Jesus makes as strong a contrast as
possible between the ways of the world and the ways of his followers at this
point. For him, it meant losing his life even though he had the power to save
it. His followers, of course, cannot give their lives as a substitutionary atone-
ment for the world's sins, but they may need to follow him to the cross or its
equivalent (Mark 8:34). Thus the apostle Paul learns from experience that
God's grace is sufficient for him in the midst of the severe trial of his famous
thorn in the flesh because God's "power is made perfect in weakness." So Paul
delights "in weaknesses, in insults, in hardships, in persecutions, in difficulties."
He concludes, "For when I am weak, then I am strong" (2 Cor. 12:9–10). How
many Baby Boomers in positions of leadership, even in churches or Christian
organizations, would say the same thing?

To be sure, both Jesus and Paul can have very sharp words for those who
so pervert the gospel that it becomes a message that damns rather than saves
(Matt. 23:13–14; Gal. 1:8–9). But even then, Paul gains the reputation for
being far more forceful in his letters than when he is physically present with
his congregations (2 Cor. 10:10). To the terribly immature Corinthians,
who present such a potpourri of problems, he writes out of his unique
relationship to them as their spiritual father, offering them a choice: "Shall
I come to you with a rod of discipline, or shall I come in love and with a
gentle spirit?" (1 Cor. 4:21). It is clear that he prefers that it be the gentle
spirit.[6] Or again, in 1 Thessalonians 2:7–11, Paul employs both maternal
and paternal imagery to express his deep devotion to his congregants. "Just
as a nursing mother cares for their children, so we cared for you. Because
we loved you so much, we were delighted to share with you not only the
gospel of God but our lives as well. Surely you remember, brothers and
sisters, our toil and hardship; we worked night and day in order not to be
a burden to anyone while we preached the gospel of God to you" (vv. 7–9).[7]
This is the demeanor that we Boomers must inculcate more and more in
Christian leadership today rather than anything that smacks of authoritarian or autocratic behavior.

5. Many would credit Robert K. Greenleaf, *Servant Leadership: A Journey into the Nature
of Legitimate Power and Greatness,* rev. ed. (Mahwah, NJ: Paulist Press, 2002) with launching
the movement.

6. In contrast to the prevailing view in that day about discipline. David E. Garland, *1 Corinthians* (Grand Rapids: Baker Academic, 2003), 149.

7. On Paul's surprising and positive use of this metaphor, see Beverly R. Gaventa, "Our
Mother St. Paul: Toward the Recovery of a Neglected Theme," *Princeton Seminary Bulletin*
17 (1996): esp. 33–36 and 42.

Paul then adds, "For you know that we dealt with each of you as a father deals with his own children, encouraging, comforting and urging you to live lives worthy of God, who calls you into his kingdom and glory" (1 Thess. 2:11). Paul has earned the right to speak plainly to his converts because they have seen him "up close and personal" as children see their parents, and he has been as involved in their lives as good parents are involved with their children.[8] Access to Paul is not limited to a few office hours or as part of a large crowd watching a performer at a distance.

As a final example from Paul's letters, we may consider his appeals to Philemon for Onesimus's well-being on the basis of their close relationship rather than Paul's apostolic authority (vv. 1, 8–9, 14, 17, 20).[9] It is true that the letter to the Hebrews commands believers to "have confidence in" and "submit to their [leaders'] authority" (Heb. 13:17a), but the author is talking about leaders whose lives are worth imitating (v. 7). And the motive for this deference and cooperation is not so that the leaders can be more exalted in people's eyes but "because they keep watch over you as those who must give an account" (v. 17b). The author concludes, "Do this so that their work will be a joy, not a burden, for that would be of no benefit to you" (v. 17c).

Technology and the Internet

To the extent that Boomers can remember life without the latest technology, they are in the best position to analyze how it can be used for God's glory and not abused. New inventions, especially costly ones, should not be embraced unthinkingly until it is clear their value will outweigh their cost. There is wisdom in Christians emulating what in the business world is called being a "fast second." In other words, we should rarely trumpet any new technology as the panacea to a problem without it first being carefully tested. But when it does appear that its strengths considerably outweigh its weaknesses from a Christian perspective, then we should be quick rather than reluctant to get on board. To take just one example, Boomers are clearly least well represented among the generations on Facebook (not surprisingly, since it began with university students barely over a decade ago). But given the number of people

8. For the significance of the parallelism between the maternal and paternal imagery, see Linda McKinnish Bridges, *1 & 2 Thessalonians* (Macon, GA: Smyth & Helwys, 2008), 52–54.

9. Contra the view that Paul is being manipulative here, see Andrew Wilson, "The Pragmatics of Politeness and Pauline Epistolography: A Case Study of the Letter to Philemon," *Journal for the Study of the New Testament* 48 (1992): 107–19. Carl R. Holladay (*A Critical Introduction to the New Testament* [Nashville: Abingdon, 2005], 383) calls it "a diplomatic masterpiece because of its sensitive handling of a delicate situation."

around the world who value it and appreciate learning from older, wiser individuals, the potential for its use in evangelism, discipleship, and mentoring is almost unlimited. It is no substitute for physical presence and face-to-face relationships, but it can be a powerful supplement to them.

Theologically, the key is to ascertain what uses of any technology are good, bad, or neutral. First Corinthians 8:1–11:1 and Romans 14:1–15:23 are well known in Christian circles as giving believers freedom in countless amoral areas of life and establishing principles for when restraint is wise.[10] Many activities in life are not inherently evil but can become detrimentally addictive. Believers have a responsibility not to use their freedom to entice others, even unwittingly, to sin. But those who refrain from certain activities likewise have the responsibility not to judge those who practice them. Boomers have watched the Silent Generation, including their parents, apply these principles to areas of life such as drinking, entertainment, and dress and outward appearance, sometimes in quite imbalanced ways.[11] Perhaps as a reaction against the misuse of these texts, Boomers are not as accustomed to applying these passages to new cultural developments. In the case of technology alone, there are countless possibilities. Do we avail ourselves of the latest optional medical procedures when resources are scarce, and are some tempted to feel compelled to try every new test or treatment that comes along? Must we always get the latest upgrade, the newest model, or the fastest version of the digital devices we use, when what we have is completely adequate for our needs? What examples do we set for others who can truly become addicted to technology? When we send electronic messages that are retrievable by others forever, do we think about the possible effect of our insulting rants, even in fun, on more sensitive friends (or their friends) who stumble across our posts? Of course, these issues are by no means limited to Baby Boomers. But as long as we are the generation "in charge," we should lead the way in asking and answering such questions in nuanced ways, true to Scripture but avoiding the unnecessary absolutism that many of us experienced in our past with respect to other morally neutral issues.[12]

Television gave Boomers unprecedented access to information from every corner of the globe, but the television industry still made very narrow

10. The most helpful book-length studies of these two passages remain Robert Jewett, *Christian Tolerance: Paul's Message to the Modern Church* (Philadelphia: Westminster, 1982); and Wendell L. Willis, *Idol Meat in Corinth* (Chico, CA: Scholars, 1985).

11. For a great diversity of such applications see Garry Friesen with J. Robin Maxson, *Decision-Making and the Will of God*, rev. ed. (Colorado Springs: Multnomah, 2004), 378.

12. For excellent help on a broad range of current issues, see Scott B. Rae, *Doing the Right Thing: Making Moral Choices in a World Full of Options* (Grand Rapids: Zondervan, 2013).

selections from among all the items it could have reported on and rarely ever informed the populace about the news of Christianity at home or abroad in any detail. Even *Christian* television has expended very little effort to this end, favoring mediocre preaching and supposedly entertaining talk shows instead. Now the internet magnifies the information available about events of our world exponentially. But how many people are availing themselves of the resources at their fingertips? As a Boomer, I confess that too frequently I read internet headlines without even clicking and waiting to read any of the stories they go with. When my news came primarily from a newspaper, I could instantly skim the article under a headline and decide whether I wanted to read it more carefully. I could also mentally block out all the ads on the page in ways I can never do online because these ads float past, covering up the text of what I am trying to read until I close them (and that's *after* I have blocked pop-ups!). Boomers may be the most globalized generation compared to the generations that preceded them—a good thing from the perspective of wanting to engage in properly contextualized Christian mission—but with each new technological development, they have to assess whether that objective is enhanced or diminished.[13]

Walter Cronkite—and Beyond

Boomers may not realize the degree to which they were hoodwinked in the era of Walter Cronkite. Television had the same demands then as now—to keep ratings high enough to be financially viable. Cronkite read from a teleprompter just as news reporters do now, even if it was a "lower tech" version. If he succeeded in communicating integrity and trust, it wasn't because the choice of news items was necessarily any better than those on other channels. There is no question that he exuded a certain unique level of trustworthiness, especially with his famous closing line, "And that's the way it is," followed by the date. But channel surfers among the three major networks at the time heard pretty much the same collection of stories if they listened to Chet Huntley and David Brinkley on NBC or Harry Reasoner on ABC. And each of those networks had plenty of viewers too. It is an interesting mystique of Cronkite that leads Boomers to remember him that much more and to mark *his* retirement as so significant a sign of the end of an era.

13. See esp. Neil J. Ormerod and Shane Clifton, *Globalization and the Mission of the Church* (London: T&T Clark, 2009); and Matthew Cook, Rob Haskell, Ruth Julian, and Natee Tanchanpongs, eds., *Local Theology for the Global Church: Principles for an Evangelical Approach to Contextualization* (Pasadena: William Carey, 2010).

Conversely, while there is more "wasted time" on television news reports today, with more time spent on commercials and inane banter among the broadcasters, the accuracy of the news isn't necessarily any worse than a generation ago. Indeed, with all the different networks and outlets, there may be even more accountability than in past eras. Calling an election prematurely and wrongly, for example, leads to even greater embarrassment today when a dozen other stations get it right than when there were only two other stations competing for viewers. And throughout Baby Boomers' lives, none of the main media outlets in this country have had much to say that was positive about Christian contributions to society. Evangelical churches and church leaders comparatively rarely make the news except when they are involved in some scandal. Boomers' wistfulness may simply be a part of the human propensity for suppressing the bad and remembering what they enjoyed, so that they look back fondly to the "good old days," which actually weren't always so good. Biblically, we should commemorate key ways God has worked in our lives in the past and seek his fellowship and guidance in the present, but our eyes should be firmly fixed on the future, with its ultimate hope of new heavens and a new earth (Rev. 21–22). There we will experience eternal, unbroken communion with him and with all the company of the redeemed. Grasping just how earthly (but perfected) eternity will be offers a key antidote to aging Boomers' wishing they could turn back the hands of time.[14]

At the same time, there is demonstrable deterioration in recent decades of the trustworthiness of authority figures, whether in the media, politics, education, or religion. Believers should not be surprised by this if they have a robust, biblical doctrine of human sin and an awareness of the possibilities for evil that lurk inside all of us (see esp. Rom. 3:9–20, with its barrage of Old Testament quotations to this end).[15] The Old Testament is unique among the world's sacred literature in the extent to which it acknowledges the sins and failures of God's chosen people.[16] The Gospels, especially Mark, are replete with the egregious betrayal and denial of Jesus by his closest followers (Mark 14:43–46, 66–72, and parallels). A surprisingly large percentage of the contents of the Epistles confront theological heresy and ethical immorality in churches

14. For a book on eternity, at the popular level, see Randy Alcorn, *Heaven* (Carol Stream, IL: Tyndale House, 2004). For a more theologically thoughtful work, see N. T. Wright, *Surprised by Hope* (New York: HarperOne, 2008).

15. G. C. Berkouwer, *Sin* (Grand Rapids: Eerdmans, 1971), remains unsurpassed as a comprehensive treatment of the topic from biblical and theological perspectives.

16. Dennis Prager, "Jews, Christians, Muslims, and Self-Criticism," *Jewish Journal*, October 6, 2010, http://www.jewishjournal.com/dennis_prager/article/jews_christians_muslims _and_self-criticism_20101006.

(esp. 1 Cor. 5–7; 2 Cor. 10–13; Gal. 1–4; Phil. 3; Col. 2; 1 Thess. 4–5; 2 Thess. 2; 1 Tim.; Titus; 2 Pet.; 1–3 John; and Jude). Christians of all generations need to remind each other again and again never to put their absolute trust in any mere mortal, no matter how godly he or she may seem, lest they be devastated by that person's sins or failures. Our trust must be solely in the Lord. Nor dare we blame Jesus for the horrible things people occasionally do in his name. Heroes can be inspiring and some, like Billy Graham, live their whole lives comparatively untarnished (though Graham was violently criticized in his early years for being too "ecumenical").[17] But the Bible constantly points our vision away from the human leaders of God's people to God in Christ himself.[18]

Self-Identity and Values

It is intriguing that Boomers alone seem to be particularly proud of their cohort. There is a healthy pride in one's accomplishments in life, carried out for God's glory and the advancement of his kingdom, which is biblical (Rom. 11:13; Gal. 6:4). But both Testaments stress that we should boast only in the Lord (Jer. 9:23–24; 1 Cor. 1:31). Exalting oneself, especially at the expense of others, has become endemic in our society, particularly among Boomers, whether in business and advertising, in education and grades, or in the workplace, with its performance reviews. God's people need to find ways to create oases from performance-based evaluations, since we owe all we have and do to God's grace (1 Cor. 4:7). The good works Scripture does call us to practice should be done not in hopes of receiving rewards or avoiding punishments so much as out of gratitude for God's amazing love shown to us wretched sinners and offered to us freely in Christ's atoning death, which we deserved to suffer instead.[19]

Boomers' return to valuing social justice is on the whole healthy. They have indeed put social action back into the gospel. Of course social justice was always there in Scripture, but North American fundamentalism (from the 1920s to the 1950s in particular) had unduly marginalized it because the "social gospel" (during the transitional period from the nineteenth to the twentieth centuries) frequently excluded evangelism.[20] James 1:27 links what too few

17. For an excellent biography with key lessons derived from his life, see Harold Myra and Marshall Shelley, *The Leadership Secrets of Billy Graham* (Grand Rapids: Zondervan, 2005).

18. Strikingly, even when Paul encourages people to imitate *him*, it is only to the extent that he imitates Christ (1 Cor. 11:1).

19. See further Craig L. Blomberg, "Degrees of Reward in the Kingdom of Heaven?," *Journal of the Evangelical Theological Society* 35 (1992): 159–72.

20. The manifesto, however, was drafted by the key Christian leader and thinker of the Silent Generation, Carl F. H. Henry, in *The Uneasy Conscience of Modern Fundamentalism* (Grand Rapids: Eerdmans, 1947).

throughout church history have kept together: "Religion that God our father accepts as pure and faultless is this: to look after orphans and widows in their distress and to keep oneself from being polluted by the world." Personal piety and social action jointly define true religion. Orphans and widows were those who lacked fathers or husbands to provide for them in highly patriarchal societies and so represented the most easily dispossessed and marginalized in the biblical worlds. James 2:14–17 makes it clear that those who overlook the most acute physical needs of fellow believers in close proximity to them cannot be genuine Christians, whatever their professions of faith may claim.[21] John puts it almost as bluntly in 1 John 3:17–18: "If anyone has material possessions and sees a brother or sister in need but has no pity on them, how can the love of God be in that person? Dear children, let us not love with words or speech but with actions and in truth."

Nevertheless, even if humanity could eradicate all poverty and illness in this world, it would count for nothing if people died without asking God for forgiveness for their sins, to be reconciled with their Maker from whom they are alienated and estranged, which is made possible only through the death of Jesus Christ. Jesus sums it up succinctly, "What good is it for someone to gain the whole world, yet forfeit their soul?" (Mark 8:36).[22] If one lives forever in eternity separated from God and all things good, even the greatest happiness in this life will pale compared with one's eternal sorrow.

Boomers' characteristic values of integrity and loyalty are also strengths and much to be preferred to duplicity and faithlessness, even if not all Boomers trust in Jesus. Promise keeping is a key biblical value rapidly disappearing from society at large; anyone who practices it is to be praised. James 5:12 quotes Jesus's words from the Sermon on the Mount (see also Matt. 5:34, 37): "Above all, my brothers and sisters, do not swear—not by heaven or by earth or by anything else. All you need to say is a simple 'Yes' or 'No.' Otherwise you will be condemned." Boomers have already lost earlier generations' more radical practice of this principle. My grandfather liked to recall how throughout most of his working life in the Midwest, well into the mid-1960s, a gentleman's word and handshake were as good as a contract, and he often lamented the demise of that practice. But Boomers have on the whole adhered to contractual commitments better than younger generations. Paul is concerned in 2 Corinthians 1:15–20 that the Corinthians would find him fickle because of the changes in his travel plans. He reassures them that his

21. The Greek is clearer than most English translations because it uses the negative particle *mē*, implying a negative answer to the question, "Can such faith save them?" in v. 14.

22. "Life is precious; one's eternal soul is beyond calculation." Craig A. Evans, *Mark 8:27–16:20* (Nashville: Nelson, 2001), 26.

delay was because he did not want to come back to them until he could come celebrating their renewed obedience, even though now he is once again en route to Corinth.[23] Sometimes one set of expectations must be left unmet in order to be faithful to more foundational principles. This, too, can represent integrity and loyalty.

Boomers, however, were the first generation to begin to renege in huge numbers on their wedding vows, the most solemn of all interpersonal commitments. So they may not have exhibited quite as much loyalty as they think, at least as an overall cohort. Malachi 2:16 needs to be revisited repeatedly, especially in the best translation of the Hebrew, reflected in versions like the 2011 NIV: "'The man who hates and divorces his wife,' says the LORD, the God of Israel, 'does violence to the one he should protect,' says the LORD Almighty."[24] The New Testament does *permit* divorce in the two lone instances of adultery and abandonment (Matt. 19:9; 1 Cor. 7:15–16), but it never *mandates* it, as all the surrounding Jewish, Greek, and Roman cultures did.[25] The texts are consistently phrased in terms of a man staying faithful (or not) to his wife because in the patriarchal societies of the day, women only rarely had the right to divorce. The appropriate interpretation of the text for today, especially given the consistently reciprocal language of 1 Corinthians 7, would include the censure of "the woman who hates and divorces her husband." Divorce is not an unforgivable sin, but its consequences for damaged relationships can be severe, especially among children of divorcees. Today's society and today's churches on the whole take divorce far too lightly. To put it deliberately harshly, if a person's word cannot be trusted in what they promise before God and his people "until death do us part," how can they be trusted in any lesser area of life? Of course, they can repent and be transformed and become trustworthy, but too few do, which is why second marriages dissolve at a much more rapid rate on average than first marriages.[26]

23. See also Margaret E. Thrall, *A Critical and Exegetical Commentary on the Second Epistle to the Corinthians* (Edinburgh: T&T Clark, 1994), 1:142–43.

24. Similarly, the ESV states, "For the man who does not love his wife but divorces her, says the LORD, the God of Israel, covers his garment with violence, says the LORD of hosts." The HCSB reads, "'If he hates and divorces his wife,' says the LORD God of Israel, 'he covers his garment with injustice,' says the LORD of Hosts." The 2011 NIV goes one step further, indicating the probable meaning of the metaphor on covering one's garment with violence, since a spouse was often likened to a protective garment. See, in detail, E. Ray Clendenen, "Malachi," in Richard A. Taylor and E. Ray Clendenen, *Haggai, Malachi* (Nashville: B&H, 2004), 359–70.

25. See also David Instone-Brewer, *Divorce and Remarriage in the Bible* (Grand Rapids: Eerdmans, 2002), 143–46.

26. Mark Banschick, "The High Failure Rate of Second and Third Marriages," *Psychology Today*, February 6, 2012, http://www.psychologytoday.com/blog/the-intelligent-divorce/201202/the-high-failure-rate-second-and-third-marriages.

Self-sufficiency, another Boomer value, is a desirable biblical trait when it is employed so that others do not have to be unnecessarily burdened in helping people who could have helped themselves. Thus 2 Thessalonians 3:10 recalls Paul's "rule" that "the one who is unwilling to work shall not eat."[27] In a similar spirit, Paul writes in 1 Thessalonians 4:11–12 that the Christians in Thessalonica should mind their own business and work with their own hands so that they will be respected by outsiders and dependent on no one. Christians who are known as "mooches" are seldom popular; in fact, Christians who consistently take advantage of others bring disgrace to the larger faith community. So, too, Galatians 6:5 insists that all believers should carry their own load. But three verses earlier, Paul commanded, "Carry each other's burdens, and in this way you will fulfill the law of Christ." The word for "burden" in the Greek is different from the word for "load." The "burden" (*baros*) is an excessively weighty encumbrance, whereas a "load" (*phortion*) was a normally sized backpack that a given person could have been expected to carry.[28] When life becomes oppressive, we need each other; when we have the opportunity to alleviate others' heavy burdens, it is our responsibility to do so. And not letting others know about our most serious needs, or not allowing others to help us when they learn about them, may prevent them from exercising *their* God-given spiritual gifts. The Spirit is thereby quenched (1 Thess. 5:19), and the church is not built up in the ways that it should be (Eph. 4:11–12). Boomers have a decidedly mixed track record on these issues. Boomer self-sufficiency can easily become a detriment rather than a strength.

A discussion of the Boomers' separation of spirituality from religion belongs at this juncture because it also represents a characteristic value. On the one hand, one of the great contributions of parachurch organizations (like Youth for Christ, Young Life, Campus Crusade for Christ, InterVarsity Christian Fellowship, the Navigators, and Fellowship of Christian Athletes) to the Boomers' generation was to separate coming to faith in Jesus from involvement in the institutionalized church. Countless individuals who never would have darkened the door of church buildings came to faith in private homes, on college campuses, on community sports fields, and the like. In many instances, those people were eventually encouraged to be involved in local churches as

27. On which, see esp. Robert Jewett, "Tenement Churches and Communal Meals in the Early Church: The Implications of a Form-Critical Analysis of 2 Thessalonians 3:10," *Biblical Research* 38 (1993): 23–43. Indolent Christians refusing work for pay when it was available may have been excluded from the Lord's Supper.

28. Leon Morris, *Galatians: Paul's Charter of Christian Freedom* (Grand Rapids: Eerdmans, 1996), 180n12.

well—but not always, and not always successfully. Seeker-sensitive churches managed to bring into their buildings some unbelievers who wouldn't have attended traditional services, but only some.[29]

Today, we see aging Boomers dropping out of churches that have hurt them and not necessarily seeking any further Christian fellowship.[30] What had been a strength of the movement has become a weakness. A handful of strong Christians can indeed survive on their own, but not many. The Bible does not envision God's people apart from assemblies of like-minded worshipers (Heb. 10:24–25). We were not created to go it alone. New Testament gatherings of believers were characterized by devotion to the apostles' teaching (today found in Scripture), fellowship (including the sharing of finances), the breaking of bread (at least referring to the Lord's Supper, but probably also to a complete shared meal), and prayer (Acts 2:42).[31] Of these four elements, only two—the reading of Scripture and prayer—can occur without the presence of other people, and even then those experiences are truncated. Every believer, moreover, has at least one spiritual gift (1 Cor. 12:7, 11) given for the edification of the church (Eph. 4:12). If believers remove themselves from church for any significant period of time, then by definition they are not exercising their spiritual gifts in their divinely intended way. This kind of self-sufficiency, as the defining feature of a worldview, of being able to go it alone as a rugged individualist, was central to Stoicism in the ancient Greek world.[32] But it is fundamentally contrary to Judeo-Christian values. From a biblical perspective, we are to seek a "God-sufficiency" that requires we interact with and depend on others among his people.[33]

As those who have lived through and sometimes fought the battles of the civil rights and women's liberation movements, Boomers have had decades of exposure to the concept of treating racial equality and gender equality as exactly parallel. In Scripture, however, they are not quite treated identically. Slavery in biblical times was not racially based but imposed on conquered peoples across racial lines or voluntarily entered into for a limited time as a

29. One of the most balanced and thoughtful works to come out of this movement was Sally Morgenthaler, *Worship Evangelism* (Grand Rapids: Zondervan, 1998).

30. See esp. William D. Hendricks, *Exit Interviews: Revealing Stories of Why People Are Leaving the Church* (Chicago: Moody, 1993). Hendricks wrote primarily about Boomers and often heard the claim that people were leaving religion to find spirituality. Clear definitions of that spirituality, however, are almost nonexistent.

31. See also Darrell L. Bock, *Acts* (Grand Rapids: Baker Academic, 2007), 149–51.

32. Abraham J. Malherbe, "Paul's Self-Sufficiency (Philippians 4:11)," in *Friendship, Flattery and Frankness of Speech*, ed. John T. Fitzgerald (Leiden: Brill, 1996), 125–39.

33. Ben Witherington III, *Friendship and Finances in Philippi: The Letter of Paul to the Philippians* (Valley Forge, PA: Trinity Press International, 1994), 129.

way to get out of debt.[34] How one addresses the biblical teachings on slavery, then, proves largely irrelevant to the question of racial equality today, though often that has not been recognized.[35] The relevant question is, do we see any texts treating people differently on the basis of race? The curse on Canaan, son of Ham, in Genesis 9:22–27 has nothing to do with a God-ordained inferiority of black people; this was decisively debunked a long time ago.[36] The New Testament contains no texts that could easily be twisted to support discrimination on the basis of race. What it does contain is the exact opposite—the pervasive emphasis on the equality of Jew and gentile in Christ across racial lines (see esp. Eph. 2:11–22). Some older Boomers were at the forefront of the civil rights movement of the early 1960s through the early 1970s and learned this lesson a long time ago. Others, however, at the time were part of an ideology in evangelical Christianity that viewed such causes as "liberal," and these Boomers still harbor a fair amount of racism. American churches, as has often been pointed out, are still too often bastions of segregation, especially when they do not adequately represent the racial diversity of the neighborhoods in which they are located.

The issue of gender roles is trickier. On the one hand, we can cite texts like Galatians 3:28, where racial unity is juxtaposed with the unity of slave and free and male and female in Christ.[37] On the other hand, Paul's letters contain famous texts that preclude women, at least in the first century, from exercising the ultimate, "buck stops here" roles of spiritual authority in church and home. In fact, the pattern seems to span the canon. In the Old Testament, women could hold every leadership office except the priesthood. In the Gospels, Jesus gives women remarkable countercultural affirmation and responsibility but never designates one to be among his twelve closest followers, the apostles. In Acts, women appear in an impressive array of leadership and teaching roles, especially in view of the customs of the cultures in which the fledgling church grew up, but never as elders/overseers of local churches. In the Epistles they are again permitted, and even encouraged, to use the whole range of spiritual gifts and function in all roles or offices of leadership and ministry in any church

34. David W. Pao, *Colossians and Philemon* (Grand Rapids: Zondervan, 2012), 349.

35. Thus, e.g., the misapplications, like the charges against Paul, continue sporadically throughout church life. See Matthew V. Johnson, James A. Noel, and Demetrius K. Williams, eds., *Onesimus Our Brother: Reading Religion, Race, and Culture in Philemon* (Minneapolis: Fortress, 2012).

36. For past abuses here and elsewhere, see Willard M. Swartley, *Slavery, Sabbath, War and Women: Case Issues in Biblical Interpretation* (Scottdale, PA: Herald, 1983), 31–37 and 46–50. For rebuttal, see pp. 37–46 and 50–53.

37. It often goes unnoticed that Paul's focus is more on unity than on equality. See esp. Richard Hove, *Equality in Christ? Galatians 3:28 and the Gender Dispute* (Wheaton: Crossway, 1999).

context, save that of the most senior role of authoritative teaching.[38] It is, of course, possible that situation-specific factors explain even these restrictions, but Paul's repeated appeal to creation ordinances (how God made man and woman before the fall) suggests some timeless differentiation between the genders (1 Cor. 11:8–9; Eph. 5:31; 1 Tim. 2:13).[39] Those restrictions, nevertheless, are probably far fewer than most complementarians care to acknowledge, even while still unsatisfactory to egalitarians because they leave men and women without completely interchangeable roles.

The same is true with the family. We may need to create a third label for a position that is neither classically complementarian nor egalitarian.[40] For a husband to love his wife as Christ loved the church and gave himself for her (Eph. 5:25) is a far cry from most complementarian insistence on the man leading the home; being the decision maker, in charge, and "wild at heart"; and exercising special privileges.[41] But the call for women to submit to their husbands as to the Lord (Col. 3:18; Eph. 5:22–24) distinguishes Paul from full-fledged egalitarianism as well. Philippians 2:4 reads literally, "not looking each to the things of yourselves, but each of you to the things of others." Many manuscripts add a *kai* (possibly to be translated "also") to the second of these clauses, but there is no "only" in the first clause. Yet quite a few translations cannot accept either the grammatical awkwardness of "not . . . but also" or the radical theology of "not to your own things, but to others' things," so they insert an "only" in the first clause—"not *only* to your own things, but also the things of others." A better explanation of the *kai* is that *alla kai* without *monon* ("only") in the previous clause means "but actually" or "but rather," not "but also."[42] The KJV captured the correct sense with its rendering, "Look not every man on his own things, but every man also on the things of others," though its generic use of "man" is

38. See further Blomberg, "Women in Ministry: A Complementarian Perspective," 128–72.

39. As argued esp. by Linda L. Belleville, "Women in Ministry: An Egalitarian Perspective," 19–103, and Craig S. Keener, "Women in Ministry: Another Egalitarian Perspective," 203–48, both in Beck, ed., *Two Views on Women in Ministry*.

40. Craig L. Blomberg, "Neither Hierarchicalist nor Egalitarian: Gender Roles in Paul," in *Paul and His Theology*, ed. Stanley E. Porter (Leiden: Brill, 2006), 283–326.

41. *Wild at Heart* is the title of a disturbing yet bestselling book by John Eldredge (Nashville: Nelson, 2011) that describes the fallen state of male humanity more than that which Christians should be cultivating! His wife, Stasi Eldredge, makes the same mistake for women in her book, coauthored with her husband, titled *Captivating: Unveiling the Mystery of a Woman's Soul* (Nashville: Nelson, 2010). A seminary student in her twenties (herself a complementarian) who worked in the Denver Seminary bookstore when the first edition of *Captivating* appeared in 2005 summarized her take on the work very succinctly: "A largely accurate summary of what women want *in their fallen nature*"!

42. Markus Bockmuehl, *The Epistle to the Philippians* (Peabody, MA: Hendrickson, 1998), 115–16.

not as readily recognized today. But the NKJV, NASB, RSV, ESV, HCSB, NET, and NLT all have added "only" or "merely" to the first clause, misconstruing the contrast. The updated NIV, NRSV, NAB, NJB, and CEB, however, all get it right. In short, all believers should be putting others' interests above their own, not just on an equal level, and should certainly do so in a marriage relationship. Overall, evangelical Boomers are probably still more hierarchical than the biblical ideal, even as Gen-Xers and Millennials may at times take egalitarianism for granted without examining the full teaching of Scripture.

Materialism, Consumerism, and a Work Ethic

If there is one Boomer value that deserves a section all by itself, it is materialism.[43] No other generation has successfully worked so hard to attain as high a standard of living for as large a percentage of its cohort. Prosperity, however, did not occur equally among all races, but disproportionately among the Anglo and Asian communities in contrast to the Black and Hispanic ones. Boomers likewise produced most of the megachurches of our land, which have sunk billions of dollars into facilities and staff salaries that could have gone to ministry and missions instead. To their credit, however, they have attracted people looking for "full-service churches," meeting almost every possible spiritual need of every family member under one roof. And many megachurches have been well equipped and very generous in giving to meet the spiritual and physical needs of those outside their four walls.

Statistics on Boomer giving show, on the one hand, a marked decrease from the generations preceding them with respect to the percentage of income given to the Lord's work. On the other hand, they are funding church and parachurch ministries considerably more generously than the generations coming after them. Biblical theology, as is increasingly being recognized, does not teach a tithe for New Testament–era believers.[44] Instead, it enjoins generosity, even sacrificial giving, which for most Boomers in the middle class or above may mean more than 10 percent of one's annual income. A case can be made that to apply Paul's principles in 2 Corinthians 8:13–15 about equity or fairness, a graduated tithe is needed.[45] The more one makes from year to year above

43. For further information about most of the points in this and the next paragraph, see Craig L. Blomberg, *Christians in an Age of Wealth: A Biblical Theology of Stewardship* (Grand Rapids: Zondervan, 2013).

44. See esp. David A. Croteau, *You Mean I Don't Have to Tithe? A Deconstruction of Tithing and a Reconstruction of Post-Tithe Giving* (Eugene, OR: Cascade, 2010).

45. See esp. Ronald J. Sider, *Rich Christians in an Age of Hunger: Moving from Affluence to Generosity*, 5th ed. (Nashville: Thomas Nelson, 2005), 187–90.

and beyond mere cost-of-living increases, the higher percentage one should probably give. Hopefully, Christians will join churches that themselves follow biblical priorities of generosity in giving to others, balancing needs for evangelism with those for helping the poor and other areas of mercy and social justice. If Christians cannot find any such congregations in a given community, they may need to give above and beyond their generous contributions to their churches to help support parachurch work that more directly targets those priorities.

Boomers likewise have amassed record levels of debt. Parachurch ministries helping people get out of debt are finally flourishing, and some of them are spilling over into local churches; but they have still only helped a small portion of those who need to change their spending habits.[46] Except for items that are likely to grow in value and often cannot be acquired in any other way, like homes and higher education, Christians should be very reluctant to go into any kind of debt. "Let no debt remain outstanding, except the continuing debt to love one another" (Rom. 13:8a). Paul does not mean never to accrue any financial debt. But he does suggest that we do so sparingly and do our best to pay off loans as quickly as possible.[47] In an age of such exponentially higher interest rates on credit card debt, every other financing option should be exhausted before resorting to not paying off all of one's credit card bills at the end of each month.

There is no question that numerous Proverbs inculcate the value of hard work (Prov. 6:6–11; 12:11; 14:23; 20:13; 21:5; 27:23–24). All other things being equal, industriousness leads to greater wealth than sloth and laziness do.[48] But all other things are seldom equal. The Proverbs (and Psalms and Prophets) likewise describe plenty of wealthy people who acquired their riches unethically, including by exploiting the poor, even among God's people (e.g., Prov. 15:16–17; 16:8; Ps. 37:16–17; Amos 5:11–12). There are plenty today (as in previous eras) who are poor through no significant fault of their own, just as there are those who are rich through no significant merit of their own.[49] The "prosperity gospel"—the notion that God will grant his people economic wealth (and physical health) if they just work hard enough, trust him, and obey

46. Esp. Crown Ministries and Dave Ramsey's Financial Peace University.

47. Douglas J. Moo, *The Epistle to the Romans* (Grand Rapids: Eerdmans, 1996), 812. See also Thomas R. Schreiner, *Romans* (Grand Rapids: Baker, 1998), 691.

48. See further Timothy J. Sandoval, *The Discourse of Wealth and Poverty in the Book of Proverbs* (Leiden: Brill, 2006).

49. There *are* truly "worthy poor." See Robert Lupton, *Theirs Is the Kingdom: Celebrating the Gospel in Urban America* (New York: HarperCollins, 1989), 60–61. On how and to whom to give (or not), see his *Toxic Charity: How Churches and Charities Hurt Those They Help (and How to Reverse It)* (New York: HarperOne, 2011).

his commands—is an insidious heresy when applied across the board to all people irrespective of their circumstances. Boomers did not invent this heresy (the postwar generation did), but they have developed it into a fine art.[50] The secular equivalent is the concept that those who simply work hard enough and follow the best principles of the business world can expect financial prosperity, but all it takes is a sizable recession to give the lie to that generalization. "You can't take it with you" summarizes a large swath of biblical teaching, even if it is not a quotation of a text that can be identified by chapter and verse. Or, more colloquially, "You've never seen a hearse pulling a U-Haul!"

The same consumerist attitudes that prevail throughout the Boomers' quest for material prosperity easily transfer over to church. The Silents were the first generation to have good enough cars and roads and enough choice so that at least a few of them would choose to attend a church other than the one that was closest to them. But it was the Boomers who turned this trickle into a flood tide. The two most fundamental reasons that Christians over the centuries and throughout the world belonged to one local congregation rather than another were (1) denomination or theological tradition, and (2) geographical location—the parish to which one belonged. With Boomers, neither of these were the main reason any longer, as a consumerist mindset led them to drive however far they had to in order to find a church that fit their denominational or theological tradition.[51] As denominationalism waned and nondenominational or interdenominational churches exploded in number, it became more common for Boomers to drive to where they could find "good preaching," their preferred style of worship and music, the right programs to educate their children, and so forth. Scripture acknowledges, sadly, that at times there do have to be divisions when true Christianity is no longer taught or practiced in a particular denomination or congregation (see 1 Cor. 11:19 on the profanation of the Lord's Supper).[52] But a major purpose of the public assembly of God's people is *koinōnia*—a term far richer than the average English-speaking person's concept of "fellowship."[53] It involves the building of

50. For a state-of-the-art description and critique, see David W. Jones and Russell S. Woodbridge, *Health, Wealth and Happiness: Has the Prosperity Gospel Overshadowed the Gospel of Christ?* (Grand Rapids: Kregel, 2011).

51. See Bruce L. Shelley and Marshall Shelley, *The Consumer Church: Can Evangelicals Win the World without Losing Their Souls?* (Downers Grove, IL: InterVarsity, 1992). Father and son, Silent and Boomer, respectively, raise key questions fairly early in the era of Boomers championing consumerism.

52. For both interpretation and application of this verse and the entire, often misunderstood passage in vv. 17–34, see Craig L. Blomberg, *1 Corinthians* (Grand Rapids: Zondervan, 1994), 228–40.

53. See J. Schattenmann, "*koinōnia*," in *New International Dictionary of New Testament Theology*, ed. Colin Brown (Grand Rapids: Zondervan, 1975), 1:639–44.

sufficiently intimate and trusting relationships with fellow church members so that one will freely share material possessions and even sacrifice some of one's own to help others far needier (Acts 2:44–45). This almost never occurs when Christians regularly church "shop" and "hop," never staying more than a few years in any one congregation. It's as if the popular praise chorus declared, "It's all about me, Lord; it's all about me," rather than "It's all about you, Lord!"

God and Country

Americans have classically exhibited an intensity of patriotism that often leaves overseas visitors baffled. Of our three cohorts, Boomers definitely excel in putting country a close second after God—unless of course they put country even before God! This overemphasis on patriotism baffles many Xers and Millennials.[54] In Christian circles, all it takes is an election year to see how religion gets co-opted, particularly by Boomers, for all kinds of campaigns that are essentially political at heart. When our preferred party is in power, or a piece of legislation is enacted or a court verdict is rendered in keeping with our political sympathies, Romans 13:1 is regularly and resoundingly cited: "Let everyone be subject to the governing authorities, for there is no authority except that which God has established. The authorities that exist have been established by God." When another party is in power and legislative or judicial decisions cut against our convictions, reference to this text is conspicuously absent from our conversations. Yet there is nothing in this text that limits its application to political officeholders we personally prefer.[55] In fact, it was the megalomaniacal emperor Nero who was on the throne in Rome as Paul wrote these words to Christians in the capital of the "evil empire" of the late fifties in the first century AD![56]

At the same time, Revelation 13 describes two beasts, one depicting the antichrist and one the false prophet, which represent government gone as bad as it ever can. Here believers, or anyone else who will not acknowledge

---

54. One very mature Millennial Christian woman I know well recently began singing the famous patriotic hymn, "God Bless America," and then reworded the second line, "Land that I pretty much like most of the time." This is a more biblical evaluation of the United States of the twenty-first century!

55. This is the most commonly cited passage in Wayne Grudem, *Politics according to the Bible* (Grand Rapids: Zondervan, 2010). This passage appears whenever he wants divine endorsement for his Republican and even libertarian positions. When existing legislation is not to his liking, though, he never cites the passage but calls for Christians to behave differently than what the government dictates.

56. For sober exegesis of this text, see esp. Stanley E. Porter, "Romans 13.1–7 as Pauline Political Rhetoric," *Filología Neotestamentaria* 3 (1990): 115–39.

the evil empire's sovereignty and the emperor's deity and absolute lordship, will be severely persecuted and discriminated against.[57] Christian Boomers probably need to temper their patriotism with a dose of biblical realism, acknowledging that their citizenship is in heaven (Phil. 3:20), while at the same time recognizing that things are far from as bad as they could be in America. In fact, compared to most of the world, we still have enormous spiritual freedoms and opportunities. Yet Boomers have lived through and helped perpetuate as intense a flurry as history has seen of apocalyptic predictions about the end of the world (or at least the end of democracy as we know it), and to date 100 percent of those predictions have proved to be wrong.[58] This should inspire a much more profound humility in end-times watching and prognosticating, as should Jesus's own declaration to his followers, "It is not for you to know times or seasons the Father has fixed by his own authority" (Acts 1:7). I choose this passage rather than the better-known text in Mark 13:32 and parallels ("But about that day or hour no one knows, not even the angels in heaven, nor the Son, but only the Father") for two reasons. First, it contains the most general terms for "time" in the Greek language (*chronos* and *kairos*).[59] Second, and as a result, this passage is not susceptible to the misinterpretation that sometimes has been offered for Mark 13:32, which suggests that one might not be able to know the day or hour, but one can at least predict the month, week, year, or generation!

Boomers desperately need a globalized perspective on the role of the American military. This will not solve the age-old debates in their various forms between just war and pacifism, but it will temper some of Boomers' Rambo-like rhetoric.[60] Even just-war theory has always made it clear that war should be embarked on as an absolute last resort after every conceivable alternative has been exhausted.[61] It is not obvious that any of America's military excursions around the world, from Vietnam to the present, have

---

57. Craig S. Keener (*Revelation* [Grand Rapids: Zondervan, 2000], 327) has profound insight into the possible need for Christian martyrdom before faith will proliferate in some of the most resistant cultures of our twenty-first-century world.

58. See Francis X. Gumerlock, *The Day and the Hour: A Chronicle of Christianity's Perennial Fascination with Predicting the End of the World* (Atlanta: American Vision, 2000), 297–331.

59. "One should probably not look for a difference in meaning between the two near synonyms. . . . *Any knowledge* related to the time of the restoration of Israel is not the prerogative of the disciples." Martin M. Culy and Mikeal C. Parsons, *Acts: A Handbook on the Greek Text* (Waco: Baylor University Press, 2003), 8, emphasis added.

60. See esp. Robert G. Clouse, ed., *War: Four Christian Views* (Downers Grove, IL: InterVarsity, 1991); Richard S. Hess and Elmer A. Martens, eds., *War in the Bible and Terrorism in the Twenty-First Century* (Winona Lake, IN: Eisenbrauns, 2008).

61. Gary M. Simpson, "Just-War Theory," in *Dictionary of Scripture and Ethics*, ed. Joel B. Green (Grand Rapids: Baker Academic, 2011), 446.

unambiguously qualified as a just war by this criterion. Inconsistencies in where we have intervened, moreover, abound. Perhaps the government will almost by nature default to where *national* interests are most threatened, but Christians must occupy higher moral ground. Where basic human rights are repeatedly and egregiously violated, it shouldn't matter how much oil a country has to offer the West. If injustice demands military intervention in one location, then other, less-strategic settings with similar injustice likewise require our help.

Even more than with issues of just war, Boomers seem to rally behind the idea that the United States is a Christian nation. Therefore what is in our best interest must be godly, as if America were the new Israel, God's new chosen country. Dispensationalists and covenant theologians can debate to what degree the role of ancient Israel is or is not fulfilled today in the church, but there is no biblical case to be made for any *geopolitical* entity replacing biblical Israel![62] Much more important, just-war theorists and pacifists, overly zealous patriots, and severe national critics alike can and should embrace Glen Stassen's repeated calls for "just peacemaking"—taking proactive steps to peace and reconciliation that can forestall armed conflict, just as organizations like "Peacemakers" can help end conflict at the local level in individual churches and communities.[63] The Truth and Reconciliation Commission of South Africa was an amazing Christian model that needs more widespread emulation, even as it has been used with varying degrees of success in numerous places.[64]

Pay Your Dues and Mentoring

Is there anything inherently biblical about the notion that young adults must languish for a period of time in settings of work or church for which they are overqualified, simply waiting for the older generation to retire or die off before they can maximize the use of their gifts? Not that I am aware of! A period of apprenticeship was common in the biblical cultures and continues to make good sense. Paul includes among the criteria for deacons that "they must first be tested; and then if there is nothing against them, let them serve" (1 Tim. 3:10). But once it is clear that someone is adequately trained and has

---

62. For an excellent overview, see Larry R. Helyer, *The Witness of Jesus, Paul and John: An Exploration in Biblical Theology* (Downers Grove, IL: InterVarsity, 2008), 84–120.

63. Glen H. Stassen, *Just Peacemaking: Transforming Initiatives for Justice and Peace* (Louisville: Westminster John Knox, 1992); Ken Sande, *The Peacemaker: A Guide to Resolving Personal Conflicts*, 3rd ed. (Grand Rapids: Baker Books, 2004).

64. See esp. Priscilla B. Hayner, *Unspeakable Truths: Transitional Justice and the Challenge of Truth Commissions*, rev. ed. (New York: Routledge, 2011).

proved trustworthy over a reasonable period of time, those in charge, whether in the workplace or in church, should exhaust every possibility to find places for them to use their skills and talents to the fullest.

In biblical cultures, students were not greater than their teachers in two senses. First, where the teacher was the sole repository of information or skill to be passed on to the student, then obviously the student was limited by the teacher's knowledge and ability (Luke 6:40). Second, if teachers suffered for their commitments, students, dedicated to those same commitments, should not imagine they would be exempt from similar suffering (Matt. 10:24).[65] But even in the New Testament world, those who learned to read had access to books and libraries and could gain more information and training than just what living teachers could provide. Today's world, saturated by ever-increasing information overload, should lead teachers to *expect* their students to outstrip them in a whole raft of ways. Boomers should not view this as a threat if they see themselves and their work in the context of kingdom ministry rather than just their personal mission.

What about the reverse of paying your dues? Do Boomers owe it to Gen-Xers and Millennials to retire at a reasonable age in order to open up more opportunities for their younger contemporaries? Some Christians like to trumpet the fact that "there is no retirement in the Bible."[66] This can be misleading in several respects. First, it is an argument from silence. There is no reference to elementary education outside the home in the Bible either, but Jews consistently practiced it through their local synagogues. There is no reference to graduation ceremonies; are they then forbidden? There is no reference to term limits for church leaders, or search committees or professional consultants, or orders of service, or announcements, or Sunday school. Are all these bad? The list could be lengthened almost endlessly. Second, there are ages mentioned beyond which it is assumed people wouldn't be able to work. The reason widows had to be at least sixty to be eligible to be enrolled in a church list for material support (1 Tim. 5:9) was probably because it was assumed they couldn't engage in enough work to provide for themselves at that age in their society, nor were they likely to remarry and come under the care of a new husband.[67] Third, seven times in Numbers 4, Levites who are to

---

65. For both of these points, see David E. Garland, *Luke* (Grand Rapids: Zondervan, 2011), 284.

66. Freeman Miller, retired Mennonite bishop, responds to the barrage of his friends who have accosted him with this claim in "Is Retirement Biblical?," *The Mennonite*, February 1, 2012, http://www.themennonite.org/issues/15-2/articles/Is_retirement_biblical.

67. I. Howard Marshall with Philip H. Towner, *A Critical and Exegetical Commentary on the Pastoral Epistles* (Edinburgh: T&T Clark, 1999), 583, 593.

be counted for service in the tabernacle are required to be between the ages of thirty and fifty, and in 8:25 it is stated as a command that "at the age of fifty, they must retire from their regular service and work no longer." So here is at least one text about retiring from ministry among God's people. Fourth, people on average, with important exceptions, died at a younger age in the biblical worlds, leaving fewer individuals to live to an age when retirement would be a viable option.

Today's world offers God's people many more choices. Where positions for a highly specialized skill are scarce, it may be a very loving and compassionate move for Boomers to retire at an age that makes it possible for younger, talented colleagues to occupy their positions. There are plenty of biblical models for Christians and churches training their successors. Literature on mentoring regularly mentions Moses and Joshua or Elijah and Elisha in the Old Testament. Even more obviously, Jesus was constantly training the apostles to take his place in proclaiming the gospel to the ends of the earth. Paul never traveled alone, as far as we know, but always with younger, less experienced coworkers who were learning to imitate him. Second Timothy 2:2 may be the most important text in all of Scripture for the responsibility of Christian leaders to ensure that godly and gifted people succeed them: "And the things you have heard me say in the presence of many witnesses entrust to reliable people who will also be qualified to teach others."

It is true that Christ has promised that he will build his church and that the gates of hell will not prevail against it (Matt. 16:18). The church worldwide cannot be extinguished. But he also warned the seven churches of Revelation that their local "lamps" might indeed go out if they proved faithless (Rev. 2:5). We all have seen far too many examples of local congregations or ministries of various kinds that were vibrant at one moment and in a distressingly short period of time had to close their doors. Various elements factor into such events, but central is often inadequate care in replacing good leaders with equally good ones. The slogan that Christianity is only ever one generation away from potential extinction *is* true for any given ministry. So we see Paul concerned for four generations or cohorts of individuals in 2 Timothy 2:2, even if each does not necessarily span the approximately eighteen years that the modern technical definition of the generations of Boomers, Xers, and Millennials does. First comes Paul, then Timothy, who accompanied him throughout much of his second missionary journey and ministered in Ephesus for a number of years after that. Timothy in turn is charged with teaching other reliable people who can carry on after him, even while he is still present. Finally, those people must be taught and qualified to teach others also—a fourth generation. Not only must Christian leaders do their best to ensure that trained and gifted leaders succeed them, but they must inculcate the vision in those leaders to keep replicating the process.[68]

Two key reasons for failing to implement this vision are fear of loss of power or control and fear of not having enough money in retirement. In the latter case, we need to review all that the Bible has to say about material possessions. Whether through insurance, Social Security, investments and savings, or simply "working until one drops," the quest to secure one's future materially against all possible calamity can never be fulfilled.[69] One must set reasonable goals, be prepared for a potentially simpler lifestyle, let others know of special needs, and trust God. In the former case, such fear suggests one has an unbiblical approach to power and control already. One is apparently not using leadership responsibilities to serve and train others. Paul's model throughout his missionary career is instructive here. He could announce that "from Jerusalem all the way around to Illyricum," he had "fully proclaimed the gospel" (Rom. 15:19) when he and his coworkers had established fledgling churches in each major geographical region in the arc from Israel to modern-day Albania, Montenegro, and Croatia. Then he entrusted those congregations to the Lord to continue the ministry of reaching their immediate vicinities as he moved on to preach in entirely unevangelized areas (v. 20; see also 2 Cor. 10:16). In other words, his goal was to work himself out of a job and move on to the next one.[70] More Boomers facing retirement might need to think in similar terms.

What Kind of Mentor?

The three kinds of mentors Elisabeth describes in chapter 1 correspond to three kinds of teachers, pastors, and employers as well. Boomers have excelled at the ministry of proclamation, the delivery of lectures and top-down mandates, and the like. The dominant biblical model is one of unidirectional instruction, so we dare not lose sight of the value of such training. I have even heard compelling and creative *lectures* about how to teach in ways other than by lecturing! When one is imparting information or training in skills that others don't yet have, there is invariably an element of "do as I tell you, and

68. See also Samuel M. Ngewa, *1 & 2 Timothy and Titus* (Grand Rapids: Zondervan, 2009), 208–10.

69. "If we hold that true wisdom is to be rich toward God, then work will have a limited place in our lives. *We shall work hard enough to provide the necessities; we shall leave the future in God's hands.* We will not make work a means of securing our lives against all possible calamities." John Purdy, *Parables at Work* (Philadelphia: Westminster, 1985), 48–49, emphasis in original.

70. For a book-length elaboration, see Eckhard J. Schnabel, *Paul the Missionary: Realities, Strategies and Methods* (Downers Grove, IL: InterVarsity, 2008).

do as I model for you" that must occur. But Paul's theology of spiritual gifts cuts against the grain of cookie-cutter models that imagine all Christians need exactly the same education in every area of life. None of the spiritual gifts is given to all believers (1 Cor. 12:29–30). Christians need to discover the unique ways God has wired them and nurture their specific gifts. Formal or informal mentors, therefore, need to facilitate conversations and experiences that enable mentorees to discover their gifts, learning styles, personality traits, and what works best for them, even if that turns out to be quite different than what works for their mentors.[71]

Beware, then, of extensive teaching on the full range of spiritual gifts or the diversity of the members of the body of Christ without making opportunities available for all people to exercise those gifts and talents for the building up of the body. Too often churches concentrate only on a small range of gifts and gifted people, leaving those who don't fit in quite frustrated. At best, they will go elsewhere to other churches or ministries; at worst, they may leave the visible church altogether. And even when people have direct questions that suggest straightforward "lectures" by way of response, notice how often Jesus, in good rabbinic fashion, answers similar questions with additional questions (e.g., Matt. 9:14–15; 15:2–3; 15:33–34; 19:3–5; etc.).[72] Of course there are times to make solemn pronouncements, but only after as many of the facts as possible are known and carefully understood (see 1 Cor. 4:5). This usually requires a prolonged period of questions and answers, which may allow mentorees to discover their giftings for themselves. If they wrestle through questions to come up with their own answers, they are more likely to own their discoveries than if they merely had been handed it on a platter, as it were, by someone else. Here is where Christian counseling, with its techniques of asking good questions, can be extremely helpful. Boomers have come a long way in removing the stigma of counseling and of even learning from counselors' methods, but in general they have not yet embraced it as fully as younger generations have.[73]

It's All Good until You Hear Otherwise

Boomers learned this assumption that they don't need to provide liberal praise to mentorees or coworkers from at least one generation before them.

71. A standard resource is J. Robert Clinton and Richard W. Clinton, *The Mentor Handbook: A Detailed Guide for Christian Mentors and Mentees* (Altadena, CA: Barnabas, 1991).
72. See esp. Conrad Gempf, *Jesus Asked: What He Wanted to Know* (Grand Rapids: Zondervan, 2003).
73. For the strengths and weaknesses of the main approaches, see esp. Eric L. Johnson, ed., *Psychology and Christianity: Five Views*, 2nd ed. (Downers Grove, IL: InterVarsity, 2010).

My parents were both public schoolteachers, and I attended public schools from kindergarten to twelfth grade, followed by a private college, a private seminary, and a public university (in Scotland, no less). In every setting, the teacher grading my papers commented far more on what was wrong than on what was right. It was only when the Millennials came to dominate our seminary's student body not that many years ago that I started to realize their expectations and their experiences were quite different. They did not assume that everything *not* commented on was fine; they needed specific and repeated words of affirmation. At first, I resisted this because it made my job harder and more time consuming. But extending affirmation is a biblical value. God the Father even goes out of his way to publicly commend his Son at his baptism (Mark 1:11 and parallels) and then again at his transfiguration with an audible voice (Mark 9:7 and parallels). The laws of Moses regularly balance God's rewards for obedience alongside his punishments for disobedience (esp. Deut. 28). The narrator of 1–2 Kings ends with a summary assessment of each king as to whether his reign was primarily good, primarily evil, or a mixed bag. Jesus publicly praises those who show great faith in him (Matt. 8:10; 9:2, 22; 15:28; etc.). Paul commends his faithful coworkers, especially when others have deserted him (1 Cor. 16:10–18; Col. 4:10–15; 2 Tim. 4:9–18). In Philippians he draws special attention to a man we might never have otherwise heard of, Epaphroditus, who risked his life to help Paul (Phil. 2:25–30).[74]

On the other hand, it still remains true that the Old Testament is filled with far more correction of the Israelites when they wander from the right path of following God than praise for when they obey him. Jesus's words of rebuke to his disciples are more prominent than his words of commendation for them. Paul's letters provide considerably greater instruction about what to think and how to behave when his churches are not believing but doing the wrong things. Someone who has not internalized Christian values enough to know what is right to do in most situations, and to realize that God is smiling down on them and affirming them when they do it whether or not any human ever commends them, probably has a faulty view of God.[75] The more Christianity in the West becomes an embattled minority, the more his people are going to have to learn to follow biblical belief and practice not only when

74. "In light of Paul's positive recommendation of Epaphroditus, we can infer that he had a positive view of his strong emotions of longing for friends during his prolonged separation and distress when he underwent the traumatic experience of serious illness complicated by the inability to clarify reports his friends have heard of his illness." G. Walter Hansen, *The Letter to the Philippians* (Grand Rapids: Eerdmans, 2009), 204.

75. J. I. Packer, *Knowing God* (London: Hodder & Stoughton, 1973), remains a classic with its balance of the love and justice of God, but it ends with a main section on "if God be for us who can be against us?" from Rom. 8:31 (pp. 161–254).

they don't receive affirmation, but even when they are being criticized, and perhaps even persecuted, for doing so. Both Testaments are replete with examples of how such hostility can come not only from the outside world but from within the camp of those who profess to be God's people, whether from those who disobey the Torah, oppose righteous kings, counter the prophets, crucify Jesus, or introduce false teaching into the apostolic churches. If we are not to become like those rocked by a wave of the sea, "blown and tossed by the wind," "double-minded and unstable" in all we do (James 1:7–8), we will have to learn to adhere to biblical values even when a majority of the church is not following them.[76] One thinks, for example, of the rampant premarital or extramarital sex in many evangelical congregations, or the capitulation to the gay lobby in otherwise orthodox churches.[77] How tragic it is when the very people who should remain faithful to biblical sexual values ridicule or oppose them instead! Biblically faithful people then need to rely on the affirmation of God and on their own consciences all the more rather than counting on other humans to praise them. Boomers can still remember when biblical sexual ethics were the norm and not the exception in churches, even in many non-evangelical ones, so they must take the lead in teaching and modeling for others that those ethics are still possible to obey.

Family, Religion, and the Public Square

If they have been in evangelical churches for any length of time, Baby Boomers have often heard that one's biological family is the second most important place for one's time and loyalty only after God himself. Jews in Jesus's day typically believed the same thing, which is why it would have been so shocking to hear him rebuff his mother and brothers with the rhetorical question, "Who are my mother and my brothers?" The Gospel of Mark continues, "Then he looked at those seated in a circle around him and said, 'Here are my mother and my brothers! Whoever does God's will is my brother and sister and mother'" (Mark 3:33–35).[78] Worse still, he will later say to the crowds following him, "If anyone comes to me and does not hate father and mother,

---

76. Referring to those who waver between different "gods," not to those who are unsure of how God will choose to act. See further Craig L. Blomberg and Mariam J. Kamell, *James* (Grand Rapids: Zondervan, 2008), 62–63.

77. Contra both of which, see esp. Linda L. Belleville, *Sex, Lies and the Truth: Developing a Christian Ethic in a Post-Christian Society* (Eugene, OR: Wipf & Stock, 2010).

78. See also Andreas Köstenberger, "Marriage and Family in the New Testament," in *Marriage and Family in the Biblical World*, ed. Ken M. Campbell (Downers Grove, IL: InterVarsity, 2003), 247.

wife and children, brothers and sisters—yes, even their own life—such a person cannot be my disciple" (Luke 14:26). Fortunately, a parallel passage in a different setting in Matthew explains Jesus's probable meaning here in Luke: "Anyone who loves their father or mother more than me is not worthy of me; anyone who loves their son or daughter more than me is not worthy of me" (Matt. 10:37).[79] This is challenging enough; the form of the saying in Luke is downright shocking—hardly conducive to a (positive) "focus on the family"! Jesus appears to have diagnosed the Jewish culture of his day as having overemphasized family ties and underemphasized ties across extended family and kinship lines within the people of God. It is arguable that Boomers have often made the identical mistakes today. Alternately, among ministry *professionals*, the view that ministry regularly comes before family has done great damage to the families of those Christian leaders.

The desire to give one's kids everything possible may stem in large measure from the overemphasis on family over spiritual kin. There are definite advantages, of course, of promoting a healthy self-image in our children and in providing financially for them. If those children have internalized Christian values themselves, if the money enables them to receive the kind of education or training needed to maximize their giftedness (whether directly for the Lord's work or indirectly in the secular workplace), then such parental help honors God. But if it teaches kids to expect handouts, if it fosters irresponsibility on their part, or if it leads to workaholism on the part of their parents and thus to broken or dysfunctional families, then those parents are trying much too hard to help the next generation! There are good lessons about life to be learned through diligent (but not debilitating), wholesome work and through healthy independence from families of origin, which cannot be gained when parents provide everything for their children.[80] In the same vein, "helicopter" parents prevent adolescents from transitioning in healthy ways to young adulthood, for instance, developing the ability to fend for themselves, learning how to be accountable, and learning how to accept the consequences for their own choices. Helicopter parents also make life inappropriately difficult for both educators and employers.[81] Most young adult children resent overly invasive parenting that thwarts their growth toward independence, even if they may

---

79. See also Cynthia Long Westfall, "Family in the Gospels and Acts," in *Family in the Bible: Exploring Customs, Culture, and Context*, ed. Richard S. Hess and M. Daniel Carroll R. (Grand Rapids: Baker Academic, 2003), 135–37.

80. For an excellent, concise biblical theology of work, see Ben Witherington III, *Work: A Kingdom Perspective on Labor* (Grand Rapids: Eerdmans, 2011).

81. On this and other approaches to parenting, see Jim Fay, *Helicopters, Drill Sergeants and Consultants: Parenting Styles and the Messages They Send* (Golden, CO: Love and Logic, 1995).

(think they) appreciate being "rescued" out of some difficult situations they could have handled themselves. Ephesians 6:4a comes readily to mind: "Fathers [or "parents"], do not exasperate your children."

Children, of course, need to know that their parents love them and care for their well-being. Mom and Dad need to think through in advance reasons for how they will parent and then explain those reasons to their children as they progress toward adulthood, so that the children can own those reasons. A good case can be made from Christian and secular sources alike that parenting should seek to move children from the highest levels of protection and nurture, ever so gradually, to increased degrees of freedom and responsibility to prepare them for adult living. After all, especially for anyone who marries, the biblical goal is that children "leave father and mother" to be united with their spouses (Gen. 2:24; see also Matt. 19:5; Eph. 5:31). This isn't necessarily a geographical departure; extended families often lived together in the biblical worlds. So it must refer to close interpersonal allegiance.[82] This doesn't happen overnight; preparation for a healthy marriage requires learning to live as an emotionally independent adult. Only then can one voluntarily enter marriage ready to give more than to get.

On the other hand, modern Western living has often fostered too much independence between parents and children. A parent who has the ability to offer substantial help toward the costs of higher education for a talented and responsible young adult (who could not access that education otherwise) is understandably perceived as unloving if he or she withholds that help. But parents who sacrifice time with their spouse or children (in the name of providing the best financial resources for the family or serving a certain ministry) so that the family ends up being estranged, have also failed miserably by biblical standards. A grown child who refuses to help in finding ways of providing care for his or her increasingly needy older relatives is "worse than an unbeliever," Paul declares (1 Tim. 5:8), because even pagans in the ancient Mediterranean world recognized the importance of such family responsibilities.[83] But the approach of Bill Gothard's *Basic Youth Conflicts* curriculum (which many evangelical Boomers will remember from their young adulthood), which teaches that the nature of honoring parents does not change when children are adults and permission is still sought from or obedience rendered to parents in every walk of life, proves equally unhealthy.[84]

82. Craig L. Blomberg, "Marriage, Divorce, Remarriage and Celibacy: An Exegesis of Matthew 19:3–12," *Trinity Journal* 11 (1990): 166–67.
83. See the sources listed in Marshall with Towner, *Pastoral Epistles*, 591n53.
84. Bill Gothard, *Basic Youth Conflicts: Research in Principles of Life,* rev. ed. (Oak Brook, IL: Institute of Basic Youth Conflicts, 1981).

Turning to matters of civil religion, Boomers are to be commended for having brought their faith back into the public square. The year 1976 saw the election of Jimmy Carter to the presidency, which led to *Time* magazine dubbing it the "Year of the Evangelical."[85] The election of Ronald Reagan to two terms of office in the 1980s was due in significant measure to Jerry Falwell's leadership in mobilizing what was dubbed "the Moral Majority." Evangelical leaders, especially in the Baby Boomer generation, have played a "loud, proud" role in every election, even if they haven't always succeeded in being "in charge" through the election of their (invariably Republican) candidates. The Moral Majority similarly began the campaign against *Roe v. Wade*, which to date has been largely unsuccessful but has had many high-profile dimensions to it. Anti-abortion lobbying should remain a high priority for coming generations because it does indeed involve the taking of human life on a massive scale.[86] But it is not yet clear whether Xers or Millennials will carry the torch with the same enthusiasm. Younger generations have never known the country without legalized abortion. To them, the issue has been decided legislatively, and they would rather fight it in a preventative/pre-pregnancy way. Boomers often feel that this approach is unacceptable in the church unless it is an abstinence-only message. And as Elisabeth highlights, Boomers have a legacy more generally of fighting "the system" (or "the man," as they liked to call it) that younger generations to date do not. The most publicized forms of Boomer efforts to apply their religious values to the public square have tended to focus on *distinctively* Christian values, but they have been only marginally successful. Younger generations may need to create or recover other approaches.

Conclusion

Boomers have demonstrated numerous leadership gifts that fit biblical models. In Christian circles they have accomplished great good for the advance of God's kingdom. Sometimes that leadership has not always been sufficiently oriented toward servanthood; sometimes it has seemingly excelled in servanthood at the expense of fostering unhealthy dependence on the part of those served. In many ways they have carried on the best of the legacies of their forefathers and foremothers, spiritually speaking, without the rigid institutionalization

85. Jonathan Devine, "Honor vs. Obey," *Recovering Grace*, September 2, 2011, http://www .recoveringgrace.org/2011/09/honor-vs-obey/.

86. For sensitive yet biblically faithful reflections, see John Stott, *Issues Facing Christians Today*, 4th ed. (Grand Rapids: Zondervan, 2006), 389–406.

and stultifying legalism that sometimes characterized the Silent generation. Boomers have often displayed a healthy sense of their own identity, worked for self-sufficiency, and shown commendable loyalty and commitment over long periods of time to their work and their calling. They have developed and utilized numerous forms of technology that have made our world more of a global village. They have fought for the rights of others and put social justice issues, along with broader matters of faith and religion, back on the public radar.

At the same time, in loosening some ties to previous generations' values and in undervaluing certain commitments, both in the church and the family, they have opened the doors to what has become a veritable flood of theologically or ethically unbiblical beliefs and practices in many segments of society. Their can-do optimism, rooted in a strong self-image, can work against the relinquishing of control, the sharing of power, and the preparing of younger generations to maximize their gifts and talents in both the private and public sectors. What will characterize Boomers' retirement years, as they begin to form the largest generation in history to retire and to live longer and healthier lives? One thing seems sure: even if they think they can go it alone, inevitable encounters with their mortality will make them ultimately dependent on Xers and Millennials in ways many of them do not currently imagine.

3

Priorities for Ministry
with Boomers

Not so loud, not so proud, and not as much in charge! This is the inevitable future Baby Boomers face, and some of the oldest among them are experiencing it already. Perhaps more than with previous generations, it terrifies them. By pitting themselves years ago against "the establishment," they left themselves no recourse but to chart their own independent way. By distrusting "the man," they forced themselves to become their own authorities. Many, perhaps most, have moderated over time, but those original defining urges lie deeply embedded in Boomers' psyches. Therefore, these realizations must be kept front and center when conceiving and implementing strategies for successful ministry to aging Boomers.[1]

Confronting Mortality

More than one analyst has generalized the Boomers' plight (without too much hyperbole) as believing they are immortal (or at least believing they will stay

1. Craig K. Miller (*Baby Boomer Spirituality: Ten Essentials Values of a Generation* [Nashville: Discipleship Resources, 1993]), identifies the following defining characteristics exhibited variously across the cohort: brokenness, loneliness, rootlessness, self-seeking, godliness, supernaturalism, adventurousness, millennialism, globalism, and wholeness.

forever young).[2] Of course, no one seriously thinks they will not die; death is just not on their radar screens. If we think of an analogy from the world of construction, Boomers consciously or unconsciously have built a fortress that for some time has seemed impenetrable. Exceptions appear if they have already had a life-threatening illness or injury, or if people very close to them in their cohort have had one *and* if they have allowed it to truly sink in that it could just as easily have been *they* who were in danger of dying. But Boomers have watched astonishing developments in health and medicine prolong the lives of so many in recent years that they often envision these processes continuing at a similar or even faster rate. But no one will be able to postpone death indefinitely.

With Christians

Ministry with aging Boomers, therefore, needs to prioritize sound biblical teaching about the life to come. Dying may or may not be accompanied by prolonged, acute physical pain, but it certainly need not entail spiritual distress. Far more than is common in typical evangelical pulpits in the Western world, preachers need to be addressing what Scripture promises about life after death and, to quote Tom Wright, "life *after* life after death."[3] Preachers, teachers, small group facilitators, counselors, missionaries, and other Christian leaders need to paint again and again the glowing portrait of life with Christ in heaven, and especially the joy of the new heavens and new earth after that. All Christians need to be reminded that Paul also uses a building metaphor to speak of the life to come—"an eternal house in heaven, not built by human hands" after our "earthly tent we live in is destroyed" (2 Cor. 5:1). They need to be reminded, too, about the very earthly delights of a renewed cosmos, which will be so perfected that there will be no more loss—no death, no mourning, no crying, and no pain (Rev. 21:4). We need to be prompted to long for the perfect community of all God's people reflected in the metaphor of the New Jerusalem (v. 2). As has often been pointed out, we began in a garden (Gen. 2), but we end in a city.[4] Yet none of the evils often associated with cities, indeed often pitted against the virtues of the countryside, will linger. We were created for perfect community with God and one another, and every obstacle to fully enjoying these relationships will be removed.

2. Gary McIntosh, "Trends and Challenges for Ministry among North America's Largest Generation," *Christian Education Journal* 5 (2008): 296, 298–99.

3. E.g., N. T. Wright, *Surprised by Hope: Rethinking Heaven, Resurrection, and the Mission of the Church* (New York: HarperOne, 2008), 148.

4. E.g., Donald Guthrie, *The Relevance of John's Apocalypse* (Grand Rapids: Eerdmans, 1987), 119.

As a result, we must theologize far more creatively than simply speaking about heavenly choirs, angels with halos, and floating on clouds. Rather, we must think through what meaningful work and activity offered in service to our God in the company of fully redeemed people could look like. If the universe is infinite, and the universe is recreated, there will be an infinite amount of joyous activity, in a perfect rhythm of work and rest, to make our eternal lives more glorious and desirable than anything we could ever conceive or imagine (Eph. 3:20). Our art, our cinematography, our rhetoric, our literature, and the way Boomers live out their lives on earth all must be permeated by this joyous hope, with all of our skills and talents offered to facilitate it.[5] If, as many scientists think, our universe is infinitely *expanding*, we must imaginatively reflect on the infinite amount of time that will be required for us to explore and enjoy it.

None of this is to return to the eras and contexts that birthed the slogan that certain people were "so heavenly minded that they were no earthly good." That has decidedly *not* been the problem for Boomers. We set out to change the world for good, but most of us became disillusioned, some sooner and others later. We realized it was hard enough to change our own waistlines! We need to recapture the biblical vision that we *can* change the world through the Spirit's power and that we *will* experience a transformed world partly in this life and fully in the life to come. But all this change comes as we stay in touch with and surrender to what God wants to do through us. We must preserve the important emphasis on social justice we have reinserted into the evangelical movement after its disappearance in the wake of the fundamentalist-modernist controversy of the early twentieth century. But we must never fool ourselves into thinking that improving the lot of people in this life, as important as it is, is the sum total or even the main part of our call. People who die in rebellion against God will not spend eternity with him, no matter how much more tolerable we have made life for them here on earth.[6]

With Non-Christians

Even when I (Craig) was a teenager, it always amazed me that when people, whether young or old, referred to "reaching this generation for Christ," they

5. See esp. Randy Alcorn, *Heaven* (Wheaton: Tyndale House, 2004). See also Paula Gooder, *Heaven* (Eugene, OR: Cascade, 2011); and Anthony C. Thiselton, *Life after Death: A New Approach to the Last Things* (Grand Rapids: Eerdmans, 2012).

6. See the impassioned blog post by the CEO of Lifeway Christian Resources and longtime professor of missions and evangelism at several institutions of higher education, Thom S. Rainer, "Last Chances for Churches to Reach 50 Million Americans," http://thomrainer.com/2013/01/28/last-chances-for-churches-to-reach-50-million-americans/.

often meant leading to the Lord people who were between the ages of about fifteen to thirty.[7] It continues to amaze me four decades later. Of course, I understand the appropriate concern that every age group needs to be reached and that winning young adults proves particularly crucial for the ongoing life of the church down the road. I recognize that teenage rebellion of all different kinds (now with delayed adolescence often extending well into one's twenties) makes young adults particularly vulnerable to being lost to Christianity and that, conversely, this age group is often particularly ripe for receiving the gospel message positively. But as Boomers retire, we will have the largest generation of retirees thus far in the history of the world. Are they not also part of "this generation" (if the expression basically refers to all people alive at a given moment in history)?[8]

Recognizing the debilitating factors of aging and the inevitability of death makes older adults the *second* ripest category of people for coming to Christ. The church should not lose its opportunity to reach them, especially since there are more unchurched and more non-Christian Boomers than in their parents' and grandparents' generations. Time for them to respond positively to Jesus is indeed running out. Will the church simply turn a blind eye to this reality as it rushes headlong to enfold as many younger adults as it can? Will aging congregations merely turn inward, content to take care of their own members' growing needs? Then the fortress mindset will have triumphed again. Or will we seek to move outside the four walls of the church and the homes of church members to see where the fields are white for harvest among the aging? Studies have shown that retirement alone does not automatically make a person more open to the Christian message, however. A variety of specific events must typically occur. For example, a spouse or close friend may die, an individual may get a potentially terminal illness or sudden physical disability, or a divorce or serious financial loss may take place.[9] In other words, aging by itself does not make a person more open to the gospel; it usually takes a more significant event that reminds a person that life is not going to continue on indefinitely with only very gradual declines in its quality. They must see

7. Thus the excellent introduction to youth ministry edited by Richard R. Dunn and Mark H. Senter III is titled *Reaching a Generation for Christ: A Comprehensive Guide to Youth Ministry*, rev. ed. (Chicago: Moody, 1997), and a parachurch youth ministry is explicitly named "This Generation for Christ" (http://thisgenerationforchrist.org/). But such a title seems never to be used for any ministry with middle-aged adults or with seniors!

8. See Angela Coleman, "How to Incorporate Baby Boomers in Your Church," *Yahoo Voices*, February 8, 2013, http://voices.yahoo.com/how-incorporate-baby-boomers-church-11993094.html?cat=12.

9. Charles Arn, "Factors Affecting Late-Life Conversion," *Christian Education Journal* 5 (2008): 330–45.

that their fortress does not just have a few cracks in it but is in danger of collapsing altogether.

At the same time, enough seniors do experience precisely such events that churches and parachurch organizations need to be preparing to come alongside those who undergo these traumas. First, they must provide the genuine, caring help that anyone so afflicted might need or want, irrespective of their openness to following Jesus. Second, as opportunities permit, contextually sensitive, autobiographical reflections on the help Christ has provided for the caregivers themselves can prove very encouraging for others. These are the opportune moments that researchers suggest leave many particularly open to considering (or reconsidering) Jesus, especially when he is lovingly and redemptively presented to them.[10]

The "Good Life" for Aging Boomers

In light of these realities, how should Boomers live out their last laps around the track, so to speak?[11] Many today speak of never retiring. After all, they claim, there is no retirement in the Bible (though we saw earlier that this is not quite accurate).[12] Yet, if we live long enough, eventually our bodies do not permit us to continue the kinds of work at the same level for which society normally pays people. Should Boomers aspire to push themselves so hard that they work right up to the moment they die and, indeed, speed the day of that death by how hard they keep pushing themselves? This cannot be biblical stewardship of our bodies—a key part of God's good material and physical resources he has given us to take care of! It certainly is not the way Boomers normally treat their houses. When paint peels, roofs leak, and foundations begin to sink, repairs are made or people prepare to move to a new residence. Physically, believers can make only so many repairs to their bodies, so they need to be preparing more for life to come and the eternal state.

With Finances and Service

The kernel of truth in the "no-retirement" movement is that most people can and should find ways to serve God meaningfully, use their gifts, and

10. Frank Newport, *God Is Alive and Well: The Future of Religion in America* (New York: Gallup, 2012), 103–40.

11. For a reasonably good set of recommendations balancing service and renewal, see David Yount, *Celebrating the Rest of Your Life: A Baby Boomer's Guide to Spirituality* (Minneapolis: Augsburg Fortress, 2005).

12. E.g., Eric Tiansay, "John Piper: 'Retire' Is Not a Biblical Word," *Charisma News*, January 7, 2013, http://www.charismanews.com/culture/35140-john-piper-retire-is-not-a-biblical-word.

further his kingdom as long as they can as they get older. Old homes can often continue to be used for a long time, though not always as much as they once were able to be utilized. Whether Boomers should be entitled to continue to get paid for their work, or paid at the same levels they once were, is another matter altogether, especially if they are not able to work as hard or as well. The problem is compounded by Boomers amassing record levels of debt (at least compared to previous generations), often having little in savings and reliable investments, and continuing to want to live at the same, if not a higher, standard of living as they have already achieved.[13] These three factors lead them to believe that they cannot retire, even partly, and still be able to cope financially. The fortress mentality thus stays intact.

Little wonder that Christian ministries that help people get and stay out of debt, live within a budget, and even have money left over for savings, investing, and stewardship have skyrocketed in popularity in recent years.[14] Whether through these formal parachurch ministries or simply through good church teaching and modeling by its leadership, these trends must continue and even increase. The more Boomers realize retirement is inevitable, the more crucial it will become for them to think biblically about the stewardship of all their material resources. The secular world will continue to advertise all the luxuries with which we should pamper ourselves after a lifetime of work, since we now "deserve" them. Christian circles must thus rebut these claims with equal frequency and fervor as both unbiblical and, in the long run, unhelpful to the people who indulge in them. Like every addiction, "affluenza" only very temporarily creates good feelings and produces ever-growing longings for the replication of those feelings accompanied by an ever-decreasing ability to satisfy them.[15]

13. Already twenty-five years ago, Mike Bellah wrote an entire book on *Baby Boom Believers: Why We Think We Need It All and How to Survive When We Don't Get It* (Wheaton: Tyndale, 1988). Many still have not learned the lessons of his work, as each new cycle of economic-boom years refuels hope that "this time" things will work out well enough! See Roman Shleyn, "Generation Debt Turns Out to Be Baby Boomers," *Fox Business*, November 20, 2012, http://www.foxbusiness.com/personal-finance/2012/11/20/generation-debt-turns-out -to-be-baby-boomers/. For the growing demand for "swanky" retirement living, at least in Colorado, where the authors of this book live, see Jessica Farmwald, "The New Golden Years: How the Baby Boomers Are about to Change Retirement," *5280: The Denver Magazine* (April 2014), 89–91, 159.

14. Esp. the Financial Peace University. For a book-length summary, see Dave Ramsey, *Financial Peace University: 91 Days to Beat Debt and Build Wealth* (Nashville: Vaughan, 2004).

15. John de Graaf, David Wann, and Thomas Naylor (*Affluenza: The All-Consuming Epidemic* [San Francisco: Berrett-Koehler, 2001], 2) define this as "a painful, contagious, socially transmitted condition of overload, debt, anxiety, and waste resulting from the dogged pursuit of more."

The Silent Generation on the whole understood that retirement meant downsizing and being content with less material prosperity. It is not a coincidence that some of the most joyful Christian communities worldwide are some of the most materially impoverished ones. It should not cause surprise that per capita and in terms of percentage of income, the lower middle-class in the United States has been the most generous financial givers to churches and Christian ministries over the years.[16] In each instance, circumstances have never raised these people's hopes that they might sufficiently prosper in this life so as to secure their futures against all possible calamities. As God meets their needs in the short term, they recognize the need to give generously back to him. Individuals in higher income brackets must see Christian leaders teaching and modeling appropriate downsizing in their contexts so that they can learn how it is possible.

At the same time, a fair number of Boomers will continue to have discretionary income that previous generations did not. Downsizing does not mean trading places with the poor, as Paul makes clear in 2 Corinthians 8:13–15.[17] Ministry and enjoyment of life do not always have to be pitted against one another. Many Boomers will be able to retire and still be active in volunteer work at home and abroad, finding new ways to follow the Great Commandment and the Great Commission along the way. Frequently they will be able to work part-time in either the secular or the church world in ways they couldn't when they were working full-time. Many will remain in good health for quite a while and will want to stay active, not least to be good stewards of that health. It has often been reported that churches may be sorely disappointed if they assume that programs and activities that met the needs and wants of the Silents in their retirement years will work well with Boomers.[18] We do not want to sit around in homogeneous groups being entertained, playing games with one another, or even being passively taught by others. We want to serve and make a difference where we can, while we can. The success of such missions-supporting organizations as the Finishers Project, which target those retiring or wanting to change careers later in life and get *more* involved in explicitly Christian ministry, well attests to these Boomer distinctives.[19] Even

16. See the annual reports on American giving published by John and Sylvia Ronsvalle of empty tomb, inc., in Champaign, Illinois.

17. Craig L. Blomberg, *Neither Poverty nor Riches: A Biblical Theology of Material Possessions* (Downers Grove, IL: InterVarsity, 2001), 194.

18. McIntosh ("Trends and Challenges," 303) advocates building ministries for Boomers that are adventurous, fun, challenging, educational, and spiritual. See also Scott W. Jones, "Baby Boomers and Beyond: Tapping the Ministry Talents and Passions of Adults over 50," *Christian Education Journal* 8 (2011): 429–33.

19. See, e.g., John W. Kennedy, "A Boom for Missions: Early Boomer Retirees Are Giving Back in Big Numbers," *Christianity Today* 51, no. 2 (2007): 20–21.

the number who return to school for formal degrees in order to be licensed or ordained to pastoral office is burgeoning.[20]

With Identity

As we have seen earlier in this book, Baby Boomers, more than many other generations before and after them, derive a disproportionate amount of their identity from their work.

When they retire, voluntarily or involuntarily, a significant portion of their identity comes under siege. Here the "fortress" that Boomers often want to stay within is the office or the workplace, or at least a comparable activity, even if in a different location. Where companies or organizations permit retirees to continue to work part-time, many expect to avail themselves of these opportunities, both for the extra income afforded and, more important, so that they feel like they are still contributing to society in the ways to which they have grown accustomed. Churches and Christian ministries, however, will have to become increasingly attuned to the signs of depression, both formal and informal, that may accompany those who feel they have lost their identity and are "at sea" in determining who they are and what they should be doing with their retirement years. Watch for those who answer questions about what they will do with their newly found free time and make it clear they have thought only in terms of very small tasks that will not occupy much time at all. Those who retire and then shortly afterward also lose a significant measure of their health or independent living skills will be particularly at risk, especially if they have lived thus far relatively unencumbered by loss of work or physical abilities.[21]

For churches not already accustomed to regular teaching on Christians' identity in Christ, some shifts in priorities in instruction may be needed.[22] People who have spent a lifetime hearing that their work is what gives their lives meaning will need a steady dose of Paul's teaching about spiritual giftedness and the spiritual disciplines. As long as a person is even moderately healthy,

---

20. Jeff Strickler, "Baby Boomers Are Flocking to Church Ministry," *Minneapolis Star Tribune*, October 4, 2013, http://www.startribune.com/lifestyle/226387701.html.

21. For several of the points in this paragraph, see Hal Pettegrew, "Perspectives on the Spiritual Development of the 'Aging' Boomers," *Christian Education Journal* 5 (2008): 305–20. For the issue of who is more and less ripe for depression, see Neal Krause, "Parental Religious Socialization Practices, Connectedness with Others, and Depressive Symptoms in Late Life," *International Journal for the Psychology of Religion* 22 (2012): 135–54.

22. A small book that has helped many Boomers to this end, along with the similarly named parachurch ministry, is Neil T. Anderson, *The Steps to Freedom in Christ* (Ventura, CA: Gospel Light, 2001).

almost every gift in Paul's lists in Romans 12, 1 Corinthians 12, and Ephesians 4 can be exercised for the building up of the church and for the glory of God. This is what Christ has always wanted us to be about, whether or not we have ever been paid for using our gifts. If we haven't learned to separate the value of an activity from whether or not it is remunerated, it will be time to learn how to do so. If churches are not in the habit of empowering the laity for a whole spectrum of works of service, it is time now for them to start doing so. If it is a psychological truism that one way to stop feeling sorry for oneself is to help others still needier, then many Boomers will be prime candidates for ministering to and among the still older and more infirm people of their cohort, along with those still alive from the previous generation.[23] Boomers may need to prioritize ministry in independent and assisted living facilities, where they can help and encourage residents to find ways to continue to cultivate their spiritual gifts.

With Mentoring and Grandparenting

In past eras and in various majority world cultures still today, it has been pretty much taken for granted that older people will pass on their work skills to the younger generation. It is also assumed that parents and children will live near extended families so that the wisdom and love of grandparents can be transmitted to their grandchildren as well, and other relatives will probably live nearby also. A fortress is more appropriate when there are large numbers of people protected within it. In the so-called developed Western world, neither of these assumptions about family relationships can any longer be taken for granted. The fortress may house only one or two people! Boomers' characteristic individualism sometimes leaves them surprised when younger generations prove eager for apprenticeships or other informal mentoring relationships. In cultures like ours, in which nuclear families dissolve and may or may not be reconstituted as blended families, and in which single parents remain common, there is often a dearth of good older role models for growing children or young adults. As Christian Boomers watch their children's marriages likewise dissolve, or even remain intact but without the same values as their parents had, they may need to take a more active role in passing on the faith to their grandchildren.[24]

As Elisabeth has already noted, not all who want to mentor know how to do so, even when they may think they do. Churches may need to organize basic

23. Roy M. Oswald, "Ministry to and with Older Adults," *Congregations* 30, no. 2 (2004): 44.

24. Amy Hanson, *Baby Boomers and Beyond: Tapping the Ministry Talents and Passions of Adults over 50* (San Francisco: Josey-Bass, 2010), 52–60.

lay-mentor training programs. Parachurch organizations have often taken the lead in this respect, with various groups matching adults with at-risk children, supplying tutors for kids struggling in school, or creating cross-generational accountability partners.[25] More local congregations may need to think in terms of pairing Boomers in their first years of retirement with children within their own churches who are not already receiving enough love and guidance for healthy living. They may need to match Boomers with Gen-Xers or Millennials who are already immersed in the working world but need extra spiritual and emotional guidance for everything that life throws at them. Of course, the younger partners in each of these pairings will need to show some desire and willingness to be so conjoined, but all the evidence suggests that these younger cohorts do have a strong desire for such relationships (recall the preface).

In the workplace, including in the leadership of churches and parachurch organizations, Boomers need to think in terms of training their successors. When he was rector of St. Aldates, an evangelical Anglican church in Oxford, Michael Green used to like to say that churches should do everything possible to raise up their own ministers, following the model of 2 Timothy 2:2. This included teaching them Greek, Hebrew, theology, church history, and so on. St. Aldates, under Green's tutelage, was able to model these practices. But Green recognized that not many churches could do this, so he stressed that seminaries were needed for the so-called classical disciplines—Bible, theology, philosophy, and history.[26] Today we would need to add disciplines like counseling that prepare people for professional certification. But what *can* be taught in the context of ministry should be learned there. And if a church can help to support ministerial candidates from its own fellowship, especially during their seminary years, and bring them back to contexts with which they are familiar afterward, how much smoother the period of adjustment will be. All of the time needed for new pastors from the outside having to learn to know completely new congregations (and vice versa) is significantly curtailed, and the likelihood of serious misunderstandings minimized.

At a public conference near the end of his life, Carl F. H. Henry, in many people's minds the dean of American evangelical theologians of the Silent Generation, was asked who he saw as his protégés. Who were the individuals he saw as carrying the torch for the next generation—the Boomers—in keeping with his spirit, sentiments, and priorities? Henry seemed startled by the question. His response saddened me when I heard it in person. He replied

25. As, e.g., in Campus Life's Teen Challenge, Young Life, Serve Our Youth, Save Our Youth, Whiz Kids, Crosswinds, and many similar organizations.
26. International Mentoring Conference, Denver Seminary, Englewood, Colorado, spring 1997.

by saying that he had never consciously thought of passing his legacy on to younger theologians. He just did his work, tried to be as faithful to God and his discipline as he could, and hoped it would be of help to others.[27] There is no question that his work was enormously helpful to many others, but just think what could have happened had he *consciously* poured himself into a small collection of individuals eager to follow in his footsteps.

Contrast a recent book by Gordon MacDonald, which is all about the "great idea" that grew on him toward the end of his time in local church ministry: gathering a dozen or so individuals (and their spouses, if they had them) for regular times in his home, over a couple of years, as he and his wife, Gail, intentionally mentored them to carry on the theological and ministerial commitments that the MacDonalds had stressed and modeled in their local churches. He describes how a number of years later all remain active and successful in church as they multiply his legacy in powerful ways.[28] Every Boomer who has acquired a skill worth passing on to someone else should think about finding people he or she can intentionally nurture and equip, both as those Boomers near retirement and when they have additional discretionary time after retirement. Younger colleagues will be the better for it. In Christian contexts, such mentoring should be viewed as virtually mandatory. Retirements from and transitions to jobs and ministry should be timed so as to maximize the chances that younger protégés can actually be hired or appointed to fill the roles for which they have been trained and placed in the positions vacated by their mentors.

Church Life

Ageism

The literature suggests that in many Western contexts, Xers and Millennials have made substantial progress in reducing racism, ethnocentrism, and sexism. Ageism, however, has grown.[29] The message would appear to be that if older people often want to hole up in a fortress, metaphorically speaking, then let them. The movers and shakers will just move to a different neighborhood! Already fairly early in the twentieth century, advertising began to exploit the

27. Conference on African-American Evangelicalism, Geneva College, Beaver Falls, Pennsylvania, summer 1993.

28. Gordon MacDonald, *Going Deep: Becoming a Person of Influence* (Nashville: Thomas Nelson, 2011).

29. Margaret M. Gullette, *Agewise: Fighting the New Ageism in America* (Chicago: University of Chicago Press, 2011).

outward attractiveness of young adults for marketing products of all kinds. Over the course of the past century, there has been less and less necessary connection between the content of advertising and the merits of a product, so long as attractive people sell it.[30] Unfortunately, these trends often caught on in the church in unbiblical and counterproductive ways.[31] The same churches that are filled with young adults and are proving particularly successful at reaching twenty- and thirty-somethings with the gospel and maturing them in Christ are often the very churches that do not accommodate Boomers well. There may be so many young adults that middle-aged members and seniors get lost in the shuffle. A critical mass of homogeneously grouped individuals is often necessary if a church is going to reach a certain target population effectively. But leaving individuals grouped forever in those homogeneous gatherings stunts their growth and witness (see also Eph. 3:10).[32] Churches with traditional Sunday schools or small group ministries who want to inculcate in young adults relevant, biblical values or techniques of good parenting, for example, had best bring at least a few Boomers into their midst who have had a long track record of success in these arenas. Millennials can learn a lot from each other, to be sure, but they glean even more from Boomers who have just lived longer, experienced more, and been able to look back from a greater distance and recognize the long-term consequences of their choices.

Not many years ago, a popular slogan in certain church growth circles was "No age on stage!"[33] In other words, after years of church choirs populated increasingly by aging individuals, it was time to turn exclusively to young adults to lead cutting-edge praise teams, worship bands, and other informal groups of singers and instrumentalists. What an insult to the older generations! Two wrongs hardly make a right. Doubtless, in many instances a greater breadth of ages *was* needed "up front" so that members and visitors alike could see that the church comprised all generations. But to focus exclusively on the young borders on idolatry, and it is a more dangerous mistake than

30. One thinks, for example, of countless beer or insurance ads that capture and retain one's attention with stimuli unconnected to any potentially desirable feature of the product. For the history of advertising, see esp. Mark Tungate, *Adland: A Global History of Advertising* (Philadelphia: Kogan Page, 2007).

31. For wide-ranging reflections on a number of these and related issues, see Tom Beaudoin, *Consuming Faith: Integrating Who We Are with What We Buy* (London: Sheed & Ward, 2003). Still helpful also is Bruce L. Shelley and Marshall Shelley, *Consumer Church: Can Evangelicals Win the World without Losing Their Souls?* (Downers Grove, IL: InterVarsity, 1992).

32. See esp. Bruce Milne, *Dynamic Diversity: Bridging Class, Age, Race, and Gender in the Church* (Downers Grove, IL: InterVarsity, 2007).

33. Frequently reported from Catalyst Conferences for younger pastoral leaders in the mid- to late 2000s.

to focus solely on the old. At least older adults can often help younger ones avoid the mistakes that come from following one's impulses without giving matters adequate thought. Enthusiastic, magnetic young leaders may draw big crowds, and people may flock to the Lord (or at least to the church), but what happens when those leaders move on to other ministries, drop out of Christian work, disclose their theological shallowness, or fall into serious moral failure? When churches composed mostly of young people skyrocket in attendance under outwardly glitzy programs and externally attractive icons, they often plummet just as quickly when those icons fade or fall.

Intergenerational Ministry

During the "worship wars" of the 1990s and early 2000s, one common solution to the generation "gaps" was to create separate services, different congregations, and homogeneously grouped ministries based on the personal preferences of a church's diverse cohorts.[34] This often stopped the infighting, but it didn't promote healthy Christian growth that learns from all generations. Today, a growing minority of churches are starting to recognize that even if they are large enough to subdivide into all sorts of homogeneous groupings, and even if a few of those groupings are helpful for the sake of the effectiveness of the very focused purpose of the group (e.g., helping older divorcees, creating a competitive Christian sports team, or facilitating student-to-student ministry in a school), Christians should regularly be interacting with those in different walks of life, races, socio-economic brackets, and ages whenever possible.[35] One almost always learns and grows more when one is challenged by someone who is different than when one associates solely with those who are most like oneself.

Boomers will therefore bring different issues to the discussion table of a small group Bible study than other generations. Each can learn from the questions the others raise and from the life experiences brought to bear on their applications. Just like it is silly at best and counterproductive at worst for Boomers to be the sole strategists for ministry decisions that largely affect Xers or Millennials, few groups of exclusively younger adults will ever figure out all by themselves the best ways to minister to Boomers. We all need each other. A medical missions team will benefit from the wisdom of

---

34. Thomas G. Long, *Beyond the Worship Wars: Building Vital and Faithful Worship* (Herndon, VA: Alban Institute, 2001), 2. Long refers to this solution as the Balkanization of worship, far less than ideal.

35. John Roberts, "Our Future Is Intergenerational," *Christian Education Journal* 9 (2012): 105–20.

experienced medical personnel alongside the energy and stamina of youth-ful recruits. College ministry requires young adults still close enough in age to the majority of the students to know their subculture and relate to their feelings, hopes, dreams, fears, and insecurities, but it also needs older adults who can see pitfalls and dangers that younger staff can't and who can provide a long-term perspective on following Jesus. Our examples could be multiplied at length.[36]

Equipping and Caregiving for the Neediest Boomers

In Response to Deteriorating Health and Material Circumstances

Many of us have heard draconian predictions about the long-term solvency of Social Security. As we write this book, our nation remains very polarized over the most appropriate forms of health care for Americans and the most appropriate ways to finance it. Statistics about the decreases in the numbers of potential caregivers to the number of elderly from the present through 2050 prove downright scary.[37] Will the poorest of the Boomers die on the streets homeless, unable to pay their bills, evicted from housing, and having to beg for money just to feed themselves, even after a lifetime of wage earning? If that were to happen, would younger cohorts care? The fears at the moment may seem extreme and ill-founded, but it doesn't keep aging Boomers from having them! When the fortress finally crumbles, will there be another shelter for those holed up inside it?

Christians who are politically conservative often suggest that churches should step in where government and social services are often counted on today. For the sake of argument, let's assume they are right. Which congregations are prepared to fill that gap? Which have adequate resources to address the plight of the uninsured who are ill and failing even just in their own midst? More important, which ones would be willing to radically change their budgets in order to meet those needs if public funds were dramatically curtailed? It is easy to *claim* that the church could or should meet needs the government now addresses; it is much harder to envision it actually doing so![38]

36. See esp. Holly Catterton Allen and Christine Lawton Ross, *Intergenerational Christian Formation: Bringing the Whole Church Together in Ministry, Community and Worship* (Downers Grove, IL: InterVarsity, 2012).

37. Sally Abrahms, "Help! Who Will Care for Baby Boomers When They Need It?," *AARP Bulletin*, August 26, 2013, http://blog.aarp.org/2013/08/26/sally-abrahms-help-who-will-care-for-baby-boomers-when-they-need-it/.

38. See further Craig L. Blomberg, *Christians in an Age of Wealth: A Biblical Theology of Stewardship* (Grand Rapids: Zondervan, 2013), 194–242.

When Boomers were young, the big news was that they were dropping out of church at record rates compared to previous generations.[39] Then, especially when they had children, a significant number (though by no means a majority) returned.[40] Now a surprising number who had remained faithful all along are leaving as the institutional church has worn them down or out. They have been hurt too often by legalism, narrow thinking, or authoritarian leadership. They don't understand how much the church needs them, and they perceive that they don't need the church. After all, few preachers in local churches will ever produce the quality of messages that proliferate online. Few musicians will ever lead worship as powerfully as what is readily accessible in recorded media. As long as we keep inculcating a consumer mind-set toward church, these realities will be hard to counter.[41] Only when we demonstrate the importance and value of live community will we be able to bring the dropouts back. Or maybe we take the community to them, with the growth of the house-church movement. Of course, small groups in larger congregations can function similarly, but only when they leave room for the intentional meeting of interpersonal needs instead of just becoming another teaching time in a different venue. Some evidence suggests that retirement and aging will bring some of these lapsed churchgoers back, but not in huge numbers.[42]

From one point of view, it should not be too surprising that longtime Boomer churchgoers can drop out and think that they are not hurting themselves or others in serious ways. Boomers, after all, were the generation that defined Christianity apart from the church in the first place. Countless numbers of them came to faith through parachurch organizations like Youth for Christ, Young Life, Campus Crusade for Christ, InterVarsity Christian Fellowship, the Navigators, the Fellowship of Christian Athletes, and the like. Many were

39. James Bell, *Bridge over Troubled Waters: Ministry to Boomers—A Generation Adrift* (Wheaton: Victor, 1993), 21–27; see also Gary R. Collins and Timothy E. Clinton, *Baby Boomer Blues: Understanding and Counseling Baby Boomers and Their Families* (Nashville: Thomas Nelson, 1992), 15–16, 51–52.

40. Doug Murren, *The Baby Boomerang: Catching the Boomer Generation as They Return to Church* (Ventura, CA: Gospel Light, 1990); see also Hans Finzel, *Help! I'm a Baby Boomer* (Wheaton: Victor, 1989), 140–46.

41. Twenty years ago this was identified as a particular characteristic of Boomers that needed to be challenged. See Kenneth H. Sidey, "Boomer Boom or Bust: Churches Now 'Service' the Consumer Generation, but the Challenge Is to Convert It," *Christianity Today* 37, no. 9 (1993): 14–15. Now it appears to be ubiquitous. For both plight and solutions, see esp. Skye Jethani, *The Divine Commodity: Discovering a Faith beyond Consumer Christianity* (Grand Rapids: Zondervan, 2009). See also Fran Blomberg, "Living Hopefully in a World of Instant Gratification," *Journal of European Baptist Studies* 3 (2012): 26–38.

42. Eric Nagourney, "Why Am I Back in Church?," *New York Times*, October 3, 2012, http://www.nytimes.com/2012/10/04/booming/04question-booming.html?_r=0.

discipled and nurtured for years through these organizations before becoming active in local churches. So it is natural for them to imagine that if they find informal networks of Christian fellowship, continue to engage in spiritual disciplines, and find outlets in the community for Christian service, they can maintain their religious maturity. And a few can. But studies have shown that it is more likely that the less they stay involved in local congregations (including house churches that engage in the full range of Christian worship and activity), the more likely they are to drift away from believing the essential truths of the faith as well. Perhaps surprisingly, it is actually more common for Boomers to leave church and then begin to doubt the central doctrines of Christianity than for them to begin to doubt the truths of the faith and so leave church.[43]

If this is happening even in the latter years of Boomers' working lives, what will retirement hold in store for them? Will they have the faith to go it on their own when the challenges of aging become particularly acute? Will they become embittered because the church does not reach out and help them, even though they were the ones who left the church? Will they decide that God does not exist because they no longer experience the "abundant life" (John 10:10) that was often wrongly defined as health and wealth in this life?[44] Will they stand fast if Christians even in the West experience increasing persecution for their faith?

Despite the differences between Calvinism and Arminianism, one point of theological agreement remains crucial. Both agree that it is possible to profess faith in Christ, engage in activities and experiences with true Christians at times over decades, reach a point in life in which for whatever reasons a person renounces all vestiges of belief, and so be lost for all eternity. Calvinism insists that when certain individuals follow that spiritual path, it demonstrates that they were never truly saved in the first place, though they may have fooled many *and even fooled themselves*.[45] Arminianism holds it is more natural to view them as having sufficient freedom as human beings to have truly embraced Christianity and then truly rejected it.[46] This is an important theological debate, but not as important as the point on which they agree—such people are lost.

---

43. Kevin Ward, "'No Longer Believing'—or—'Believing without Belonging,'" *Modern Believing* 46, no. 2 (2005): 35–45.

44. The context of v. 9 makes it clear that the abundant life is salvation, not some particularly enjoyable form of earthly life, other than that our rich communion with Christ begins in the here and now. See, e.g., Colin G. Kruse, *John* (Grand Rapids: Eerdmans, 2004), 235.

45. See esp. D. A. Carson, "Reflections on Assurance," in *The Grace of God, the Bondage of the Will* (Grand Rapids: Baker, 1995), 2:383–412.

46. See esp. William J. Abraham, "Predestination and Assurance," in *The Grace of God, the Will of Man* (Grand Rapids: Zondervan, 1989), 231–42. Note the numerous items on which Carson and Abraham agree.

Boomers' Christian lives have been characterized by an enormous emphasis on "getting people saved," on crossing the threshold of faith or entrance into the Christian life. But none of the numerous statistics that churches and parachurch organizations worldwide have amassed over the past generation about professions of faith, baptisms, and numbers of members count for nearly as much as how many people are believing in Christ and following him *as they approach their deaths*. This is the only statistic that matters for standing before the judgment seat of Christ (2 Cor. 5:10). If for no other reason than this, Christian ministries had better make tending to Boomers a huge priority over the next generation since it is they who will be dying most frequently!

Of course, one has to factor in a lot of grace when individuals contract dementia, Alzheimer's, and other mental illnesses. Most Christians, of whatever theological stripe, make allowances for the significantly mentally disabled when it comes to how much, if anything, they must be able to understand and articulate about the gospel in order to be right with God. Christians often treat them with the identical theological understanding that they do infants who pass away.[47] A person who shows reasonable signs of having been a Christian prior to end-of-life mental disabilities most likely is one, no matter what they may say or do as a result of debilitating illnesses as they approach death. Indeed, Boomers who will increasingly be wrestling with the eternal destiny of spouses and close friends who precede them in death need to be encouraged with the many accounts of those who have had Jesus or an angel appear to them in their dying moments. No matter how incorrigible a person has seemed throughout life, we have no way of knowing what God's Spirit may have done to change their hearts toward Christ in their last days or hours. When we hear about the instances in which apparently comatose people were still able to perceive some of what was happening around them, or have had experiences of Jesus or heaven while flatlining on the operating table, we are encouraged to believe that many more may have had similar experiences that we will never know about in this life because they never regained consciousness to tell us.[48]

This is a much more biblical and theologically responsible approach to the question of the grace and justice of God than the currently more popular beliefs in certain circles of universalism, a finite hell, purgatory, pluralism,

---

47. E.g., Ronald Nash, *When a Baby Dies: Answers to Comfort Grieving Parents* (Grand Rapids: Zondervan, 1999).

48. See the examples noted and the literature cited in Craig L. Blomberg, *Can We Still Believe the Bible? An Evangelical Engagement with Contemporary Questions* (Grand Rapids: Brazos, 2014), 184.

or varying degrees of reward or separate kingdoms in the afterlife.[49] Salvation remains entirely by grace through faith in Jesus to those who choose to receive it. At the same time, aging Boomers must continue to be challenged, while they are of sound mind, to persevere to the end. This too is a biblical definition of those who are saved (Matt. 24:13). Christians are those who "overcome" (Rev. 2:7, 11, 17, 26; 3:5, 12, 21). Millions throughout church history have had to overcome poverty, chronic physical sickness, incapacity, and persecution, sometimes throughout their entire lives. Many Boomers in the Western world have never suffered anything remotely as severe as this; so if old age becomes hard, there will be the temptation to renege on their faith commitments and baptismal pledges. Some theological traditions that errantly teach you can accept salvation as a free gift without ever making Jesus Lord of your life, without ever demonstrating any living transformed by the Spirit, have offered false hope to people who may not truly be believers at all.[50] They may well be the first to take refuge in a cheap grace—for instance, surrounding themselves with creaturely comforts at all costs, no matter who else remains deprived—when times get tough as they age.

The issue of scarce medical resources, however, is likely to afflict far more than the theologically miseducated. As technology continues to develop, as new medicines are invented, as the population of the world continues to soar, and as politicians and economists wrangle over the best solutions to health care while current disparities and injustices go unaddressed, the numbers of individuals without access to decent medical personnel, hospitals, surgery, pharmaceutical drugs, and residential care facilities will increase, even as the wealthiest few still consume a disproportionate amount of the resources available. Since few Christians today seem upset by the current situation, and even fewer are willing to enter into negotiation with those who see different solutions as more effective or humane, it is hard to be optimistic about the response of the church as matters grow worse. Yet unless Christians become significantly more involved in redemptive ways with the suffering elderly, Boomers will feel justified in turning their backs on the church when it is their turn to face the same challenges of old age. Bitterness and resentment may wash over them much more rapidly than with their parents because they have spent a lifetime feeling entitled to so much more. Once again, Christian leaders will need to lead the way in helping them undergo a paradigm shift in their thinking, with massive doses of

49. For solid but not overly narrow biblical theology of the life to come, see Michael Bird, *Evangelical Theology* (Grand Rapids: Zondervan, 2013), 244–339.
50. Particularly associated with movements like the Grace Evangelical Society and the ministry of pastors/writers like Zane C. Hodges.

biblical truth about how little we are entitled to in this life but how much we are promised in the life to come.

In Response to Perennial End-Times Excitement

Is the fortress on fire? Is it just about to catch fire? We'll be able to escape it when it does, right? Baby Boomers ranged from six to twenty-four years of age when Hal Lindsey published his *Late, Great Planet Earth*, which became the bestselling book of "nonfiction" throughout the entire English-speaking world for the decade of the seventies.[51] And I am referring to *all* books, not just religious literature! Most of us Boomers were in our teens and twenties during the years of its most profound impact, and scarcely a denomination or parachurch ministry was unaffected by its huge popularity and the proliferation of copycat literature it spawned. Many young adults came to faith precisely through these creative descriptions of the alignment of the nations in the Middle East and elsewhere with Lindsey's understanding of biblical prophecies about the end times. Without ever making the mistake of explicitly setting a date for the return of Christ, Lindsey made it very clear that he believed Jesus would come back within one "generation" of the reestablishment of the state of Israel in 1948.[52] Biblical generations were often considered to be thirty or forty years in length but sometimes could be as long as one hundred years, so we are not yet out from under the specter of these end-times watchers' prophecies.

While Christians from the first century onward have regularly tried to predict the time of the end of the world, a more intense flurry than ever of such predictions has permeated the last half of the twentieth century, especially during the run up to the turn of the millennium.[53] Because of our collective amnesia and distaste for studying history more generally, we fail to realize how many hundreds of such predictions have proved wrong over the centuries. Fortunately, we do not stone false prophets in our age. But amazingly, we allow and even encourage the Lindseys, LaHayes and Jenkins, and Joel Rosenbergs of our world by purchasing, reading, and promoting huge quantities of what should properly be classified as "fiction" without realizing that it all stems from a theological novelty created by J. Nelson Darby, the founder of the Plymouth

---

51. Hal Lindsey, *Late, Great Planet Earth* (Grand Rapids: Zondervan, 1970). As reported by Adela Yarbro Collins, "Reading the Book of Revelation in the Twentieth Century," *Interpretation* 40 (1986): 232.

52. See Hal Lindsey, *There's a New World Coming: An In-Depth Analysis of the Book of Revelation* (Eugene, OR: Harvest House, 1984), 92.

53. Francis X. Gumerlock, *The Day and the Hour: Christianity's Perennial Fascination with Predicting the End of the World* (Atlanta: American Vision, 2000).

Brethren, in 1830.[54] What came to be known as "dispensationalism," at least in its classic form, complete with a pretribulational rapture, cannot be found unambiguously in previous Christian history.[55]

But today, especially in its most extreme forms as promoted by Lindsey and others, in many Christian circles dispensationalism is the *only* understanding of the end times that is even known, or at least the only one to be believed to be consistent with orthodoxy! Historic or classic premillennialism, amillennialism, and postmillennialism, however, are the three forms of eschatology that competed with each other in the first eighteen centuries of church history, none of which believes in a secret rapture of the church separate from the welcoming party that believers on earth will create when Christ publicly returns in triumph *after the tribulation*.[56]

All of this might seem like an arcane debate were it not for its effect on Boomers' response to hard times in this life. An escapist mentality pervades Boomer evangelical Christian thought, which has tricked many into believing that we will escape the most difficult times that earth-dwellers can face because Christ will rapture his church before we have to undergo them. Boomers often fail to reflect on the excruciating suffering God has already permitted his people to endure in many eras and many parts of the world, even should belief in a pretribulational rapture turn out to be well founded. The result is an anemic theology of suffering.[57] One wonders whether Boomers really will be able to cope with the debilitating effects of aging, to say nothing of the very real possibility that the tribulation might be imminent and that we might be called to live through it.

Avoiding the Myth of the "Good Old Days"

Every generation seems to have the tendency to forget the worst of its youth and idealize the best. "Oldies" radio stations no longer play big band music

54. Esp. Tim LaHaye and Jerry B. Jenkins's Left Behind series (Wheaton: Tyndale House, 1995–2007); Joel C. Rosenberg, *The Tehran Initiative* (Wheaton: Tyndale House, 2011); and *The Damascus Countdown* (Wheaton: Tyndale House, 2013).

55. See Donald Fairbairn, "Contemporary Millennial Debates: Whose Side Was the Early Church On?," in *A Case for Historic Premillennialism: An Alternative to "Left Behind" Eschatology*, ed. Craig L. Blomberg and Sung Wook Chung (Grand Rapids: Baker Academic, 2009), 61–87.

56. See further Craig L. Blomberg, "The Posttribulationism of the New Testament: Leaving 'Left Behind' Behind," in Blomberg and Chung, *Case for Historic Premillennialism*, 61–87.

57. For good examples of a good theology of suffering, see D. A. Carson, *How Long, O Lord? Reflections on Suffering and Evil*, 2nd ed. (Grand Rapids: Baker Academic, 2006); Philip Yancey, *Where Is God When It Hurts?*, rev. ed. (Grand Rapids: Zondervan, 1990); C. S. Lewis, *The Problem of Pain* (London: Whitebriars, 1940).

as they did when Boomers were younger but rather classic rock of the 1960s and 1970s. Debates about whether this was the greatest music of all time are usually benign, but Boomers will need to resist the urge to idealize the hippie culture with its free sex and experimentation with drugs. There is good reason that almost all Boomers who were caught up in these activities were unable to continue to live that way for very long! Living in the past so that one misses out on the present is never healthy; but Boomers of all people should know better since they, more than most cohorts, have severely criticized their parents' generation for not changing with the times.

Where there are enduring values to be preserved, retirement may give Boomers the opportunity to demonstrate these values in ways younger generations can learn from. Healthy social activism, a discontent with negative status quos, and a willingness to protest unjust authorities can all become part of Baby Boomers' legacy to pass on to those who will follow in their wake. We Boomers have often spoken what we believed to be the truth but not always with enough love, while Xers and especially Millennials often excel at love but not always with enough truth. Chastened Boomers, who learn from younger generations and who have extra discretionary time afforded by healthy years of retirement, can model the biblical mandate of speaking the truth in love in the public square.[58]

But Boomers dare not assume that they have a corner on the truth. When biblical submission to governmental authorities gets replaced with an overly zealous patriotism or a Rambo-like support of the military, Baby Boomers need younger cohorts to temper their excesses. When Boomers view politics rather than the church as providing the ultimate solutions to social problems, they need to listen to voices of other generations as well. While there are issues of racism and sexism yet to be adequately addressed, Boomers dare not go ballistic when Xers and Millennials seem reasonably happy with the advances already made and don't share the zeal for civil rights and women's rights that the 1960s and 1970s displayed. And no cohort dares allow the numerous debates surrounding the practice of homosexuality to monopolize anyone's agenda.

Conclusion

The antidote to looking in the rearview mirror too much is, of course, to pay attention to the road ahead. Great homes can be built again, and they don't need to be fortresses. Boomers who spend too much time reminiscing about

---

58. For a plethora of ideas, see throughout Hanson, *Baby Boomers and Beyond*.

the past need to be challenged to look to the future. The best days could still lie ahead. For Christians, at least, the best days absolutely lie ahead. "Let us run with perseverance the race marked out for us, fixing our eyes on Jesus, the pioneer and perfecter of faith. For the joy set before him he endured the cross, scorning its shame, and sat down at the right hand of the throne of God. Consider him who endured such opposition from sinners, so that you will not grow weary and lose heart" (Heb. 12:1–3). Or in the words of the chorus of an amazing song performed and made famous by Boomer icon Steve Green, "Oh may all who come behind us find us faithful. / May the fire of our devotion light their way. / May the footprints that we leave lead them to believe / and the lives we live inspire them to obey."[59]

Faithfulness entails keeping our promises—to our God, to our families, to our churches, and to our callings. But it means dissociating those commitments from the quantity of our income, the length of our career, or the amount of our productivity. We must reclaim our fundamental identity as beloved children of God destined for a glorious eternity and reflect on temporal realities increasingly in that light. We dare not hide our struggles from those around us, but we must certainly and humbly let our spiritual triumphs be visible to encourage others who have yet to come as far in their journeys. Then we can look forward to our Lord's words, "Well done, good and faithful servant" (Matt. 25:21, 23)!

59. Words and music by Jon Mohr. Copyright by Birdwing Music/Jonathan Mark Music, 1988.

4

Generation X

The Lost Middle Child

Music is a powerful way in which a culture or group of people can communicate their heart, soul, passions, and concerns. As with any cultural artifact, one song or genre can never fully capture a culture, but once in a while you stumble across something that serves as a quintessential example. As a younger Xer himself, pop singer and songwriter John Mayer, on his *Continuum* album, captures the sentiment of Generation X better than just about anything I (Elisabeth) have heard, specifically in his song "Waiting on the World to Change." Speaking of how Mayer's generation (Xers) is perceived by others, Mayer writes: "they say we stand for nothing and / there's no way we ever could / now we see everything that's going wrong / with the world and those who lead it / we just feel like we don't have the means / to rise above and beat it . . . / so we keep waiting / . . . on the world to change."[1]

While it isn't a perfect synopsis, it does communicate much of the underlying heart and struggle that characterize this cohort.

1. John Mayer, "Waiting for the World to Change," *Belief*, CD, Sony, 2008.

The smallest, quietest, and most overlooked of the generations, Gen-Xers have a near and dear place in my heart as the lost middle child of today's American culture. Unlike the Boomers who came before them or the Millennials after them, who were seen and talked about from the moment of their inception, no one really took notice of this cohort until the 1990s when researchers started realizing, "Hey, these guys aren't Boomers anymore!" A cohort of 61 million people, Xers are significantly smaller than the generations that surround them, but we will see that their quiet place in the "family" system is just as critical and pertinent as the places of their larger and louder siblings.[2]

The label "Generation X" is often credited to Douglas Coupland and his novel *Generation X: Tales for an Accelerated Culture*, published in 1991, twenty-six years after the cohort first made its appearance in American society.[3] Our American culture does not often consider or recognize the significance of names, but I can't help but ask people to stop and consider what this generation's name might actually represent. Baby Boomers were named because of the unique space they occupied in American society, as members of the largest "baby boom" in history, and Millennials were also named because of the uniqueness of their historic location in time (coming of age in the new millennium). Xers by contrast were given a name that functions as a "non-label," a name that communicates the cohort's desire to be undefined as well as the larger society's struggle to understand them.[4]

Before we go much further, I must admit and embrace my Gen-X identity. Although I am a cusper, born in the final year of the Generation X cohort (1981), I fit this generational identity much more than I fit the Millennial identity. As Craig mentioned in chapter 2, personal bias and generational affiliation likely cloud how I see this cohort, but I will do my best to communicate who they (we) are in a way that is honest, fair, and forthright.

The Middle Child

Without question, Xers function as the middle child within the family that is American culture today. Often the middle child is described as being the "lost" member of the family, overshadowed by the eldest child and out-prized and adored by the youngest child. The genius of middle children, though, is

2. Lindsay M. Howden and Julie A. Meyer, "Age and Sex Composition: 2010," *2010 Census Briefs* (May 2011): 2.

3. Douglas Coupland, *Generation X: Tales of an Accelerated Culture* (New York: St. Martin's, 1991).

4. Claire Raines Associates, "10 Most Frequently Asked Questions," *Generations at Work* (2009), http://www.generationsatwork.com/faq.php#2.

that they are quite creative and adept at figuring out how to find a place for themselves without having to compete for power, status, or position, and Xers have fit this description perfectly.[5] Psychologists often describe the middle child with traits we will unpack as we explore who Gen-Xers are as a group. These traits include the following characteristics: "mediator, compromising, diplomatic, avoids conflict, independent, loyal to peers, has many friends, a maverick, secretive, [and] used to not having attention."[6]

Generally quiet nonconformists, Xers often come into my presentations skeptical, making small comments under their breath about how they can't be defined and are their own unique and independent persons. It always makes me smile. In keeping with their middle-child traits, Xers quietly recoil at the insinuation that you can explain, define, or predict them, for they are independent individuals.[7] For the Xer, this is not a desire to stay hidden or elusive but rather a lived experience of feeling misunderstood, taken for granted, and even unseen that perpetuates their sense of privacy. As we have said about all the cohorts, while there are some strong commonalities that help to describe the culture or collective personality of Gen-Xers, not every Xer will fit these descriptions as each person brings their own lived experiences, personality, and broader cultural influences to the table.[8]

Xers' Place in the World

Born between 1965 and 1981, Generation X takes up the smallest amount of space out of the three cohorts, both chronologically and numerically. Born to members of the Silent generation (1925–45) and to older Boomers, Xers total 61 million in membership, significantly smaller than the 83- to 85- million-member cohorts on either side of them.[9] The end of the Baby Boomer generation and the beginning of the Xers was marked by the annual birth

5. On the power of middle children, see Catherine Salmon and Katrin Schuman, *The Secret Power of Middle Children: How Middleborns Can Harness Their Unexpected and Remarkable Abilities* (New York: Hudson Street, 2011).

6. Kevin Leman, *The Birth Order Book: Why You Are the Way You Are*, 3rd ed. (Grand Rapids: Revell, 2009), 18.

7. Inevitably, Xers do find themselves described within the presentation given, often commenting that they thought "it was just me" and finding a sense of ironic validation in knowing they are not alone in their individuality.

8. As was stated regarding Baby Boomers, the values, beliefs, worldviews, and descriptions of Generation X summarized in this chapter, unless otherwise noted, reflect key themes found in the research conducted for my dissertation. See Elisabeth A. Nesbit, "Generational Affiliation as a Component of Culture: Focus Group Perspectives of Three Generational Cohorts" (PhD diss., University of Arkansas, 2010), 17–36, 76–106.

9. Howden and Meyer, "Age and Sex Composition: 2010," 2.

rate dropping below 4 million, to 3.7 million, in 1965. The birth rate would not again start on a continual upswing until 1980.[10]

There is a variety of reasons for the birth rate of Gen-Xers being so low, and they span the personal to the political. On the personal side, Gen-Xers were being born into American society when self-help and the pursuit of personal growth were taking off. Where previous generations had seen the family as the marker of personal success, the parents of Xers were coming of age in a time when professional development was more the marker of their success. As such, children were at times seen as a hindrance to their parents' (particularly their mother's) personal pursuits and development, with pregnancy being postponed beyond the age that had been the norm in previous generations. Between 1946 and 1965 the average number of children born to a woman was consistently above 2.5, reaching nearly 3.7 in the mid-1950s.[11] The year 1965 saw that number drop below 2.5 and continue dropping into the mid-1970s to approximately 1.7, not reaching over 2.0 again until 1989.[12] Additionally, on the political front, with the birth control pill obtaining FDA approval in 1960 and the *Roe v. Wade* decision legalizing abortion in 1973, Xers were the first generation in American history to be born fully into an era that legally allowed for the prevention, and later the termination, of pregnancy. On a societal level, this combination of political climate with personal environment facilitated an atmosphere in which children were seen as hindrances to their parents' personal development, contributing greatly to a lower birth rate. Peter Menconi referred to this phenomenon as "an unwanted generation," while M. J. Stephey in his *Time* magazine article calls Xers "ignored" and "invisible."[13]

If the atmosphere in which Gen-Xers were born was less hospitable than that which Boomers encountered, their adult world did not prove any more welcoming either. Whether it was the Vietnam War, Watergate, Jonestown, the Iranian hostage crisis, the highest divorce rates in American history, Three Mile Island, the emergence of HIV/AIDS, the Challenger explosion, or the Chernobyl disaster, Xers I interviewed identified primarily disheartening or traumatic experiences as the significant historic events that shaped their view

10. Info Please, "Live Births and Birthrates, by Year," *Information Please Database* (2007), http://www.infoplease.com/ipa/A0005067.html.

11. Center for Disease Control, "Achievements in Public Health, 1900–1999," *Morbidity and Mortality Weekly Report* 48, no. 47 (December 3, 1999): 1073.

12. Center for Disease Control, "Achievements in Public Health," 1073; The World Bank, "Fertility Rate, Total (Births per Woman)," *Data* (2014), http://data.worldbank.org/indicator/SP .DYN.TFRT.IN?page=4.

13. Peter Menconi, *The Intergenerational Church: Understanding Congregations from WWII to WWW.com* (Littleton, CO: Mt. Sage, 2010), 91; M. J. Stephey, "Gen-X: The Ignored Generation?," *Time*, April 6, 2008, http://content.time.com/time/arts/article/0,8599,1731528,00.html?artId =1731528?contType=article?chn=arts.

of the world, clearly creating a sense that the world and its leaders were not safe or to be trusted.[14] Coming after the sexual revolution and the age of free love, HIV/AIDS was a game changer for adults in American society, and the oldest Gen-Xers were on the verge of adulthood when it hit the scene in 1981. This epidemic can be seen as a symbolic representation of how Xers felt about the world Boomers handed them: they had been told about and promised a lifestyle that assumed the economy would continue to increase and pursuits of personal gain and pleasure were generally rewarded without significant consequence. Instead they walked into a situation where the job market was scarce, an oil crisis was ever just around the corner if not upon them, and the consequences of pursuing personal gain and pleasure were now being felt. Tragically, what was a lived history of hope, prosperity, and endless possibilities to Boomers was a thing of storybooks and fairy tales to Xers.

The world of pop culture looked very different for Gen-Xers as well. Cultural norms such as the Beatles, Jimi Hendrix, *I Love Lucy*, and *Get Smart* were replaced with heavy metal, grunge rock, MTV, and *The Simpsons*. The music and media of Gen-X reflected their disenchantment, disappointment, sense of angst, and desire for independence from the culture Baby Boomers had created for them. Stating, "We were taught to respect the media but we've learned not to," Xers "don't trust the media," "don't believe the media," and generally "think media makes you more skeptical . . . [because] you always get so many different messages . . . and then you think you believe in one health study, and then the next year [one] comes out and says no, and there [is] just an unending amount of things that get proven and disproven."

Furthermore, while Xers take a vested interest in the concerns of those around them, they also say that the media have made them feel overwhelmed and powerless to combat the sadness and negativity they see broadcast on a regular basis. For Boomers, this introduction to the world being in their living rooms occurred gradually over time.[15] But for Xers, the world has continually

14. National Center for Health Statistics, "Advance Report of Final Divorce Statistics, 1988," *Monthly Vital Statistics Report* 39, no. 12, supp. 2 (May 21, 1991): 2. Even though Boomers also experienced these same events, the significance lies in when such events happened in the developmental processes of a generation. For Xers these events took place during their childhood and adolescence, serving to shape and influence the foundations of their worldview, whereas these same events took place after Boomers were already into adulthood with their foundational sense of self in the world already established. Furthermore, the significant events listed by Boomers, although also potentially seen as traumatic, are not talked about as such by Boomers, possibly because Boomers had a stronger familial and societal foundation upon which negative life events were filtered. For Xers, there was no positive foundation upon which to ground themselves when the negative events transpired.

15. Whether by radio or television, both Boomers and Xers have grown up with some form of media in their living rooms providing news and information about the world. The significant

been available to them on such an up-close and personal level, causing them to retreat at the weight of all they see and embark on what feel like more tangible and seemingly effective efforts on a more personal or local level. As one member in a group of Xers summarized in reference to the role of the media on their generation,

> We see death and destruction happen on even small and grand scales live. We [have] grown up with this so it's kind of like, if something happens somewhere across the world, when we're visually exposed to it, it makes us [feel] like, "Well, I can't do that. I can't fix it, I can't make it better." It's desensitized us too. And it's made us feel, like, powerless and that's why they say we're the "why not" generation, that we're so jaded because, we . . . feel that powerlessness in a sense that I don't think the younger kids feel.

In addition to feeling the weight of the events media broadcast and their powerlessness to do anything about them, Xers repeatedly spoke of not knowing where to turn for truthful information and of seeing the media as a representation of this existential uncertainty.

A Sense of Self in Comparison to the Others

I must admit that I went into researching Gen-Xers with some level of skepticism—spoken as a true Xer myself! I had read the anecdotal writings about how independent, apathetic, noncommittal, and generally unmotivated Xers are, and I was curious to see whether or not this cohort could clearly and collectively define itself.[16] What I discovered really surprised me. Where Boomers tended to overexplain themselves—going back and forth between how they used to be to how they are now, filling in with stories, examples, and anecdotes—Xers were incredibly succinct, poignant, and clear. They answered questions in a matter-of-fact way that carefully used personal, historical, and cultural examples to support their points while simultaneously communicating the sense that this self-awareness had been intentionally pursued and constructed. In keeping with their middle-child nature, Gen-Xers presented themselves as the child who has had to be intentional about

---

difference here was in the quantity and availability as well as the type of news coverage that was made available from one generation to the next.

16. E.g., Andrew Brownstein, "The Next Great Generation?," *Chronicle of Higher Education* 47, no. 7 (2000): 71, compares the main anecdotal themes of Boomers, Xers, and Millennials, highlighting key traits of each cohort. See also Jimmy Long, *Generating Hope: A Strategy for Reaching the Postmodern Generation* (Downers Grove, IL: InterVarsity, 1997), 38; and Ron Zemke, Claire Raines, and Bob Filipczak, *Generations at Work: Managing the Clash of Boomers, Gen Xers, and Gen Yers in the Workplace* (New York: American Management Association, 2013), 90.

developing their sense of self in order to have a clear identity separate from their more outspoken older sibling. When expressing who they were, it was as if they assumed their time in the spotlight was limited; if they wanted to be heard, they needed to get to the point.

A skeptical "collective of individuals" succinctly captures this generation's sense of self. "Independent," "skeptical," and "individualistic" are the descriptors that underlie the identity and motivations of Xers, and we will see these characteristics permeate the conceptualization of the world around them as well as how they engage that world. In all their independence and individualism, it is important to remember that Gen-Xers are not isolationists; being a part of a collective is still important to this cohort.

What an Xer means by a collective identity differs greatly from what a Boomer means by it. For a Boomer, collective identity is broad and generally reflects a macro-level affiliation with their generational cohort, a religious denomination, or some other large-scale social group. For Xers, a collective identity is understood on a much smaller, subcultural scale and is coupled with a fierce sense of individualism. As one Xer put it, "Everyone wanted to be an individual but then you wanted to have friends, so you had to find those friends who . . . wanted to be just like you, [who] could be individuals with you."

Interestingly, Gen-Xers spent more time talking about their identity in relationship to the generations surrounding them than either Boomers or Millennials did. In this way, Xers define themselves by what they *are not* almost as much as by what they are.[17] They carry with them conflicting feelings as they look at the generations around them, trying to balance resentment with understanding as well as skepticism with hope. As they look back at Boomers, Xers express passing appreciation for many of the social justice battles initiated and fought by Boomers but describe the older generation as being self-indulgent, self-absorbed, and selfish; they feel Boomers impose their values and causes on Xers while also expecting Xers to "fix everything." As Xers look forward at the Millennial generation, they express more hope and optimism, seeing them as activists who are full of potential. On the other side, Xers also looked at Millennials with disappointment, describing them as entitled, selfish, sheltered, indifferent to religion, and unable to think for themselves. While Xers can relate to and appreciate the collectiveness of identity found in the surrounding cohorts, they see both Boomers and Millennials as lacking the strong sense of individualism and independence that they hold so dear.

17. Zemke, Raines, Filipczak, *Generations at Work*, 89.

Independent and Alone

Gen-Xers do not see their independence or individualism as a selfish pursuit but rather one of self-protection and preservation. On both the collective and individual levels, Xers see themselves as being alone in the world, unable to depend on others for support and needing to make their own way in life.[18] Where Boomers carry with them a sense of needing to pull themselves up by their bootstraps while the community is there to support, affirm, and encourage them in their endeavors, Xers feel more that "I have to do it myself; no one's going to help me, and I'm going to do it my way." This sense of being alone in one's journey is rooted in Xers' historical location in both American society and the home. Time and experience have shown Xers that they generally *are* alone, and while their family or community might not actively oppose their efforts, they are unlikely to experience much direct support.

This sense of having to self-protect often comes out in Xers' apprehension of commitment, particularly their fear of marital commitment. Carrying with them the sense that they are the only protectors of their future welfare and well-being, and having seen the relational effects of what they viewed as their parents' poor decisions, Xers are deeply afraid of making the "wrong choice" and finding themselves stuck—unprotected, unhappy, and unfulfilled. This fear is then coupled with a belief that there is always something "better" to be had. This tension between fear of choosing poorly and a belief that one should be able to find something better at all times impacts the way Xers go about choosing everything from jobs to life partners. Their skepticism is well founded, although incomplete, as they look at marriage or any other commitment and wonder, *What if someone who seems great now only proves "good" later on, and I meet someone "better"? How can I know that the person I choose is really the person I can be with forever?* Given the models they grew up with, their fears may be seen as somewhat understandable and not necessarily without merit.

Heroes

Xers' sense of having to make their own way in the world is also seen in their response to the question of who their heroes are. For Xers, heroes are individually chosen. As if quoting a Boomer parent or older authority figure, one Xer captured the cohort's view of role models and heroes by stating, "We're not going to give you role models because every role model we've ever given you we've deconstructed for you." Whether it was a political leader such

---

18. William Mahedy and Janet Bernardi elaborate on this construct in their book *A Generation Alone: Xers Making a Place in the World* (Downers Grove, IL: InterVarsity, 1994).

as President Nixon and Watergate, a military leader like Ollie North, or Jim Bakker as a religious leader, Xers have seen leaders and would-be heroes fall from grace in ways not experienced by Boomers.[19] (Interestingly, the Boomers I interviewed spoke of seeing this cultural shift as well and noted that they are aware that their childhood heroes were not so iconic or infallible; this awareness came in hindsight.) For Xers, anyone lifted up is asking to be taken down, and he or she is ultimately not trusted until his or her flaws are revealed. While reality television is seen often as a Millennial trend, it is Gen-Xers who propelled this phenomenon, having written, produced, and starred in the reality shows in which celebrities and average people alike reveal their flaws to the public.[20] This valuing of seeing all sides of public figures continues within the Millennial generation, but Xers were the first to champion it.

While Xers vehemently rejected the idea of corporate or collective heroes within their generation, each person I interviewed could give me the name of at least one individual in their life whom they considered a hero. For Xers, a hero is not some mythical figure who appears larger than life or who holds celebrity status. Instead, a hero is a person Xers have watched in an up-close and personal way, a person they have seen rise above adversity, champion a cause, accomplish personal goals, and still take the time to invest in the Xer as an individual. In the absence of community-based role models or heroes, one Xer summarized the cohort's sentiment by stating,

> Another thing is the reliance on family as a replacement perhaps for that model of guidance and the model for your belief systems and whatnot . . . maybe more central than an outside influence. That maybe the older generations might have had, "I look up to my president; I look up to the police officer; I look up to the teacher." And now it's your family, and I would throw in friends.

For this generation, a hero is not a person who is unscathed or unscarred but rather a person who has the strength and humility to make it through hard times and pass on hope to those with whom they share their story.

19. Even though Boomers also experienced the downfall of these same leaders, the significance lies in when such failings happened in the developmental processes of a generation.

20. For example, shows such as MTV's "The Real World" (which debuted in 1992 and was arguably the first popular reality TV show) and CBS's "Big Brother" brought "normal" Xers on screen for the world to watch. Celebrity reality shows such as E!'s "Keeping Up with the Kardashians" and MTV's "Newlyweds" put young Xer stars on display for their audiences to see. (Kourtney Kardashian was born in 1979, Kim Kardashian in 1980, Jessica Simpson in 1980, and Nick Lachey in 1973.) See http://www.imdb.com for information and statistics on the above listed shows, actors, and actresses.

Gen-Xer Values

Individualism, independence, freedom, skepticism, interconnectedness, and responsibility are core values of most Gen-Xers. The pursuits of this generational cohort are not rooted in outspokenness and protest on a macro-level but instead focus on the power of individual choices and micro-level changes, both for oneself and for one's community. They fiercely pursue and protect the freedom to choose for themselves who they want to be and how they want to live life, but they do so in a way that is less outspoken or assertive than either Boomers or Millennials and with a deeper sense of skepticism and doubt.

Both/And

As mentioned above, Xers often carry with them seemingly dichotomous values, such as seeing themselves as collective individuals, but this dualistic nature is also profoundly seen in their ability to simultaneously hold skepticism and hope. Their skepticism is not rooted in an oppositional attitude or an "Eeyore-esque" pessimism but instead reflects their lived experiences in which authority, institutional structures, and information sources have proven untrustworthy and unreliable. When asked what their beliefs are, Xers struggled more than any other cohort, again rooted in their skepticism that, in regards to collectively agreed-upon truths, "We Xers don't believe anything! We wouldn't dare, it would be a lie! It would be, it would be a lie."

John Mayer's *Continuum* album and his song "Belief" capture much of Xer sentiment regarding this concept. The lyrics read, "Is there anyone who ever remembers / changing their mind from the paint on a sign?. . . / Everyone believes, / from emptiness to everything . . . / We're never gonna beat this / if belief is what we're fighting for . . ."[21]

It is important to note that the ideas in these lyrics, which came out loudly in my interviews with Xers, are not describing a lack of belief, for "everyone believes." This is not in conflict with the quotation above about not believing anything but speaks rather to a different kind of belief—a belief that is individualistic rather than collective or universal. This belief is different than that of Boomers; belief to an Xer is an incredibly individually defined construct, and the more a belief system is perceived to be shoved at them, the more an Xer will be skeptical of its trustworthiness or truthfulness.[22]

21. Mayer, "Belief."
22. The word "shoved" was intentionally chosen here, as it was the word Xers repeatedly used during my interviews to describe the influence they felt Boomers *tried* to have on them. To many Xers, anything that must be "shoved" or adamantly insisted upon causes doubt, leaving the Xer to question why so much convincing is needed if something is truly that "right" or "good."

This struggle to identify absolute beliefs means that many Xers carry with them a greater value and appreciation for the things that they perceive as "gray" in life, and conversely a rejection of things that are presented as "black and white." One Xer put it almost exactly that way: "I believe the difference in our generation is that we are more okay in the gray area," and with that they leave more room for individuals to decide for themselves what is right or wrong. Skeptical of authority, the media, and established religion, Xers counter their uncertainty with a hope that the future will be better, that they can make even a small difference in the world, and that their strivings in life will result in greater balance, life fulfillment, and happiness than their parents experienced.

Innovation and Freedom

This value and appreciation for the gray makes Xers the innovators in most workplaces.[23] They are not going to be your inventors; that role more often belongs to Millennials. Instead, Xers are the ones who have learned to find their way within a system; they are adaptable, and yet they are constantly trying to discover new ways of doing things, new ways of making the old more effective or efficient. "Generation X [has] become adaptive. While the letter X can have negative connotations, it is also an algebraic term, a variable that can be adaptive to new situation."[24] "The 'X' . . . can represent any number infinitely positive or negative. I believe God's plan for this generation is to fill in that 'X' with his abundant grace in order to see us rise to our potential."[25]

Connected to their value of being independent and their desire to carve out their own unique path and identity in life, Xers strive to find ways of making their work their own. This may be expressed in outward initiatives such as going to a boss and asking for the freedom to accomplish a task in a new way, so long as it still meets the necessary deadlines and requirements.[26] This may also be expressed as an internal conviction or awareness that the Xer carries inside them. As one Xer captured it, "I might act like I'm following the rules for a while, but I always have the freedom, you know? Inside I'm not really following the rules; I make my own rules! That's part of being unconfined, part of being independent."

23. Long, *Generating Hope*, 39.
24. Ibid., 38.
25. Jeffrey Bantz, "Generation X: Implications," paper for Latin American Mission (1995), 193, quoted in ibid.
26. This, by the way, causes great stress for many Boomers who feel that an Xer's request to change the process is a request to change the outcome or change the system.

For any boss or supervisor, it is important to remember that just because an Xer employee may appear to be passive or compliant, it does not mean that internally they aren't holding on to a variety of new ideas or innovations, just waiting for you to ask for their input. They have generally remained silent out of respect for the hierarchy and the system that they know Boomers so highly value, but they are simply waiting to be asked, to be invited, to be seen, to be heard.

Sphere of Influence

To their surrounding cohorts, Gen-Xers often appear less socially and politically active but are often not given credit for the creative, alternative, and subtle ways in which they engage and contribute to the needs around them.[27] Challenging again the Boomer notion of large-scale change and activism and choosing instead to look on a more micro-level, Xers prefer to focus on their "sphere of influence." As some Xers have described it, "I need to be responsible for my sphere of influence, my part of the puzzle. And then your sphere of influence goes out and explodes forward—overlaps into other people's. So it's a *huge* responsibility. It is! But it starts individually; we start individually."

To Xers, a sense of responsibility for the environment is also connected to the value placed on one's sphere of influence. More than any other cohort, Xers spoke of environmentalism and their personal efforts to be responsible with the resources they have. Tying in to their emphasis on sphere of influence, one Xer captured the cohort's sentiment by stating, "The only thing that I can do is local," and that by focusing on the micro-level of change they counter their feelings of being "overwhelmed with all the problems" in the world.

In the midst of their individualism a sense of interconnectedness permeates the Xers' sense of responsibility. This belief that "everything is interconnected" speaks to both a relational interconnectedness between people and an interconnectedness between life choices; one decision will not just influence those around them but will impact future choices and decisions as well. One Xer

27. Social Science Data Network, "Voter Turnout," http://www.ssdan.net/content/voter-turnout. In 2008 Gen Xers were 25–44 years old and had a voter turnout for the presidential election at just over 50 percent. In 1988 and 1992, when Baby Boomers dominated that age bracket, voter turnout was closer to 55 percent. Michael Winerip ("Boomers, Millennials, and the Ballot Box," *The New York Times*, October 29, 2012, http://www.nytimes.com/2012/10/29/booming/voter-turnout-for-boomers-and-millennials.html?_r=2&) demonstrates how "unseen" Xers are, as he compares Boomer and Millennial voting rates but doesn't even address Xers. See also National Conference on Citizenship, "Two Special Generations: The Millennials and the Boomers" (2008–2014), http://ncoc.net/226. According to Jon D. Miller, "Active, Balanced, and Happy: These Young Americans Are Not Bowling Alone," *The Generation X Report* 1, no. 1 (Fall 2011): 5, a full 44 percent of Xers are actively involved in volunteer organizations.

captured the cohort's perception of this phenomenon by stating, "It really overwhelms me. Just that, even the interconnected thing, I think I do believe that we're interconnected, but my goodness it feels really overwhelming. It's too big. The responsibility is too big." What I personally found interesting in my conversations with Xers is that the sense of being overwhelmed by the responsibility to whatever they are connected did not seem to deter Xers from still striving toward their goals and doing so with hope.[28]

The values of individualism, independence, freedom, skepticism, interconnectedness, and responsibility that Xers carry permeate nearly every part of their life—the work they do, how they spend their recreational time, and whether they choose to have a family. It is important to note that to whom or for what an Xer is responsible is not likely to be discerned by an outside observer; it must be understood from the perspective of each individual Xer. In particular, where a Boomer perceives responsibility through the lens of their life roles and tasks, an Xer's sense of responsibility is not tied to life roles; it is instead intricately influenced by their values of individualism, independence, freedom, interconnectedness, and skepticism, and their sense that they have to make their own way in life.

Xers: Up Close and Personal

As we did with Boomers, it is now time to bring the focus out of the general and into more specific areas of Xer life. In particular we are going to explore how Xers engage their community and social relationships, their workplace, their homes, and their churches or religious communities. As with each generational cohort, the values, worldview, and lived experiences of Gen-Xers deeply influence the ways in which they express themselves within each context.

Xers in Community

Community for Xers is a unique thing, and like many other concepts for Xers, it is individually defined and pursued. As I reviewed literature on this topic, I was confronted time and again with the fact that Xer community does not look or sound like Boomer or Millennial community. In fact, in all the interviews that I did, very few Xers talked about friends, family, or community

28. Where Baby Boomer hope is an optimistic and idealistic hope of what could be, an Xer hope is more pragmatic and practical. What is significant in these findings is that the pervasive hope that Xers spoke of in interviews counters much of the stereotypes and anecdotal assumptions about Xers and shows that Xers' skepticism is not necessarily pessimism.

unless directly asked, while Boomers and Millennials interwove such affiliations into much of what they talked about. It is not fair to Xers to say they lack community as a generation; rather, they see its role differently than the generations that surround them. Much of this likely goes back to their historic location and their lived experiences as latch-key kids, only children, and being such a smaller cohort. Instead of viewing community as group affiliation, for Xers their social and interpersonal connections are about *individuals* with whom they connect and choose to go through life.[29]

Unlike Boomers, who describe themselves as "citizens of the planet" and see their community as the people with whom they regularly interact, Xers truly focus their sense of community on their sphere of influence and those with whom they are interconnected. For the Xer, community is not simply the people around you but more specifically the people to whom your life choices ripple out and affect. In this way, community for Xers is not a concept that is as critical to their identity as it is for Boomers. For Boomers, their sense of self is partially defined by the groups or the community they are a part of, but for Xers, their individualism stands out as a larger definer of who they are.

In true middle-child fashion, much of who Xers are is defined by what they are not, or where they differ from their "older sibling." Xers' sense of national identity is one such situation in which Xers have generally rejected what they see as Boomers' extreme patriotism, stating, "We've never been proud to be Americans—our political memory stretches back only as far as Vietnam, Watergate, and Reagonomics."[30] This is not necessarily an anti-American sentiment, but like many other Xer perspectives, there are conflicting emotions. They are aware of and grateful for the freedoms that come with being an American while also expressing disappointment and disapproval for the way the country as a whole, and the government in particular, has handled various issues.

Partially out of their dislike and distrust of authority and anything corporate, Xers prefer to engage in social justice causes that allow them direct access to those they are serving. Their deep sense of fairness and equality motivates much of their philanthropic endeavors, but their lived experiences have taught them to be skeptical of any organization's ability to truly follow through on their promises or to ethically manage their finances.[31] This does not mean that Xers will not give to or participate with nonprofit organizations,

29. Zemke, Raines, and Filipczak, *Generations at Work*, 110.
30. Sarah E. Hinlicky, "Talking to Generation X," *First Things*, no. 90 (1999): 10–11.
31. Zemke, Raines, and Filipczak, *Generations at Work*, 92.

but it does mean they are more likely to give and participate if they have a personal connection to the organization.[32] That personal connection may be through a friend who trusts the organization, a family member who once received benefits from such an organization, or an organization that offers direct access between the people giving time, money, or services, allowing the Xers to personally connect with the people on the receiving end. Their philosophy in caring for others is expressed in the following statement by one cohort member: "What I do for you will hopefully make you a better person, which in turn will make you better somebody else, which will hopefully make them act better. Kind of like a domino effect, you know, that's kind of how I see it. That's how I think about my ability to make the world better."

Equality is a value that Xers bring into nearly every sphere of their life, and they see it as something bigger than just the racial or gender equality that Boomers championed. For a cohort that struggles to identify collective core beliefs, equality is something they easily rally around and talk extensively about. As one Xer summarized, "I believe [in] equality, that's what I stand on the most. I want it fair for everybody. If these rules apply to this person, then they better apply to that one." In true Xer form, they simultaneously hold a seemingly contradictory understanding that "life is unfair" even though the pursuit of "fairness, oftentimes more than justice" motivates their social justice and community involvement. Whether in work, education, health care, or any other context, Xers are passionate about everyone being "equal" and everyone having "equal opportunities" because "everyone has value and significance, and purpose."

This issue of equality and fairness is both of personal and political importance to Xers. On a larger political level, Xers see themselves as "the first generation where . . . we were just more on equal footing; even though there were different cultures around us, we were not taught to, as a whole, think any differently about different cultural groups or ethnic groups. You know, it was just we're all here."

On the personal level, Xers see themselves as being less discriminatory and less bound by social categories. Movies like *The Breakfast Club* captured this sentiment as students from all social groups (jocks, preps, stoners, etc.) could

---

32. Generation X is credited with approximately 20 percent of the estimated $143.6 billion in charitable giving, according to a 2013 report. Boomers accounted for 34 percent, the Silent generation contributing 26 percent, and Millennials accounting for only 11 percent. See also Deborah L. Jacobs, "Charitable Giving: Baby Boomers Donate More, Study Shows," *Forbes.com,* http://www.forbes.com/sites/deborahljacobs/2013/08/08/charitable-giving-baby-boomers-donate-more-study-shows/.

come together as friends.[33] In speaking of equality and fairness as it pertains to social class, a group of Xers collectively made the following statement.

> Maybe we were the ones to dissolve it when you really look at it, I mean, the ability to intermingle, to have football friends, to have hippie friends, to have, you know, those kind of friends—to have class not be so much of an issue too. That where you come from and your money isn't what defines who you are and who you hang out with—it's not necessarily class equality but something about materials instead of people having more. Yeah, it was more about what clothes you wore, stuff like that. Instead of, "Oh, I come from this neighborhood or something"—oh yeah, I didn't care if you lived in a trailer home if your stuff was cool; that's what mattered to me. I didn't care if you lived in a dumpster if your stuff was alright, man, then that's where I was going to be.

While Baby Boomer materialism is often expressed in big toys (houses, cars, high-end electronics, etc.), Gen-Xer materialism is seen in the little things (trendy jeans, a high-end pair of shoes, etc.). For Xers, smaller markers of status do not undercut their value of equality, as smaller items are seen as more easily attainable for all. They allow for individualism in how they want to represent themselves and with which collective of individuals they want to affiliate. In this, status or popularity for Xers can be defined by a single item or attribute rather than collective wealth: "You could be poor as hell and spend all your money on Girbaud jeans and be cool."

While community, or connection to other people, is part of being human and pertinent to the human experience, each generation pursues and defines it quite differently. For Xers, it is important to remember that their sense of self is deeply rooted in the concept of a collective of individuals in which equality and being responsible within one's sphere of influence are core values. While they may not be joining the Boomers in picketing, marches on Washington, DC, or large-scale protests, Xers still carry with them passion and concern for the world around them, seeing their role and responsibility being expressed on a more micro-level.

Xers at Work

Remember how we said that each generation takes for granted the good, reacts against the bad, and responds within their historical context? For Xers, the workplace and the home are the two primary arenas in which this plays

---

33. *The Breakfast Club*, DVD, directed by John Hughes (Universal City, CA: Universal Studios Home Entertainment, 2008; original release date: 1985).

out. We'll start with the workplace. Xers were born at a time when professional growth and success were often seen as higher pursuits than family or relationships. Whether that philosophy was consciously believed or simply lived out is up for debate. They watched their parents strive to reach higher rungs on the corporate ladder, all in the name of securing a nice pension and comfortable retirement and pursuing their version of the American dream. But then something happened, and the promise that working hard today (and being absent from family) would pay off tomorrow crashed with the economy. Xers watched their parents, who had invested twenty to thirty years in a company or career, get "downsized" and saw their parents' investments go under. Xers saw their skepticism validated and in turn decided their lives had to be built on something other than career, other than professional identity and development. They had watched hope disappear as their parents struggled to rebuild their sense of self (and their bank accounts), and they were going to therefore pursue career from the perspective of change, freedom, and self-protection, never being bound, in case something better came along.

COMPETENCE AND ENJOYMENT

Let's go back to that neighborhood block party where you again meet your new acquaintance, Joe, but this time Joe is an Xer. Wanting to get to know your neighbor a bit better, you say, "So, Joe, tell me about yourself." Unlike Baby Boomer Joe, Gen-Xer Joe will likely stall for a moment as he tries to assess your age and what you might mean by that statement. Joe may answer you with something like, "Umm, what do you mean? Are you wanting to know what I do for a living or how I like to spend my time?" Or, Joe might respond with, "Well, for my job I work in marketing, but in my free time I like to ski and fix old cars." These responses are vastly different than our Boomer response of career field, job title, and company. For Xers, their view of work is one way in which they very clearly push against what they see as the bad (workaholism) of the previous generation.

I often say that we as Xers don't care how young you are; you can be twelve, as long as you can do your job. Now, there's a bit of tongue-in-cheek in this statement, but it reflects the Xer sentiment that rejects the Boomers' "pay your dues" approach to leadership. While Xers may take for granted the good that comes with history and longevity in a position or company, this sentiment reflects the desire to react against the bad in which Xers have seen people (Boomers) rise to power simply because they *outlasted* everyone else. Xers have seen the obstinate, ruthless, and mean person rise in status because their dysfunction forced the "good" people to quit, and have seen the well-intended, semi-incompetent but oh-so-sweet person continually make it past their annual review because their loyalty to the company secured their position—even if they were lacking in competency. Both of these processes feel deeply unjust and impractical to an Xer, whose pragmatism and sense of fairness trumps loyalty or tenacity, especially in the workplace.[34]

To an Xer, work is not identity in the way that it is to a Boomer. For an Xer, work is multifaceted. While the work ethic of Xers looks different than that of Boomers, it is no less strong; it is just redirected into different areas.[35] Xers, like Boomers, assume that they must work for what they want, and they do not expect things to be handed to them. But where Boomers put the majority of their efforts into their professional identity development, Xers spread out those efforts between professional and personal development. While both generations hold values of loyalty, a Boomer expresses much of that loyalty in their career and to their employer, while an Xer's loyalty is more likely to be dedicated to chosen family and friends. Seeing a career as an expression of one's broader values and interests, Xers stated that it is "more important that you enjoy the work, that it's something you want to do, [and it's] not about the money," and that if you pursue "something that you love, just make sure you'll be able to support yourself" while simultaneously doing something that will "help the world."

Xers began entering the workforce as teenagers in the early 1980s, when Boomers were in the early to middle stages of their careers. Additionally, a recession in the early 1980s, the stock market crash in 1987, and an unemployment rate hovering around 7 percent for much of the decade (reaching as high as 10.8 percent in 1982) made for an unpredictable economy that was primarily saturated with workers who belonged to the then-largest generation in American history.[36] The Xers who now needed to make a living for themselves had to rely on their creativity and out-of-the-box ways of thinking and so turned to at-home businesses, entrepreneurial endeavors, and jobs that were more about facilitating time for personal pursuits than they were about professional success. The name of the game was pragmatics: what is effective, efficient, and still meets my needs?[37]

34. Valerie I. Sessa, Robert I. Kabacoff, Jennifer Deal, and Heather Brown, "Generational Differences in Leader Values and Leadership Behaviors," *The Psychologist-Manager Journal* 10, no. 1 (2007): 68.

35. Thom S. Rainer and Jess W. Rainer, *Millennials* (Nashville: B&H, 2011), 11.

36. Bureau of Labor Statistics, "Household Data Annual Averages: Employment Status of the Civilian Noninstitutional Population, 1943 to Date," *Employment and Earnings* (January 2008), http://www.bls.gov/cps/cpsaat01.htm; Michael A. Urquhart and Marilyn A. Hewson, "Unemployment Continued to Rise in 1982 as Recession Deepened," *Monthly Labor Review* (February 1983): 1.

37. Neil Howe and William Strauss, *Millennials Go to College* (Great Falls, VA: American Association of Registrars and Admissions Officers and LifeCourse Associates, 2003), 13.

I still see the effects of this as I walk around the halls of various universities and graduate schools and see a bimodal distribution of faculty members, with one large cluster being those over the age of fifty and a growing cluster being those of us under the age of thirty-five, with very, very few in between. When the majority of my fellow Xers graduated from college and looked to enter academia as a profession, there were few openings and little prospect of there being openings for years, if not decades. Boomers had filled those gaps in the previous decades and were not looking to retire or step away from their loyalty to the institution any time soon. As I sought out an academic job in 2010, only a small handful of Boomers were beginning their retirement, leaving few spaces for us younger Xers except in instances where new positions were being created. Xers older than me who have come to academia have generally come as a second career as spaces have been created or started to open up. They first worked in other fields that provided them with the means to meet their financial and personal needs. This has been the employment experience for many Xers, driving them to find alternative ways of using their gifts, training, and passions and postponing their actual career goals until later in life. Where Baby Boomers often had one career during their lifetime, the average adult today changes jobs every three to four years.[38] Where a Boomer might ascribe that to a lack of dedication, an Xer is more likely to see that as an expression of the economic situation they find themselves in, as well as their desire to see a job as that which facilitates the *expression* of their holistic sense of self rather than being that which *gives* them a sense of self.[39]

Today as I consult with various businesses and nonprofit organizations, I see a similar split, particularly in ministry contexts. Positions of highest leadership are still held by Boomers or are being given to older Millennials that Boomers perceive to be up-and-coming leaders, even though older Xers are well into their late forties and could be seen as having "paid their dues" by now. In both the secular and the religious sectors, Xers continue to be the lost middle children who are present and serving, often quietly doing their job well but not striving to be seen as the front-runner in the ways that Boomers and Millennials do. This is often mistakenly understood by surrounding cohorts as the Xers' inability or lack of desire, drive, or passion, while Xers see themselves as (1) having patiently waited their turn to execute the desire, drive, and passion to lead; (2) trusting that, in the end, fairness will mean

38. Carl Bialik, "Seven Careers in Lifetime? Think Twice, Researchers Say," *The Wall Street Journal*, September 4, 2010, http://online.wsj.com/news/articles/SB10001424052748704206804575468162805877990.

39. Zemke, Raines, and Filipczak, *Generations at Work*, 95.

the best person gets the position based on competency; and (3) simultaneously holding a skepticism that anyone really sees or values their contribution
anyway. Nevertheless, they hope that their years of quiet steadfastness will
finally be recognized.

Free to Be

Differences in leadership preferences and management styles are evident
across generational cohorts as well.[40] As we've discussed, Baby Boomers tend
to prefer a more hierarchical, top-down type of leadership that is perceived
by younger cohorts as micro-managing, with too many meetings and not
enough positive feedback. Most people enter the workforce expecting their
relationship with this new authority figure (the boss) to be somewhat similar
to the relationship they have had with previous authority figures (their parents
and teachers), and Xers are no different. Coming from a childhood of extremely hands-off parenting where they were left to raise themselves in many
ways, Xers expect a similar dynamic at work. Xers thrive best in a workplace
where they are given clear bounds and job descriptions but then are left with
the freedom to figure out *how* they want to accomplish the necessary tasks,
tapping into their values of freedom, choice, and individualism, while still
honoring that they are a part of a collective (the workplace).[41]

For Xers, following the step-by-step way something has always been done
is impractical and downright frustrating if they can find a new approach that
cuts time or resources, or allows them the freedom to cultivate other areas
of their lives. They are not necessarily looking to skirt responsibility or do a
half-hearted job but are instead striving to seek out ways in which they can
fulfill both their personal and professional responsibilities. For example, where
Boomers often see their work responsibility in hours per week and dedication
to a company, Xers often see their work more as a series of tasks that need to
be accomplished, giving them the freedom to leave or do other things once
those tasks have been completed.

Remember, for Xers, their work is a *part* of their identity, not their core
source of identity. This plays into what motivates Xers as well as the type of
feedback they desire from employers. Xers prefer to be defined by their personal pursuits, whether that be family and friends, hobbies, or volunteerism,
and they appreciate when an employer validates the world outside the office.
This can be as simple as a boss asking an Xer, "So, do you have any fun plans
for the weekend?" While an Xer is likely to respond only with, "Yeah, I think

40. Sessa et al., "Generational Differences," 47–74.
41. Zemke, Raines, and Filipczak, *Generations at Work*, 106, 112.

some friends and I might grill out or something," this simple question can validate and affirm that the employer recognizes the Xer has a life outside the office. Additionally, as I've talked with Xers across the country, they have said time and again that they would prefer more vacation time over a higher salary, as this speaks to their values of freedom, choice, and individualism and aligns with their rejection of Boomer materialism and financial pursuit.[42]

Xers at Home

During their childhood, the outside world was changing and uncertain, leaving many Xers feeling unsafe and unknown. Sadly, home didn't prove much different. While many Xers grew up in stable two-parent homes, the "normal" home situation across the United States was shifting.[43] For starters, during this generation's developmental years, a drastic change in the age at which people married occurred. By 2009 the median age for marriage in the United States was 28.1 for men and 25.9 for women, having steadily climbed up from 23.2 for men and 20.8 for women in 1970.[44] Meanwhile, between 1965 and 1980, birthrates were generally declining while the number of divorces in the United States jumped from just over 400,000 to nearly 1.2 million each year.[45] With so much divorce taking place within this generation's key developmental years, personal identity as well as social identity was undoubtedly shaken.[46]

GROWING UP XER

To Xers, family is not the same foundational institution that it was and is for Boomers. Boomers often speak of their families having distinct roles and expectations. But for Xers, family offered a very different context; they often spoke of almost living lives of parallel personal development with their parents. For example, one Xer made the following comment in a focus group interview.

Who has divorced parents? [Five out of six group members raise their hand.]
I think that's a big thing too; we became more open to our parents having

42. These findings are in keeping with the generational descriptions given by Hart, "Generations in the Workplace," 26.
43. Robert Wuthnow compiles a wealth of statistics, charts, and sociological data on this generational cohort in his book *After the Baby Boomers: How Twenty- and Thirty-Somethings Are Shaping the Future of American Religion* (Princeton: Princeton University Press, 2007).
44. Gary R. Lee and Krista K. Payne, "Changing Marriage Patterns Since 1970: What's Going On, and Why?," *Journal of Comparative Family Studies* 41, no. 4 (2010): 538.
45. National Center for Health Statistics, "Divorce Statistics," 2.
46. See Andrew Root, *The Children of Divorce: The Loss of Family as a Loss of Being* (Grand Rapids: Baker Academic, 2010), for an excellent analysis and explanation of the deeper effects of divorce.

alternate lifestyles too. Like we kind of had to adjust to, well, my parents are going to get divorced, and my dad's going to have three more wives. Or, my mom's going to have a wife. You know, we had to be open to our parents being individuals too, and you know, more open to their journey. I think that may have shaped the way we thought about adulthood. You know, 'cuz we would see our parents go through these major changes that their parents didn't go through.

For Xers, family refers to your immediate family or to those you have chosen to consider family, whether they are related to you or not. For this generation, emotional bonds, mutual caring, and dependability in hard times are the underlying traits of "family."[47] While biological family ties for this generation are loose and focused mostly on immediate family members, their valuing and pursuit of relationships is of top priority, in many ways because of the instability they experienced in their biological family units.[48] Long captures the Xer perspective on family and its impact on their worldview:

> Their longing is for a place to belong, a place to call home. As we have already seen, Generation X is suffering from the effects of the dysfunctional family, which are causing them to search for new places to belong. The traditional family, because of its dysfunctionality, has become a place many Xers feel they no longer belong.[49]

For many Xers, their lived experience with or even exposure to such demise within the American family has tapped into both their skepticism and their hope as they have embarked on making families of their own. As the "latch-key kid" generation, Gen-Xers often came home from school to an empty house as dual-income families and absentee parenting were becoming more and more commonplace.[50] Today, approximately two-thirds of Xers have married and 71 percent report having minor children in their home.[51] The most current divorce rate now stands at the lowest it has been since 1970, 18 percent lower

47. Participants in my focus groups confirmed the thematic findings of the Barna Group's research on Gen-Xers nearly fifteen years earlier. See George Barna, *The Invisible Generation: Baby Busters* (Glendale, CA: Barna Research Group, 1992).

48. Mahedy and Bernardi, *Generation Alone*, 46; Alene Dawson, "Study Says Generation X Is Happy and Balanced," CNN.com, October 27, 2011, http://www.cnn.com/2011/10/26/living/gen-x-satisfied.

49. Long, *Generating Hope*, 83.

50. Bryan E. Robinson, Bobbie H. Rowland, and Mark Coleman ("Taking Action for Latchkey Children and Their Families," *Family Relations* 25, no. 4 [1986]: 473) define "latchkey children" as "unsupervised youngsters who care for themselves before or after school, on weekends, and during holidays while their parents work. They commonly carry house keys to let themselves in and out of their homes."

51. See Miller, "Active, Balanced, and Happy," 2.

than its peak in 1981.[52] Specific to generations, in 2009, 27.4 percent of Xer women who had ever been married (ages thirty-five to thirty-nine) had been divorced, in comparison to 32.4 percent of Boomer women of the same age in 1996.[53] And while this instills hope in many Xers that they may be able to do this marriage and family thing better than their parents did, they are not naive to the weight or cost of building their own family.

THE HOUSE THAT XERS BUILT

Xers more than any other cohort spoke of the weight, tension, and significance they feel around the decision to have a family of their own. Having felt, directly or indirectly, that they came second to their parents' professional development goals, Xers shared with me a deep sense of responsibility to put the role of parent as a top priority *if* they were to choose to have children. With the lowest birthrate in American history and approximately one in five Xer women ending their childbearing years childless, I was surprised by the consistency I heard from Gen-Xers in my interviews regarding their sentiment about getting married and having children.[54] Consistently, the cohort spoke of the importance, weight, and significance of both marriage and parenting, but with that they also did not take for granted that marriage or parenthood was a necessary step in their experience as adults. True to their values of freedom, choice, and individualism, Xers have approached marriage and parenthood with a similar ethos. One female Xer, born in 1979, summarized the cohort's thoughts:

> I guess I just never felt it [getting married and having kids] was something I had to do. I really love my family, and so I feel like I had a good model for parenting and for a good marriage model as well. But, I'm still single, so I don't know. I don't feel like [I'm] desperate, like I *have to* have this. And I do feel like there have been times where I would have felt like it would make me stuck. Actually, I kinda still feel like that.

52. In 2011 there were forty-one divorces for every one hundred marriages (Center for Disease Control and Prevention, "National Marriage and Divorce Rate Trends," *National Vital Statistics System*, February 19, 2013, http://www.cdc.gov/nchs/nvss/marriage_divorce_tables .htm), compared to fifty divorces for every one hundred marriages in 1981. Info Please, "Marriages and Divorces, 1900–2009," *Information Please Database* (2007), http://www.infoplease .com/ipa/A0005044.html.

53. Similar comparisons between Boomers and Xers exist across age groups, demonstrating the decline in divorce. See Rose M. Kreider and Renee Ellis, "Number, Timing, and Duration of Marriages and Divorces: 2009," *Current Population Reports: United States Census Bureau* (May 2011): 6, http://www.census.gov/prod/2011pubs/p70-125.pdf.

54. Lauren Sandler and Kate Witteman, "Having It All without Having Children," *Time*, August 12, 2013, 38.

A male Xer, born in 1968, added to this sentiment of feeling as if a family of his own would limit his life journey:

> I swore I was never going to have a family. Literally. My parents got divorced and I just was like, I'm not even going there—I mean I have an infant daughter now and things have changed. But that wasn't, like, how I saw myself—I saw family as something that kind of confines you almost. Until the last, you know, pretty recently actually. Honestly I had relationships and stuff, I don't know, I just valued being able to be mobile and not confined. And I picture family, like, something confining.

Whether coming from a family with good models or from a broken home, Xers communicate this sense that to embark on creating their own family would be confining. Now, from an outside perspective, this may appear selfish or hedonistic: a generation who just wants to do their own thing and not be encumbered by anyone or anything else. While that may be part of it, remember the context, and listen to the rest of the story. Xers did not come into adulthood at a time when they had the financial or social opportunities that their parents had at the same age. No longer could a single income provide the same standard of living that it once did, forcing many Gen-Xers to maintain a dual-income household in order to survive.[55] Now, this is where the Xer sense of responsibility comes into play. For many, the choice not to have children, or to delay having children, is rooted in a sense that they do not have the means to provide for children in the way they feel they should, whether that be with finances or with time.[56] Therefore they see it as their choice and *responsibility* not to bring a child into the world unless they can parent, provide, and continue their other passions to the degree that they feel is necessary. The following interview comment came out of my focus group interviews with Gen-Xers.

> People are making tough choices. And it started with our generation, like a lot of us women are choosing not to have kids for one reason or another. Sometimes it's economics, and sometimes it's just, I don't know that I want to bring a child here . . . and we have that choice now. That seems like a really heavy burden to me to say, "Yeah, I want to get pregnant and have a child and bring them here."

55. Mahedy and Bernardi, *Generation Alone*, 18.
56. In 1970, the average age at which a woman had her first child was 21.4 years old. By 2006, the average age was 25 years old. See T. J. Matthews and Brady E. Hamilton, "Delayed Childbearing: More Women Are Having Their First Child Later in Life," *NCHS Data Brief* 21 (August 2009): 1.

At another point in the interview, a cohort member in her forties spoke of a tension between being loyal to the environmental and societal commitments she had made and felt passionate about and the social pressure to have a child, saying,

> When I talk about not having kids, and I don't know where you are with that, I'm talking about like, seriously, like I wouldn't be able to do some of the sustainable things in my lifestyle that I do now because I would have to be pouring everything that I could into the child, which is very little. Well, what if you wanted to have a child and wanted to maintain your, the things that you believed in, and you just ended up not being able to?

Of the Xers I interviewed who had children, the responses were split as to whether they felt that having children had left them feeling limited in their choices. Regardless of parenthood status, Xers communicated clearly that they understood that a choice made today impacts future choices and opportunities, and that personal responsibility must be maintained in that choice-making process. But, as stated before, a definition of responsibility or values must not be imposed on any one generation from the surrounding generations, as an Xer's sense of responsibility is connected to different values or priorities than those of Boomers and Millennials.

As I put together this section, I was again struck by how little Xers talked about their families in comparison to Baby Boomers and Millennials. The time they did spend talking about family was in relation to their hesitation and tensions about having their own children, often rooted in either their own family background or the cultural climate in which they would be raising children. Interwoven within these discussions was the Xers' theme of striving for and pursuing something for which they had hope—hope for the future, hope "that you can always make something better," hope for happiness. Whether about a career or a family, the Xer mentality is, "Just be sure you do it 100 percent, whatever it is that you choose," because personal happiness is a value that supersedes most others. Xers ascribe this wholehearted pursuit of happiness to their parents, who they felt sacrificed their own personal happiness for too long in life, costing both parents and children in the long run. In speaking of the decisions many of their parents made to "stay together for the kids" but still ultimately divorcing, one Gen-Xer states,

> In terms of personal sacrifice and my happiness, I just don't know that I could do that—not for a moral code where there's a little bit more of a, "yeah I know I promised to stay together forever. I promise this, and I promise that, and I made this vow, but my happiness isn't there anymore." And that trumps almost

[everything], and I hate to even say that, I think that is something that the past generation did differently. That their moral code trumped their happiness, their personal happiness, and that doesn't exist anymore.

While studies have shown that the parents who divorce often feel that the decision has made their life better, the children rarely agree.[57] Interestingly, the Xers in my study seemed more concerned that their parents had stayed together as long as they did over their concern for themselves or the ripples the divorce produced in their lives. The value they placed on happiness wasn't "necessarily the me-happiness and my happiness, it's other people's happiness too that we're concerned about."

Parenting

We have said that each generation takes for granted the good of the previous generation, reacts against the bad, and responds within their historical location, and Xers too utilize this formula in their approach to parenting. Having felt alone in their developmental process, many Xers strive to be very active and present parents.[58] As I have interviewed Xers, there seem to be two primary approaches they have adopted in order to rectify what they perceive as the bad approaches of their parents. A third is beginning to quietly emerge but has yet to gain a large following. In all cases, Xers tend to value higher levels of direct parental involvement, but the first group takes the approach of trying to be their child's friend first and foremost. Compensating for what they feel was a lack of emotional and relational attachment between them and their parents, generally older Xers have pursued parenting from this model as they strive to detach from the authoritarian parenting style they experienced.[59]

The second group also pursues a higher level of engagement in their parenting style but tends to do so more from a perspective of setting a high bar for performance and achievement for their child, getting equally involved in their child's sports, volunteerism, or academic endeavors because they see their participation as a way of joining with their child and showing that what the child is interested in is of value to the parent as well. The Xer parent's goal in this approach is to compensate for what they felt was parental ambivalence, disinterest, or devaluing of their own childhood pursuits. Both of these two

57. Judith S. Wallerstein, Julia Lewis, and Sandra Blakeslee, *The Unexpected Legacy of Divorce* (New York: Hyperion, 2001), 39.

58. Miller, "Active, Balanced, and Happy," 3.

59. Shows like *The Gilmore Girls* on the WB network epitomize this model of parenting in which hierarchical lines between parent and child are often blurry at best but capture the hearts of viewers who experienced more estrangement from their parents.

types of Xer parents can appear to be helicopter parents, like Boomers, as both cohorts are parents to Millennials.

Primarily among younger Xers I have started to hear rumblings of a third type of parent, one who also desires an increased emotional engagement between themselves and their children. But their approach is more a reaction against the type of parenting by older members of their own cohort than it is a reaction against their own parents. This third group sees helicopter parenting as overly protective, and, while they too will encourage their child's participation in extracurricular activities, they nostalgically talk about the days when it was okay to skin a knee or fall off the monkey bars without it being a major life crisis. For this third group of Xers, their primary value in parenting is raising self-sufficient children in keeping with the Xer value of independence.[60]

It will be interesting to see how this final, youngest wave of Xers approaches marriage and parenting more generally, given this initial trend. Each person's childhood and experiences with marriage and family impact their expectations and desires as they consider such contexts for themselves. It is important to recognize not just the behavioral choices of each generational cohort but also to understand the reasons and the values behind those choices. The Xers' differences in attitude toward marriage and family compared to previous generations are deeply rooted in the pain, disappointment, and stark realities they directly experienced in their own lives and childhoods.

Xers in Church

The Gen-Xer approach to the topic of religion is steeped in skepticism, as they place a high value on spirituality but react very negatively to the concept of religion. As one Xer put it, "It seems like we all believe in God, or the spiritual or something higher. There's some kind of intention to all of these systems that are in the universe, you know, that it's not chaotic or happenstance. But I don't want that defined."

Xers were incredibly passionate in discussing their spiritual views and were equally as passionate about explaining how they came to their convictions as they were about sharing those convictions. As two Xers collaborated to express that they, as a cohort, are "not indifferent" to religion and spirituality, they explained that "we have an opinion about it. Whether we're skeptical

---

60. See also Anne Boysen, "4 Reasons Why P&G Ad Featured Resilience Parents—Not Helicopter Parents," *After the Millennials: With Futurist Consultant Anne Boysen,* January 12, 2014, http://afterthemillennials.com/2014/01/12/4-reasons-why-pg-ad-featuring-resilience-parents-not -helicopter-parents-is-well-timed/.

of it, [or] whether we espouse a religion, we take it seriously. It's serious stuff to us." In keeping with the rest of their values and lived experiences, Xers' skepticism is only perpetuated when "people talk about Christian values and Christian principles but then, they're not very Christian." In a world where Xers value close relationships of authenticity, transparency, and equality, any religious or spiritual community that presents a holier-than-thou persona or attempts to elevate one member of the community or congregation above the others will be viewed with much skepticism if not outright rejection.

Outside organized religion, Xers have explored and pursued various forms of spirituality. While this is not new to any generation, Xers were able to embark on this journey with much more openness and acceptability than previous generations had known. For this generation, what they care about, what they want to know, is whether someone has intentionally chosen their religious beliefs in an informed and deliberate manner, that is, whether they are pursuing their beliefs as a marker of individualism rather than conformity. It is a topic of serious concern, interest, and conversation.

Don't Box Me In

The values of freedom and independence underpin much of Gen-Xers' approach to spirituality as they vehemently push against the idea of someone or something, especially an institution, telling them what to think or believe. Their entire lives they have been left to raise themselves, make their own way, and strive toward independence, and with such a background the idea of going blindly into any religious belief feels foolish.[61] The opportunity to make one's own decisions, to decide for oneself what to believe, and the freedom to pursue those beliefs (even if they lead to an organized religion) is of critical importance to Xers who passionately say, "Don't tell me how to think, don't tell me what to say, don't make rules; we can make our own decisions."

Recall our discussion of Gen-Xers as adapters in the workplace; we'll bring those same concepts into this discussion of religion and spirituality. This generation is not necessarily looking to alter religious beliefs so much as they are seeking to modify the *expression* of the beliefs that they hold into a more authentic and intimate experience.[62] They are not nearly as denominationally aligned as Boomers often are, seeking instead a collective of individuals that

---

61. Richard Flory and Donald E. Miller (*Finding Faith: The Spiritual Quest of the Post-Boomer Generation* [New Brunswick, NJ: Rutgers University Press, 2008]) explore how Xers' lived experiences contribute to their pursuit of religious expression and experiences.

62. Ibid., viii. Flory and Miller describe four different types or forms of religious action, with "reclaimers" and "appropriators" best fitting the above description of Xers being innovative in their approach to religious pursuits.

not only hold similar beliefs but also want a similar type of aesthetic and experiential worship experience and expression.

A search for absolute truth is not something that captures the hearts of Xers. Their values of freedom, choice, and individualism lead them to find greater appreciation for the things in life that are gray rather than black and white, as we saw earlier.[63] As Menconi articulates, "To many Gen-Xers the worship experience in Boomer churches is overproduced, contrived, and not appealing. They are often put off by cutting-edge productions and seeker-service manipulations that impress them as slick and insincere."[64] Instead, Xers are looking for a spiritual experience that engages them aesthetically, speaks to them with an authentic transparency and rawness, and allows for intimate community. In this space, they must be able to trust that the truth they are hearing can be applied to their specific context as an individual, for they feel a mutual sense of intimacy. The combination of truth, context, and the intervention of the Holy Spirit can lead to change.[65]

PERSONALLY RELEVANT

For Xers, the context in which they are exposed to proclamations of truth and the speaker's ability to communicate that truth in the Xer's context are both of critical importance. For their whole lives they have seen authority figures make promises or pronouncements about what is right, good, truthful, and the like, only to see such claims disintegrate under reflective scrutiny or simply over time. They are hungry for something that speaks to their skepticism and hope while inviting them into authentic community.

While the "emerging church" is often spoken of in connection with Millennials, the postmodern approach to religion in general and Christianity specifically reflect the underlying values and worldview of the Gen-X cohort. Popular Christian authors such as Donald Miller and Shane Claiborne capture and write to the heart of Xers who still affiliate themselves with Christianity but desire a different approach to or discussion about the expression of their faith. For many Xers, the Boomer way of doing church and religion feels disconnected from the rest of their life and just too big. Xers are instead

63. Menconi, *Intergenerational Church*, 104–5.

64. Ibid., 116.

65. My senior pastor, Nick Lillo (Waterstone Community Church, Littleton, CO), once preached a sermon in which he explained that for Generation X a three-part mixture was needed to produce change: *Truth + Context + Holy Spirit*. This differed from the Baby Boomer mixture of *Truth + Holy Spirit = Change* and the Millennial mixture of *Truth + Context + Relationship + Holy Spirit = Change*. Neither Nick nor I can remember when he gave this sermon or what it was titled (and I've heard something like it somewhere else, so I suspect he didn't make it up from scratch).

seeking something more intimate, personal, integrated with the rest of their lives, and focused on serving and connecting with their sphere of influence, and less focused on presentation, performance, and show. In many ways they are looking for

> communities that practice the way of Jesus within postmodern cultures. This definition encompasses nine practices. Emerging churches (1) identify with the life of Jesus, (2) transform the secular realm, and (3) live highly communal lives. Because of these three activities, they (4) welcome the stranger, (5) serve with generosity, (6) participate as producers, (7) create as created beings, (8) lead as a body, and (9) take part in spiritual activities.[66]

The description of emerging churches captures well the heart of many Xers as they look for a faith community to be a part of. While one in three Gen-Xers reports active membership in a religious organization, with most of these attending at least one religious activity per week, we need to be asking about the other two-thirds.[67] What about those who look around at mainstream American Christianity and do not see a place to create, a place to live authentic life together beyond Sunday mornings, a place where they can invite their non-Christian friends, or a place that invites them to be participants in their own spiritual journey rather than simply being passive receivers of a sermon? We will see Millennials champion these questions even more loudly and with greater energy simply because of their size (and partly because their parents have joined the cause for fear of their Millennial children leaving the faith), but these were initially the questions of Xers. Sadly, in many places and relationships, these questions went unanswered and often unheard, contributing again to Xers' sense of being the lost middle children: not outspoken enough to get attention like the older siblings or prized enough to get attention like the babies.

As in many business organizations, the leadership torch in our churches is often being handed down from Boomers to Millennials, skipping over Xers, who are not seen as being active leaders. While this may be partly true, Xers are also giving their time, money, and other resources to faith-based and humanitarian organizations that let them have more direct involvement in the missions about which they are passionate. Having spent the majority of their lives being overlooked or told, in one way or another, that the Boomers have it handled, Xers are unlikely to assert themselves into places of leadership

---

66. Eddie Gibbs and Ryan Bolger, *Emerging Churches: Creating Christian Community in Postmodern Cultures* (Grand Rapids: Baker Academic, 2005), 45.

67. Miller, "Active, Balanced, and Happy," 4.

or notoriety. They instead need to be invited, and their creative avenues of service need to be affirmed and legitimized by the older cohorts.

In his book *You Lost Me*, David Kinnaman speaks to various types of Millennials who have left their Christian faith or simply left the church.[68] Although Kinnaman's research speaks more to Millennials (and we will explore more of it when we talk about ministry to and with the youngest cohort), I cannot help but wonder how many Xers feel like "exiles": people of faith and conviction left alone in their efforts to radically impact their surrounding culture because their methods and vision do not fit the established notion of doing "church" or "ministry."[69] This generation is still an active and influential part of both our churches and our society; it is imperative that we stop overlooking them and learn to engage them in their spiritual journeys.

Conclusion

The lost middle child, Gen-X is sandwiched between two generations significantly larger and louder than they are. Nonetheless, they provide a significant bridge between the Boomers and the Millennials and offer the larger culture an opportunity to see activism on a micro- as well as a macro-scale. A collective of individuals, Gen-Xers strive to make their own way in the world while still pursuing close interpersonal relationships of depth and authenticity with the people they have chosen to see as family.

Often overlooked, or looked at through a Boomer lens, this cohort has intentionally lived out their values of individualism, independence, freedom, skepticism, interconnectedness, and responsibility while maintaining a reserved optimism or hope about what the future may bring. Fighting against the Boomer mentality that placed career above virtually all other life roles, Xers strive to maintain a greater sense of work-life balance, often seeing their jobs as the means that facilitate their personal interests outside of work. Furthermore, their values of freedom and responsibility weigh heavily as they contemplate and engage in their own pursuits of marriage and parenting.

The silent participants in many churches, Gen-Xers bring with them a profound sense of spirituality and place a high value on one's personal religious beliefs. Religious or spiritual affiliation for this generation is rooted in research, reflection, and individualism, and they reject the thought that any institution can ask them to conform in the name of belonging. Spirituality

68. David Kinnaman, *You Lost Me* (Grand Rapids: Baker Books, 2011).
69. Ibid., 75, 246.

is both deeply personal and simultaneously public as they desire to express their beliefs in creative, caring, and outwardly expressive ways. Approaching mid-life, Xers are still in a position to shape and influence the culture around them and to make decisions for themselves about who they want to be and the legacy they want to leave. Where will they bless the younger and older generations around them? Where will they bemoan the younger (and older) generations? How will they choose to influence those who follow?

5

Xers in Light of the Bible

I (Craig) belong to a church that was planted in 2000 specifically to reach members of Generation X. My wife serves on staff there half-time. It began by particularly targeting urban, artistic, and disaffected twenty-somethings. One of our slogans is that we try to minister among the "right-brained and left out." Today those twenty-somethings are in their thirties, many of them have married, and some have children. A handful of Boomers have joined over the years, and an ever-increasing number of Millennials are swelling our ranks. Only recently has the church leadership begun to recognize how different the two groups of younger adults are based on generational distinctives.[1]

As a Boomer with two Millennial daughters in their twenties, Generation X is the cohort I have the least amount of experience with. But as a seminary professor who has taught numerous students in every cohort over the years and who is deeply involved in a church that has at times been dominated by Xers, I still have a fair amount of experience with this generation. Once again I resonate very much with Elisabeth's descriptions and analysis. They fit well with all that I have observed.

1. For the story of the first decade of the church's history, see Mike Sares, *Pure Scum: The Left-Out, the Right-Brained and the Grace of God* (Downers Grove, IL: InterVarsity, 2010).

The Younger of Two Children and the Older of Two Children

To my knowledge, the Bible says nothing generalizable about middle children in families of three or more children. Treating a middle child like a younger child in a family of two or like the older child in a family of two is often unhelpful or misleading, though the more there is an age gap among the children in question, the more there can be some similarities.[2] The same is true if one compares the oldest Boomers, mid-range Gen-Xers, and the youngest Millennials. It is also the case that a variety of life contexts do not bring all three cohorts into simultaneous contact with one another, so that there may be certain settings where the middle child relates like a younger sibling to an older brother or sister or like an older sibling to a younger brother or sister.[3]

Elisabeth's chapter repeatedly made me think of Jesus's classic parable of the prodigal son and his older brother (Luke 15:11–32). Trying to carve out his own identity and not wanting to conform to either his parents' or his older brother's values, the younger son makes some very shocking and damaging decisions for the sake of his independence. He asks for his share of his inheritance in a context in which such a request was tantamount to saying he wished his dad were dead.[4] He goes to a far country, meaning that he leaves Jewish lands for unclean gentile territory. He squanders his father's wealth in dissolute living and bottoms out working for a pig farmer, unable to feed himself during a famine even with the pigs' food. To appreciate the dark humor here, from a Jewish perspective, one must realize that he longs to eat the ritually unclean food of the most ritually unclean animal while working in a ritually unclean occupation in a ritually unclean land after choosing the most morally unclean set of activities.[5] One cannot imagine a worse situation for a Jew to find himself in.

Fortunately, he comes to his senses. He repents, returns home, and, to his astonishment, is welcomed back by his father with lavish festivities and no strings attached.[6] In other biblical texts, as we saw in chapter 2, God chooses

2. Then oldest and youngest siblings might barely interact at all, and they might not even live in the same home at the same time. The middle child functions simultaneously as a younger sibling and an older sibling.

3. See further Kevin Leman, *The Birth Order Book: Why You Are the Way You Are*, 3rd ed. (Grand Rapids: Revell, 2009), 149–65.

4. Kenneth E. Bailey, *Poet and Peasant: A Literary-Cultural Approach to the Parables in Luke* (Grand Rapids: Eerdmans, 1976), 161.

5. For probable details of the arrangements, see J. Albert Harrill, "The Indentured Labor of the Prodigal Son (Luke 15:15)," *Journal of Biblical Literature* 115 (1996): 714–17.

6. Some have questioned whether he truly repented, but see Greg Forbes, "Repentance and Conflict in the Parable of the Lost Son (Luke 15:11–12)," *Journal of the Evangelical Theological Society* 42 (1999): 225–26.

younger siblings for privileges over their normally privileged older counterparts for no apparent reason other than his sovereign grace. To whatever degree, therefore, that Gen-Xers resemble younger siblings, we must take care not to imagine them as any less loved by God.

Although there are plenty of exceptions, first children are often more introverted, studious, and independent than second born, who tend to be extroverted, social, and dependent.[7] To the extent that Xers are more independent, quiet, and thoughtful than the younger Millennials, a few analogies with firstborn children may prove relevant. Sticking with the parable that is probably better titled "The Lost Sons," the older brother only appears to be true to his father's values. He has been a dutiful, loyal, stay-at-home, and hardworking son, to be sure. But his resentment of his father's welcome of his younger brother contrasts sharply with his father's joy. Counselors would probably call his outburst a sign of passive-aggressive behavior. What appears to have been his entirely voluntary embracing of his father's values, even after his brother left home, has been boiling up into deeply seated anger at the "fun" his brother got to have. Now that this prodigal is also rewarded upon his return, with no retribution from his father or even a probationary period in which he has to prove himself before he can be fully accepted, the older son discloses his profound jealousy.[8] To the extent that Gen-Xers compare themselves favorably to Millennials as holding and implementing better values, they run the risk of mimicking the Pharisaic attitudes of the older brother in this parable (see also Luke 15:1–2).

The self-initiated comparisons of Xers with both Boomers and Millennials reflect, of course, a perennial human temptation. Compare yourself with those you deem less exemplary than yourself so that you can take pride and boast in your superiority. Compare yourself with those to whom you see yourself as inferior so you can indulge in a pity party or excuse yourself from certain responsibility. To the extent that Xers intentionally compare themselves favorably or unfavorably with the generations before and after them more than the other two cohorts do, they in particular need to reflect on 2 Corinthians 10:12–13, in which Paul explains,

> We do not dare to classify or compare ourselves with some who commend themselves. When they measure themselves by themselves and compare themselves with themselves, they are not wise. We, however, will not boast beyond

7. Leman, *Birth Order Book*, 78–99, 166–88.
8. Ruth Etchells, *A Reading of the Parables of Jesus* (London: Darton, Longman & Todd, 1998), 41.

proper limits, but will confine our boasting to the sphere of service God himself has assigned to us.

At first it sounds like there is nobody else involved but the Corinthians Paul is rebuking, but what Paul means is that some in Corinth are making themselves the ideal standard of comparison. Of course they measure up to themselves, but no one else does. Paul's introductory statement makes it clear that he avoids comparing himself with *others*, while his final statement clarifies that his self-assessment is based on what God has assigned *him* to do, which is at least partially unique from what God has called others to do. Every person's gifting and calling from God is in part unique to them because no two persons are exactly alike.[9] We must cut Xers some slack, because a lot of their comparisons with their surrounding cohorts have to do with their quest to carve out their own identity in the midst of feeling ignored by others due to their size, temperament, and approach to life. But their comparisons can nevertheless become unhealthy.

Romans 12:3 supplements these remarks precisely in the context of Paul's teaching that every member of the body of Christ has a different function (v. 4). In verse 3 Paul declares, "For by the grace given me I say to every one of you: Do not think of yourself more highly than you ought, but rather think of yourself with sober judgment, in accordance with the faith God has distributed to each of you." At first glance, it might sound like Paul is imagining different amounts of faith given to different people, just as God gives each person different gifts.[10] There is no question that Christians, subjectively, have different levels of ability to believe or trust God in various settings, but it seems doubtful that Paul would credit that diversity to something God gives, as if he makes less faith available to some people and more to others. It would make very good sense for Paul to mean that everyone should assess him- or herself according to the same standard—the faith that God has given to everyone equally.[11] But does this do justice to the context, which emphasizes individual Christians' diversity? Perhaps Grant Osborne explains it best, drawing on elements of both these interpretations: "Paul is saying that we will have a proper humility when we examine ourselves in keeping with the different gifts God has apportioned to us. There can be no pride, for all gifts are equally important to God and must be received by faith."[12]

9. For detailed analysis, see Margaret E. Thrall, *A Critical and Exegetical Commentary on the Second Epistle to the Corinthians* (Edinburgh: T&T Clark, 2000), 639–47.
10. E.g., Thomas R. Schreiner, *Romans* (Grand Rapids: Baker, 1998), 652–53.
11. E.g., Douglas J. Moo, *The Epistle to the Romans* (Grand Rapids: Eerdmans, 1996), 760–61.
12. Grant R. Osborne, *Romans* (Downers Grove, IL: InterVarsity, 2004), 324.

Taking Sin Seriously

I am always amazed when I meet people who think human beings are inherently good by nature. Even if they have never been exposed to any biblical teaching, I just wonder what world they live in. Are they oblivious to the horrors and tragedies of humanly perpetrated evil, or those that kill or maim countless individuals every day of every year? Are they living in willful denial of their own thoughts and lusts, which even when kept firmly in check remain poised to explode into shocking action if the right trigger is pulled? Are they blind to the way people spend so much time dwelling on what John summarizes as the essence of this fallen world, "the lust of the flesh, the lust of the eyes, and the pride of life" (1 John 2:16)? It is rare to find anyone of any cohort who can honestly say that they don't frequently focus on the delights of fulfilling bodily appetites above and beyond anything that is necessary for their existence and well-being. Who isn't regularly attracted to unnecessary material possessions that appear pleasing (especially in light of our advertising-saturated culture)? Which individuals don't consistently take action on what is required to secure their own survival and happiness and much more—that which will enable them to take pride in having a better standard of living than many?[13]

To the extent that members of Generation X learn the proper lessons from their unrelenting experience with authority figures who let them down, with heroes who turn out to have lead feet, and with media who mislead or misinform, they are uniquely positioned to agree with biblical teaching on human sin and depravity. Barely after beginning to enjoy the unfathomable blessings of the Garden of Eden, Adam and Eve succumb to Satan's temptations, which strikingly resemble the triad of sins enumerated in 1 John 2:16.[14] The unnamed forbidden fruit (no, the Bible never calls it an apple) is "good for food and pleasing to the eye, and also desirable for gaining wisdom" (Gen. 3:6). Not one of these three qualities is inherently bad, but they are when God has declared something off limits and we use those qualities to justify disobeying him! Then they morph into the *lust* of the flesh, the *lust* of the eyes, and the *pride* of life. This is precisely what happened to the first human couple. Theological truths such as this remain the key points of Genesis 2–3 no matter how one interprets the genre of these two chapters (literal history, religious myth, or some combination of the two).[15]

---

13. This, of course, was the point made powerfully in William Golding's classic novel *The Lord of the Flies* (New York: Penguin, 1954), and in the movie of the same name produced from the book.

14. See Daniel L. Akin, *1, 2, 3 John* (Nashville: Broadman and Holman, 2001), 108.

15. For the debate, see Craig L. Blomberg, *Can We Still Believe the Bible? An Evangelical Engagement with Contemporary Questions* (Grand Rapids: Brazos, 2014), 152–55.

Jeremiah 17:9 is rightfully famous for its observation that "the heart is deceitful above all things and beyond cure. Who can understand it?" Of course what is impossible for humans is possible for God (Mark 10:27). The salvation made possible through the work of Christ initiates a process of curing the heart, a process that continues throughout a Christian's life but will only be complete in the life to come. But the New Testament affirms as certainly as Jeremiah that every human being who is ever born is sinful both by nature and by choice.

Romans 5:12–21 forms the classic text for both of these complementary truths. Verse 12 begins Paul's paragraph with a sentence that is never completed (at least not until he restarts it in verse 18): "Therefore, just as sin entered the world through one man, and death through sin, and in this way death came to all people because all sinned—." In this sentence fragment, Paul insists both that Adam's sin guaranteed that sin would spread to all of his descendants and that everyone freely chooses to sin.[16] Theologians have debated the puzzling particulars of these affirmations in ways we can abbreviate here. Prior to our modern understanding of the transmission of DNA, learned "doctors" of the church vied with one another by claiming either that God used Adam's sin to *represent* how the rest of the human race would be treated or that all humans were somehow already *present* in Adam when he sinned.[17] In the famous Calvinist-Arminian debate, theologians have alternately argued that humans are totally depraved, unable even to choose salvation when God freely offers it to them so that it is wholly by his sovereign choice that he saves some, or that people are universally enabled through "common grace" to choose him, but only some do. Both camps, however, agree that every person who is ever born is seriously tainted by sin and that everyone needs the regeneration made possible only by God's Spirit.[18]

In any scenario, God's wrath is justifiably unleashed against sinners because God's existence is deducible from creation and because his moral standards that we all inevitably violate are inscribed on our hearts. But individually and as societies, we so suppress this "general" or "natural" revelation that we worship the creature (including ourselves) rather than the Creator (Rom. 1:18–25).[19] So, from a Christian perspective, we have no legitimate reason to

---

16. Colin G. Kruse (*Paul's Letter to the Romans* [Grand Rapids: Eerdmans, 2012], 242) observes a growing consensus among commentators to acknowledge both of these causes simultaneously.

17. G. C. Berkouwer, *Sin* (Grand Rapids: Eerdmans, 1971), 436–65.

18. Gregory A. Boyd and Paul R. Eddy, *Across the Spectrum: Understanding Issues in Evangelical Theology*, 2nd ed. (Grand Rapids: Baker Academic, 2009), 145–60.

19. "Pagans are not judged for choosing not to avail themselves of knowledge of God but for rejecting the knowledge of God they actually have—knowledge that God exists and is powerful."

be surprised when any human being, however beloved, lets us down, betrays us, hurts us, or shatters our dreams. If the Israelite judges, kings, and other Old Testament leaders were evil in God's sight more often than not, if the Jewish leaders in the first century were frequently regaled as "hypocrites," and if one of Jesus's closest followers could betray him and another one deny him, then we should scarcely be surprised when our political and religious leaders, or our parents and their friends, do the same today. As we mentioned in chapter 2, our trust should never be in any mere human being but only in Jesus.[20] Xers' lifelong disillusionment, therefore, with those whom other generations might have at first idolized is actually a more responsible and realistic reaction, from a biblical perspective.

What *should* surprise us, however, is the great power for good that many Christians *have* been able to exert in our world through the power of the Spirit. Xers may need to help balance their understandable disenchantment with others by imbibing and then sharing an adequate dose of this good news. What needs explanation is not the depth of human depravity in the doctrine of original sin—what Reinhold Niebuhr liked to call the only empirically verifiable doctrine of Christianity—but the progress of civilization in the centuries since Jesus's followers began to transform the Roman Empire.[21] Study the history of the development of Western science, medicine, law, government, and education, and you will discover how disproportionately responsible Christians have been in the growth and humanizing of these institutions, working with explicitly Christian presuppositions about the rationality, justice, and goodness of God.[22] And because all humans are created in God's image and likeness (Gen. 1:26), which remain present, even if corrupted, after humanity's fall into sin (Gen. 9:6; James 3:9), people of other worldviews and ideologies can and have also contributed to these developments.[23] However helpful various particulars of evolutionary theory may or may not be in explaining parts of the biological history of the universe, "survival of the fittest" fails

---

Again, "the root problem is not ignorance but suppression of knowledge" (Ben Witherington III with Darlene Hyatt, *Paul's Letter to the Romans: A Socio-Rhetorical Commentary* [Grand Rapids: Eerdmans, 2004], 66).

20. What was somewhat legitimately surprising was how highly Boomers touted themselves as exemplary models, making their failures that much more striking and the let-downs for those who trusted in them too much that much greater.

21. Reinhold Niebuhr, *Man's Nature and His Communities* (New York: Scribner, 1965), 24, quoting the *Times Literary Supplement*. G. K. Chesterton made much the same point even before Niebuhr.

22. See esp. Jonathan Hill, *What Has Christianity Ever Done for Us? How It Shaped the Modern World* (Downers Grove, IL: InterVarsity, 2005).

23. In detail, see G. C. Berkouwer, *Man: The Image of God* (Grand Rapids: Eerdmans, 1962), 119–93.

to explain altruism when it comes specifically at the expense of a person's well-being and even survival. Gen-Xers should be the best of our cohorts at recognizing all of this if they reflect carefully on the significance of all their disappointing experiences with authorities and others they have trusted and also scrutinize all that is good in our world as well.

Structural Evil and the Groaning of Creation

Reflection on the evil that can be perpetrated by governments and churches as institutions lands us squarely in the field of systemic or structural evil. To the extent that Xers have identified this phenomenon better in general than Boomers or Millennials, they have provided our society, and particularly Christian society, with a crucial insight. Commentators, especially on Paul's letters, have frequently delved into the language and contexts in which he speaks about "principalities and powers" (KJV) or "rulers/powers and authorities" (NIV) (Eph. 3:10; 6:12; Col. 1:16; 2:15; Titus 3:1).[24] Clearly, the biblical writers believed in the world of the demonic—of unseen, evil beings seeking to wreak havoc throughout God's creation. But Paul in particular appears to envision somewhat distinctive evil potentially perpetrated by systems or structures of organizations, which may or may not be overtly diabolical but certainly transcend the wickedness intended by even the worst of the individuals enmeshed in those systems. For example, the most well-intentioned American Christian cannot help but participate through taxes in evils occasionally inflicted by our government, and through purchases participate in injustices at times inflicted by multinational corporations in various places around the globe.

When the nineteenth-century English baron Lord John Acton made his famous declaration that "power tends to corrupt and absolute power corrupts absolutely," he enunciated a principle that seems to be very close to biblical teaching on this topic.[25] Unlike the nations around it, ancient Israel was a theocracy—the kings were not divine but subject to God, and prophets had the right to challenge royal behavior in the name of God (see classically 2 Sam. 12:1–14). The more hierarchical or top-down the corporation or institution, the more there is potential for abuse, even unwittingly, thus requiring checks

24. See esp. Clinton E. Arnold, *The Powers of Darkness: Principalities and Powers in Paul's Letters* (Downers Grove, IL: InterVarsity, 1992). On the theme of Jesus and the New Testament more broadly, see esp. the trilogy of works by Walter Wink: *Naming the Powers: The Language of Power in the New Testament* (Philadelphia: Fortress, 1984); *Unmasking the Powers: The Invisible Forces That Determine Human Existence* (Philadelphia: Fortress, 1986); and *Engaging the Powers: Discernment and Resistance in a World of Domination* (Minneapolis: Fortress, 1992).

25. In a letter to the Bishop of Peterborough, Mandell Creighton, in 1887.

and balances on power. The egalitarian intuitions of Gen-Xers are therefore, at heart, very good ones. As we saw in chapter 2, there are times in Scripture when God does not give identical roles to all people, but the *essential or inherent* equality of all individuals in God's eyes is foundational to Christianity. Every human being is created in God's image, giving them immense value in his sight. Even if certain roles may be limited to certain individuals, we must constantly exercise caution that we never treat others as if they were in any way inferior to anyone else. Xers should again be uniquely poised to model proper biblical behaviors in this arena.

But other types of institutional evil exist as well. Both hierarchical and egalitarian institutions can erect roadblocks that prevent people from thriving as much as they might, simply due to policies or practices that stifle creativity, growth, accountability, and the like. Moses wasn't freed up to do what he was called to do because he was judging too many cases (Exod. 18:13–27), and the apostles had to delegate some of their tasks to individuals who created the precedent for the office of deacons (Acts 6:1–6). In those two instances, too much power and responsibility in one or a small group of leaders created problems. But democracies frequently create too much bureaucracy. Create a committee to study every significant issue in a local church, and routine decisions that could have been made by elders and simply approved by the congregation can take forever, lead to wrangling and dissension, and stifle church growth and health. There is actually New Testament support for all three major forms of church government that have divided Christians throughout their history: presbyterian, congregational, and episcopal.[26] Elders or overseers clearly appear in 1 Timothy 2:1–7, Titus 1:5–9, and Philippians 1:1, as in the presbyterian model. Decisions made by entire congregations appear when all the believers in Jerusalem chose the seven "deacons" to help the apostles (Acts 6:1–6) and when the church in Antioch selected and commissioned Saul and Barnabas for their missionary service following the Spirit's guidance (13:1–3). The itinerant roles and overarching authority of apostles and missionaries like Paul and his coworkers, finally, represented the beginnings of larger geographic oversight of multiple congregations, as in episcopal models. Generation X, with its creativity and independence from tradition, should take the lead in seeking the right models for the right situations, perhaps even inventing new

26. See Chad O. Brand and R. Stanton Norman, eds., *Perspectives on Church Government: Five Views of Church Polity* (Nashville: Broadman & Holman, 2004). Elements of all the perspectives treated here (two of which are "mutations" of the classic three) are clearly biblically founded, so it is not a matter of choosing one model as "the right" one but recognizing when each model serves the church and its mission better than the others. Unfortunately, most Christians have not thought this way on this topic, usually leaving the task unaddressed.

ones altogether, once they recognize that none of these first-century practices is absolutized in Scripture.

Indeed, in today's world of rapid change, growth, and diversification of Christian congregations and ministries, great sensitivity and careful reflection are needed to determine, with God's help, the structures that will best support and not stifle God's work among his people. That such stifling can occur so quickly and so commonly among people with a fair amount of goodwill suggests some kind of potential for evil in institutions that outweighs the sum of the personal evils of the individuals within those institutions. A fair dose of anti-institutionalism is healthy for the church (see the model of 1 Cor. 14:26, in which everyone employs their spiritual gifts in the community gathered for worship), though it can be taken too far (Paul and Barnabas still appointed elders in every church they planted; Acts 14:23).[27] Xers will need the balancing emphases of the other cohorts, but evangelism and church growth typically require a substantial influx of fresh thinking from each new context to the next. Xers should lead the way in helping fashion models of ministry that will advance and not hinder God's kingdom.

The environmental concerns of Generation X remind us still more about the nature of sin in our universe. The fall of Adam and Eve affected not just all subsequent humanity but the entire universe. Romans 8:19–22 personifies creation's response with memorable language.

> For the creation waits in eager expectation for the children of God to be revealed. For the creation was subjected to frustration, not by its own choice, but by the will of the one who subjected it, in hope that the creation itself will be liberated from its bondage to decay and brought into the freedom and glory of the children of God.
>
> We know that the whole creation has been groaning as in the pains of childbirth right up to the present time.

Paul goes on to stress humanity's longing for the consummation of all of God's purposes, which will culminate in new heavens and a new earth. But Paul, like all the biblical authors, recognized an "already" as well as a "not-yet" dimension to the redemption of humanity and the restoration of all creation.[28] Just as it is incumbent on believers to participate in the Spirit's work in the conversion and discipleship of fellow human beings, it is also

---

27. For a detailed and balanced account of the developments in the first century, see Arthur G. Patzia, *The Emergence of the Church: Context, Growth, Leadership and Worship* (Downers Grove, IL: InterVarsity, 2001).

28. See esp. throughout George E. Ladd, *A Theology of the New Testament*, rev. and ed. Donald A. Hagner (Grand Rapids: Eerdmans, 1993).

important for them to seek to restore creation to positions and patterns of health and well-being. What should distinguish Christian creation care from certain other forms of environmentalism is not a lack of concern for animals, plants, and the geosphere more generally but a refusal to elevate nonhuman forms of creation to the same level as humanity.[29] Only men and women are created in God's image. So it is a perverse reversal of God's intentions, for example, when people clamor to save baby whales but refuse to care about unborn baby humans, thinking that they are merely extended pieces of tissue within a human body to be discarded at will. That said, we *should* care about the needless and cavalier destruction of baby whales or any other form of destruction of the animal kingdom or rape of the environment. May Gen-Xers lead the Christian world in helping all of us to care!

Independence versus Community

The most accurate way I have heard a member of Generation X summarize their desires for community in my church, only partly tongue-in-cheek, is, "I want community, but I want it on my terms." As a result, as Elisabeth points out, Xers can take a long time to commit—to friendships, small groups, marriage relationships, and even social invitations. My wife and I have experienced this commonly when we invite people for a meal and/or fellowship at our home (a practice that seems to be dying out along with Boomers). Boomers used to tell us right away if they were free and interested. If they said they would come, they would be there. With all of today's technology making communication so easy and constant, now most Boomers want a reminder, or they contact us to make sure an event is still "on" in ways they never used to. But they still mostly keep their commitments. When we invite Xers, a common response is, "Can I get back to you?" Sometimes it's not until the day before or the day of the event that we find out that they are or aren't coming because they've been weighing their options. If something "better" comes up, they go to that instead. If nothing better emerges, they come to the Blombergs' home! As a Boomer, I find this amazingly rude, but I am learning to adjust and trying to be less offended.[30]

---

29. For two excellent evangelical treatments of environmental ethics, see Richard Bauckham, *The Bible and Ecology: Rediscovering the Community of Creation* (Waco: Baylor University Press, 2010); and Noah J. Toly and Daniel I. Block, eds., *Keeping God's Earth: The Global Environment in Biblical Perspective* (Downers Grove, IL: InterVarsity, 2010).

30. For some Xers, Elisabeth informs me, this vacillation is a reflection of social anxiety. Having not had parents who were actively engaged in their lives, these Xers missed out on older adults who could model how one is to conduct oneself in various adult social settings. Elisabeth

Biblical cultures shared various traits from both Boomers and Xers in this regard. In a world without even the forms of communication that anyone alive from World War II onward took for granted, messengers were sent out days, weeks, or even months in advance of special events with the equivalent of our "save the date" emails. Then the day before or the day of the event, there would be a follow-up summons to come at such-and-such a time.[31] Attention to starting and finishing times in the biblical cultures, like in many more traditional parts of the majority world today, was very loose. In societies in which the sundial was the most accurate timekeeping device, this was perfectly understandable.[32] In today's Western world, a host and hostess may have a hot meal ready to serve at six o'clock in the evening only to receive a text that an invitee will be thirty minutes late, for no better reason than that they didn't budget their day and travel time well. Questions of discourtesy loom again.

Once more the parables of Jesus come quickly to mind. The parables of the great supper (Luke 14:16–24) and wedding banquet (Matt. 22:1–4) both describe initial invitations sent out a long time ahead of a festive day. Those originally invited proceed to reject the followup calls to come to the banquet on the day it is prepared. One or two emergencies are not unexpected, but it would be unheard of for everyone to cancel.[33] Jesus is obviously telling a story with a spiritual meaning; he is *not* primarily discussing time management and interpersonal etiquette concerning hospitality and social gatherings. It is ludicrous to reject God's invitation to the kingdom—submitting to his sovereign and gracious reign. Even the seemingly most important of earthly affairs pales compared to the urgency of responding to *this* invitation.[34]

---

has talked with many Xers who get just such an invitation but are worried about accepting because they are afraid that they won't know how to conduct themselves "properly": *What do I bring? What do I wear? How long am I expected to stay? What will we do? What will we talk about? Is it expected that I reciprocate?* These and similar types of questions can often paralyze Xers (and many Millennials for that matter) who have not had the opportunity of growing up in families who modeled such social interactions.

31. Kenneth E. Bailey, *Through Peasant Eyes: More Lucan Parables* (Grand Rapids: Eerdmans, 1980), 95–99.

32. Moreover, time was "not a resource in short supply" like almost everything else, so people could take their time and enjoy themselves. For the cultural elites like the banquet giver, there were few fixed boundaries between work and play. See Bruce J. Malina, *Christian Origins and Cultural Anthropology: Practical Models for Biblical Interpretation* (Atlanta: John Knox, 1986), 42.

33. See Arland J. Hultgren, *The Parables of Jesus: A Commentary* (Grand Rapids: Eerdmans, 2000), 336: "Each is, in effect, a flat refusal to come to the banquet that has been prepared. Their refusals are extremely offensive since they had accepted the invitation previously."

34. See Klyne R. Snodgrass, *Stories with Intent: A Comprehensive Guide to the Parables of Jesus* (Grand Rapids: Eerdmans, 2008), 316: "What could possibly be so important about mundane affairs that they keep one away from God's celebration? To reject the invitation is to exclude oneself from the eschatological meal."

Yet the cavalier attitude of some people, especially Xers, toward social gatherings here in this world often does carry over to spiritual matters. If I can't unequivocally respond to an invitation to go to someone's home in two weeks' time, how could I possibly commit to something as serious as a promise to follow Jesus for the rest of my life? What about when it gets hard? What about when it seems to be boring? What about when life, the church, and people let me down? Doesn't that mean God is letting me down? I'd love to try Christianity for a few years, but then I might like to try Buddhism for a few. So I just won't make up my mind for now. There have always been individuals afflicted with this disease, but there do seem to be a disproportionately large number among Xers who have caught it. (And some Millennials may have turned the disease into a pandemic!) The Scriptures are blunt in their consistent teaching that this represents extreme folly because we could meet our Maker at any moment (e.g., Luke 12:21; Matt. 24:45–51).

The dynamic of the parable of the great supper in Luke 14:16–24 is particularly instructive here. The three representative excuses Jesus uses for the people who originally agreed to come to the banquet but who refuse on the day it is celebrated are (1) "I have just bought a field, and I must go and see it"; (2) "I have just bought five yoke of oxen, and I'm on my way to try them out"; and (3) "I just got married, so I can't come" (vv. 18–20). The first two excuses are ridiculous enough, akin to someone in the Western part of the United States buying land in Florida sight unseen from a door-to-door salesman they know nothing about. Everyone in Jesus's world would visually examine a field and test any oxen for skills at pulling a plow if they were considering purchasing them. As for excuse (3), ancient weddings were scheduled months in advance as they typically are now, so no one would ever agree to attend a banquet in the first place if they knew they were getting married the same day, and no one would plan a wedding on a day they had already committed to an important banquet. Social calendars just weren't that full in the ancient Mediterranean world! It is clear that the originally invited guests are deliberately snubbing the host.[35] Those who refuse God's gracious invitation to join his "forever family" of those he gave his Son to die for are proving equally rude and rebellious. There is no better offer; indeed, there could never be any better offer than the new heavens and new earth that all the company of the redeemed will one day enjoy. Hedging one's bets in case a better offer comes along and not becoming a Christian sold out for God's service and glory resembles C. S. Lewis's famous analogy of children content to make mud pies in the slums

35. Bailey, *Through Peasant Eyes*, 94–95.

when offered a holiday at the seashore![36] If this is a particular characteristic of Gen-Xers, then it is time they "get over it" in a hurry.

In short, independence and creativity can be positive traits when they lead to helpful thinking "outside the box" that enables ministry to be released from stifling traditions. But when these traits stem from the desire for autonomy— from God or from God's people—then they fight against everything we were created to be. Apart from serving God, we are lost. Apart from serving others, we fail to achieve God's designs for us even as Christians (see Matt. 22:34–40). Community can only occur when each person submits his or her personal desires to the will of the entire congregation and asks how they can best fit in and help others (Acts 2:42–47; 4:32–37; contrast 5:1–11). Of course, there is a degree to which self-protection and preservation are necessary. But Xers are scarcely alone in the world. If no one helper proves completely trustworthy, a multiplicity of helpers can certainly meet specific needs throughout one's life journey. A foundational role for God's Holy Spirit is as our "Paraclete"—the most fundamental meaning of which may be Advocate—a Helper who inter- cedes on one's behalf before the relevant authorities (see esp. John 14–16).[37] Xers who feel too alone may need to cultivate the spiritual disciplines more, so that they recognize how near and dear God, through his Spirit, can be to them even if every human being sooner or later lets them down.

Skepticism, Relativism, Postmodernism

Somewhere in the 1980s, "existentialism" as the label for a worldview largely disappeared, and "postmodernism" took its place.[38] While not identical, the two ideologies have proved strikingly similar. Both reject theological and moral absolutes. Both deny that there are any metanarratives—overarching stories about human existence that are true for all people. Both call people to

36. "It would seem that Our Lord finds our desires not too strong, but too weak. We are half-hearted creatures, fooling about with drink and sex and ambition when infinite joy is offered us, like an ignorant child who wants to go on making mud pies in a slum because he cannot imagine what is meant by the offer of a holiday at the sea. We are far too easily pleased." C. S. Lewis, *The Weight of Glory, and Other Addresses* (London: HarperCollins, 2000), 26.

37. Note the growing trend to use this translation in English versions, including the updated NIV, NRSV, REB, NAB, NET, and NLT. For the requisite historical background, see Craig S. Keener, *The Gospel of John: A Commentary* (Peabody, MA: Hendrickson, 2003), 2:956–61.

38. The oldest hit for "Postmodern," "Postmodernist," or "Postmodernism" under a title search in the database for all entries in *New Testament Abstracts* appears in 1985, but the terms do not start commonly appearing until the 1990s. Hits for "Existential," "Existentialist," or "Existentialism" are more diverse, but those more recent than the 1980s tend to be about the philosophical perspectives of earlier writers.

live more in the present, recognizing the gifts of life in each moment and to be true to oneself above all. Existentialism's gurus included Jean-Paul Sartre and Albert Camus, writers from the G. I. Generation (those born between 1901–1924) who profoundly influenced the situation ethics, free love, and anti-"establishment" cultures of Boomers' young adult years.[39] Postmodernism became the term of preference for Xers, who took their cues from Jacques Derrida and philosophical "deconstructionism." This movement more consciously rebels against "modernism"—everything that takes the aesthetic, spiritual, personal, artistic, and contemplative out of life and culture.[40] Reinstating all of these elements into settings in which they had been lost may represent the greatest gifts postmodern thought and practice have bequeathed to us.

The recovery of these aspects of life has come at a price, however, and a very costly one at that. Postmodernists consistently disavow any truth or interpretation of a text that claims to be true for all human beings and any narrative that purports to make sense of every individual's personal story.[41] As has often been pointed out, however, every denial of all absolutes is itself an absolute statement. If there are no absolutes, then the statement "there are no absolutes" cannot be true, and thoroughgoing relativism implodes on itself. True to form, some postmodernists have thus responded that they believe only in partial relativism.[42] Oxymoronic as this may at first sound, it is actually consistent with biblical teaching. The Bible is a complex mixture of timeless and situation-specific truths, sometimes intermingled in ways that make it hard to separate them (recall our comments on 1 Cor. 8–10 and Rom. 14–15). There are principles that can be abstracted from every scriptural passage, but the processes by which they are identified are often more nuanced than one imagines on first glance. The art and science of biblical hermeneutics explores these processes and the presuppositions that guide them.[43]

The point of insisting on at least a few absolutes is not so much to create a confessional statement of faith or creed of nonnegotiables that Christians should believe. The point is not to craft a document of unassailable lifestyle requirements to which Christians should adhere. Such collections of

39. See esp. Joseph Fletcher, *Situation Ethics: The New Morality* (Philadelphia: Westminster, 1966).

40. For an excellent primer with critique, see David S. Dockery, ed., *The Challenge of Postmodernism* (Wheaton: Victor, 1995).

41. See Robert P. Carroll, "New Historicism and Postmodernism," in *The Cambridge Companion to Biblical Interpretation* (Cambridge: Cambridge University Press, 1998), 62.

42. See esp. Umberto Eco, *Interpretation and Overinterpretation* (Cambridge: Cambridge University Press, 1992).

43. See further William W. Klein, Craig L. Blomberg, and Robert L. Hubbard Jr., *Introduction to Biblical Interpretation*, rev. ed. (Nashville: Nelson, 2004), esp. 477–504.

affirmations have their place in certain contexts, but they neglect the *form* of God's revelation to humanity in inspired Scripture. Above all else, the Bible is a *narrative*. Its contents are couched in story form. Even long lists of laws, powerful proverbs, or exemplary epistles are all set in the larger context of the accounts of God's mighty acts throughout history and his constant, quiet working in the lives of all his people. No other religion or worldview has sacred Scriptures that effectively give a metanarrative that spans creation to new creation. No other "holy book," even if it provides reasons for the frustrating mixtures of good and bad in *every* era of human history, goes on to describe God's plans to save humanity from its alienation from him *by claiming that God has already accomplished this through the death and resurrection of a historical individual.* Only Christianity successfully crafts a story that moves in narrative sequence from creation to fall, to the selection of a people group through whom all the peoples of the world would be blessed (Gen. 12:3), to the appearance of a Messiah or Savior whose life and death can be documented in human history, to the creation of a community of that individual's followers who appropriate salvation by God's grace as they await the end and climax of the ages, to the recreation of the entire cosmos.[44] *Every* human being's existence and every portion of each human life takes its place and finds its meaning in that story. These are the absolutes worth clinging to. Xers dare not jettison the concept of one metanarrative that explains all of our individual narratives, for that is precisely what the Bible provides.

At the same time, Xers provide an important wakeup call to their fellow cohorts by pointing out how much of our world falls into the "gray areas." Much of biblical teaching does too, perhaps more than Boomers and Millennials regularly acknowledge. How do Old Testament laws apply in the New Testament age? Which New Testament teachings carry over into other times and cultures unchanged, and which require contextualizing and how? What does it mean to call nonhistorical genres of literature inerrant or infallible? For example, what does it mean to say that an imprecatory psalm is without error? Which parts of the Bible's historical literature are merely descriptive, and which parts are prescriptive? What would it look like if believers today imitated both Jesus and the apostles and got the most upset over the ultraconservatives in their midst whose legalism, traditions, and censorious attitudes stifle the growth of true disciples?[45] What would happen if we imitated Jesus

---

44. See esp. Christopher J. H. Wright, *The Mission of God: Unlocking the Bible's Grand Narrative* (Downers Grove, IL: InterVarsity, 2006).

45. For scriptural details, see Craig L. Blomberg, "The New Testament Definition of Heresy (or When Do Jesus and the Apostles Really Get Mad?)," *Journal of the Evangelical Theological Society* 45 (2002): 59–72.

and the New Testament authors in making surprisingly solicitous overtures to the most notorious sinners in our societies? Freethinking Xers should be challenged to draw on the strengths of their cohort in helping the church address all these issues more creatively while also remaining true to Scripture.

Acting Locally with Liberty and Justice for All

A common slogan in missions circles over the last twenty years or so has been to "think globally, but act locally."[46] If technology has enabled Boomers to be the first generation to consistently *act* globally, traveling the world with unprecedented ease for countless enterprises, Gen-Xers may be needed to keep the church's feet on the ground so that it acts locally as well. Many congregations led by Boomers do much better at sending missionaries overseas to help fulfill the Great Commission (Matt. 28:18–20) than they do at impacting the neighborhoods and communities immediately surrounding them and fulfilling the Great Commandment (Lev. 19:18; Mark 12:31 and parallels). Some Gen-X churches have significantly compensated for that gap with ministries of outreach, mercy, and justice at home while struggling to determine what, if any, responsibility they have to people elsewhere in the country and world.

The ministry of God's people must encompass both near and far, like and unlike, evangelism and social action (division of labor and a holistic gospel is commended in Gal. 2:1–10, esp. vv. 8–10), though that doesn't necessarily mean that every congregation, however small, must always undertake all of these. But where size and resources permit, a balance between the two elements in each of these pairs of opposites is usually good.[47] If one area has been underserved, then more emphasis may need to be placed on it for a while. After all, the central topic of Jesus's ministry—the kingdom of God—was an amazingly broad concept. Andrew Kirk comprehensively defines its meaning when he writes,

> The kingdom sums up God's plan to create a new human life by making possible
> a new kind of community among people, families and groups. [It combines]

---

46. The slogan appears to have begun in secular contexts, esp. in the United Nations. This then led to the creation of the hybrid word "glocal." Both were then appropriated in Christian circles. See, e.g., Bob Roberts Jr., *How Glocal Churches Transform Lives and Change the World* (Grand Rapids: Zondervan, 2006). On the specific issue of principles for an evangelical approach to contextualizing the gospel, see esp. Matthew Cook, Rob Haskell, Ruth Julian, and Natee Tanchanpongs, eds., *Local Theology for the Global Church* (Pasadena: William Carey, 2010).

47. As particularly in Paul's missionary model, on which see esp. Eckhard J. Schnabel, *Paul the Missionary: Realities, Strategies, Methods* (Downers Grove, IL: InterVarsity, 2008).

the possibility of a personal relationship to Jesus with man's responsibility to manage wisely the whole of nature; the expectation that real change is possible here and now; a realistic assessment of the strength of opposition to God's intentions; the creation of new human relationships and the eventual liberation by God of the whole of nature from corruption.[48]

Boomers in their young adult years tended to learn mostly about the personal relationship to Jesus of which Kirk speaks. Some Xers have overly stressed the environmentalism and social justice parts of his definition. It may be up to the Millennials to try to capture the right balance of the two. The same may be true for the balance between global and local action, along with the probable consequences of each set of actions.

Somewhere in my grade-school years, when public-school children still pledged allegiance to the flag at the beginning of each school day, I learned a version of the pledge in simplified English language. It hasn't stuck with me because I recited the regular version far more often both before and afterwards. But I do remember that it ended with "with freedom and fairness for all." That phrase came back to me as I read Elisabeth's comments about Xers' love of independence and about how fairness at times trumps even equality for many of them. But the American pledge to the flag is not found in the Bible, even if that comes as a surprise to a few Boomers (nor was our Constitution or Bill of Rights ever a part of inspired Scripture!).

The framers of the simplified pledge that I learned obviously understood "fairness" as an adequate synonym for "justice" and an easier word for children to grasp. I suspect they were right that it was easier, but for a different reason; the two concepts can be slightly different. "Justice" appears 134 times in the ESV, whereas "fairness" occurs only twice, both times in 2 Corinthians 8:13–14, where the term is the Greek *isotēs*, referring to something more akin to "equity" than to "equality" (the rendering in the majority of translations).[49] Herein resides the difference between the two English words: equality typically means treating everyone identically, whereas fairness means treating everyone equitably. While in some contexts the words are used interchangeably, fairness or equity can mean treating people unequally, but according to what they deserve or merit. This is exactly what Xers in Elisabeth's studies said they wanted.

48. J. Andrew Kirk, *A New World Coming* (London: Marshall, Morgan & Scott, 1983), 47. Published in the United States as *The Good News of the Kingdom Coming* (Downers Grove, IL: InterVarsity, 1983).

49. Wayne Grudem, *Business for the Glory of God: The Bible's Teaching on the Moral Goodness of Business* (Wheaton: Crossway, 2003), 53.

The parable of the workers in the vineyard (Matt. 20:1–16) illustrates this perfectly. The landowner decides to pay all the workers a full day's wage even though they have labored for dramatically different percentages of the workday. When the workers discover this, they complain. The master replies, "I am not being un*fair* to you" (v. 13). Equal pay for unequal work seemed very unfair because fairness is *not* always the same as equality.[50] To the extent that Xers want fairness even more than equality, if this is the kind of distinction they envision, they had better think again. No one should ever want God to be fair with them. Whether they realize it or not, they are asking to be condemned! Because no human being can ever come remotely close to God's perfectly holy standard for living, everyone must trust in Jesus, the perfect sacrifice for human sins, who lived a sinless life and took our place on the cross in receiving the punishment we deserved. Of course, we should serve him and seek to obey him throughout our lives, but only as a profound act of gratitude to him for doing for us what we could never have done ourselves, not because we think we can merit anything in the process. The equality we have in Christ is not fair, nor is it earned, but given entirely by God's grace.[51]

In a social justice context, however, Xers often want equity, in the biblical sense, more than equality. They are pushing against the Boomer idea that everyone should or does have equal access to the good life in America. Xers are very aware that just because we are technically "equal" doesn't actually mean that everyone has the same starting point in life or the same access to resources. To the extent that Xers recognize this and are not asking for fairness at the last judgment but just in this life, the question then becomes how much we should expect just treatment in so deeply flawed a world as ours. Perhaps we all need to exercise more grace to others who grant *us* less than a fair shake at times, while still moving heaven and earth to seek justice for others!

Work, Personal Time, and Identity

In eighth grade, I was required to take a semester-long class called "Guidance" in my public junior high school in Illinois. It might have had a longer official title, but that's what we all called it. The purpose of the class was to help us explore a wide variety of possible careers, what they entailed, and, as we moved on to high school, how best to start preparing for them if we so chose. One comment by our teacher has particularly stuck with me throughout

50. Jan Lambrecht, *Out of the Treasure: The Parables in the Gospel of Matthew* (Grand Rapids: Eerdmans, 1992), 76.
51. Michael J. Wilkins, *Matthew* (Grand Rapids: Zondervan, 2004), 666.

the years. On one occasion he talked about how some European countries were already starting to move to slightly less than a forty-hour work week. He predicted that before too long, and certainly not long after we were all employed adults, the United States would move to a thirty-five-hour work week and quite possibly eventually to one with only thirty hours. The biggest challenge Americans would have would be with how to spend their leisure time. After all, the speed of improvement and the invention of all kinds of technology were creating "labor-saving devices" that would make all of our jobs so much easier and faster.

Little did anyone realize in the late 1960s that what was being invented and honed were "labor-*creating* devices." The faster I can do what filled all my work hours a generation ago, the more work I will be given to do today! I suppose we shouldn't complain. After all, immediately after the commandment about remembering the Sabbath to keep it holy, God declares, "Six days you shall labor and do all your work" (Exod. 20:9). In a largely agrarian society, people typically worked from sunup until sundown, averaging twelve hours a day, six days a week—a seventy-two-hour work week. Even though average American workers today work about forty-six hours a week, the highest figure in the developed world, they still fall well below seventy-two![52] But especially for Christians who do not keep a literal Sabbath (because, after all, it is part of the ritual law fulfilled in Christ; Col. 2:16), it remains incumbent that they budget adequate time for both rest and worship.[53]

Biblically speaking, moreover, Christians are identified by who they are in Christ—beloved, redeemed, empowered creatures made in God's likeness to serve him and his mission in the world. Xers are right not to define themselves or find their identity solely or even primarily in their work. But neither would they be adopting the appropriate alternative if they defined themselves by their hobbies, interests, or recreational activities outside work. They are gifted children of God. What distinguishes one believer from another is the specific package of gifts God has given them for building up the church and so furthering God's work in the world (Eph. 4:11–12). Personal time and work are both important. But most important of all is kingdom activity. God's reign can often be advanced even as people work or relax, but only the gathered

52. See Alan Pearcy, "Most Employed Americans Work More Than 40 Hours per Week," *Ragan's PR Daily*, July 12, 2012, http://www.prdaily.com/Main/Articles/Most_employed_Americans _work_more_than_40_hours_pe_12123.aspx; and G. E. Miller, "The U.S. Is the Most Overworked Developed Nation in the World—When Do We Draw the Line?," *20 Something Finance*, October 12, 2010, http://20somethingfinance.com/american-hours-worked-productivity-vacation/.

53. See further Craig L. Blomberg, "The Sabbath as Fulfilled in Christ," in *Perspectives on the Sabbath: 4 Views*, ed. Christopher J. Donato (Nashville: B&H, 2011), 305–58.

community of the people of God can fully implement God's vision for what the church is to do and to be for each other and the world.

Failure to understand the context of a verse like Matthew 6:33 brings this issue into sharp focus. In the Sermon on the Mount, Jesus commands us, "Seek first his kingdom and his righteousness, and all these things will be given to you as well." In the preceding verses, it is clear that "these things" refer to the basic necessities of life—food, shelter, and clothing. God promises to meet our needs, not our greeds. But what about faithful believers who have starved to death, gone homeless, or died of curable diseases because they didn't have access to any medicine? Here we need to recognize the significance of the second-person plural verbs and pronouns in the Greek. God promises his disciples as a community (see also 5:1) that as they implement God's righteous and just requirements, there will be no acutely needy person among them (see also Acts 4:34).[54] If Xers are profoundly suspicious of all institutions, *including the church*, it is only because Boomers and older generations have failed miserably to implement Christ's vision for the church. There are, of course, pleasant exceptions; however, in general, Mormons are better at caring for their own, physically and materially, than are evangelical Christians![55] Perhaps Xers can step up to the plate and build on their disappointment to start to transform today's churches into what God wants them to be. And, if they do not yet have the power to affect an entire congregation, let them do what they excel at: working quietly in small ways with their own cohort, setting the example that could in turn challenge and inspire the rest of the body of Christ.

At the same time, Xers, like all cohorts, need to recover a fully-orbed biblical theology of work. Work is not just something to endure while longing and living for discretionary time. God created human beings for work, as demonstrated by his placing them in the garden with the explicit instructions to care for the earth (Gen. 1:28–30). Work became onerous only after the fall (3:17–19). But like every other element of creation, it too is in the process of being redeemed. Christians fulfill God's purposes for them as they work, wrestle with how best to glorify God, exhibit exemplary service, and bring a Christian ethic to the workplace. Colossians 3:23 deserves repeated reflection in each position of employment: "Whatever you do, work at it with all your heart, as working for the Lord, not for human masters."[56]

---

54. See Robert A. Guelich, *The Sermon on the Mount: A Foundation for Understanding* (Waco: Word, 1982), 373.

55. See the statistics in Craig L. Blomberg, *Christians in an Age of Wealth: A Biblical Theology of Stewardship* (Grand Rapids: Zondervan, 2013), 23–32.

56. David E. Garland (*Colossians and Philemon* [Grand Rapids: Zondervan, 1998], 268) rightly notes the dangers of applying principles surrounding the institution of slavery to

Church and Family

Elisabeth's discussion of those in Generation X who have already begun to create new, interactive, authentic communities of worship proves profoundly encouraging. I have experienced a fair amount of this in my own church. It is very difficult for me to return to the stereotypical suburban megachurch without feeling that most everything is "staged." I have little chance to get to know the people up front and find out what they are really like, but what I see seems all about musical talent and the skills taught in the local high schools' speech and drama classes. Musicians walk to their places while everyone is praying (but then *they* don't have a chance to pray much), so there is no "downtime," even for a few seconds, between portions of the service. Tech flow charts time each element of the service down to the minute, while digital clocks on large screens count down the seconds until the start of worship. If the Spirit wanted to do something unplanned, would there be even one spare moment for him to do so? It's great "staging," but that is a theatrical term not an ecclesiastical one.[57]

I like it that often the musicians in my church have only dim lights on above them. Sometimes one or more have sat down behind others so that they can't be seen as easily. The point is to draw attention away from themselves so that hopefully people can worship *the Lord*. If the podium for the preacher isn't in just the right place, no one gets upset if someone takes a short time to move it into place. The sound system isn't great, but it's adequate; and it's all we can afford. God is pleased with every good-faith effort to worship him with singing, liturgy, preaching, teaching, fellowship, and sacraments/ordinances that stay true to fundamental Christian doctrine, foster just and loving Christian behavior, and bring men and women closer to Jesus.[58] He cares next to

---

workplaces in a democracy but does stress principles that can legitimately be derived, including the avoidance of dishonesty, negligence, or shoddy work. "The temptation may be to work only to attract attention or to get by with as little as possible. The Christian, by contrast, must give wholehearted service in the workplace in all circumstances, because our work is something done for the Lord. We work in the confidence that it will not be wasted but that it will be gathered up by God, who brings everything to its successful culmination." For good introductions to a Christian theology of work more generally, see Ben Witherington III, *A Kingdom Perspective on Labor* (Grand Rapids: Eerdmans, 2011); Darrell Cosden, *The Heavenly Good of Earthly Work* (Peabody, MA: Hendrickson, 2006); and Miroslav Volf, *Work in the Spirit: Toward a Theology of Work* (Eugene, OR: Wipf & Stock, 2001).

57. There is still a whole range of God-honoring worship styles and practices. See Paul A. Basden, ed., *Exploring the Worship Spectrum: 6 Views* (Grand Rapids: Zondervan, 2004).

58. For a full treatment of the Bible's teaching on the topic, see Allen P. Ross, *Recalling the Hope of Glory: Biblical Worship from the Garden to the New Creation* (Grand Rapids: Kregel, 2006).

nothing for just how much polish it all has; indeed, he berates Israel when it takes pride in its worship while neglecting matters of justice (e.g., Isa. 1:10–20; Jer. 7:1–26; Mic. 6:1–8). Xers' passion for authenticity should stand them in good stead here. As they move more and more into positions of leadership, it will be incumbent on them not just to lament the frequent absence of authenticity from Boomer-led activities but to model it themselves. And then they will need to wrestle with what best creates authentic Christianity for the next cohort after them. Already I am observing some older Xers unwilling to trade in what was cutting edge and powerfully effective for them fifteen years ago for what will function similarly for Millennials today.

Spirituality outside a Christian church but still Christian in content (e.g., the Ignatian exercises or centering prayer that repeats a phrase like "Christ, have mercy") can transform the lives of various Xers (and members of other cohorts) in powerful ways. Psalm 119 is an amazingly repetitive, 176-verse testimony to the creativity of its author to keep extolling his delight in God's Word and its capacity to transform every area of his life. Psalm 136 repeats the refrain "His love endures forever" no less than twenty-six times, so that those who spoke or sang it might finally let the message sink in![59] Spirituality outside Christianity should be viewed as "pre-evangelism" rather than something hazardous. Paul builds on the abundant spirituality he discovers in Athens in order to lead people toward a knowledge of the one true God of the universe (Acts 17:22–31).[60] It is always sad when Christians seem more threatened by those of other religious or sectarian worldviews than by outright agnostics or atheists. We need to delight in Xers' deep spirituality and build on it so that it can become redemptive faith as well.

To the extent that Xers' commitments to marriage play a significant role in the decrease in the divorce rate nationwide, they should be heartily commended. To the degree that this greater level of commitment stems from their waiting to marry and/or choosing not to have children, or to have fewer children, these trends too must be praised. Boomers never adequately took 1 Corinthians 7 to heart. Paul makes it abundantly clear that being married is no higher form of Christian living than the single life (esp. vv. 7–8). Indeed, he would like everyone to commit themselves as wholeheartedly to God's work in the world as an unmarried person has the opportunity to do (vv. 32–35). He wants to spare people as many hardships as possible, so he

---

59. "Here is the unchanging certainty which Israel flung defiantly in the face of the ever changing and often testing experiences of life." Robert Davidson, *The Vitality of Worship: A Commentary on the Book of Psalms* (Grand Rapids: Eerdmans, 1998), 437.

60. See esp. Susan Campbell, "Scratching the Itch: Paul's Athenian Speech Shaping Mission Today," *Evangelical Review of Theology* 35 (2011): 177–84.

encourages those already married to live as simply as possible, almost as if they were still single (vv. 28–31). As I have asked elsewhere, "How often do Christians contemplating getting married ask the question of whether a prospective partner will enable them to serve the Lord better? If they cannot realistically imagine ways in which this could happen, they are probably not ready to 'tie the knot.'"[61]

When members of Generation X become more committed and involved parents of their children in healthy ways, this is also positive. Christian Boomers throughout their lives may have heard a dozen times as many messages about obeying their parents (Eph. 6:1) than they heard about parents not exasperating their children but bringing them up "in the training and instruction of the Lord" (v. 4). But the pendulum must not swing too far in the opposite direction so that biological family takes precedence over spiritual family when the two conflict. Recall our earlier discussion of Mark 3:33–35, Luke 14:26, and their parallels. A couple's decision not to have children at all because they don't believe they can be the kinds of parents those children would need should also be respected as a potentially godly choice. It will not do just to keep repeating Genesis 1:28, in which God blesses Adam and Eve and then declares, "Be fruitful and increase in number; fill the earth and subdue it." As a human race, we have done very well at obeying these commands! With the depletion of the earth's resources, it could be good if population growth slowed.[62]

Unfortunately, sometimes Xers' decisions about faith and family seem more selfishly than biblically motivated. A person might not want to be married or have children so that they can remain as much of a workaholic as any Boomer. Or they might want to have tons of discretionary time free for travel, recreation, hobbies, and the like but don't factor in serving fellow human beings in any significant way.[63] Perhaps they are terrified of commitment, like the younger Xer we used to know who described her life experience as "reinventing herself every two years." She never had trouble finding boyfriends, but she couldn't keep them. Finally she married one, a godly young pastor, but ditched him for a different man two years after their wedding and moved two thousand

---

61. Craig L. Blomberg, *From Pentecost to Patmos: Acts to Revelation—An Introduction and Survey* (Nottingham, UK: Apollos, 2006), 179. Published in the United States as *From Pentecost to Patmos: An Introduction to Acts through Revelation* (Nashville: B&H, 2006).

62. This, however, is in no way to sanction the perverse use of this text and this logic in some circles to support abortion or euthanasia.

63. One of Elisabeth's interviewees explained that she did not want children because she did not know how she could afford to provide for them financially while continuing her full-time commitment to environmentalism. This is certainly a wise decision if one is unprepared to relinquish any of the latter, but at some point people, created in God's image, must take priority over nature, which is not so created.

miles away. She ditched the new live-in boyfriend (that she never married) two years after that, only to discover that he shortly thereafter committed suicide. Although an extreme and perhaps even pathological example, she serves as an illustration and warning of what the pendulum swing can look like for Xers pursuing their own individualistic desires.

I think also of another acquaintance, an older, nominally Catholic Xer who has no trouble finding girlfriends but eventually gets bored with them. For him, it's all about the hunt. As soon as he finds someone and the relationship might be moving toward marriage, he discovers some way in which the woman is less than perfect or less than fully compatible with him, and he's on the prowl again. He does not acknowledge his own flaws, but he has a long mental checklist of what qualities each woman he dates should have; and he trots this out to justify each breakup.[64] First Corinthians 13 needs repeated attention and study. True Christian love is not primarily an emotion but a freely chosen commitment to "the unsolicited giving of the very best you have on behalf of another regardless of response."[65]

Conclusion

As with the Baby Boomers, members of Generation X display an intricate cluster of strengths and weaknesses when evaluated biblically. Their desires for less workaholism and less striving after material wealth, coupled with greater commitments to issues of justice and creation care, match key biblical themes. The conservative evangelical world, still run by Boomer power brokers, too seldom recognizes this. Gen-Xers' fierce independence and suspicion of authority and its manipulative power are strengths when the authorities truly are warped, but these can turn into weaknesses in other contexts. Gratitude for the many choices Gen-Xers have keeps this independence from becoming as damaging as it might be, but fear of commitment can become paralyzing or worse. Keeping as many options open for as long as possible to maximize the good for oneself is a strength when one has few really good choices, but it becomes a weakness when it prevents people from making *good* choices for fear of missing out on the *best*. A vague, pluralist spirituality need not be condemned; it can be seen as a preparation for the gospel. But it must not be viewed as an adequate substitute for saving faith in Jesus Christ.

64. There was a *Friends* episode in which Chandler played a man very like this one as the noncommittal Xer: https://www.youtube.com/watch?v=TwjvrButSok.

65. Richard Walker, AMOR Ministries' motto (Murray, KY). Walker was a longtime Southern Baptist pastor and missionary to the upper Amazon basin in Brazil.

The strengths of Generation X have indeed yet to be fully appreciated. Their potential for good remains in large part yet to be unleashed. What might it look like for the church of Jesus Christ if this were still to occur? How can we make sure we don't leapfrog over this generation in our youth-obsessed culture and move directly to engaging Millennials without having tapped into what Xers can and want to offer? Our next chapter will focus particularly on these questions as we turn to Christian ministry with this cohort.

6

Priorities for Ministry with Xers

Waiting—waiting for the world to change. After more than four decades, these lost middle children are coming into their own mid-life and have the hope of finally getting the chance to make the changes they have longed to see. Currently in their thirties and forties (with the first having reached fifty in 2015), Gen-Xers are in key positions to influence younger generations as they raise children and shape businesses, organizations, and ministries while changing the face of evangelicalism. The question to our churches today is whether we will give them the space and the opportunity to make the changes they see as necessary and live out the faith experiences with which they resound.

Successful ministry to and with Generation Xers must engage their skepticism, relate to their need for individual community, and participate in an experiential journey that connects head, heart, and hands in authentic faith. With only one in three Xers reporting active membership in a religious organization, churches and parachurch ministries would do well to heed the characteristics, concerns, and needs of this generation or else risk losing them and the impact they have on their own spheres of influence.[1]

1. Jon D. Miller, "Active, Balanced, and Happy: These Young Americans Are Not Bowling Alone," *The Generation X Report* 1, no. 1 (Fall 2011): 4.

A Change in Worldview

Relativism, postmodernism, constructivism—whatever "-ism" you use to describe the shift in worldview over the last fifty years, it is the reality of Generation X, regardless of whether they are inside the church or outside it. For these over sixty million people, truth is primarily understood through experience. Anything or anyone who purports to have a corner on any kind of absolute must either be a fool or a con, for almost nothing in Xers' experiences has given them reason to believe in absolutes. Older generations, or those with a more modernist view of the world, can bemoan and attempt to refute this perspective until they are blue in the face, but it will not change the foundational perspective from which Xers approach life. Ministry with Xers (and with Millennials too for that matter) needs to recognize them as a new and distinct culture from those who have gone before them. This is similar to the idea that missionaries who are looking to minister to a village in rural China or to post-Christian France would not go in assuming that the people they are hoping to minister to hold the same worldview, values, or philosophical perspectives as the missionaries themselves. Instead, the missionaries would go in with an attitude of openness, curiosity, and respect as they learned the values, beliefs, and worldview of the new culture. The same attitude must be true as ministry leaders seek to connect with American Gen-Xers—Xers are not simply younger Boomers, and they should be pursued, understood, and engaged as their own cultural group.[2]

In tandem with this, Xers are often times more easily understood by what they are not and by what they do not want or need. We will unpack more of this as we proceed but, as an overview, Xers

- do not like large group affiliation, but prefer instead a smaller, more intimate sense of collective identity;
- do not respond well to arguments made from a purely rational perspective, and instead value an argument that is contextually and experientially relevant;
- are not disinterested in or apathetic about spiritual things.[3]

2. Literature on recognizing that other cultures sometimes have better insights into biblical meaning and truth than our own abounds. A particularly good recent example is E. Randolph Richards and Brandon J. O'Brien, *Misreading Scripture with Western Eyes: Removing Cultural Blinders to Better Understand the Bible* (Downers Grove, IL: InterVarsity, 2012). Now we have to recognize generational cohorts as different cultures, even if sometimes not to the same extent, and ask how often Xers (and Millennials) might recognize biblical and theological truth better than Boomers. Premodernist and postmodernist cultures have numerous similarities.

3. See Roland D. Martinson, "Spiritual but Not Religious: Reaching an Invisible Generation," *Currents in Theology and Mission* 29, no. 5 (2002): 326–40.

This smaller, lost middle child of generational cohorts has a lot to offer the church and the culture at large, but they must be invited to share what they have seen, what they understand, and how they envision getting that mission done. What would it take to create a space where Xers feel at home?

Creating Home

In true Xer form, I (Elisabeth) would like to use a metaphor, specifically the metaphor of a home, to talk through what ministry to and with Xers needs to look like. From the foundation and walls to the individual rooms, this generation is looking for a place of safety, acceptance, and warmth, a place to call home. You will notice that the church is not a separate space or a unique room; instead it permeates the entire house. There are few distinctions between life roles and callings, but a holistic sense of self is simply expressed to varying degrees and with different purposes within each room of the home. Picture it with me, if you will.

The Yard

Your yard is the very first thing guests experience about your home. It's public, it's open, and there's really no good way to hide it. Your yard can be an outward expression of the things that matter to you, but it is still appropriate for public viewing and discussion. For Xers the theme of their yard is practical theology. To extend the lawn analogy even further, Xers are not the generation to have tacky and unnecessary lawn ornaments—everything that they do with their yard is likely to have a practical use or purpose. An example of this practicality is the number of churches run by Xers that meet in schools or other public buildings even when they can technically afford a building of their own. In these situations, their practical theology guides their financial stewardship and their selection of a building that is pragmatic and accessible within their community.

Conceptualizing life within their sphere of influence, Xers look to care for the world around them. In missions and community service, this often takes a much more local rather than global perspective. Missions among Boomers often focused on global outreach and international missions. True to family roles (what the oldest is good at is likely not what the next child will pursue), Xers brought the focus to a more local level. In my church some examples of this include a community garden on the church grounds, which donates all produce to local food banks; partnering with local county agencies to provide hotel vouchers for the homeless during cold Colorado winter nights; and packing backpacks with school supplies for low-income children in our community. We still support global missions, but the emphasis in our ministries is much more local and directly connected to the needs and relationships around us.[4]

Many Xers' yard space also includes practical theology as it pertains to issues of social justice. In a ministry capacity this is not as likely to take on a political face as it is a face of activism and advocacy. For example, my church has partnered with a local, non-faith-based nonprofit organization that provides resources and training to help prevent teen suicide. This organization seeks to uphold the inherent value and worth of all people, honoring the life that God has given them. While not expressly Christian, there is nothing about this organization that contradicts the gospel message, and it actually passionately supports the worth that Scripture places on human life.[5]

Whether you want to call it environmentalism or creation care, taking care of the resources that God has entrusted to people is a yard-space issue for Gen-Xers. Having grown up with Earth Day, and with recycling programs becoming more and more prevalent throughout their developmental years, Xers have a keen awareness of environmental concerns and often feel responsible to attend to what is within their sphere of influence. As a ministry, you will make Xers feel more at home if you too embrace a recycling program at your facility and take steps to conserve energy.[6] Too often I have heard more conservative Boomers connect environmentalism with evolutionary science; but the issue is one of stewardship, and Xers are right to pursue it.[7] Churched or not, many Xers see the world as a resource that must be wisely stewarded rather than used up or exploited. For this generation, bigger is not always better; brighter and shinier are not always more appealing; and practical, functional, and responsible use of space and resources is often of higher value. As such, yard space—that which is the most public and visible—should

4. See further Sammy Campbell, *The New Urban Missions: Local Breaching for Global Reaching* (Nashville: CrossBooks, 2010).

5. The Second Wind Fund: http://www.thesecondwindfund.org/.

6. An organization such as the Evangelical Environmental Network may be a beneficial place for ministries to look to find out more about creation care: http://www.creationcare.org/.

7. Particularly helpful for the biblical and theological underpinnings is Richard Bauckham, *The Bible and Ecology: Rediscovering the Community of Creation* (Waco: Baylor University Press, 2010). Bauckham is a Boomer but also British, and the UK has been about a generation ahead of the United States on this issue. More briefly, see American Xer Jonathan Moo, "Continuity, Discontinuity, and Hope: The Contribution of New Testament Eschatology to a Distinctively Christian Environmental Ethos," *Tyndale Bulletin* 61 (2010): 21–44. Xer authors who give a myriad of practical insights along with having a good theological base include Jonathan Merritt, *Green Like God: Unlocking the Divine Plan for Our Planet* (Nashville: FaithWords, 2010); and Tracy Bianchi, *Green Mama: The Guilt-Free Guide to Helping You and Your Kids Save the Planet* (Grand Rapids: Zondervan, 2010).

speak to practical theology, a generally pragmatic approach to most areas of life, and community care whenever possible.

The Foundation and the Walls

As an Xer, I grew up in a larger culture where constructivism was simply a given; this was the *foundation* of our cultural "home." Everything was built upon this foundational premise that truth is relative and subjective.[8] At school and in the media, Xers listened to things such as "Free to be you and me"[9] and heard multiple talks, shows, and messages about how it is important to be your own unique self. When these messages ran up against the absolutist messages of the church, Xers as a generation turned to what they knew to break the tie: experience. Experience, as the *walls* of the home, provided the bounds by which they assessed information and claims of truth. Experience taught Xers that one individual's understanding of a situation would likely differ from their friend Sara's, which would likely differ from their friend Scott's—those unique experiences were grounded on constructivism, and then conceptualized within the framework of their own experiences. Experience showed Xers that those proclaiming absolutes weren't necessarily living by them, and so hypocrisy and basic human fallibility supported the claims of relativism and constructivism while undermining messages of absolute truth. In an environment that lacked invested, relatable mentors to provide the walls by which to assess truth, Xers sought the messages that affirmed and validated their unique and individual experiences. As the church now seeks to re-engage this generation, it must take into consideration the background and framework they bring: truth without contextual relevance will be left unheard and unexplored, while opportunities to consistently *experience* truth in the context of relationship will allow for a personalized understanding and acceptance of that same truth.[10]

8. There is an inherent irony in a "foundation" being built on something subjective and relativistic rather than on something concrete and absolute (i.e., objectivism). Nonetheless, constructivism is the foundational framework for the Gen-Xer worldview and must be understood as such. For an overview of constructivism, see Jonathan D. Raskin, "On Essences in Constructivist Psychology," *Journal of Theoretical and Philosophical Psychology* 31, no. 4 (November 2011): 223–39.

9. *Free to Be You and Me*, DVD, directed by Bill Davis, Fred Wolf, and Len Steckler (Henstooth Video, 2001; original release date 1972).

10. Influential works in this vein that have received a better hearing among Xers than Boomers (though written by Boomers) include Carl Raschke, *The Next Reformation: Why Evangelicals Must Embrace Postmodernity* (Grand Rapids: Baker Academic, 2004); and Stanley J. Grenz and John R. Franke, *Beyond Foundationalism: Shaping Theology in a Postmodern Context* (Louisville: Westminster John Knox, 2001). More briefly, see Craig van Gelder, "Postmodernism

As with other types of missions, we do not enter someone's home and immediately criticize them for building a house out of clay and straw and try to sell them on the benefits of aluminum siding. Instead, we recognize that context and culture dictate how a home is built, and we enter another's home with grace and kindness, thankful for their hospitality. As we enter into this metaphorical home of Xers, let us enter with the same spirit, eager to learn how they turn a house into a home.

The Threshold

The threshold of any house can vary. For some, you walk through the front door and immediately enter the living space, and for others you pass through a vestibule or entryway before entering into the rest of the home. Regardless, the entrance of any home provides an immediate first impression, a glimpse into the atmosphere and climate of a home. You cannot get further into the home without passing through and experiencing the threshold—in our metaphor this serves as the shared experiences, worldview, and understanding of our Gen-X "home." Part of the Gen-X entrance is understanding and embracing the concept of being a collective of individuals. To enter into the Xer home, you must gain some understanding that the individual's unique lived experiences and perceptions are important *and* that a given individual finds identity in being a part of something bigger than herself or himself. The collective is not necessarily the entire generational cohort, but instead a sphere of influence or a small cohort of other "individuals" who have something in common.

Another part of entering the Gen-X "home" is recognizing the language that is used, as language becomes the expressed representation of values and worldview.[11] Xers had less organized religion in their upbringing than previous generations, and instead were exposed to spirituality as a more general concept. As such, their language is more geared toward the "spiritual" than toward the religious or "Christian-ese" of mainstream evangelicalism.[12] Beginning spiritual conversations with this generation means starting with the broadly existential and generally universal rather than the specific language and concepts of Christianity. This requires churches, ministries, and Christians in general to be familiar with spiritual concepts outside Christianity

and Evangelicals: A Unique Missiological Challenge at the Beginning of the Twenty-First Century," *Missiology* 30, no. 4 (2002): 491–504.

11. Julia T. Wood, *Communication Theories in Action: An Introduction*, 2nd ed. (Belmont, CA: Wadsworth/Thompson Learning, 2000), 218.

12. For a humorous look at "Christian-ese," check out the online video entitled "Stuff Christians Say," http://www.crosswalk.com/video/stuff-christians-say.html.

to the degree that they can be "bilingual"—speaking spiritual truth without having to use Christian language until a mutually understood foundation has been laid. Overly "Christian" language will not be welcomed in this "home" and will be perceived as disrespectful, pushy, and egocentric until a closer relationship is developed in which all parties involved have a shared faith, understanding, and appreciation of the language used.[13] In counseling, we teach students to listen to the language used by their clients and adjust their reflections to match the client's level of vocabulary, slang, formality, and the like. For example, let's say I have an adolescent client who comes into my office and says, "Man, school totally sucks!" It would be completely inappropriate and inconsistent with who my client is if I replied with, "My dear boy, it sounds like you had a rather disagreeable day receiving your education. Do tell me what transpired that evokes so much negative emotion." Instead, I'm going to mirror my client's language and reply with something more along the lines of, "That sounds awful; what happened today that made school feel so sucky?" Often in churches we use language that makes *us* feel comfortable rather than listening to the language of our audience and using their vocabulary and way of understanding to communicate the truths that matter. If we, as a church, only have one way of communicating the truth that we know, then we don't actually have a deep grasp of that truth. We should be able to communicate something near and dear to us in multiple ways in order to be clear to a wide variety of audiences.

The final, and possibly the most important, piece when crossing the threshold of the Xer home is to be authentic.[14] This generation will be much more hospitable, receptive, and appreciative of someone or some ministry that is willing to be imperfect and honest about their life experiences. Transparency and vulnerability will be seen as the litmus test for authentic interaction. In past generations, the expectation was often focused more on saving face and presenting oneself as a "good Christian"—a testimony was welcomed *after* the person had "made it through" the trial or difficulty and could then talk about how faithful or good God was in the outcome of the process. Xers are intimately aware of the reality that life is difficult, that suffering happens, and that no one *really* has it all together. They are looking for others who are

13. A recurring theme in Bob Whitesel, *Inside the Organic Church: Learning from 12 Emerging Congregations* (Nashville: Abingdon, 2006).

14. See Steve Rabey, *In Search of Authentic Faith: How Emerging Generations Are Transforming the Church* (Colorado Springs: WaterBrook, 2001); Donald Miller's book *Blue Like Jazz* (Nashville: Thomas Nelson, 2003) was one of the first books to model some of this discussion. He sparked controversy among more conservative Christians because of his lack of overtly Christian language, his willingness to engage secular concepts and perspectives, and his incorporation of biblical concepts without the use of chapter and verse.

willing and able to share in the midst of their experience rather than waiting until the end. For example, an Xer will appreciate a pastor who can appropriately share from the pulpit what he or she is currently learning or wrestling with in their faith. A leader who appears to always have it all together or always have all the answers will be perceived as a fraud and untrustworthy. Xers will also appreciate a church or ministry that allows members to share stories in the midst of the journey, not just at the end. My church did this for a while a few years ago. They periodically showed a video of someone in the church who was going through something significant (job loss, child's severe illness, chronic mental illness, etc.). Some of the stories had "happy" endings, but many were unresolved or still in process. The stories served to help members of the congregation get to know others in the church and also helped foster a culture that made it "normal" to be in process.[15] Hypocrisy is one of the greatest sins, if not *the* greatest sin, in the eyes of an Xer. Don't be something you're not; own and embrace what you are—strengths, flaws, and all. Authenticity from leaders and peers is a critical expectation as you cross the threshold into the Xer home.[16]

As with any home, passing through the entryway is a critical step before being welcomed further into the home. Anyone, from strangers to family members, may step across the threshold, but it is only those who pass this initial test—who are seen as safe enough—who are able to then enter into the more personal, private, and sacred spaces of a home. Understanding and respecting the values of "a collective of individuals" who use spiritual rather than religious language, and who place high priority on authentic interactions, lead the way into the rest of the Xer home.

The Living Room

In most homes the living room is the gathering space for friends, family, and even some acquaintances. It is a personal space—not the most intimate part of a home, but the part of the home that is open to guests. It is the place in the home to welcome, entertain and get to know others. The living room allows

15. It would still be important for church leadership to choose participants wisely for this type of activity. In each of the stories I saw, those sharing had a solid faith and were able to authentically balance the hurt, pain, fear, and disappointment in their stories with a deep conviction in the sovereignty and goodness of God. They did not sugarcoat or overspiritualize their stories but modeled what mature and honest integration could look like.

16. Even Xers, however, will eventually tire of repeat chronic offenders, however authentic and transparent they are. See, e.g., Alan Prendergast, "There's Nothing Holier-than-Thou about Gil Jones," *Westword*, August 22, 2013, http://www.westword.com/2013-08-22/news/gil-jones-the-village/.

for the homeowners and guests alike to decide whether they want to learn more or invest more in the people with whom they are sharing space. Carrying with you the principles learned in the entryway, the living room is where the right to be heard and to speak into one another's lives is *earned*. The value placed on authenticity means that any church, ministry, or individual Christian still gets to show the truth of who they are and what they believe, but *how* they communicate those things is what becomes critical to Gen-Xers. It also means starting with topics you know will most likely find common ground among participants, rather than immediately going for what could be perceived as controversial. From the pulpit, this could mean sermons (well-grounded in Scripture) that speak to practical concerns and passions such as care for those in need, love for family, personal responsibility in life matters, and the like.[17] This is a tricky balance as Xers also deeply long for an authentic experience from the pulpit. A pastor who is authentically intellectual, philosophical, and heady will be of greater appeal than one who is trying to be "cool" and "relevant" in ways that are incongruent with her or his own personality. To an Xer, there is often a perceived relationship between them and their pastor, and as such the relationship requires both parties to give and take—not changing *who* they are but being willing to learn, grow, and modify *how* they express themselves in order to connect with the other person. Too often those in our churches expect prospective parishioners to do all the adapting and conforming; instead, we need to know our audience and become like them whenever possible, just as Paul described in 1 Corinthians 9:19–23.[18]

From a ministry standpoint, this could look like offering a book club on parenting or finances or healthy relationships. The challenge, though, is that the book chosen should *not* be written by a Christian or from an overtly Christian perspective, but it should still offer good counsel nonetheless. These books do actually exist![19] The purpose of the book club would

17. This should not be misunderstood as a desire for only topical sermons. Xers still want and need teaching that is deeply rooted in the exposition of Scripture but are also looking for concrete applications of that truth to their distinctive subcultures. It is not enough for them to know what the Bible says about something unless they know *why* that knowledge matters in their "real world." For an outstanding example of a Denver-area church that grew out of an original Xer base and seeks to do precisely that, see Mike Sares, *Pure Scum: The Left Out, the Right-Brained, and the Grace of God* (Downers Grove, IL: InterVarsity, 2010).

18. For good suggestions, see Graham MacPherson Johnston, *Preaching to a Postmodern World: A Guide to Reaching Twenty-First Century Listeners* (Grand Rapids: Baker Books, 2001); and Scott M. Gibson, ed., *Preaching to a Shifting Culture* (Grand Rapids: Baker Books, 2004).

19. For example, Melody Beattie's *Codependent No More* (Center City, MN: Hazelden, 1992) offers a well-grounded discussion of what it means to have healthy versus codependent relationships. Books by John Gottman, such as *The Seven Principles for Making Marriage Work* (New York: Random House, 1999), offer research-based guidance on healthy marriages.

be to create "living room space" that allows for getting to know each other. The book club should still be led and facilitated by a member of the church or ministry so that as spiritual conversations arise, they may be attended to in a manner that is scripturally sound while still being relationally and contextually respectful.

Another example is one that I am aware of at my church, called Night Lights. Night Lights is a monthly program in which the church hosts childcare for children with special needs and their siblings so that their parents can have a few solid hours away. There is a special training for all volunteers, and the church pays to have nurses on site for those children with special medical needs. There is no cost to the families that participate, there is no agenda to directly communicate the gospel, and there is no requirement that participants ever attend the church—it is simply a way to welcome in the community and to do so in a way that earns the right to be heard at a later time.

This, by no means, is asking that we be ashamed of the gospel, nor is it a call to dumb down or dilute the message of the gospel. In fact, Xers are more likely to respond to something radical and challenging than to something that appears too good to be true (remember the authenticity value?). This generation is well aware that life is hard, that suffering exists, and that few (if any) are immune to difficulties in life. They are not looking for a message that sugarcoats their perspective on life; they are looking for something that meets them in suffering, gives meaning and purpose to their trials, and simultaneously casts a vision for something bigger.[20] The living room is the space not to tackle these issues but rather to initiate the conversation that communicates awareness and understanding that such issues exist. For too long the evangelical church in the United States has wanted to pretend that by becoming a Christian, all troubles, trials, and difficulties magically get better because now you have Jesus. We successfully communicated within our churches that, as good Christians, we must "give thanks in all circumstances" (1 Thess. 5:18) but struggled to affirm that such a profession could go hand-in-hand with an honest confession that "I do believe, help me overcome my unbelief" (Mark 9:24). In an attempt to make Jesus and the gospel appealing, we have made it unrelatable to a generation that is not looking for a magical solution but rather for meaning, purpose, and support within the challenges of life.

---

20. For a blend of excellent biblical, theological, and practical studies, see Christopher W. Morgan and Robert A. Peterson, eds., *Suffering and the Goodness of God* (Wheaton: Crossway, 2008). For a poignant personal account of his experience with cancer, punctuated with his wife's reflections from her diary and their theological reflections, see Jeff Wisdom, *Through the Valley: Biblical-Theological Reflections on Suffering* (Eugene, OR: Wipf & Stock, 2011).

I had a theology professor in seminary who once said something along the lines of, "'Jesus loves you and has a wonderful plan for your life' is the biggest bait-and-switch in church history. Instead, we should be telling people that yes, Jesus loves you, but while the plan he has for you will be the most beneficial and purposeful thing you could ever do, it will also be the most challenging, painful, difficult, confusing, and costly thing you've ever done. So, are you in?"[21] To present the gospel as nothing more than "Jesus loves you and has a wonderful plan for your life" will feel hollow, shallow, and manipulative to this generation.[22] For a generation that feels alone and insignificant, the gospel meets them in their need for purpose, intimacy, and a sense of being known. The living room space is not necessarily where we get into the nitty-gritties of these things, but it is where they get introduced—where relationships of safety, mutual respect, and authenticity are developed so that deeper, more intimate conversation can take place in other rooms as relationships grow.

One of the challenges of the living room space is the need for patience and pacing within this room. Sure, there are people who seem to instantly feel like family and you seem to be able to immediately dive into the depths of life together while sitting over coffee on the living room couch. But, more often than not, that sense of intimacy grows over time and multiple coffee talks or shared meals (branching into the dining room). Ministry with and to Xers is no different; it takes time, repeated experiences, and earning the right (as they define the process) to speak into such intimate spaces as faith and belief. The ways of creating a living room space with and for Xers are endless so long as this space offers a mutual give-and-take of ideas, perspectives, and get-to-know-you opportunities without the pressure to join, agree, or sign up. One way of engaging this process is to attend community lectures, gatherings, and activities with your Xer friends. Attend activities that are of mutual interest to you and your friend, whether they be activities regarding politics, music, poetry, or social change, and attend for the sole purpose of building

21. Many thanks to Dr. Craig A. Smith for this perspective—it has absolutely changed the way I see the gospel in my own life and how I present it to others. Check out Dr. Smith's ministry website, http://www.shepherdproject.com, for podcasts, articles, and other ministry resources that help to facilitate "strategic intersections of faith and culture."

22. Even in the heyday in the 1970s of the use of Campus Crusade for Christ's "Four Spiritual Laws," the first of which was "God loves you and has a wonderful plan for your life," staff workers in the British Commonwealth discovered that they had to rephrase the law as "God loves you and wants to have a personal relationship with you." Now even this language may have become somewhat hackneyed. Some have suggested that the (more biblical) "union with Christ" should replace a "relationship" with him. Is it a coincidence that *Christianity Today*'s 2012–13 book of the year in the area of Bible and theology was by the artist and jazz musician turned New Testament scholar, Xer Constantine Campbell, *Paul and Union with Christ: An Exegetical and Theological Study* (Grand Rapids: Zondervan, 2012)?

relationship and creating shared experiences. Unless directly prompted, this will *not* be the time to evangelize or present the gospel but a time to develop an authentic, mutually respectful, and beneficial friendship.

The Dining Room

From the living room, the next place we often bring guests is into the dining room. The dining room is a slightly more intimate and personal space in the home, but is not quite at its center. The dining room is a space of practical care for those who have been invited in. From a ministry perspective, the dining room is the space in which we care practically for the needs of those around us *while simultaneously nourishing ourselves*.

When you invite dinner guests over to your home, you don't make a lovely meal, serve your guests, and then insist on simply serving and staring at them while they dine. It would be considered incredibly rude and a violation of the developing relationship. Instead, the dining room is a place of service that still meets the personal needs of the hosts. The dining room experience may have some formality around it, but it ultimately leads to laughter, conversation, and shared experience around a meal. The dining room of Xer ministry is no different—this space needs to facilitate experiences of caring for the needs of those already a part of the family but also of reaching out and drawing in those who are not yet a part of the family. This, literally, could involve the sharing of a meal.

In the fast-paced world that is American society today, food is often something grabbed on the go, and we forget or neglect the relational value that can be built and shared when enjoying a meal together. Caring for the needs of others is important to Xers, but their scope of care is often focused on those within their "sphere of influence" or those with whom they would more naturally have dinner (both literally and figuratively).[23] The dining room experience offers slightly more intimate conversation and relationship than that which takes place in the living room, but it is often built on the conversations and relationship that were begun in the living room. While it is possible to jump immediately from the entryway to the dining room, it is a rare occurrence without some sort of preexisting relationship between host and guest.

If the goal of the dining room is to care for the needs of all involved, then the activities and focus need to be quite practical, pragmatic, and relevant.

23. See further Craig L. Blomberg, *Contagious Holiness: Jesus' Meals with Sinners* (Downers Grove, IL: InterVarsity, 2005), 164–80. See also Margaret Feinberg, *Scouting the Divine: My Search for God in Wine, Wool, and Wild Honey* (Grand Rapids: Zondervan, 2009). Feinberg is one of the most creative and prolific Xer Christian writers on the popular level; she is worth reading on just about any topic she addresses.

This is the space where theology is first lived and *then* spoken, not the other way around. For many churches and ministries, the dining room experience looks like in-home small groups (often called home groups, life groups, etc.) that meet in people's homes on a regular basis to literally share a meal and then engage in a Bible study or some other service activity together. These groups have a core number of participants but remain open to new people and have a primary emphasis on building relationships while still being authentic, transparent, and up-front about the beliefs and convictions held by the group. It is also critical that these groups do not meet at the church but in homes; this speaks to the Xers' preference for spirituality over religion and allows an up-close-and-personal look into the authenticity of those involved. In comparison to traditional Sunday school classes that focused first on teaching, in-home small groups see relationship development as the primary goal, and then truth is taught within the context of relationship building. Again, authenticity is key in this endeavor; some in-home small groups may be more or less academic depending on the personality, giftings, and values of those involved.[24]

As with actual dinner guests, we try to meet the dietary needs of our guests in the dining room, but there are bounds as we seek to find a common ground between what the host likes to eat and what the guests like to eat. In ministry to and with Xers, the same concept holds true. You, as the host, are unlikely to serve something that you are "allergic" to or have no taste for, but you may serve something that is not your favorite or preferred food because you know your guest likes it and it will enable your guest to feel welcomed and comfortable without compromising your own health. As churches and ministries seek to create dining room experiences, that same mentality should hold true. We should ask, "What is something we can serve our guests that will not violate our own convictions and needs, still nourish us, but simultaneously nourish our guests and make them feel welcomed?" An example of this might be to host a family movie night and show a secular film that is still "appropriate" for your target audience rather than only showing "Christian" movies. The purpose of the event would not be evangelistic, and there would not be a "Christian critique" of the film following its viewing. Instead, the purpose of the event would be to allow families from the community (churched and unchurched) to come together, socialize (it's always helpful to have snacks!),

24. The literature on small group ministries is large. Excellent contributions include Randy Frazee, *The Connecting Church 2.0: Beyond Small Groups to Authentic Community* (Grand Rapids: Zondervan, 2013); Andy Stanley, *Community Conversation Guide: Starting Well in Your Small Group* (Grand Rapids: Zondervan, 2013); and Steve Gladen, *Small Groups with Purpose: How to Create Healthy Communities* (Grand Rapids: Baker Books, 2011).

and find common ground together. Movies could be those that often raise spiritual or metaphysical questions in people's minds; out of countless possibilities just from the last fifteen years, almost at random one thinks of *Inception*, *Avatar*, *The Matrix*, *The Fighting Temptations*, *The Truman Show*, *Crash*, *The Lord of the Rings* trilogy, and *The Book of Eli*.[25] Families from the church should be encouraged to invite their non-Christian friends and neighbors for a low-cost (or free) family night, and to see this event as a way of building relationship around the dining room table. This event could be held at the church, at a local community center, or even outdoors given the right climate and resources.[26]

Bringing "church" into homes is a critical piece of engaging Xers. It allows for the tearing down of walls between the sacred and the secular while offering an opportunity for greater transparency and authenticity of relationship. (It's a lot harder to hide who you are when people are in your home week after week, rather than just sitting together in a sanctuary from time to time!) In-home small groups should offer three specific kinds of nourishment.

1. Physical nourishment: That means food! Preferably a dinner, not just snacks, and preferably a potluck. You may set a theme for each night, but it is important that everyone (or at least most people) contribute, which allows for a mutual sharing of oneself, one's preferences, and one's resources. Contributing should not be a condition of participation, but it should be encouraged as it provides a sense of ownership and togetherness.[27]

2. Emotional nourishment: This means engaging with one another outside scheduled small group times—going to movies, taking walks, having child play-dates, and the like. This also means following up mid-week to find out how someone's job interview went, how their big exam turned out, or how the doctor's appointment went. (Or better yet, offer to go with them!)

25. Not all of these movies are appropriate for children, and some include rather mature themes. In addition to a "family night," consider a "movie club" with other adults. Similar to a book club, the group would meet to watch a movie and discuss it together over dinner, dessert, or drinks.

26. I knew of a church that had a family with a barn and a lot of acreage. In the summers they got a large white sheet and draped it over the side of the barn to create a "screen" and then projected the film on the side of the barn. Speakers were set up in the viewing area, and families brought lawn chairs and blankets to enjoy the movie under the stars—their own kind of "sit-in" movie theater!

27. In situations where finances or means are limited, contributing should never be a hindrance to participation, nor should participants ever be made to feel inferior to others because of what they can or cannot contribute.

What is critical here is that this emotional nourishment is not just provided by the leader but reciprocally provided by all (or most) participants. For many ministries, this can be a difficult norm to set and may require the leader "delegating" such responsibilities to different members of the group until it becomes a more natural ethos for the group as a whole.

3. Spiritual nourishment: Here is where we delve a bit more deeply than what took place in the living room. This is where ministries often have difficulty. In many small group or Bible study contexts, the curriculum or topics of discussion are focused *either* on "seekers" *or* on the "churched." But if we continue the analogy of a meal, a good meal should include foods for various appetites. Again, we are not looking to dilute or in any way be ashamed of the gospel, but neither are we looking to make the material so dense and complex that steak knives are needed for every bite. Just as a good meal has balance, so should a good dining room ministry experience. This takes greater work, skill, maturity, and patience on behalf of a leader. It requires an ability to engage and incorporate Scripture and theological truths while coupling that depth with practical application.[28]

What about from the front of the church? In some churches this looks like adding new elements to their worship services, such as art, dance, liturgy, candles, and other experiential activities that engage the senses. For example, in a sermon focused on building intentional relationships with our neighbors, my church passed out small custom magnets that had nine squares on them, like a tic-tac-toe board. At the center was a house, representing your individual home. The surrounding eight squares represent your neighbors. The challenge to the congregation was to identify and get to know the people in each "square" over the coming week or weeks, write their names in the squares, and then begin to pray intentionally for those neighbors, being open to the opportunities that God might provide to connect more personally. Additionally, I attended a service one time that was meant to share with the congregation the missionary connections that the church had. It wasn't a "missions fair" as many churches have; it was interwoven into the Sunday service following worship and a brief message of introduction, and it was held in the sanctuary in place of the sermon.[29]

28. The worldwide Alpha Course that brings people together for extended periods of time (often over weekends) in people's homes to consider aspects of Christian faith may well owe much of its stunning success to the incorporation of many of these principles. See http://www.alpha.org.

29. A traditional missions fair often involves information booths set up in a gym or large classroom where people "make the rounds" from booth to booth, gathering information about

Instead of having someone stand at the front and talk about missions, stations were set up throughout the sanctuary where parishioners could see, touch, and smell items from the various locations. Few if any of the stations had people to talk to; instead they had short snippets of information, powerful pictures, and personal but simply stated prayer requests. What was particularly unique about this setup from other missions fairs that I have attended was that this was not primarily a cognitively focused, information-gathering activity—it was aesthetically designed to be an experiential worship act in which participants did not only take time to pray for the church's missionaries but were welcomed into an experience that engaged their emotions and their senses along with their minds.

The dining room is a unique space in the home. It is intimate and personal, and yet it can still be rather formal and structured. It invites guests beyond a surface knowledge and experience of who we are, but it still does not bring them into the heart of our home. Nonetheless, it is a critically important step in building relationship and earning the right to speak more personally, profoundly, and reciprocally into someone's life.

The Kitchen

As I was growing up, the kitchen was the place in our home where all the significant conversations took place. As a child, I'd hop up on the counter while Mom made dinner, and we'd chat about the day. When I became a teenager, my friends would gather in the kitchen, some sitting on countertops and some on the floor, and it was in that space that we spent hours discussing the latest drama in our adolescent lives. The kitchen is the heart of the home, the place where tradition is lived out, created, and changed, often in very profound ways.

The kitchen is the most creative space in the house—at least in my house. For many people, making a meal is a function of practical necessity, but for others of us making a meal is an endeavor in creative artistry that nourishes the body and the senses. The kitchen ministry to and with Xers is no different. It is a place of creativity, engagement, and care, a place that lives out old traditions while creating new ones. The big question within this kitchen space that ministries must address is, What is biblical, and what is merely habitual?[30]

---

the locations, people groups, and needs of particular ministries. While food samples are sometimes included, these fairs are generally cognitively focused and allow parishioners to take a more passive role.

30. Again, the question is a commonplace one in cross-cultural ministry. See, e.g., Craig L. Blomberg, "We Contextualize More Than We Realize," in *Local Theology for the Global*

To use a food example, in my family we have this one dish that is served every Christmas (and sometimes at Thanksgiving) that is made of pickled red cabbage, currant jelly, and sugar. In all honesty, few of us really like it, but it's tradition—you just must have red cabbage at Christmas! So each Christmas a batch is made and simmers on the stove as the rest of the meal is put together. The smell is quite distinct, and while some of us experience it as a "happy memory smell," others find the pickled vinegar smell quite nauseating. A few of us will have a spoonful at dinner and then call it good, but no one ever really goes back for seconds (except for maybe my mom). In all reality, red cabbage does not define a Christmas meal—it was something from Denmark that my family brought over when they emigrated in the 1950s, carrying a bit of old home into their new home. That generation is now gone, and the tradition, although valuable and well-intended, no longer carries the same significance as it once did.

In many of our churches and ministries, we keep serving red cabbage. We have ways of doing a worship service, small groups, Sunday school classes, or evangelism that at one time served a great and significant purpose, but they have become outdated. Xers (and those even younger) no longer have a taste for doing things that way and may even find them nauseating. What gets really tricky is that for those who like the tradition, it can feel as if change is a disregard of history.[31] Instead, we must recognize that at one point in time, how we did things was new and broke someone else's tradition. For example, there is no scriptural passage that says a worship service should start with twenty minutes of songs, followed by three to five announcements, the offering, a thirty-minute sermon, a final song, and the benediction. Also, there's no scriptural passage that says pews are better than chairs, or vice versa. By making tradition, habit, and preference akin to scriptural instruction, we force younger generations to continue to eat red cabbage at every meal, not just for Christmas dinner.

We need to look at the kitchen as a place of innovation. Rather than imposing old recipes and traditions on Xers, we should be inviting them into the

---

Church: Principles for an Evangelical Approach to Contextualization, ed. Matthew Cook, Rob Haskell, Ruth Julian, and Natee Tanchanpongs (Pasadena: William Carey, 2010), 37–55. Can we now raise it more consistently with cross-generational issues?

31. Indeed, one characteristic of postmodernism is its recovery of certain premodern expressions of the faith. Just as many Boomers left the institutional church, many Xers began to recover key elements of tradition that they found valuable. See esp. the books by Robert E. Webber: *Ancient-Future Faith: Rethinking Evangelicalism for a Postmodern World* (Grand Rapids: Baker, 1999); *Ancient-Future Evangelism: Making Your Church a Faith-Forming Community* (Grand Rapids: Baker Books, 2003); *Ancient-Future Time: Forming Spirituality through the Christian Year* (Grand Rapids: Baker Books, 2004); and *Ancient-Future Worship: Proclaiming and Enacting God's Narrative* (Grand Rapids: Baker Books, 2008).

creative process and allowing them to be cocreators in the design, production, and execution of ministry. As with cooking, there are rules and bounds—a marinara sauce, by definition, needs tomatoes, but the exact spices and the proportion of spices used can vary according to the cook. For example, in a worship service it can be scripturally supported that Christians are to come together for teaching, singing, the exercise of various spiritual gifts, and mutual encouragement (1 Cor. 14:26–33; Eph. 5:19–20). Beyond that, there's considerable flexibility.[32] So, as a congregation or ministry, let that be your guide, and let tastes, preferences, and context influence the logistics.

The kitchen also introduces issues of succession. Many families have a tradition that certain family gatherings are hosted by the matriarch or the patriarch, who sets the expectations and structure for such gatherings. But at some point in time, the matriarch or patriarch must pass the torch and allow a new generation to lead. In some families, that torch is passed only upon death, at which time some valuable traditions and values can be lost because the handoff never allowed for an explanation or introduction to what was being done and why. A more effective plan is for the older generation to bring the younger generation into the planning and execution of tradition before a handoff is a necessity, allowing for stories, explanations, and purposes to be more thoroughly passed down. It is time to invite Xers into this role, passing on the mantle of leadership in a proactive and intentional way.

In churches, this could be done two to five years before a pastor's retirement, by bringing on an apprentice who will take over the pastor's role upon his or her retirement. The new person needs to have been intentionally selected by the church leaders as someone who seems to "fit" with the church in vision, personality, and style, but who also seems to offer skills and perspectives that would facilitate growth. This person should be a paid employee (like any other person on the ministry team) and have an active ministry role for part of their time. But the other part of their time should be intentionally spent observing the church and meeting with the pastor for mentorship and purposeful discussion about why and how things are done at the church. Over the course of the apprenticeship time, visibility and decision-making power should shift from the retiring pastor to the incoming apprentice pastor. While this requires a relatively healthy church and an outgoing pastor who is

---

32. Acts 2:42 also describes four key elements of worship that have persisted throughout the centuries: "the apostles' teaching, fellowship, the breaking of bread, and prayer." Scripturally based preaching or instruction, the sharing of lives and resources, the Lord's Supper (and other meals), and prayers are among the most consistently adopted activities of the many branches and manifestations of the church throughout the world and throughout its history.

mature enough to pass on his or her position, it can create an ideal transition.[33] Realistically, there is no guarantee that the younger generation won't amend or tweak what is being passed down. But marinara sauce is still marinara sauce, whether you like more basil in it than Grandma did or not. Whether in a pastoral position or in a lay ministry leader role, invitation is important to this generation; they are unlikely to bulldoze their way into positions of leadership and authority. They will not overrun the matriarchs and patriarchs still in positions of leadership, but they nevertheless have insights, skills, and abilities to offer that our churches and ministries desperately need.

I think that the kitchen is often the most challenging room in the Xer house for older generations. As we discussed previously, Boomers are often reluctant to retire or step down from leadership roles, seeing their identity and worth wrapped up in their work and accomplishments. This is functionally the kitchen space. It is the heart of the home, the center of creativity and innovation for a family, and it is often the place of authority. Giving up or passing on roles of power can either be a challenge or a joy, depending on how one sees one's identity connected to that power. We often choose homes based on the functionality and design of a kitchen, and our churches are no different. If a ministry's "kitchen" is a place that is open and welcoming to younger generations, allowing them to be cocreators and innovators, then the church itself is more likely to be perceived as safe and welcoming—a place Xers can call home. Having "town hall meetings" or open forums where congregants are encouraged to come and share ideas and ask questions about church direction is one way of communicating a safe and collaborative "kitchen."

From a practical standpoint, invited mentorship is another way that a ministry can open up their kitchen space to Xers. In my church this looks like a leadership development program that selectively invites a set number of people to be mentored, discipled, and invested in by church elders and leaders over the course of a year. The expressed purpose of the program is to develop leaders, thus placing participants in positions of apprenticed leadership during and after the program. As Xers have often felt like an afterthought to parents and other authority figures, intentional individual mentorship or discipleship for the sole purpose of an Xer's personal and spiritual development is also a critical component of inviting Xers into the kitchen space of a ministry. Whether a structured program or an initiative engaged on an individual basis, this concept of mentorship is critical to passing on tradition and training

33. See esp. Mark Conner, *Pass the Baton: Successful Leadership Transition*, 2nd ed. (Melbourne: Conner Ministries, 2010).

Xers so that they not only have a place in the kitchen but are invited to be innovators and cocreators in that space.[34]

From the pulpit or the worship stage, this means inviting Xers (and Millennials, as we'll see later) to again be cocreators in the service. Multigenerational worship teams, for example, allow for all members of the congregation to feel "represented" and connected to the worship experience. This does *not* mean separate services for each generational cohort! While well intended, separate services often communicate to younger generations that there is something wrong, immature, or less important in the way they prefer to worship. And, simultaneously, it can communicate to older generations that there is nothing more to learn, no further ways to grow, and no other ways to experience their faith. We need each other, and we need the encouragement along with the discomfort that comes with engaging in a worship experience that stretches us and asks us to relate to the Lord in new or diverse ways.[35]

As we navigate the kitchen space, welcoming Xers into a space of cocreation, innovation, and helping to shape future traditions, we must remember the values of the threshold. As a collective of individuals, Xers want and need to be individually seen, affirmed, and invited, but they also want others they care about to feel equally valued, even if that gets communicated in different ways. Additionally, remembering that spiritual language is of higher value than "Christian-ese" and Christian clichés is of critical importance. Xers are very aware that members of their generation outside the church have no knowledge of or interest in Christian language, and they also recognize that

34. There are a myriad of models of mentorship or discipleship that focus on various areas of personal and spiritual development. My preference is for models that allow for personal modification and adaptation and do not pigeonhole the participant into only one acceptable outcome. Having been spiritually trained in the Navigators' campus ministry, I readily look to their resources as starting points when meeting with mentorees. Another good resource is Jeff Myers, *Cultivate: Forming the Emerging Generation through Life-on-Life Mentoring* (Dayton, TN: Passing the Baton International, 2010). Furthermore, seminars such as The Integrated Life (http://www.theintegratedlife.org) offer churches and ministries the opportunity for understanding the unique gifts and passions of their participants in a way that then asks participants to identify how their community and ministry need them and can use them.

35. We recognize that this could create an entire conversation on the theology of worship, what the purpose of worship is perceived to be, and who the beneficiary of worship is. We would suggest that churches who desire to be more multigenerationally engaged *do* embark on such conversations from the pulpit and within small group settings, as changing the look and feel of a worship service is, for many people, like saying there will be no turkey at Thanksgiving dinner. For excellent biblical and theological resources, see D. A. Carson, ed., *Worship: Adoration and Action* (Eugene, OR: Wipf & Stock, 2002); Sally Morgenthaler, *Worship Evangelism: Inviting Unbelievers into the Presence of God* (Grand Rapids: Zondervan, 1999); and Allen P. Ross, *Recalling the Hope of Glory: Biblical Worship from the Garden to the New Creation* (Grand Rapids: Kregel, 2006).

if a truth can only be expressed using such insular language, it must not be that profound or relevant of a truth—in other words, if it is worth saying, there should be multiple ways of communicating the message. And finally, transparent authenticity must be ever evident. To an Xer, a good mentor is not someone who has it all together. Instead, a good mentor is one who is willing and able to share the successes as well as the failures and struggles in their life and in their relationship with Jesus.[36] We cannot truly love or respect another person if we know only a part of them; true love and respect comes as we grow in our understanding of who they are. This is why authenticity in mentorship is so critical for Xers.

The Bedroom Space

The bedroom is the most private and intimate space in any home. The bedroom is the room to which we escape when we feel vulnerable, afraid, sick, or exhausted by the world. It is our personal space, a sacred and treasured space, but it is also our most vulnerable space. In ministry, the bedroom space has to do with those topics, concerns, and issues that hit closest to home and closest to our core identity. The bedroom space addresses topics that have the potential to be the most divisive or the most affirming; they tap into the depths of who we see ourselves to be. While other topics may be relevant within the bedroom space, I think it is particularly important that ministries to and with Xers understand how to navigate issues related to relationships, sexuality, and family life. As we embark on these topics, it is crucial to remember the foundation and walls that built this Xer house and therefore influence the structure of this bedroom space—*relativism* and *experience* constantly interweave as we help this generation find their place.

Xers today are in their mid-thirties to their late forties (with the oldest Xer having turned fifty in 2015), placing them squarely in the middle of what many would consider prime child-rearing years. In past generations this was definitely more the norm. But for many Xers, children of their own are not a part of their chosen families, as "43 percent of Gen-X women and nearly a third (32 percent) of Xer men do not have children at all."[37] Furthermore,

36. It actually warms my heart when I show up to my mentor's house and her response to my question of "How are you doing?" is something along the lines of, "Eh, it's been a rough day; my husband and I got in a fight right before you came." My heart goes out to my mentor and her husband that they have had conflict, but I am honored and encouraged by her willingness to be honest and share the real-life struggles that are a part of normal living.

37. Sylvia A. Hewlett and Lauren Leader-Chivée, *The X-Factor: Tapping into the Strengths of the 33- to 46-Year Old Generation* (New York: Center for Work-Life Policy, 2011), 27. This

"24 percent of college-educated women had not had a child at age forty."[38] Similarly, approximately one-third of Xers are not married.[39] What does this mean for ministries to and with Xers? A lot. Defining adulthood around the concept of marriage and children is no longer relevant for a large percentage of this generation. And even if Xers have married, they did not do so until twenty-six to twenty-eight years of age, leaving a good eight to ten years after high school to struggle to find a place in today's churches, which tradition-ally build Sunday school classes and small groups around marital status and/ or parenthood stage. For many in this struggle, they simply left church after getting the clear message that they were not welcome in the kitchen. Whether married or not, or parents or not, how might we create a space where Xers feel wanted, needed, and welcomed; a place where they feel invited into the kitchen?

For example, at thirty-three and single (as of mid-2014),[40] I often struggled to find my fit in churches, particularly if they had not yet changed their struc-ture to reflect cultural realities. Too often church ministries progress something like this: junior/senior high youth group, college (or college/career),[41] young marrieds, and then adult Bible study. Now, for the Xer who either isn't mar-ried or doesn't have children, where do they belong? At thirty-five, forty, or forty-five years of age, they definitely do not fit in the "college/career" group, but too often the "adult Bible study" category assumes married *with* children. In my experience, the same occurs with women's ministries. Gatherings are often held at ten o'clock on a weekday morning, or are marketed to "women of all ages," but their descriptions include the phrase "from young marrieds to empty-nesters."[42] Such subtleties in language can send a very powerful message about who is and who is not seen or heard in a congregation.

---

study classified those born between 1965 and 1978 as Generation X, cutting short three years of Xers in comparison to the current discussion.

38. Ibid.

39. Miller, "Active, Balanced and Happy," 2.

40. When I wrote the first draft of this chapter I was not dating anyone. Between then and this book's publication I have gotten married, so I write this part now in the past tense from my vantage point in mid-2014!

41. Can we be honest here? An eighteen-year-old college student is in a very different life stage than a twenty-six-year-old who is getting established in her career. The existence of "college/career" groups often only communicates to their participants that the church does not actually understand who they are. According to neuroscientist Dr. Sandra Aamodt, the average brain is not fully developed until age twenty-five (with women's brains developing approximately two years earlier than men's). See Tony Cox and Sandra Aamodt, "Brain Maturity Extends Way beyond Teen Years," *Tell Me More,* NPR Network transcript, October 10, 2011, http://www.npr.org/templates/story/story.php?storyId=141164708.

42. A helpful distillation of these and related problems, along with constructive suggestions for addressing them is Kristin Aune, *Single Women: A Challenge to the Church* (Carlisle, UK: Paternoster, 2002).

What about the Xers (and Millennials) who do not fit these more traditional categories? Similar to the argument made about multigenerational worship experiences, the bedroom space calls for ministries to recognize the changing landscape of single adults, meeting them in their personal and vulnerable spaces without inadvertently communicating that being unmarried or childless disqualifies them from being "adults" within the congregation. What is needed is a both-and solution in which there are times and places for people of a similar demographic to gather together. But more important, there should be times and spaces where *people* gather with other *people*, welcoming the wisdom, experience, and understanding that comes with being at different life stages. A space is needed that is simply defined by "people who love Jesus and want to do life together." It is in spaces like these that the biblical instruction for the younger to learn from the older, and for the younger to share their own wisdom and knowledge with the older, can take place (1 Tim. 4:12; Titus 2:4). If we never engage in cross-generational ministry, how is the body to benefit from the wisdom of those more experienced and the vibrancy of those new in their faith?[43]

The issue of sexuality is a sensitive and personal one, and it can be highly divisive. But, it is also a topic of deep theological significance, and it must therefore be addressed. For a generation that was taught to value individual freedom and to question any teaching or instruction that came with absolutes, biblical instruction on sex and sexuality struggles to find a landing pad on the relativistic foundation of the Xer worldview. In this worldview, I am the maker of my own rules and the designer of my own standards because there are few if any absolutes, and sin is what I define it to be. To tell someone that the Bible says that sex before or outside marriage is unacceptable goes against an Xer's belief and experience that (1) I am the decision maker for what is "acceptable" in my life; (2) my sexual experiences are part of what shape and define my identity as an adult and even more fundamentally as a person; and (3) I have the right to express my sexuality in whatever ways I deem appropriate, so long as I maintain the responsibility not to use my sexuality to harm or disrespect another person. In light of these foundational assumptions, to simply look at an Xer and say, "Don't have sex before or outside marriage" is received as (1) your opinion and (2) highly judgmental and disrespectful of those who may differ from you. This bedroom-space topic needs to be addressed much like the living room and dining room space conversations, in which dialogue rather than instruction is the primary means of conversation. Remember

---

43. E.g., Ross Parsley, *Messy Church: A Multigenerational Mission for God's Family* (Colorado Springs: David C. Cook, 2012).

that bedroom space is a personal, private, gentle, and vulnerable space, and good bedroom conversations involve a mutual dialogue of kindness, respect, and reciprocal interest in what the other person has to say. Topics that get discussed in the bedroom space of ministry must be discussed with patience and gentleness and come with layers of explanation that unfold over time.[44]

For example, as a church, we should be unwavering on what we understand Scripture to say regarding sexuality. But we must also recognize that those precepts are put into place in Scripture because of how deeply personal and significant sexuality is, and therefore it must be approached with reverence as we talk with others. Just because someone has not or does not uphold the same convictions on celibacy or monogamy that we believe Scripture teaches does not make the role of sexuality in that person's life any less vulnerable or significant to their identity.[45] Furthermore, discussions about sexuality should focus more on the deeper spiritual symbolism and significance of sexuality, along with its beauty and goodness. Between 1998 and 2002, 54 percent of unmarried Gen-Xers who regularly attended church said that sex before marriage was "always wrong," and nearly another 10 percent said it is "almost always wrong." Yet "63 percent of those who thought premarital sex was always wrong acknowledged having had sexual relations in the past year."[46] Even within our churches, stated conviction does not necessarily align with personal behavior, as 69 percent of unmarried evangelical Xers (and older Millennials) report having had at least one sexual relationship in the previous year.[47]

I would argue that part of the disconnect between stated and lived conviction is that churches have too often focused on the "thou shalt nots" of sexuality, creating or enforcing rules without providing explanation beyond "because the Bible says so." On some level, that may be a good enough reason to obey, but for a generation that is grounded on experience and relativism, that reasoning has little to no relevance. One of the beautiful things about

44. For an excellent start in this direction, see Lauren F. Winner, *Real Sex: The Naked Truth about Chastity* (Grand Rapids: Brazos, 2005). That this book had some definite exegetical weaknesses and yet became such a bestseller shows how little competition it had.

45. See esp. Xer author Jenell Williams Paris's book *The End of Sexual Identity: Why Sex Is Too Important to Define Who We Are* (Downers Grove, IL: InterVarsity, 2011).

46. Robert Wuthnow, *After the Baby Boomers: How Twenty- and Thirty-Somethings Are Shaping the Future of American Religion* (Princeton: Princeton University Press, 2007), 138–39.

47. While many churches will state that sex outside of marriage is sin, very few take the time or build the relationships in which to discuss sexuality and, more specifically, a theology of sexuality that goes beyond behavioral dos and don'ts. Larger societal norms that encourage sexual experience prior to marriage are then left unaddressed, aside from an empty "don't do it" from the pulpit, rather than being met with dialogue, empathy, and acknowledgement of the challenges that unmarried adults face in the realms of sexuality.

Xers and Millennials in ministry is that they require all of us to delve into the personal, practical, and spiritual reasoning behind our convictions, which requires that we explain our convictions with understanding and relevance. We should not be threatened by this request, as God himself often provides explanation and rationale for his instructions throughout Scripture. If we do feel threatened by these requests, we should instead use the opportunity to know and understand our own faith with deeper levels of reflection, awareness, and ownership.[48]

The challenge with this discussion is that there is no easy solution to how the church *should* address the topic of sexuality. The Boomer response to show them the research (secular and Christian) about the emotional and sexual consequences of having multiple sexual partners is likely to be met with an Xer belief that *they* are the exception to that research, and that one cannot quantify their qualitative experiences. The difficult answer is likely that the church needs to be addressing a *theology* of sexuality throughout their curriculum (from children's programs through adult studies and into the pulpit). A theology of sexuality goes beyond behaviors, rules, and expectations and dives deep into Scripture and doctrine, engaging the symbolism and sacredness of sexuality. Additionally, it requires the church to take proactive steps in providing safe spaces for singles (as well as marrieds) to discuss sexuality and ask questions such as, What does it mean to be a sexual person and yet be celibate? What sexual struggles, challenges, and frustrations come with being single (or single again)? What, if anything, does Scripture say regarding masturbation? Is there a difference in the "letter of the law" and the "spirit of the law" regarding sexuality? When do you feel the most vulnerable to sexual sin? When you have engaged in sexual sin, what were your motivations, feelings, thoughts, and convictions? What do you make of the discrepancy between your convictions and your actions?

Any bedroom topic must be approached with humility and honest self-reflection. No one's sexual life (if one includes the thought life) has been perfectly pure. This does not give license, but it does call for all involved in the discussion to be gracious, understanding, and empathetic. In humility, we must also recognize that sexual sin does not cease to exist once someone gets married. If we, as the church, truly engage our *theology* of sexuality, we will find that it extends far beyond behavior and into motivation, identity, and worship—and these issues transcend marital status and outward sexual

48. For excellent models, see Christopher Ash, *Marriage: Sex in the Service of God* (Vancouver: Regent College Publishing, 2005); *Married for God: Making Your Marriage the Best It Can Be* (Downers Grove, IL: InterVarsity, 2012); and *Christianity and Sexuality* (Deerfield, IL: Christ on Campus Initiative, 2009).

activity.[49] Jesus said, "If you love me, keep my commands" (John 14:15), and, as with any other area of life, obedience in the area of sexuality will overflow out of a love for Jesus, not out of legalism or blind rule-following. It is our job, as the church, to get to know the Xer in our ministry well enough that we can help them engage their heart regarding bedroom issues, prayerfully seeking how their love for Jesus permeates into the most personal and intimate issues of their lives.[50]

A variety of other issues could arise within the bedroom space of ministry, and many of them come down to issues or topics related to what is (or isn't) sin. Sin is a difficult concept for many Xers (and Millennials) because it inherently describes an absolute standard that can be violated, countering their foundation of relativism. In light of this, starting with Xers, younger generations do not see sin as seriously as older generations do, and definitely not as seriously as Scripture sees it. In a world of relativistic standards, there are few moral absolutes, especially if there is no direct evidence that my "sin" negatively impacts someone else. For those ministering to Gen-Xers or who have Xers in your ministries, there is a very fine line to walk in this area. On the one side

49. We have intentionally not addressed the topic of same-sex attraction or homosexuality as a specific topic of interest because how a church or ministry handles that area of sexuality should also flow out of the theology of sexuality that is embraced. Again, focusing on outward behavior, struggles, or identification removes the opportunity to engage a deeper, more heart-based conversation that addresses the purpose, meaning, and symbolism found within a scripturally grounded theology of sexuality.

50. Helpful starting points could include distinguishing the reasons for sexual activity outside the norms of Scripture. What has been called pre-ceremonial sex (i.e., by engaged couples who simply couldn't or didn't wait) must surely be differentiated from multiple, habitual "one-night stands." Some couples who live together have informal plans to marry but for a variety of reasons simply aren't yet in a position to do so and eventually do go on to be married. Others live together precisely because they have no intention to marry. Without condoning any of these situations, Christian leaders could show that they are not identical or equally sinful. No Scripture proscribes self-stimulation at all; it may be far better to relieve strong urges by oneself than to engage in profoundly interpersonal relationships involving (and potentially damaging) others. The personal experiences of those with multiple sexual partners frequently testify to the problems created by one partner comparing those experiences and evaluating the other partner on their basis. One needs no empirical research to share this common experience and discover widespread agreement within audiences. Christian organizations with double standards need to rethink them: is someone summarily fired for use of pornography while those living together outside marriage are tolerated? The latter could be a more serious problem than the former. See the distinctions made in Erin Dufault-Hunter, "Pornography," in Dictionary of Scripture and Ethics, ed. Joel B. Green (Grand Rapids: Baker Academic, 2011), 607–8. Books such as Janelle Hallman, The Heart of Female Same-Sex Attraction (Downers Grove, IL: InterVarsity, 2008); Michael John Cusick, Surfing for God (Nashville: Thomas Nelson, 2012); Dan Allender, The Wounded Heart (Colorado Springs: NavPress, 1990); and Judith Balswick and Jack Balswick, Authentic Human Sexuality (Downers Grove, IL: InterVarsity, 2008) all address different aspects of human sexuality particularly well from an integrated Christian perspective.

of the line is the scriptural truth that says sin separates us from God and it is because of sin that we need a savior (Rom. 3:23; 6:23). This truth needs to never be compromised, for it is the crux of why the gospel truly is good news. But on the other side of the line, simply because every sin separates us from God scarcely makes all sins equally bad. Jesus taught that murder and anger are both sinful and make us liable to judgment (Matt. 5:21–26), but that scarcely means it is as bad for me to be mad at someone as to kill them! We need to empathize with those who get carried away prematurely in an otherwise loving, committed relationship without calling their behavior correct. We should also be quite concerned for the long-term well-being of someone who regularly "hooks up" on weekends with people they never intend to see again.[51] This is true for any cohort, but Xers form an audience who comes into the discussion with the foundational understanding that an absolute definition of sin does not exist.

As in most cross-cultural communication situations, the correct answer is not simply for one party to impose their perspective on the other but instead to slowly build a relationship in which similarities and differences can be discussed within a growing context of knowing and understanding one another. From there, discussions can take place that politely and gently challenge one another to think about an alternative perspective, to present reasons and experiences to support one's position, and to hear from the other person what about your perspective is both appealing and challenging to them. Patience, respect, mutual curiosity, and a clear understanding of both the logical and the experiential reasons for one's beliefs will be critical regardless of the issue.

Bedroom issues in ministry are at times the very ones that churches like to address boldly and loudly from the pulpit, focusing on behavior rather than conviction and understanding. Beginning with Xers, it is critical that ministries address such personal topics with grace, patience, and compassion. They should acknowledge that what is being taught is challenging, difficult, and contrary to the larger cultural teaching and experiences. It is one thing to try to talk someone into doing what everyone else is doing, but it is an entirely different task to convince someone to go against all that they have seen and known. Steadfastness of conviction (authenticity) and transparency combined with empathy, patience, mutual respect (individualism), and the ability to communicate truth in relevant and relational terms (nonreligious language) are critical for navigating the sensitive and personal issues in ministry with and to Xers.[52]

---

51. See Randy Alcorn, *Restoring Sexual Sanity: Christians in the Wake of the Sexual Revolution* (Ft. Lauderdale: Coral Ridge Ministries, 2000).

52. Indeed, an unprecedented sensitivity to relational needs may be the abiding takeaway from numerous creative experiments in ministry with Xers. See Collin Hansen, "The X Factor:

In Summary: Making a House a Home

As with any house or apartment, it takes something extra, something personal, to make it a home. Ministry to and with Xers is no different; it is not just a compilation of individual rooms or ministries or groups; something personal, integrative, and authentic is needed to bring everything together. Your understanding of a home is made through each room coming together into one holistic experience. As we engage Xers in ministry, we must be willing to holistically and authentically cocreate a space in which there is safety, honesty, and reciprocal engagement in relationship. When that happens, all involved will feel like they've truly come home.

Conclusion

Writing this chapter has been quite the experience for me. As an Xer, I thought it would be a lot of fun and easy to write. I would finally get to put onto paper what my cohort wants, needs, and has experienced. But as I sat to write, an interesting thing happened: I had no words for a long time. In counseling we talk about "parallel processes" in which the counselor presents to their supervisor the way the client presents to the counselor.[53] I feel like that is what happened with me and this chapter: Xers, as a group, are rather disillusioned with organized anything (especially religion) and have spent decades being told in one way or another that they are inferior and that the needs and voices of Boomers and Millennials matter more. Xers, therefore, often feel that expressing their ideas, needs, opinions, or preferences in a system won't really get them anywhere, so why waste their energy? So, as I sat to write this chapter, I found myself feeling disillusioned, apathetic, and prematurely discouraged that this chapter would not be as valued as those for Boomers and Millennials. The experience formed a parallel process in its own right.

Most of the Highly Celebrated, Experimental Worship Services Launched in the Nineties to Reach 'Gen-X' Are Now Gone," *Leadership* 30, no. 3 (2009): 25–29.

53. For example, a client comes in apathetic, depressed, and pessimistic that anything will really help their situation. The counselor then goes to their supervisor to get guidance on the case but appears apathetic and pessimistic that anything the supervisor might offer would actually help the counselor in knowing how to work with the client. Originally identified by H. F. Searles ("The Informational Value of Supervisor's Emotional Experience," *Psychiatry* 18 [1955]: 135–46), various counseling and psychological textbooks now see this concept as foundational to the supervisory process. Brian W. McNeill and Vaughn Worthen, "The Parallel Process in Psychotherapy Supervision," *Professional Psychology: Research and Practice* 20, no. 5 (1989): 329–33.

I was also reminded through this that the way we present ourselves influences the ways in which others experience us, and in turn the way people experience us influences the way we present ourselves. There is a responsibility on the part of Gen-Xers to put themselves out there, engage, ask for what they need (or want), and take the lead when it is possible. There is also a responsibility of those with the more powerful voice and influence (generally the Boomers) to invite Xers to speak up, invite them into positions of influence, and encourage them to make the changes that they see as pertinent. We need each other.

As we step into the homes of Xers, literally and figuratively, we must remember that this is a cross-cultural experience and that we are their guests. They have built their homes with the tools and resources they were familiar with, and for good reason. Each room of each home, just like ours, has unique purposes and norms, and we earn the right to step into more personal and intimate spaces as we respect those purposes and norms. Transparency, authenticity, grace, patience, and empathy must guide our conversations, our motivations, and our interactions as we visit this home.

7

Millennials

Apple of the Eye

The high school graduating class of 2000 marked the entrance of Millennials into the adult world, but their celebrity status was already well established by the bumper stickers placarded on their parents' cars: from "Baby on Board" to "My Child Is an Honor Student," the Millennial generation could well be the most announced and celebrated generation to date. The largest generation in American history, this cohort brings not just numbers but vision, passion, and optimism along with a belief that the world is theirs for the making.

I (Elisabeth) have to own my bias as I write this chapter. I am actually really impressed by this generation. Despite all the negative press about it being entitled or lazy or developmentally behind older cohorts, I think they have a lot going for them.[1] As we'll discover, the Millennials have their shortcomings in comparison to other cohorts, but they also bring some amazing assets. This fundamental tension between strengths and weaknesses is no different

---

1. Joel Stein, "Millennials: The Me Me Me Generation," *Time*, May 20, 2013, http://www .time.com/time/subscriber/printout/0,8816,2143001,00.html.

from the tension that Boomers and Xers bring; it's just that the tension areas differ for each cohort.

The Youngest Child

The current baby of the American family, Millennials hold a special place in our society.[2] Often the baby in a family is looked on with a special kind of fondness and delight, and is seen as holding both an elevated and protected space in the family system. This is a pretty apt description of the place Millennials occupy. Furthermore, psychologists often describe the youngest as follows: "manipulative, charming, blames others, attention seeker, tenacious, people person, natural salesperson, precocious, engaging, affectionate, loves surprises"—all traits of the collective Millennial personality.[3] A unique element of Millennials as the youngest child is their developmental age, not just their space in the American family system. Born between 1982 and 2001, Millennials currently range in age from early adolescents to early thirties, not nearly old enough as a cohort to determine who they will be once all have reached adulthood. For most of us, we are loath to be described forever as the person we were at fifteen or even twenty, and as a collective the same understanding and grace needs to be extended to this generation as they grow into who they are to become.

Additionally, each generation before them modeled two separate tracks within their rankings before reaching adulthood, one mainstream and one "deviant." For Boomers, the hippies were seen as the deviants, the subsection of the generation that seemed the most radical and least fitting within the broader society. For Xers it was the grunge rockers or the Goth subcultures that garnered that attention. Within the Millennial cohort, the deviant path is often those who are labeled entitled, self-absorbed, and materialistic.[4] As with the hippies and the grunge rockers before them, the entitled bunch does not necessarily represent the majority of the generation. I will propose later

2. The generation to follow Millennials will change the "family system" as we are currently discussing it. Born after 2001 and known as "Generation Z" or "Homelanders" (having been born after the inception of Homeland Security), this upcoming generation is not a part of our current discussion as they are yet too young to research and too early in their developmental journeys for observers to know the collective personality, role, or influence they will have as they grow into adulthood.

3. Kevin Leman, *The Birth Order Book: Why You Are the Way You Are*, 3rd ed. (Grand Rapids: Revell, 2009), 18.

4. Tomas Chamorro-Premuzic, "Are Millennials as Bad as We Think?," *The Guardian,* January 24, 2014, http://www.theguardian.com/media-network/media-network-blog/2014/jan /24/millennials-generation-gap.

that the word "expectant" needs to replace the word "entitled" in how we define and understand this generation as a whole.

Millennials' Place in the World

Millennials first graduated high school in the year 2000, giving them both their name and a unique place in American history as the first generation to reach adulthood (or at least turn eighteen) in the new millennium. The 9/11 events mark the end of the births of the Millennial generation, as any child born in 2002 or later will have never known the New York skyline with the World Trade Center buildings or life in the United States without the Department of Homeland Security. The largest generation in American history, Millennials boast a membership of 85.4 million people and because of immigration are expected to grow to nearly 90 million by 2019, when they all will have reached legal adulthood.[5]

In various places, Millennials are also referred to as Generation Y, the Echo Boom, the Net Generation, and Nexters, but I think it is really important to settle on a common name.[6] My background and research have looked at generations as cultures, allowing for each generational cohort to be seen as its own culture with distinct values, beliefs, and worldviews. In that context, an anthropologist or sociologist would never dream of going into an unknown tribe or people group and arbitrarily naming them based on what made sense to the researcher. Instead, the researcher would ask the group being explored how they self-identify, understanding that a name is more than a label and represents core values and facets of someone or something. As such, I think it is crucial to use the name that this youngest cohort has chosen for themselves: Millennials.[7]

The Millennials came into American society at a time when birth rates were rising and then stabilized, starting at an average of 1.8 children per woman in 1982, rising to 2.1 in 1990 and 1991, and stabilizing around 2.0 for the

5. Lindsay M. Howden and Julie A. Meyer, "Age and Sex Composition: 2010," *2010 Census Briefs*, May 2011, 2; Jacqueline Doherty, "On the Rise: A Lost Generation? No Way!," *Barron's*, April 29, 2013, http://online.barrons.com/news/articles/SB50001424052748703889404578440972842742076.

6. Paul M. Arsenault, "Validating Generational Differences: A Legitimate Diversity and Leadership Issue," *Leadership & Organization Development Journal* 25, no. 2 (2004): 124–41; Nicky Dries, Roland Pepermans, and Evelien De Kerpel, "Exploring Four Generations' Beliefs about Career: Is 'Satisfied' the New 'Successful'?," *Journal of Managerial Psychology* 23 (2008): 907–28; Neil Howe and William Strauss, *Millennials Rising: The Next Great Generation* (New York: Vintage, 2000).

7. Howe and Strauss report the findings of an ABC News online poll in which "Millennials" or "the Millennial Generation" took top preference. *Millennials Rising*, 6.

following decade.[8] Where Gen-Xers were born into a world where abortion was legal and birth control was widely available, Millennials entered into a world that then added the availability of *in vitro* fertilization. December 1981 marked the first *in vitro* baby to be born in the United States. With this development, Millennials were welcomed into a world where conception and birth could not only be prevented but also created, thus drastically shaping the lens through which society saw its children.

Additionally, Millennials were typically born to older parents than in previous generations. In 1982, the median age for a mother giving birth to her first child was 23.2 years old, while in 2001 it was 24.6 years old.[9] No longer were children seen as a hindrance to their parents' social or professional development; now they were seen as the pinnacle of their parents' development—something chosen, desired, and representative of all their other life efforts. The parents of Millennials were not just having children later but getting married later as well.[10] In 1982, the median age of first marriage was 25.2 for men and 22.5 for women, which rose to 26.9 for men and 25.1 for women in 2001.[11] By the time Millennials themselves started to get married in 2008, the median age of first marriages for men was 28.2 and 25.9 for women.[12]

Diverse Individuals

A unique and important element of Millennials' identity is their diversity. The most ethnically diverse generation in American history, "only 61 percent are white, 19 percent Hispanic, 14 percent black, and 5 percent Asian" in comparison with those older than Millennials (70 percent white).[13] A generation raised on *Sesame Street*, *Barney*, and *Dora the Explorer*, it has not had to *learn* multiculturalism but instead has embraced it as a core value and

8. World Bank, "Fertility Rate, Total (Births Per Woman)," *Data,* http://data.worldbank.org /indicator/SP.DYN.TFRT.IN?page=4.

9. As a point of reference, the median age in 1965 at which a mother gave birth to her first child was 21.9 years old. Centers for Disease Control, *Table 1–5: Median Age of Mother by Livebirth Order, according to Race and Hispanic Origin: United States, Specified Years 1940–55 and Each Year 1959–2003* (2003), http://www.cdc.gov/nchs/data/statab/natfinal2003.annvol1_05.pdf.

10. As a comparison, the median age of first marriage in 1947 was 23.7 and 20.5 for men and women, respectively; by 1965 those numbers had shifted slightly with men at 22.8 and women at 20.6. Sheri Stritof and Bob Stritof, "Estimated Median Age at First Marriage, by Sex: 1890 to 2012," About.com Marriage (2014), http://marriage.about.com/od/statistics/a/medianage.htm.

11. Ibid.

12. Info Please, "Median Age at First Marriage, 1890–2010," *Information Please Database* (2009), http://www.infoplease.com/ipa/A0005061.html.

13. Judy Woodruff, "Millennials Study Captures Snapshot of Young America," *PBS Newshour,* February 24, 2010, http://www.pbs.org/newshour/bb/social_issues/jan-june10/millenials _02-24.html.

norm. Millennial Jess Rainer states, "As I look back to my childhood, racial and ethnic diversity have always been a part of my life. I have known no other world."[14] In addition to being more diverse in their ethnic and cultural makeup, Millennials are generally more open to people of different religions, ages, and lifestyles. Over 70 percent report having friends of different religions, 93 percent see nothing wrong with people of different races or ethnicities marrying each other, and 87 percent expressed their own willingness to marry outside their ethnic or racial group.[15] In regard to same-sex marriage, and prior to the 2015 Supreme Court ruling, six out of ten Millennials say they have no problem with it. As one Millennial stated, "I don't tell other people how to live their lives. I don't impose a standard of morality on them."[16] More than Boomers or Xers, Millennials have grown up in a world where tolerance of the differences among people was just the beginning, and acceptance of those who are different from you became the expected norm, reaching beyond race and ethnicity and into various other domains of life as well.

Millennials place a high value on individualism and do not want to be seen as a continuation or extension of anyone or anything else.[17] As one Millennial put it, individualism is "the big capital letter title of the whole generation, the arc for everything." It is important to note that this individualism is distinct from Xer individualism. For Xers, individualism was pursued out of skepticism and was more reactionary in its nature. For Millennials, this individualism comes with less fear of being confined and instead is more of a continuation of having been seen and treated as unique and special throughout their childhoods. Where Xer individualism is in many ways an act of protest, individualism for Millennials is an act of celebration.

If each generation takes for granted the good that has gone before them, reacts against the bad, and responds within their historical context, it is hard to definitively say who the Millennials will be, given that nearly a quarter of them are not yet adults and therefore the historical context in which they will grow and develop is not yet fully known. What we can say and conclude is based on who the first two waves of this generation appear to be, knowing that the third wave may end up altering the trajectory and personality of the cohort as a whole. Interestingly, Millennials spoke the least about national

14. Thom S. Rainer and Jess W. Rainer, *The Millennials* (Nashville: B&H, 2011), 79.

15. Ibid., 89–90.

16. Ibid., 92.

17. The values, beliefs, worldviews, and descriptions of Millennials summarized in this chapter, as well as any otherwise undocumented quotations, can be found in Elisabeth A. Nesbit, "Generational Affiliation as a Component of Culture: Focus Group Perspectives of Three Generational Cohorts" (PhD diss., University of Arkansas, 2010), 15–36, 107–136.

and world events shaping their sense of self and the world around them. Their discussion of generational identity was less macro-environment oriented and more focused on the commonalities they experienced within the micro-level of life—close interpersonal relationships and experiences. An additional point of interest is that throughout my interviews with Millennials, they continuously hedged their responses with statements such as, "At least that's how I personally feel," "I can only speak for myself," "That's just how I feel," and other equivalent phrases marking their hesitation to speak on behalf of anyone other than themselves as individuals.

Connecting with the World

While the United States military has regularly been an overseas presence since World War II, there has not been a time in history where our presence has been so extended and profound. From the first Iraq War to Somalia, Bosnia, the second Iraq War, and Afghanistan, Millennials have grown up in a time of nearly constant military action, which has shaped their perspectives and expectations of the world around them. Additionally, the impact of 9/11 on this generation cannot be underestimated. While 9/11 happened to all Americans, it happened to Millennials during key developmental years, thus impacting their sense of self in more significant ways than it impacted Xers, Boomers, or Silents. For older generations, their concept of the United States, national security, and international relationships was already relatively (if not significantly) formed prior to the attacks of September 11, 2001. But for Millennials, this event happened when the oldest of them were only nineteen years old, and thus the cohort's perception of the United States, national security, and international relationships was still being formed. Other significant events to occur during Millennials' developmental years were the Oklahoma City bombing, the death of Princess Diana, the impeachment trial of President Clinton, the Columbine shootings, and the deaths of Saddam Hussein and Osama bin Laden.

Millennials, like Boomers, highlighted the role that media and technology had in shaping their identity. Where Boomers spoke of the growing presence of technology in their lives, Millennials spoke of its omnipresence. The first generation to have television, telephone, cable, computers, and internet all available in their homes from the time they were born, Millennials have never had to go find the "S" encyclopedia on the bookshelf to learn about Sudan or the sun. Instead, they google or ask Siri. This fire hose of technology and information that has always been available to Millennials is a double-edged sword, and they see it as such. As one Millennial put it,

I'm very aware that there's a lot of information and it, like, on the one hand, it makes me open-minded or, like, willing to adjust what I believe, or, like, just realize that maybe I'm wrong. And, on the one hand that's positive, but on the other hand it makes me kind of, like, insecure about what I really know, or what I can know. It's almost too much. I feel, like, as a society we're going through this transition where accessibility to information is changing and there's, like, a certain arrogance that sort of goes along with that, like, we can know so much more, be so much more informed in our decisions, but I feel like we have to figure out a way to, like, adapt to that, that at least I personally don't feel like we have.

Another Millennial added, in reference to awareness of the outside world, "I don't think we know, I think we think we know." As a professor who works primarily with Millennials, I am especially struck by the truth of this awareness that Millennials have a lot of information available to them but lack the skills or knowledge to adapt to it or decipher it. In previous generations, access to knowledge grew as the individual grew, and with that was built a schema (or structure) for how to analyze and process new information in order to determine what was trustworthy and what was not. Millennials did not grow up with the same type of scaffolding; instead they have had to learn these critical thinking and discernment skills in a more trial-by-fire way. They are essentially building the plane while it's in the air.

So much access to information and exposure to the larger world have left many Millennials caught in a tension between apathy and feelings of deep responsibility. The following comments from Millennials capture their perceptions of the effects of media and technology on their worldview: "I think we're more informed about the world than previous generations have been because of technology—we have the *opportunity* to be informed. We're more informed but we aren't necessarily more concerned because we are so used to being informed that we're like, 'okay, okay that's great.'"

Similarly, "I think that the media has, like, desensitized our view of umm, like, world poverty and stuff. Like, we'll see a hungry kid on TV and be like 'Oh, that's sad' and then watch our sitcom. I don't know, I just think we're more desensitized to it than our parents. We might be more aware of it, but that's just how I feel."

Many recognize the inundation they have experienced and speak of all the information and exposure as being "too much," as it leaves them with a greater sense of knowledge but also a greater sense of responsibility to be a part of the solution.

It's ugly that we have to see that type of stuff. But at the same time it's reality. It's ugly that we have to be exposed to it. All these terrible instances, it's ugly,

it's terrible that we have to be exposed to that, but at the same time, we have
to look at it and say, "This is what's really going on; what can we do to change
this? What can we do as individuals to make a difference for our generation?
What values do we need to show, to make a difference?"

Unlike the generations that came before them, Millennials have never known
a time when information and entertainment were not continuously at their
fingertips. Additionally, they have never known a time when one source was
looked to as the keeper of truth or the final authority on a subject matter.
Instead, there is always another news channel, another research study, or
another blog to provide a different perspective, claim, or answer.

Understanding the historical context in which Millennials were born and
are developing is a significant part of understanding who they are and who
they are becoming. This generation knows nothing of the days when they
could ride their bicycles all over town as long as they were back by dinner.
This generation knows nothing of rotary telephones, record players (unless
they're hipsters), or card catalogues. The world has not grown with them; it
was large and in many ways overwhelming from their infancy. Just as with
Boomers and Xers, it is important to recognize and understand the context
in which Millennials have grown up in order to best understand and value
what they, as a cohort, are all about.

A Sense of Self in Comparison to Others

One thing I really respect about the Millennials I interviewed was their
candor. When asked who they saw themselves to be as a generation, they
readily said that they "haven't had enough experiences" to fully answer that
question. One Millennial expressed how this uncertainty of identity spreads
across multiple domains of life: "I mean, now, we're not even sure we want
to believe in our own president and our own country. You know, we're just
not sure of it. We're hopeful, but we're not sure. I just think it's gonna take
more time for us to have that worldview."

With that being said, Millennials are not without self-concepts, self-
awareness, or self-reflection; they just recognize that it may not be as solidified as it is with older cohorts. Some of the traits and roles they have ascribed
to themselves include fixers, leaders, open-minded, tolerant, digital natives,
optimistic, and entrepreneurs.[18] At the same time, many also recognize that,

18. Adjectives came from my interviews with Millennials and Nona Willis Aronowitz, "Millennials Reject 'Lazy, Entitled' Label," Today.com, May 16, 2013, http://www.today.com/news
/millennials-reject-lazy-entitled-label-who-are-they-talking-about-1C9948170.

in comparison with previous generations, "we're incredibly immature for our age" and yet, because of their exposure to media, also "less sheltered than previous generations." In the world of counseling, psychology, and other social sciences, much discussion is taking place about "delayed" or "emerging" adulthood and the ways in which the Millennial generation is actually "behind" in its psychosocial developmental milestones in comparison with previous generations.[19] What must be remembered here is that behavior is purposeful and generally represents a cluster of causes rather than simply over 85 million people collectively deciding to be behind. While no study can definitively state why psychosocial development processes are looking more elongated in this generation, I would argue that it goes back to taking for granted the good of the past, reacting against the bad, and responding within a historical context, as well as the causes that lie within the broad culture, the way Millennials were parented, and their individual choices.[20]

Millennials see themselves as optimistic—more optimistic than previous generations—and believe that the world is theirs for the taking and the making. There is a self-focus that is unique in its expression within this generation. Part of being American, part of being human, is an individualism and selfishness that wars with altruism and philanthropy, and we have seen this tension in both Boomers and Xers in their own unique ways. The tension exists within Millennials as well, but again it takes on its own unique expression. For Millennials, the high value they place on individualism and individuality is the lens through which they see all other values and pursuits, including "equality, tolerance, family, marriage, mentors, and trust." What other generations might see as selfishness, Millennials see as balance in their pursuit of individualism. Specifically, a small group of Millennials collaborated in summarizing the cohort's focus on self and balance by stating,

> It's a valuing our own time more. Like, "No, I'm not going to work on Saturday, that's my time. Not my family time, but that's '*my* time.'" That makes us sound horrible! We're materialistic *and* selfish! But I think that's healthy in a way. It's, like, this is my time. This is when I unwind and I do things that make me healthy and happy. . . . We're more balanced as a generation. . . . Yeah, and I think that we believe that it's important to be balanced. . . . Maybe we aren't [balanced] but we believe that it's definitely something we should strive for.

19. The first to thoroughly explore and describe this phenomenon was Jeffrey Jensen Arnett, *Emerging Adulthood: The Winding Road from the Late Teens through the Twenties* (New York: Oxford University Press, 2004).

20. I chose the word "cause" and not "fault," as fault assumes that the old way was "right" and this new process is "wrong." I believe there are pros and cons to each developmental pattern, and the good and bad of each is dependent upon cultural contexts.

In reacting against what was bad in previous generations, Millennials recognize that the Boomer mentality of work, or even family, as the primary focus of life left their parents unbalanced and unfulfilled. In an attempt to compensate for a performance- or relationship-based foundation for identity, Millennials have responded to the self-esteem curriculum they have received from kindergarten to twelfth grade and have attempted to focus their identity inwardly in a pursuit of personal happiness.

In much of the literature on Millennials, a key word that is often used to describe them is "entitled."[21] At least one researcher has gone so far as to label them a generation of narcissists and honestly has the data to prove it.[22] Now, before we go any further, let's break down some concepts. Merriam-Webster defines "entitle" as: "to furnish with proper grounds for seeking or claiming something." According to the American Psychological Association, individuals with narcissistic personality disorder must have

a pervasive pattern of grandiosity (in fantasy or behavior), need for admiration, and lack of empathy, beginning by early adulthood and present in a variety of contexts, as indicated by five (or more) of the following:

1. Has a grandiose sense of self-importance.
2. Is preoccupied with fantasies of unlimited success, power, brilliance, beauty, or ideal love.
3. Believes that he or she is "special" and unique and can only be understood by, or should associate with, other special or high-status people (or institutions).
4. Requires excessive admiration.
5. Has a sense of entitlement (i.e., unreasonable expectations of especially favorable treatment or automatic compliance with his or her expectations).
6. Is interpersonally exploitative.
7. Lacks empathy.
8. Is often envious of others or believes that others are envious of him or her.
9. Shows arrogant, haughty behaviors or attitudes.[23]

21. Stein, *Me Me Me Generation*; Derek Thompson, "Adulthood, Delayed: What Has the Recession Done to Millennials?," *Atlantic*, February 14, 2012, http://www.theatlantic.com/business/archive/2012/02/adulthood-delayed-what-has-the-recession-done-to-millennials/252913/.

22. Jean M. Twenge et al., "Egos Inflating over Time: A Cross-Temporal Meta-Analysis of the Narcissistic Personality Inventory," *Journal of Personality* 76, no. 4 (August 2008): 875–902; Jean M. Twenge et al., "Further Evidence of an Increase in Narcissism among College Students," *Journal of Personality* 76, no. 4 (August 2008): 919–28; Jean M. Twenge and W. Keith Campbell, *The Narcissism Epidemic* (New York: Atria, 2009).

23. American Psychiatric Association, *Diagnostic and Statistical Manual of Mental Disorders*, 5th ed. (Washington, DC: American Psychiatric Association, 2013), 669.

In regard to entitlement, I would argue that Millennials are *expectant* rather than entitled. To be expectant means to be characterized by the act or state of anticipating or looking forward to the coming or occurrence of something. Millennials do not generally bring with them an attitude that they are *owed* certain things in life, such as certain levels of treatment, validation, or affirmation. Instead they, like all of us, assume that their future experiences will duplicate the patterns, rewards, consequences, and norms of past experiences. The past experiences of Millennials have shown them that they *are* the center of most environments (from home, to school, to advertising), that they *will* receive affirmation, validation, and rewards for every step of progress made, and that only positive reinforcement will be used to modify or correct behavior.[24]

A multiculturally competent counselor is aware that in order to assess whether someone's behavior is considered deviant, the behavior needs to be understood in light of the norms and context of that individual's culture.[25] The norms by which Millennials' narcissism is judged are based on assessments that were created in the 1970s, thus holding them to a separate cultural standard and not taking into account the cultural context and expectations in which Millennials currently find themselves.[26] With that being said, it is worthwhile to ask whether the broader American culture is to adapt and adjust to Millennial norms or whether the individual cultures of Boomers, Xers, and Millennials should collaborate and compromise together in establishing a collective American cultural norm regarding entitlement and expectancy.[27]

One of the most profound statements I heard from the Millennials I interviewed was in regard to their self-concept that the world is theirs for the

24. I was astounded to hear of a newer phenomenon occurring at the end of fifth or sixth grades, depending on the school district, in which students participate in a "Continuation Ceremony" complete with cap and gown. There is no mention of the fact that they are not legally allowed to drop out of school at this age; they are simply doing what is required of them, and yet they receive a ceremony (complete with certificate and often a "continuation party")! The fact that this also happens at the end of kindergarten is also mind-boggling to someone who is not a Millennial or someone who does not have Millennial children. For an example of positive reinforcement, see Laura Markham, *Peaceful Parent, Happy Kids: How to Stop Yelling and Start Connecting* (New York: Penguin, 2012).

25. American Counseling Association, *2014 ACA Code of Ethics* (Alexandria, VA: American Counseling Association, 2014), 11.

26. Robert Raskin and Calvin S. Hall, "A Narcissistic Personality Inventory," *Psychological Reports* 45 (1979): 590; Twenge et al., "Egos Inflating over Time," 875–902.

27. Brett McCracken, "How to Keep Millennials in the Church? Let's Keep Church Un-Cool," *Washington Post*, July 31, 2013, http://www.faithstreet.com/onfaith/2013/07/31/how-to-keep-millennials-in-the-church-lets-keep-church-un-cool/10033, provides a well-articulated argument (by a Millennial) as to what it could look like for all generations to collaborate together in making society and the church more healthy and balanced places.

taking and the making. People of older generations often mistake this for entitlement or grandiosity, and in some ways it is reflective of an inflated sense of self-efficacy.[28] But it is also reflective of the training, parenting, and feedback they have received their entire lives.

> We've been told our whole lives that we can do anything, and we believe it. But we haven't been taught how to manage our time, or manage our goals. We haven't been taught how to form priorities, you know, we've been told we can do anything we want but at that same time we've been told that you have to pick one thing. And we haven't really been taught how to do that.

The generation that was raised on participation trophies and awarded for meeting minimal standards now finds itself in adulthood, face to face with the realities that the world does not award simple participation and that they were not trained or equipped to live in this larger world of deferred gratification. Where parents of Millennials were attempting to raise children who felt validated and affirmed in their identity rather than in their performance, they unintentionally raised children who were unable to self-motivate, self-govern, or self-direct.[29] In attempting to "react against the bad" of their childhood, parents of Millennials took for granted the good that can come from coming in fourth place and feeling the desire to do better next time. They took for granted the benefits of not being the best at something and having to come face to face with your limitations, not because limitations made you less than someone else but because limitations make you human, empathic, and appreciative of the strengths you do have, as well as the strengths of others. In an attempt to make every child feel special, parents of Millennials took from their children that very opportunity, for when everyone is special, no one has particular value.

As I speak with Baby Boomers I am regularly struck by their assumption that Millennials must carry the same distrust and dislike of authority that they themselves had of "the establishment" or "the man." Because of this assumption, they often approach Millennials from a position of antagonism, assuming they have to "prove" their trustworthiness. One of the unique elements of

---

28. "Perceived self-efficacy refers to beliefs in one's capabilities to organize and execute the courses of action required to produce given attainments." Albert Bandura, "Self-Efficacy: Toward a Unifying Theory of Behavioral Change," *Psychological Review* 84 (1977): 192.

29. Jeanette Twenge, Liqing Zhang, and Charles Im explain that "people who believe they are in control of their destinies have an internal locus of control ('internals'). Those who believe that luck and powerful others determine their fate have an external locus of control ('externals')." "It's beyond My Control: A Cross-Temporal Meta-Analysis of Increasing Externality in Locus of Control, 1960–2002," *Personality and Social Psychology Review* 8, no. 3 (2004): 308.

Millennials and their place in American society is that they *like* their parents, and they generally trust authority. We'll talk more about why this is when we get into later sections, but where Boomers and Xers often speak of having to fight against the expectations and rules of older cohorts, Millennials see themselves as working alongside other generations in a more egalitarian way. Better than Boomers or Xers, the Millennials I interviewed actively articulated both the pros and cons of those who have gone before them. When specifically asked how they see themselves in comparison to other cohorts, Millennials spoke of respecting older generations (language not seen or communicated by Boomers and Xers) and of seeing them as being harder workers and more committed to things like their job or marriage. This type of language and commentary was not communicated by Boomers and Xers. Simultaneously, Millennials saw Boomers and Xers as lacking in some traits that they consider deeply important, namely, things like tolerance and open-mindedness. They look at Boomers in particular and "want to avoid whatever happened to them that made them so rules-oriented." They see the older cohort as lacking in passion, energy, and compassion for others.

The Millennial sense of self is still a work in progress—developmentally in young adulthood, it is still being formed and solidified by personal choices and life circumstances. A cohort that believes they have high self-efficacy but is aware that they may lack competency, Millennials are striving to find their place in American society. At times entitled but more often expectant, this cohort faces a bait-and-switch challenge that no previous generation encountered: the rules of the world in which they were educated and parented do not match the rules of the world in which they are expected to function as adults.

Millennial Values

Values underpin the motivations and worldview of each generation, and Millennials are no different. What is interesting to me is that while multiple generations may speak of similar values (such as individualism), their expression and motivation behind those values may be vastly different. For Millennials, values such as individualism, the personal nature of truth, expectation of (immediate and constant) feedback, and pursuit of change all capture key elements of this generation's core values.

Ironically, individualism is likely the uniting thread that holds all other Millennial values together. While individualism is also a high value for Xers, the expression and motivation of this value differ greatly between the two cohorts. For Millennials, individualism is not a stance against someone else.

Instead, for Millennials, individualism is seen as celebratory, as a natural and intentional outflow of the parenting and education they received. Individualism as "the big capital letter title of the generation" is supported by another Millennial's comment that "we are mortified by the fact that there are those in the world that can't be individuals." Another facet to Millennial individualism is their use of the word "uniqueness," and their value of seeing and honoring the uniqueness in each person. This pursuit of uniqueness is explained by one cohort member who stated,

> People who are in college and high school right now really value realness and uniqueness, and that's not something that came from our parents or their parents because they valued fitting in. That you shaped yourself to be okay with society, it was much more conservative . . . we want people to be real and honest. We value uniqueness in people.

In this way, individualism for Millennials is not an isolationist position, for they desire relationship and community with one another. They value the coming together of different kinds of unique people in one space. We will explore this concept of individuals within tribes when we discuss Millennials in community.

Me, My Stuff, My Truth

While Millennials were given the intense value of individualism from Xers, they were simultaneously given the high value of community from Boomers. These seemingly contradictory pursuits come together in Millennials' approach to materialism. For Boomers, their collectivistic materialism was seen in the acquisition of large status symbols such as cars or homes. The "in crowd" only bought the "best" brand of car or a home in the "best" area, thus allowing the individual status of a Boomer to be reflected in the community by which possessions identified them. For Xers, their individualistic materialism was seen in the possession of smaller, unique items, such as a pair of sneakers or a designer handbag. For Millennials, the game has changed. They exist in a social world with far more subcultures than previous generations experienced, allowing for multiple ways to express materialism and status without having as dominant a primary culture of materialism—materialistic expression to a hipster may look significantly different than it would to someone involved with the punk or gangster subcultures. The desire to be "cool" and fit in with the mainstream, while present, is not always seen as the only or best option for Millennials. With that being said, the materialistic pursuit that unites this generation can be seen in technology. For many Millennials, the newest iPhone is not seen as a materialistic status symbol (that comes in the *case* you buy for your iPhone) but rather a necessity. Older generations remember a time in which modern technologies were not available, and thus are now seen more as conveniences and luxuries that we may begrudgingly admit are more and more difficult to live without. But, for Millennials, items such as cell phones, computers, MP3 players, and the like are givens.

Millennials also take the Xers' sense of individualism and freedom a step further into postmodernism. For Xers, there was a time in their lived experience when someone or something was seen as the holder of truth. Granted, that truth holder was at some point deconstructed, and their skepticism toward absolute truth or authority was shaken. But, for Millennials, there has never been a time in their lived experience where the broader culture generally agreed on someone or something as a truth holder. The postmodern notion of relativism, while initiated by Xers, was in full swing by the time Millennials came around. For Millennials, truth is not just relative, it is personal. Personal truth is what *I* believe about something or someone, and it is not just some existential musing about what may or may not be true in a given space, time, or context. It is instead a conviction that is contained within the self. The Millennials I interviewed used terms like "my personal belief" and "my personal value": "It seems like we've moved toward understanding that your belief is your belief, and someone else's belief is their belief. Just like he [another Millennial] said, 'My personal belief' or 'my personal value,' and not thinking that there's one absolute."

For Millennials, personal truth may or may not be grounded in some type of science or socially accepted fact, for a Millennial sees these "truths" of science or society as no more grounded or trustworthy than someone else's musings. Tomorrow a new study may emerge that challenges or thoroughly debunks yesterday's "truth." How many times have Millennials seen news articles arguing the life-threatening effects of cholesterol in eggs, only to turn around and read an article touting eggs as a healthy source of protein? We may laugh at this example, but it is representative of Millennials' experience with "news," "truth," and "facts."

Questions and Feedback

Because truth is so personal and seemingly ever changing, Millennials place a high value on questioning. Their questions about policy, procedure, exceptions to rules, and purpose behind standards are often seen as a direct challenge to the authority of older cohorts. For Millennials, these questions often reflect a desire to buy in to the "whys" of such policies, procedures, and rules. Throughout their childhoods, Millennials were parented by Boomers and older Xers who swore they would never be the parent that said, "Do this because I said so" and instead vowed to always explain their reasoning to their children. A well-intended parenting style meant to facilitate the child's participation in their own development and discipline created a generation that has little to no experience with a hierarchical authority that expects obedience before understanding. For Millennials, obedience or compliance comes *after* understanding. In every generation, there are those who question authority out of defiance and disrespect. While that is also present within the Millennial generation, more often the disrespect that is felt by a Boomer or an Xer is meant as an attempt at joining or collaborating by a Millennial.

Connected to the Millennials' value placed on questioning is their valuing the giving (and receiving) of feedback. Growing up in a world with child-centered education, child-centered parenting, 24/7 customer-service lines, customer-satisfaction surveys, and "How's my driving?" bumper stickers, Millennials have been taught that their opinion matters (and they believe it).[30] They have lived experiences with parents and teachers who have modeled an interaction pattern in which all participants have equal voice and opportunity to provide input. It is extremely important to Millennials that everyone involved in a process or decision be heard. Conflict often happens between Millennials and older cohorts in what comes next. For Boomers, there was an inherent distrust of "the system." If Boomers were to express an opinion in opposition to that which was previously established, they were expressing that opinion in order to make change; and they expected change to happen. For Millennials, there is less apprehension and distrust of hierarchy and system. They do not trust completely or blindly, but they are less skeptical than either Boomers or Xers. Millennials expect to be heard but not necessarily followed. They will express an opinion or a dissenting voice and expect others to do so as well. They then expect that the collective will choose the best suggestions and move forward from there. Being heard is of more importance than being right or being followed. In an attempt to be heard, a Millennial is generally

30. An example of this is the rise in Montessori education in which children "learn at their own, individual pace and according to their own choice of activities from hundreds of possibilities." See "The International Montessori Index," http://www.montessori.edu.

While there are some great strengths and benefits to various approaches to parenting, anything taken to an extreme can leave a child (and a parent-child relationship) unbalanced. The swing from authoritarian parenting to emotion- and attachment-focused parenting is evidenced in books such as William Sears and Martha Sears, *The Attachment Parenting Book: A Commonsense Guide to Understanding and Nurturing Your Baby* (New York: Little, Brown, 2001).

See Twenge and Campbell, *Narcissism Epidemic*, 13–17, for a discussion of the effects of a self-focused childhood environment.

expressing engagement and ownership in a system or a process; this often challenges a Boomer's (or Xer's) assumption that vocalizing an opposing view is an attempt at redirecting power.

The feedback loop goes in both directions for Millennials, who expect not only to give feedback but also receive feedback (as long as it's positive). The expectation of mutual feedback is a stark contrast to the unseen and unheard experiences of Gen-Xers. Whether in spoken words, emails, text messages, Facebook comments, or voicemails, this cohort expects to be sought after in order to be provided with feedback, and therefore they see silence as rejection or disapproval. A common example of this is the Facebook "like" button. No button exists to "dislike" someone's status or picture, so by default to not "like" something is perceived as disapproval, apathy, or not caring enough to "follow" that person's updates. Although this example relates to only one media sphere, it represents the values and expectations of this youngest cohort: feedback should be immediate, constant, and positive.

On one hand, the Millennial expectation of feedback is about collaboration, participation, and mutual respect, but on the other hand, it is about locus of control.[31] Jean Twenge and her colleagues explored this idea of locus of control across generations and found that college students in 2002 (older Millennials) "had a more external locus of control than 80 percent of college students in 1960."[32] Interestingly, similar conclusions were found when comparing children in 1971 to children in 1998, and they calculated that 14 percent of this variance was accounted for by birth cohort (generation). In nonstatistical language, generational affiliation accounted for *a lot* of what gives Millennials a more externally directed locus of control, even more than their family environment. This expectation goes beyond an individual personality trait and views "locus of control as a generalized expectancy about life events and the workings of the world in general."[33]

Pursuing

Even with an increasing external locus of control, Millennials bring with them a value of "pursuing"—specifically, pursuing success and change. The generation that was raised to have no losers (because no one loses when everyone gets a trophy) is still deeply human—pursuing competition, status, and comparison with others. The pursuit of success is often more focused

31. One is said to have either a primarily internal or primarily external locus of control. See Twenge, Zhang, and Im, "It's beyond My Control," 308.
32. Ibid., 315.
33. Ibid.

on status than on actual accomplishment for this generation. According to one Millennial, "We value success more than hard work." Another cohort member elaborated on the value of success in connection with other Millennial values by stating, "It's like competition, success, and independence are all tied together in a way. It's like you want to be independent but you want to compete against *everybody*, even your friends and your family, to be the most successful." Garrison Keillor's description that "all the children are above average" in Lake Wobegon succinctly captures the attitude in which this cohort was born and raised and now pursues as a part of their identity.[34]

In their quest for success, Millennials also value a pursuit of change. Having lived experiences in which technology, politics, and the economy were always changing, this generation has come to expect that success plus growth equals change. Change for this generation can be on large or small scales, but change centers on individuality and one's ability to choose where, how, and in what ways one individually wants to make a difference. Millennials have hope and confidence in the idea that "we all, as a generation, believe that individuals can change the world and can make a big difference." In many ways this cohort captures the vision of the Baby Boomers with the individualism of the Xers as they work to imagine what their impact on the world will be. One Millennial explained their pursuit of change in comparison to previous generations by stating,

> That's something I think that our generation values more [making a difference]; we're more enthusiastic. Not that other generations weren't, they all had their big moments where they changed, like the civil rights movement, the feminist movement. They had big movements. I see our generation as much more enthusiastic about doing things individually and on smaller scales to make a difference.

Where Millennials will land as a cohort in regard to their social justice and civic involvement is yet to be seen. While Millennials themselves speak of a high value of change, both experiencing it and making it, the literature about their involvement in change is split. Many say that Millennials are more active in social justice and community concerns than previous generations and anticipate them to be the most civically oriented generation in modern American history.[35] But some research is showing otherwise. It is true that in high school and college, Millennials engaged in more community service

---

34. Garrison Keillor's public radio show *A Prairie Home Companion* depicted a fictitious Minnesota town in which it was said "all the women are strong, all the men are good looking, and all the children are above average." See http://www.garrisonkeillor.com.

35. Howe and Strauss, *Millennials Rising*, 216.

activities than previous cohorts, but much of that was due to curriculum requirements. Current research suggests that although Millennials had more community involvement in high school than previous generations, their overall care and concern for others, their environmentalism, and their general civic engagement declined after graduating high school, with the sole exception being an increase in political discussions and voting.[36] As Millennials enter adulthood, it will be interesting to see the level of their civic involvement and how their personal and collective development influences these areas of life as they pursue their expressed value of change.

The Millennial generation, like the Xers and the Boomers before them, encompasses a diverse set of individuals. These individuals collectively come together and hold sometimes seemingly contradictory values as they seek to express who they are and navigate their place in the larger American society. While we can identify individualism, the personal nature of truth, expectation of immediate and constant feedback, and pursuit of success and change as key values for Millennials, I think it is important to let this generation grow and develop further before we close the books on our understanding of who they are going to be.

Millennials: Up Close and Personal

As we have done with Boomers and Xers, we now turn to look at Millennials in the smaller, more intimate spheres of their lives. We will see that Millennials define community much differently than the older generations and that their lived experiences with home and family are also vastly different. Finally, their approaches to work and religion have the potential to cause more misunderstandings and conflict than any other generation we have discussed thus far.

Millennials in Community

The best word to describe Millennials in community is one they use themselves: "tribe." For this generation, they do not first primarily associate community with large organizations or institutions with whom they have affiliation

36. Jean M. Twenge, W. Keith Campbell, and Elise C. Freeman, "Generational Differences in Young Adults' Life Goals, Concern for Others, and Civic Orientation, 1966–2009," *Personality Processes and Individual Differences* 102, no. 5 (2012): 1054, 1056. *The New York Times* reported that 51 percent of Millennials in 2008 (ages 18–28 at the time) voted in comparison to 50 percent of Baby Boomers in 1976 (ages 18–30 at the time). See Michael Winerip, "Boomers, Millennials, and the Ballot Box," *New York Times*, October 29, 2012, http://www.nytimes.com/2012/10/29/booming/voter-turnout-for-boomers-and-millennials.html?_r=2&.

(like Boomers), nor do they shun the idea that they might be like some other collective that they themselves haven't selected (like Xers). Instead they readily connect themselves with various smaller groups in which they find shared interests or characteristics. As one Millennial explained,

> I think at least for me, and probably for a lot of other people, just wanting to be a part of something else and being able to, like, identify with other people around you so that you don't feel so alone in that individualism. And I think, that's the community aspect, and we've gotten that ever since, while we were growing up: doing group projects in school, and joining clubs, and doing sports, and all these, you know, "go out and be with other kids your age and hang out" type things. And then you get to college and it's all about creating community in your residence halls and creating, you know, getting involved in things and service learning.

Community for this cohort involves choices and options, allowing them to identify with various smaller groups simultaneously—and without long-term commitment, if they so choose. They may have a tribe from dance class, a tribe from their professional association, a tribe for their hiking and backpacking excursions, and so forth. Millennials "seek out tribes of specific interests, not just because the opportunity's there but because there are so many specific tribes available to us where we can say 'my interest is here, there's a tribe for that, and there's a tribe for this and there's a tribe for this.'" These tribes may be connected in time and space, with all members being in the same geographic location, or they may be spread across thousands of miles connected only by Skype, Facebook, or an online role-playing game.

Connecting back to their expectation of feedback, their value of individuality, and their tendency toward an external locus of control, Millennials enter into community with both high anxiety and high expectation. Growing up in a world where something or someone new and better was just around the corner, and where everyone had the option to choose and change their minds, Millennials are fiercely aware that tribal affiliation can change at a moment's notice, either by their own choice or by the choices of others in the tribe. Having been taught to build their sense of self around the continual feedback they receive from those around them, Millennials carry with them high levels of anxiety and a deep fear of rejection. One cohort member explained: "You're afraid. You don't want to be judged or told, you know, that [others] don't agree with it. You want the support so you're almost afraid to jump out there." Where Millennials' parents intended to raise a generation with higher self-esteem and increased experiences of affirmation, they unintentionally raised a generation that can often struggle to maintain an identity that is not dependent upon the acceptance or praise of others.[37]

Psychologist Rollo May defines anxiety as "a condition in which we feel threatened as if the very foundation of existence had been knocked out from under us."[38] This definition in many ways describes the constant state of many Millennials. Research on the changing levels of anxiety across generational cohorts is astounding. An average child's anxiety score in 1993 was higher than those of same-aged child *psychiatric* patients in the 1950s.[39] What is interesting about this study and these results is that the author rightly connects increased anxiety to decreased social connection and increased environmental threat.[40] This means that although Millennials have more of the benefits of increased social contacts through various tribes and technological resources (i.e., Facebook, Twitter, etc.), their actual level of *connection* is decreased along with their sense of safety. As such, community for Millennials is something they deeply seek, as it is part of being human to desire relationship, but they do not bring with them the sense of safety and security that previous generations had. This absence of a sense of safety transcends both the physical and the existential realms for Millennials. From the perspective of older cohorts, the community relationships that Millennials had may be wider and more numerous, but they are seen as far less intimate. And, from a Millennial perspective, they see themselves as "lonelier, [and] more isolated individually."

Beyond peer relationships, it is important to look at how Millennials see older generations and whom they regard as heroes. As father-and-son team Thom and Jess Rainer found in their research, Millennials see no reason not to respect older generations, challenging the Boomer and even Xer mentalities that often looked down upon or resented the ways of older cohorts.[41] Instead of speaking of heroes, Millennials spoke more frequently of mentors, whom

37. Brittany Gentile, Jean M. Twenge, and W. Keith Campbell, "Birth Cohort Differences in Self-Esteem, 1988–2008: A Cross-Temporal Meta-Analysis," *Review of General Psychology* 14, no. 3 (2010): 261–68. This study demonstrates the overall rise in self-esteem scores using a widely accepted self-esteem measure. The rise in self-esteem scores is so significant that the authors recommend re-norming the current scale to better reflect what is considered low, average, and high self-esteem.

38. Rollo May, "Toward an Understanding of Anxiety," *Pastoral Psychology* 1, no. 2 (March 1950): 26.

39. The average participant's age was eleven at the time of the study, making them older Millennials. Jean M. Twenge, "The Age of Anxiety? Birth Cohort Change in Anxiety and Neuroticism, 1952–1993," *Journal of Personality and Social Psychology* 79, no. 6 (2000): 1017.

40. Ibid.

41. Rainer and Rainer, *Millennials*, 59.

they saw as people of any age they allowed into their lives to both challenge and support them. More than any other cohort, Millennials bring with them a sense of egalitarianism in their relationships with other people, not adhering to older conventions regarding hierarchy, status, or age barriers. The Millennials I interviewed did make an interesting distinction in their expectations of friends versus mentors, wanting friends to be "just supportive" while mentors should be "frank and honest." One Millennial summarized the difference by explaining, "If your mom was going to be like, 'Hey, this is not good, you shouldn't do this,' you know? That'd be okay, but not from my friends." Note the example of who the mentor was for this Millennial: Mom. No other cohort sees their relationship with their parents in quite the same way that Millennials do; simultaneously, there is a collegiality and almost peer-like relationship found between many Millennials and their parents that we'll explore further when we talk about Millennials at home.

Millennials at Work

The newest members to the American workforce, Millennials are still in the process of defining and acquiring their place, and they are estimated to account for 50 percent of the American workforce by 2020.[42] Before we examine Millennials' values and approaches to work, it is important to look at the context they are finding themselves in as they enter the workforce. Like the Xers before them, Millennials are entering a workplace that is still dominated by Baby Boomers, particularly in upper management and leadership positions. Similar again to Xers, Millennials have watched their parents invest in their careers only to be let go or sorely disappointed after years of dedicated service, and therefore they do not see longevity with a company as something necessarily to be desired. Instead, they see one job as a means to another job and a means to their personal goals, and they will leave a job if they do not foresee the right kinds of growth or opportunity.[43]

Let's return to that neighborhood block party where you are chatting with Joe, but this time Joe is a Millennial. You are still interested in getting to know more about Joe, and you say to him, "So Joe, tell me about yourself." Joe the Millennial is likely to respond by saying, "Well, last weekend I went hiking with some friends, and then to a concert of this really cool local band. I really enjoy live music. I play competitive volleyball in the summers, and I'm

---

42. Jeanne Meister, "Three Reasons You Need to Adopt a Millennial Mindset Regardless of Your Age," Forbes.com, October, 5, 2012, http://www.forbes.com/sites/jeannemeister/2012/10/05/millennialmindse/.

43. Rainer and Rainer, *Millennials*, 129.

thinking about taking Spanish lessons here pretty soon. I guess that's pretty much me—oh, and I have a job in marketing, but someday I would love to be the CEO of my own PR firm that helps promote the work of nonprofit organizations." Millennials often start with the personal and include some kind of yet-to-be-obtained vision, demonstrating the fact that they are still growing into themselves. Like the Xers before them, they push against an identity that is defined by work, but in their own right they place a greater emphasis on their work being personally and socially beneficial—at least in theory.[44]

With that being said, it is false to assume that careers do not matter to this generation. Millennials can be incredibly ambitious and have high expectations of success as it pertains to their work, with over 84 percent of Millennials stating "career success is important to them."[45] What can easily be interpreted by Boomers (and some Xers) as a lack of commitment or an unwillingness to "pay your dues" is a reflection of Millennials' sense of restless ambition and the belief that they cannot depend on a company or organization to care about their professional growth, so they must take care of themselves.[46] In summarizing various studies that compare Millennial work values and attitudes to those of Gen-Xers and Boomers at similar ages, Jean Twenge states,

> [Millennials] see work as less central to their lives, are more likely to value leisure, and say they are less willing to work hard. Viewed positively, this generation places a high importance on work-life balance beginning in high school, long before they have children. Viewed negatively, the work ethic has declined . . . [however, Millennials] report higher job satisfaction than Gen X.[47]

Another false assumption that often gets discussed about Millennials in the workplace is that they do not care about money, when a better way to say it is that they care about resources that facilitate relationships. Millennials are still Americans, and Americans as a whole still like money, but Millennials differ from previous generations in what they want the money for. Where Boomers use money to buy big toys and save for retirement, Millennials tend to focus

---

44. Much verbal affirmation is given by Millennials and about Millennials regarding their social justice orientation and desire to care for those around them. It is yet to be seen in the research whether they will live up to the talk, or how they will compare in this area to other cohorts.

45. Rainer and Rainer, *Millennials*, 130.

46. Ibid.

47. Jean M. Twenge, "A Review of the Empirical Evidence on Generational Differences in Work Attitudes," *Journal of Business Psychology* 25 (2010): 208–9.

on using money to facilitate relationships with family and friends. Therefore, in the workplace, compensation is extremely important to this cohort, but compensation may be in the form of cash, a flexible schedule, or paid time off. They won't necessarily turn down a retirement package, but they will be more attracted to a higher salary with which they can decide how much to invest, how much to live off of, and how much to put toward a better cell phone, computer, or plane tickets in order to stay in touch with the people who matter in their lives.

I've spoken with various managers about their struggles and questions regarding Millennial employees, and there is one issue that continues to come up: expectations. Time and again I hear Xer and Boomer managers baffled by their need to explain, re-explain, and affirm the work of Millennials. Millennials, on the other hand, are baffled by what they perceive as the lack of clarity in their job description, and then the absence of their bosses in their process of acclimation to the job. Remember that Millennials' lived experiences have taught them to expect authority figures to be actively involved in their lives, overly explanatory, and highly affirming. Their educational experiences from kindergarten to twelfth grade have been filled with stickers, awards, comments, and consistent input, and they have been taught to expect input from a superior after nearly every action. Beyond their educational experiences, Millennials' "helicopter parents" have regularly paved a way for them, explaining and navigating everything as they went, and thus not allowing their Millennial children to develop their own base levels of general knowledge on which they themselves could build.[48]

While for some Millennials this need for clear explanation and affirmation comes from their external locus of control, for others it comes from a deep desire to do right by those in authority over them. For still others it is an attempt to build up their base level of general knowledge in order to feel competent in the Boomer-dominated work world. For many Millennials, their actual competency has yet to catch up with their perceived sense of ability.[49] As they step into the work world, quickly realizing that this system does not function like home or school, they are left with their high levels of anxiety but without the internal resources to know how to mediate that anxiety. Couple that awareness with the knowledge that nearly every media source for the last decade has touted the ineptness, laziness, and incompetence of their generation, and Millennials are left between a rock (to fail at a job that hasn't been

48. See p. 21, n. 42 for a definition of helicopter parents. See also Jennifer J. Deal, David G. Altman, and Steven G. Rogelberg, "Millennials at Work: What We Know and What We Need to Do (If Anything)," *Journal of Business Psychology* 25 (2010): 193.

49. Bandura, "Self-Efficacy," 192.

explained to them) and a hard place (to admit to their older colleagues that they do need help).[50]

Millennials, unlike previous cohorts, speak fondly of older generations and generally respect those in authority. They bring into the workplace their lived experiences with parents and teachers who walked with them through tasks step by step expecting similar types of interactions with their bosses. It would benefit any cross-generational workplace to have a discussion between boss and employee as to the type and frequency of feedback and explanations that are expected. I wholeheartedly agree with the findings of the Rainers when they say Millennials "respond well to guidance and even criticism, but they do need some clear guidelines and expectations. It will be worth the time and investment."[51] For a Baby Boomer who functions more from the perspective of "it's all good unless you hear otherwise," this approach to management and employee development is both perplexing and exhausting, but it could be invaluable in passing on one generation's legacy while launching another.

The Millennial value placed on work/life balance and having a job that allows them to maintain interpersonal relationships contributes to their valuing of the personal *with* the professional, rather than valuing one life sphere over the other. This interpersonal value can be seen in Millennials' expressed desire and appreciation for mentorship in the workplace. For a Millennial, mentorship is not simply about someone teaching them the fundamentals of a job, it is about someone with whom they can exchange ideas in a way that is authentic, transparent, and mutually beneficial. As much as they want a boss or senior colleague to lead them well, they want to know that they too have a voice in the organization and can contribute to the forward movement and development of their department and their company.[52]

On a more macro-level, Millennials appreciate a work environment that contains varied work experiences, has a goal-directed orientation, and emphasizes teamwork. The use of technology in their work is something this generation "takes for granted" as an organic knowledge and skill set, and they expect their superiors to have a similar level of competency with things like email, voicemail, and general office software.[53] Where advanced technology in

50. See esp. Chamorro-Premuzic, "Are Millennials as Bad as We Think?"; Stein, *Me Me Me Generation*.

51. Rainer and Rainer, *Millennials*, 147.

52. Ibid., 144–46.

53. Ron Zemke, Claire Raines, and Bob Filipczak, *Generations at Work: Managing the Clash of Boomers, Gen Xers, and Gen Yers in the Workplace* (New York: American Management Association, 2013), 131.

the workplace for Boomers is seen as something that allows their organization to stand out or be superior, to a Millennial the *lack* of such resources is what stands out and makes an organization inferior.

Millennials at Home

In 1982 when the first Millennials were being born, the landscape of the American family had shifted dramatically since the 1950s and 1960s, when many of their parents were growing up. Taking for granted the good, reacting against the bad, and responding within their own historical context, the parents of Millennials were bound and determined to create the best generation in American history: "We're [Boomers] not the best; the ones I just created are the best!" Having often been raised in a historical context where the parental role was more traditionally authoritarian, the parents of Millennials set out to parent in a more collaborative and relational way. They wanted to be seen by their children as friends, not just authority figures. In this, the good that was lost was a sense of hierarchy and an understanding that power and privilege come with time and responsibility; what was gained was a generation that saw parents as partners and allies rather than "the man" who needed to be fought against.

The family structure experienced by Millennials' *parents* looked vastly different than the family structure experienced by Millennials themselves. For every one hundred marriages that took place in 1950, twenty-three divorces also occurred that year; in 1965 that number was hovering right around twenty-eight divorces per one hundred marriages, but jumped to 48.5 divorces in 1975 and a full fifty divorces per 100 marriages in 1981. Throughout Millennials' childhood, the United States saw the divorce rate slowly decline throughout the 1980s and 1990s, reaching 47.6 divorces per one hundred marriages in 2001.[54] Another change in family structure has to do with extended family, as 7.3 percent of Millennials lived with a grandparent in 2010, compared to 3.6 percent of Xers in 1980 and 3.8 percent of Boomers in 1960.[55]

Approaches to parenting also look different for this generation, with the emergence of "helicopter parents." The intention in this parenting style was to ease the burden on their children, but the tradeoff came in fostering an

54. Info Please, "Marriages and Divorces, 1900–2009," *Information Please Database* (2009), http://www.infoplease.com/ipa/A0005044.html.

55. Breana Wilson, "Grandchildren: Living in a Grandparent-Headed Household," *NCFMR Family Profiles: FP-13-03* (2013): 1, http://www.bgsu.edu/content/dam/BGSU/college-of-arts-and-sciences/NCFMR/documents/FP/FP-13-03.pdf.

external locus of control in the children, a decreased ability to navigate challenges on their own, and lower levels of satisfaction in their lives due to a diminished sense of responsibility and ownership of their life choices.[56] While Millennials report feeling less sheltered than previous generations regarding media and global information, they also report feeling that they have remained "under [their] parents' umbrella" longer than previous generations and are therefore "incredibly immature for [their] age." This sentiment is in keeping with the research that exists about delayed adolescence and emerging adulthood, in which developmental stages and milestones previously associated with people in their late teens and early twenties are now being experienced in the early to mid-twenties.[57]

This cohort is incredibly family oriented, both in regard to the connections they have with their families of origin and also the families they are starting for themselves. The belief that having a good marriage and family is of high importance is virtually unchanged among high school seniors between 1976 and 2008.[58] In 2010, when asked to identify the most important things in their lives, 52 percent of Millennials listed being a good parent, 30 percent said having a successful marriage, while only 15 percent said having a high-paying career.[59] As Millennials get married and become parents themselves, an interesting shift is emerging within their homes. Cohabitation is a more common situation, and the median age of first marriage continues to rise.[60] In 1987, 27 percent of all women between the ages of nineteen and twenty-four had cohabited, but by 2008 that number had risen to 41 percent.[61] On the other side of the home front, the divorce rate for those under twenty-five

56. Eli J. Finkel and Grainne M. Fitzsimons, "When Helping Hurts," *New York Times*, May 10, 2013, http://www.nytimes.com/2013/05/12/opinion/sunday/too-much-helicopter-parenting .html?_r=0.

57. Robin Marantz Henig, "Why Are So Many People in Their 20s Taking So Long to Grow Up?," *New York Times*, August 18, 2010, http://www.nytimes.com/2010/08/22/magazine /22Adulthood-t.html?pagewanted=all.

58. National Center for Family and Marriage Research, "Thirty Years of Change in Marriage and Union Formation Attitudes, 1976–2008," *Family Profiles: FP-10-03* (2010), http://www .bgsu.edu/content/dam/BGSU/college-of-arts-and-sciences/NCFMR/documents/FP/FP-10-03 .pdf.

59. Sharon Jayson, "Study: Millennial Generation More Educated, Less Employed," *USA Today*, February 23, 2010, http://usatoday30.usatoday.com/news/education/2010-02-24-millennials 24_ST_N.htm.

60. Info Please, "Median Age at First Marriage."

61. Cohabitation is generally understood as two people who have a sexual relationship and who live together without being married. See National Center for Family and Marriage Research, "Trends in Cohabitation: Twenty Years of Change, 1987–2008," *Family Profiles: FP-10-07* (2010): 1, http://www.bgsu.edu/content/dam/BGSU/college-of-arts-and-sciences/NCFMR /documents/FP/FP-10-07.pdf.

declined by 33 percent between 1990 and 2010, meaning young Millennials
are divorcing at a lesser rate than their Gen-Xer counterparts twenty years
earlier.[62] While we know that Millennials are waiting longer than previous
cohorts to have children, how many children they will have is yet to be seen.
We do know that when asked to anticipate how many children they might
have, 47 percent said two children, 20 percent said three, 9 percent anticipated
only one child, and 13 percent said they anticipated having no children.[63] This
leaves only 11 percent anticipating having four or more children (7 percent
anticipated having four children, while 4 percent anticipated having five or
more).[64]

More than any other cohort, Millennials spoke of their parents as friends,
even identifying them as their best friends, the people they look up to, and
the people to whom they turn for advice.[65] They place a high value on family
connection and identify their family as one of the primary tribes with which
they affiliate. Millennials bring with them very different, "progressive," and
simultaneously more conventional experiences of family than Xers did before them. Their progressiveness can be seen in the ways they define family
and their openness to alternative family constellations, while their conven-
tionality can be seen in a decrease in sexual activity and number of sexual
partners among unmarried teenagers.[66] It will be interesting to see whether
the optimism and hopeful expectation regarding having successful families
and marriages of their own will become a reality as Millennials enter further
into adulthood.[67]

62. National Center for Family and Marriage Research, "Age Variation in the Divorce Rate,
1990–2010," *Family Profiles: FP-12-05* (2012): 1, http://www.bgsu.edu/content/dam/BGSU/college
-of-arts-and-sciences/NCFMR/documents/FP/FP-12-05.pdf.

63. Rainer and Rainer, *Millennials*, 68.

64. Ibid.

65. Ibid., 57; Howe and Strauss, *Millennials Rising*, 123.

66. For example, according to Gallup, in 2013, 70 percent of Americans ages 18–29 were in
support of gay marriage compared to 53 percent of those between the ages of 30–49 and 46
percent of those 50–64 years of age. Jeffrey M. Jones, "Same-Sex Marriage Support Solidifies
Above 50% in U.S.," *Gallup Politics*, May 13, 2013, http://www.gallup.com/poll/162398/sex
-marriage-support-solidifies-above.aspx.

According to the CDC, in 1991, 54 percent of high school students (Generation Xers)
reported ever having had sexual intercourse, with 18.7 percent having had sexual intercourse
with four or more people in their lifetime, in comparison to 2011, in which 47.4 percent of
Millennial high school students reported having ever had sexual intercourse, and 15.3 percent
having had sexual intercourse with more than four people in their lifetime. Centers for Disease
Control and Prevention: National Center for HIV/AIDS, Viral Hepatitis, STD, and TB Prevention, "Trends in the Prevalence of Sexual Behaviors and HIV Testing National YRBS: 1991–
2011," *Youth Risk Behavior Survey*, http://www.cdc.gov/HealthyYouth/yrbs/pdf/us_sexual
_trend_yrbs.pdf.

67. Rainer and Rainer, *Millennials*, 63.

Millennials in Church

The topic of religion was discussed less by Millennials than it was by any other cohort in my study, and others have also identified it as a topic of less importance in comparison with Xers and Boomers.[68] For Boomers, the topic is one of both history and renewed interest; for Xers, it is a topic of deep personal angst and importance; but for Millennials, it appears to simply be one more thing that people make choices about. Where 59 percent of older cohorts say that religion is very important in their lives, only 45 percent of Millennials would agree; and only 15 percent would say living a "religious life" is very important to them.[69] Similar to older cohorts, Millennials see religion and spirituality as two distinct concepts: religion refers to an institutional belief system, while spirituality is more of a personal choice and expression.

While Millennials are less likely to be religiously affiliated and are less likely to believe in God, their beliefs regarding heaven, hell, life after death, and miracles are similar to those of older Americans.[70] In the late 1970s, 39 percent of Boomers reported that religion was very important to them, not much different than the 40 percent of Millennials in the late 2000s, thus leaving us to wonder what is generational and what is developmental.[71] One-third of Millennials identify themselves as religiously unaffiliated, and 88 percent of the unaffiliated say they are not looking for a religion.[72] Compare this to 21 percent of Gen-Xers and 15 percent of Baby Boomers who claim no religious affiliation.[73] In a separate but similar study, of those who were affiliated, only 20 percent of Millennials identified as "born-again Christians," meaning "those who have made a personal commitment to Jesus Christ and believe they will go to heaven because they have confessed their sins and accepted Christ as their Savior."[74]

68. Ibid., 229.
69. Pew Research Center, "Millennial Generation Less Religiously Active Than Older Americans," *Pew Research Center* (2004), http://www.pewforum.org/2010/02/17/millennial-generation-less-religiously-active-than-older-americans/. The term "religious life" was not defined in the research report by Pew Research Center, *Millennials: A Portrait of Generation Next* (February 2010), http://www.pewsocialtrends.org/files/2010/10/millennials-confident-connected-open-to-change.pdf.
70. Pew Research Center, "Religion among the Millennials: Less Religiously Active Than Older Americans, but Fairly Traditional in Other Ways" (2010): 16, http://www.pewforum.org/2010/02/17/religion-among-the-millennials/.
71. To complete the comparison, 48 percent of Gen-Xers of the same age in the late 1990s said that religion was very important. Ibid., 11.
72. Unaffiliated includes atheists, agnostics, and those who had no preference.
73. Paul Taylor, *The Next America: Boomers, Millennials, and the Looming Generational Showdown* (New York: BBS Public Affairs, 2014), 128.
74. Rainer and Rainer, *Millennials*, 231.

The Millennial values of individualism and the personal nature of truth underpin their approaches to religion and spirituality. Statements such as "We agree to disagree; some people might be this religion, some people might be that religion, but you still have the right to choose what religion you want to be" exemplify this generation's perspective on religion. Another way this is put is, "I can have my beliefs, I can do whatever I think makes me good, and you can do whatever you think makes you good. [A] live and let live kind of attitude towards religion. I don't think we saw that a lot in past generations."

For Millennials, to even articulate a specific stance or belief system can be seen as "preaching" and disrespectful of others who may hold different beliefs. For a generation that has never collectively felt as if there was a place to turn for trusted information, facts, or truth, the thought that one religious belief system could claim such authority is almost beyond comprehension. All their lives they have been able to self-select the things that they prefer or find valuable, and religion is no different: "For some people it is much more kind of pick and choose your own, and make up your own beliefs about religion based on maybe many different ones or none of them at all, and you just pick and choose."[75]

Millennials carry with them an apparent contradiction when exploring topics of religion and belief. On the one hand, they have a deep appreciation and value for things that have a history and a heritage that are bigger than themselves.[76] On the other hand, the Millennial values of individualism and the personal nature of truth often push them to question anything that has an established history. In my conversations with Boomers, Xers, and Millennials, I have seen a misunderstanding occur across the cohorts as to *why* Millennials question established history. From a Boomer perspective, the questioning often arises out of a distrust of the institution or organization being looked at. From a Millennial perspective, the questioning arises out of a desire to understand the whys behind a given tradition or practice, and to appease their own need to feel as if they have made a decision out of an informed space. As one Millennial explained,

And now it seems like we've moved toward understanding that your belief is your belief, and someone else's belief is their belief. Just like he said, "My personal

75. Thirty years ago Robert Bellah described this as "Sheilaism" after a young woman named Sheila Larson who articulated almost exactly this sentiment. *Habits of the Heart* (Berkeley: University of California Press, 1985), 221. Then it was a shocking, almost unheard-of, personal potluck form of religion. Now it's commonplace and even has a Wikipedia article to describe it (http://en.wikipedia.org/wiki/Sheilaism)!

76. Some of this may come from their embracing of multiculturalism and the value of knowing one's personal history and lineage within one's racial and ethnic heritage.

belief" or "my personal value" and not thinking that there's one absolute. And that we tend to want to know why there's the main belief. It's, like, "Okay, I give you that you believe that, but why? Why should *I* believe that?" And, I don't know if that's a value or a belief or a worldview, but it's the kind of, it's, if someone tries to change our belief or value in some way, we want to know why they're questioning it.

Millennials have been raised to question any and all claims presented to them, or to at least not be surprised if anything presented as truth gets changed over time. As such, they come into religion with similar uncertainty and skepticism.

Where Xers pushed against the waning beliefs and philosophies of the early twentieth century, ushering in a more mainstream acceptance of post-modernism, Millennials have known no other framework than a relativistic and personally designed way of seeing the world. Everything else in the lives of Millennials was rooted in choice, options, freedom, individuality, and sub-jective experience, so why wouldn't religion be the same? A generation that places high value on relationships and personal experience, Millennials often struggle to find their place within organized religion where hierarchical struc-ture abounds, rules and regulations are expected to be universally followed, and the individual is not elevated above the collective.

The Millennial value of egalitarian relationships, as modeled by their parents, is a telling lens through which to understand their religious non-affiliation. Simultaneously, this generation brings with it a value of history, context, experience, and culture that could prove to be an inroad for churches that offer a more traditional or liturgical framework for their worship. Where Gen-Xers' cultural values and framework lead them to an emergent church model, many are finding that Millennials who do religiously affiliate are being drawn into Christian denominations with a more high-church model that has long-standing traditions, and into non-Christian faiths with ancient roots (e.g., Buddhism, Hinduism, and Wicca). In a society that is constantly pushing the "now" and emphasizing the individual pursuit of happiness, Mil-lennials carry with them a tension to keep in step with the ethos around them while also desiring to find something that connects their lives to something greater, giving them meaning and purpose beyond their temporary sense of self.

While many of the numbers look bleak, this generation stands at a cross-roads, inviting the church into a similar pivotal time of decision making and exploration. With more than 85 million in their ranks, how might older cohorts respond to the relational and spiritual needs of this youngest child?

Conclusion

The current baby of American society, Millennials are an 85 million–plus force to be reckoned with. For all the bad press of their entitlement, laziness, and materialism, this cohort brings with them a renewed sense of hope, vision, and energy. An expectant generation raised to hope, dream, and believe they could be anything they choose to be, Millennials pursue change, growth, and individuality. The largest and most ethnically diverse generation in American history, Millennials entered American society as one of the most wanted and intentionally welcomed cohorts.

Millennials are a generation that is still in the midst of their own development and on the verge of becoming fully themselves. It will be exciting to see what they become. Millennials bring to the workplace, and to society as a whole, an eagerness to question, understand, and not take for granted the way things have always been, while still respecting their elders and valuing cross-generational relationships. They were confronted with a fire hose of information and accessibility and had to learn how to accurately sift through legitimate and trustworthy sources rather than being given foundational truth upon which to build their worldview.

As they enter adulthood, Millennials are confronted with the realities of the world that Boomers and some Xers created. Well-intended parents attempted to protect this generation from hardship and disappointment, not wanting their babies to ever hear the word "no" or have limitations put on their potential. These parents left Millennials with high self-esteem but lower competency and the challenging realization that being told you can do or be anything does not endow you with the knowledge or skill to accomplish your aspirations. They are a generation, like any other, with two tracks or subcultures of their own; one embodies all the negative press of laziness, entitlement, and self-centered materialism, while the other embodies the drive, ambition, and philanthropy that define the best of American aspirations.

While valuing not just tolerance but acceptance, this cohort struggles to define right and wrong outside their own personal convictions, desiring to leave room for others to believe differently without judgment. Growing up in a society in which truth is constantly changing and subjective, religious convictions are of less importance than in previous generations, for one's individual happiness and convictions are the only things one can truly "know."

The heart of this cohort is one that beats with the compassion and grace of the gospel, but it can lack an understanding of the righteousness of God and the grievous impact of humanity's sin on our relationship with God. The least represented generation in American churches today, this cohort has the potential to dramatically shape American society. Will older cohorts bemoan Millennials' shortcomings or find ways to invest in and bless this generation as they come into their own as adults?

8

Millennials in Light of the Bible

I (Craig) like Millennials a lot. My two favorites are my daughters, delightful young women in their twenties. I have enjoyed being around almost all of their friends when they brought them home as they were growing up. A year ago, my older daughter and her husband of five years took over our basement for nine months while she completed the half of a degree at Denver Seminary that has to be done in residence. As a Boomer who could hardly wait to be old enough and financially solid enough to move *out* of my parents' home, which I did at age twenty, I would have found it very difficult to move back in with them for so long a period of time after being married for five years and after having not lived at home for eight years. I assumed I would have to give my daughter and son-in-law lots of space, lots of privacy, and assure them that I would keep up all the appropriate boundaries. Instead, I discovered that most of the time when they were home, they preferred to hang out with my wife and me upstairs, and that they often invited us along when they were going out somewhere, even though we often couldn't accompany them. The same is true of many of their friends and their families.

In other words, my experience strongly confirms Elisabeth's more empirical research. Millennials as a cohort, in general, really do like their parents.

They like teachers, pastors, and other authorities also, at least if it's clear those older individuals are making good-faith efforts to embrace them. The "generation gap," the expression that was so often applied in the 1960s and 1970s to the distance between Boomers and their parents and their parents' peers, barely exists in the same way between Millennials and older Xers or younger-to-middle Boomers.[1]

The Babies in the Family

A little bit of this may be attributable to the analogies Elisabeth has been drawing between our three cohorts and a three-child family. Parents tend to adore the youngest in a family and find it hardest to let go of them, knowing they are (usually) the last to "fly the coop," leaving their parents behind to be "empty nesters." Youngest children sometimes return this affection, but not always. If they are *too* smothered, the loving can backfire, and the children can do everything they can to leave as soon as possible.

We have already talked a little about younger children in our chapters on Boomers and Xers. Perhaps the main point to add here, from a biblical perspective, is how much Jesus valued little children. In an era when children were literally much more to be seen and not heard than in modern eras, in an era when fatherless children were a paradigm of the dispossessed (e.g., James 1:27), Jesus's concern for children stands out in striking fashion.[2] In Matthew 18:3–5, he takes the initiative to call a little child to himself to join for a moment his gathering with his disciples. Then he announces to them, "Truly I tell you, unless you change and become like little children, you will never enter the kingdom of heaven. Therefore, whoever takes the lowly position of this child is the greatest in the kingdom of heaven. And whoever welcomes one such child in my name welcomes me."

The NIV translation is particularly helpful here because while the Greek in verse 4 can be and often has been translated as "whoever humbles himself" (one children's pastor in a class of mine years ago vehemently exclaimed, "Little children are *not* usually humble!"), Jesus is not speaking of the subjective attitude of children with this comparison. Rather, he is talking about their

---

1. The term is still used, however. See, e.g., Linda Gravett and Robin Throckmorton, *Bridging the Generation Gap: How to Get Radio Babies, Boomers, Gen Xers, and Gen Yers to Work Together and Achieve More* (Pompton Plains, NJ: Career Press, 2007).

2. For the relevant historical background, see Richard S. Hess and M. Daniel Carroll R., eds., *Family in the Bible: Exploring Customs, Culture, and Context* (Grand Rapids: Baker Academic, 2003); and Ken M. Campbell, ed., *Marriage and Family in the Biblical World* (Downers Grove, IL: InterVarsity, 2003).

objective state.[3] Like it or not, little children are almost entirely dependent on the adult world for their well-being. So too converting to Christian faith requires the recognition that we ultimately owe everything good we have to God.

Verse 6 then applies the image of a little child directly to all believers: "If anyone causes one of these little ones—those who believe in me—to stumble, it would be better for them to have a large millstone hung around their neck and to be drowned in the depths of the sea." A millstone was a heavy, donut-shaped stone wheel attached to a pole, which was attached to a donkey. It was placed inside a circular stone basin for crushing grain. As the donkey walked around the basin repeatedly, the wheel turned too, and the grain was ground.[4] Affixing such a stone wheel around someone's neck and dropping them overboard in the middle of the sea was the most decisive drowning imaginable for a first-century Jew! With such severe threats, it is clear that God cares deeply about little children, including all believers who metaphorically recognize their utter dependence on the Lord for all things good.

Again in Matthew 19:13–15, we see Jesus's love for small children. People brought them to him, and he laid hands on them and prayed for them. The disciples rebuked him, reflecting the standard disregard for little ones in first-century Jewish society, at least in public. But Jesus replied with a comparison similar to the one he made one chapter earlier: "Let the little children come to me, and do not hinder them, for the kingdom of heaven belongs to such as these" (v. 14).[5] To the degree that Millennials may be compared favorably with the youngest children in a family, they may likewise be viewed as special recipients of God's love.

Youngest children, on the other hand, can be babied in unhealthy ways. 1 Corinthians 3:2 reminds us of this with respect to physical nourishment, as Paul compares the Corinthian believers to babies. When they were first converted, they were "mere infants in Christ." So he appropriately gave them "milk, not solid food" because they weren't mature enough yet for more than milk. It is appropriate to feed babies baby food! But now several years have

3. "Instead of pointing to the innocence of a child, Jesus uses the little child as an object lesson on humility that comes from their vulnerability." Again, "the humility of a child consists of the inability to advance his or her own cause apart from the help and resources of a parent." Michael J. Wilkins, *Matthew* (Grand Rapids: Zondervan, 2004), 612, 613.

4. One can still see the apparatus at the outdoor museum next to the ruins of the Capernaum synagogue in Israel. See Craig S. Keener, *The Gospel of Matthew: A Socio-Rhetorical Commentary*, rev. ed. (Grand Rapids: Eerdmans, 2009), 449.

5. "To such as these" suggests that not all children are automatically part of the kingdom, nor is Jesus limiting membership in the kingdom to literal children. Again, it is the state of one's awareness of one's need for and one's dependence entirely on God in Christ that makes the difference.

passed, and the Corinthians are still not ready.[6] A four-year-old who is still breastfeeding has problems (and his or her mother has bigger problems!). So also believers who have not started growing out of their worldliness after several years are stunted in their growth.

The same is true on a literal, familial level when adolescence is overly delayed. Some psychology textbooks today define adolescence as potentially lasting until age thirty![7] Boomers looked forward to age eighteen or twenty-one for most of their adult privileges and responsibilities, and in Bible times the *onset* of puberty around age twelve or thirteen was the point at which boys and girls were viewed as men and women and given their respective rites of initiation into adulthood.[8] Millennials, of course, aren't primarily to blame for this delay. If their parents have not been preparing them for the freedom and responsibility of adulthood, it is harder for them to become independent in a healthy way. If there are no jobs available to them, if there are no means for them to set up independent households, maturing becomes that much trickier. Biblical cultures frequently saw extended families living together, so it is not geographical separation that is being taught. Learning how to parent well, for example, while living in proximity to one's own parents, if they were good models, can be extremely helpful. But even when an ancient Israelite groom brought his new bride back to his parents' home, a separate apartment or room typically would have been built, if possible, signaling some necessary separation.[9] As we saw earlier, "Leaving father and mother and cleaving to one's spouse" (Gen. 2:24) is not first of all about geographical distance but the realigning of one's most powerful allegiance and intimate attachment from parents to spouse (see chap. 2, "Family, Religion, and the Public Square").

When Millennials respect and follow their parents' wishes, they may well be obeying the fifth commandment ("honor your father and your mother"; Exod. 20:12) better than Xers and Boomers often did. But when Millennials' parents do not provide a strategy for gradually weaning their children away from financial and emotional dependence on them, they risk embittering, exasperating, and discouraging those children (against Eph. 6:4 and Col. 3:21). They also prevent the children from following God's call on their lives. If it is the children who do not adequately desire independence with accountability, then the problem lies elsewhere, for this is the timeless pattern of human

6. See further Grant R. Osborne, *Matthew* (Grand Rapids: Zondervan, 2010), 709–12.

7. See esp. Jeffrey J. Arnett, *Emerging Adulthood: The Winding Road from the Late Teens through the Twenties* (Oxford: Oxford University Press, 2004).

8. See David E. Garland, *Luke* (Grand Rapids: Zondervan, 2011), 143.

9. Glenn Kay, "Jewish Wedding Customs and the Bride of Messiah," *Congregation Netzar Torah Yeshua*, 2010, http://messianicfellowship.50webs.com/wedding.html.

maturity across cultures. Children grow, are taught, and become those who take their places of responsibility in the world to teach the generations after them. In a passage reminiscent of 1 Corinthians 3:1–4, Hebrews 5:12 berates those who still need milk rather than solid food, even though "by this time you ought to be teachers." Instead, they "need someone to teach [them] the elementary truths of God's word all over again."[10] So also twenty-somethings who are not yet prepared to cut the strings from their parents' aprons and cultivate adult relationships with them find their path to maturity blocked.

Diversity and Tolerance

Many of the attitudes concerning diversity and tolerance valued by Millennials are healthy and biblical. With texts like Galatians 3:28 so fundamental to Christian thinking, that in Christ there is "neither Jew nor Gentile," "neither slave nor free," "nor . . . male and female," racism and sexism should be forever banished, even in jest.[11] A very bright and highly educated Christian Xer told me a decade ago that he thought his generation had pretty much abolished once-and-for-all both racism and sexism, but that the biggest difficulty he and his peers faced was ageism: writing off Boomers and Silents as those from whom they could learn little and to whom they had little obligation.[12] Perhaps Millennials, with their greater respect for their "elders," will bridge this gap as well. Certainly it is a theme that permeates the entire biblical story line.[13] Indeed, it was probably not until the twentieth century in the West that any cultures began to so idolize, glamorize, and cater to the young adults in their midst. In most other times and places, the elderly were viewed as worthy of greater respect because of the wisdom they had acquired over time.[14] Countless biblical proverbs could be listed to this end. Proverbs 30:17 proves particularly poignant: "The eye that mocks a father, that scorns

10. This is a highly emphatic verse with unusual syntax and vocabulary. "Every word in this verse stresses the unnaturalness and thus the culpability of this refusal to hear." Gareth L. Cockerill, *The Epistle to the Hebrews* (Grand Rapids: Eerdmans, 2012), 256.

11. "Paul's stance disallows any extra-Christian cultural norm from becoming identified with corporate identity in Christ." Bruce Hansen, *All of You Are One: The Social Vision of Galatians 3.28, Corinthians 12.13 and Colossians 3.11* (London: T&T Clark, 2010), 103.

12. See, e.g., the wealth of materials available on the website of the Assisted Living Federation of America, http://www.alfa.org/alfa/Ageism.asp.

13. See esp. R. Alastair Campbell, *The Elders: Seniority within Earliest Christianity* (Edinburgh: T&T Clark, 1994).

14. See, e.g., Tim G. Parkin, "The Status of Older People: Ancient and Biblical Worlds," in *Encyclopedia of Aging* (New York: Macmillan, 2002), http://www.encyclopedia.com/doc/1G2-3402200386.html.

an aged mother, will be pecked out by the ravens of the valley, will be eaten by the vultures."[15] Conversely, Leviticus 19:32 enshrines as part of the holiness code the law that commands God's people to stand up in the presence of the aged, show respect for the elderly, and revere their God. (In cultures where standing does not necessarily connote respect, other gestures may replace it.) The point is clear: at least partially parallel to revering God is showing respect for those who deserve it because of what they have experienced, what they may currently be suffering, and what they can pass on to younger cohorts.[16]

The problem comes when the concepts of diversity and tolerance are extended beyond treating people fairly and graciously across all humanly erected divisions and categories to mean endorsing, or at least not objecting to, every possible lifestyle or set of behaviors. Of course, no one actually does tolerate everything. Most people would draw the line at pedophilia, rape, murder, major theft or vandalism, torture, false witness, and the like. Many people claim to promote religious tolerance but exclude evangelical Christians from that tolerance![17] But propaganda from the media, educational systems, the church, and various subcultures or subgroups with which they affiliate can repeat certain beliefs, convictions, and slogans complete with fallacious reasoning and gross inconsistencies so often that people become oblivious to them. Pro-abortion becomes pro-choice, even if the unborn infant has no choice. Gay orientations are said to be genetically caused, even though no scientific evidence has yet found more than a small fraction of such a disposition to be based in nature rather than nurture.[18] Heterosexual freedom to copulate with any consenting adult is redefined as a human right rather than recognizing sexual intercourse as a privilege of married people to enjoy with their spouse, as most other eras and cultures in human history have affirmed.[19]

At this point, those who accept biblical authority cannot simply decide ethical questions based on what most promotes diversity or tolerance; they must wrestle with multiple texts in Scripture that bear on each topic. They

15. "Aged" appears in the Septuagint, the Syriac, and the Targum, not the Masoretic Text, but there is some evidence that the Hebrew "obey" (as in the ESV—"scorns to obey a mother") is corrupt here and originally read "gray hair." See Bruce K. Waltke, *The Book of Proverbs Chapters 15–31* (Grand Rapids: Eerdmans, 2005), 459–60n49.

16. Gordon J. Wenham cross-references Isa. 3:5 and remarks, "A society which fails to honor the old is on the brink of destruction." *The Book of Leviticus* (Grand Rapids: Eerdmans, 1979), 273.

17. See esp. D. A. Carson, *The Intolerance of Tolerance* (Grand Rapids: Eerdmans, 2012).

18. Linda L. Belleville, *Sex, Lies, and the Truth: Developing a Christian Ethic in a Post-Christian Society* (Eugene, OR: Wipf & Stock, 2010), 61–64.

19. For a comprehensive treatment of biblical sexual ethics in contrast to contemporary culture, see Daniel R. Heimbach, *True Sexual Morality: Recovering Biblical Standards for a Culture in Crisis* (Wheaton: Crossway, 2004).

must adopt and articulate a defensible hermeneutic for sifting the timeless from the culture-bound. They must incorporate all of Scripture's teaching on a topic, not just their preferred texts. William Webb's redemptive trajectories, popularized in his book *Slaves, Women and Homosexuals* in 2001, offers a good illustration.[20] Webb argues that if one traces *prescriptive* (not just merely descriptive) teaching chronologically from Genesis to Revelation, one will either find that a controversial practice is increasingly promoted or tolerated, increasingly rejected, or that there is no change in the Bible's teaching at all. With respect to the issue of slavery, it is *never* commanded in the Bible, only legislated; it becomes increasingly infrequent among God's people; and the New Testament in several places sows the seeds that point directly toward its abolition. It is therefore not only appropriate but incumbent on Christians after the first century down through church history to work for the abolition of all forms of human slavery.

With respect to women, Webb argues for the identical trajectory. Here he does see some prescriptive statements about what women cannot do, especially early in biblical history. But he perceives a growing openness to their participation in all roles in the home, church, and society, so that he believes it is right for Christians to follow this trajectory further to full gender egalitarianism throughout the church age. I personally agree with Webb on his analysis of slavery in the Bible, but I would want to tweak his summary with respect to gender roles slightly.[21] But my point in raising the example of his method is not to commend every jot and tittle of it, merely to use it as an illustration of the kind of consistency in one's hermeneutic that is needed.

I agree entirely with Webb's perceptions of the biblical teaching when he turns to homosexuality. Leaving aside possibly unanswerable questions about "orientations," Webb correctly observes that every reference to homosexual *sex*—achieving sexual climax with a person of the same sex—is in both testaments treated as outside God's will. He therefore finds no justification for this form of same-sex activity for the Christian. Celibacy is the correct option for those of homosexual orientation, just as it is for the unmarried heterosexual.[22] That our contemporary Western cultures, including too often our Christian

20. William J. Webb, *Slaves, Women and Homosexuals: Exploring the Hermeneutics of Cultural Analysis* (Downers Grove, IL: InterVarsity, 2001).

21. In other words, I would argue that the restriction of the "highest" authoritative teaching office among God's people to men, while women have freedom to function in any other role, is consistent in all parts of Scripture. See Webb's own update in "A Redemptive-Movement Hermeneutic: Encouraging Dialogue among Four Evangelical Views," *Journal of the Evangelical Theological Society* 48 (2005): 331–49.

22. For the definitive exegetical treatment of the whole topic, see Robert J. A. Gagnon, *The Bible and Homosexual Practice: Texts and Hermeneutics* (Nashville: Abingdon, 2001).

circles, routinely believe and behave otherwise does not count as evidence against this interpretation of Scripture. The Bible is replete with the prolonged idolatry and sexual misbehavior of ancient Israel without condoning it. Here is where Boomers have an advantage over Millennials. Many of us know or can remember real people who lived rich and rewarding lives but never married, Christian and non-Christian alike, who were also lifelong celibates.

The entire epistle of Jude could be subtitled "The Limits of Tolerance."[23] Tolerance cannot be the one absolute value left in an otherwise relativistic world! One who claims to submit to the lordship of Christ will place very clear limits on tolerance. Even when people right in our churches teach otherwise, we must reread Jude 4: "For certain individuals whose condemnation was written about long ago have secretly slipped in among you. They are ungodly people, who pervert the grace of our God into a license for immorality and deny Jesus Christ our only Sovereign and Lord." The thought here is not that these people outwardly or explicitly deny Jesus. No sects or heresies in early Christianity did that. They could hardly continue to claim to be following Christ in any sense if they did. Rather what Jude is saying is that those who exploit God's grace by turning it into a license to sin—not just momentary lapses, even severe ones, but a characteristic lifestyle of flouting biblical ethics—demonstrate that they do not know the Jesus they claim to be following.[24]

What, then, about Matthew 7:1 ("Do not judge, or you too will be judged")? This is one of the most misused verses in the Bible, especially by non-Christians![25] As with all scriptural texts, it must be read within its larger context. The NIV rightly includes it with verses 2–6 in a section given the label "Judging Others." Verses 2–5 proceed to ask why people try to take specks out of their spiritual brothers' or sisters' eyes when they have planks in their own eyes (vv. 3–4). Jesus then exclaims, "You hypocrite, first take the plank out of your own eye, and then you will see clearly to remove the speck from your brother's [or sister's] eye" (v. 5). If Jesus's point in verse 1 had been never to call anyone's behavior wrong, inappropriate, or immoral, then he could not have added verse 5. We are to assist our fellow believers in behaving morally, but we are to address our own immorality as well.[26]

---

23. See D. A. Carson and Douglas J. Moo, *An Introduction to the New Testament*, 2nd ed. (Grand Rapids: Zondervan, 2005), 694.

24. Thomas R. Schreiner, *1, 2 Peter, Jude* (Nashville: Broadman and Holman, 2003), 440.

25. Sandra Dimas, "A Look at 10 (or So) Commonly Misunderstood Bible Verses," *Reasons to Believe*, March 9, 2012, http://www.reasons.org/blogs/take-two/a-look-at-10-or-so-commonly -misunderstood-bible-verses.

26. "Matthew encourages believers to help other believers, but it must be done with credibility and proper decorum (cf. Matt 18:15–20)." Craig A. Evans, *Matthew* (Cambridge: Cambridge University Press, 2012), 163.

Verse 6 makes this even clearer. The Greek verb *krinō* for "judge" has about as broad a semantic range as its English equivalent. It can mean "make a selection," "pass judgment on (and therefore to seek to influence) the lives and actions of other people," "express an opinion about," "criticize, find fault, condemn," "think, consider, look upon," "reach a decision, propose, intend," "hale before a court," or "hand over for judicial punishment."[27] Clearly, not all of these meanings are negative ones. What kind of judgment does verse 1 preclude, and what kinds are not in view at all? Verse 6 clearly calls on people to analyze others' nature and assess their probable reactions to trying to teach them gospel truths. With vivid imagery, Jesus declares, "Do not give dogs what is sacred; do not throw your pearls to pigs. If you do, they may trample them under their feet, and turn and tear you to pieces." We cannot possibly obey this command without judging in order to assess who is currently acting like a dog or a pig![28]

Paul in 1 Corinthians 4 discloses that he cares very little whether he is judged by the Corinthians or any human court. Indeed, he does not even judge himself (v. 3). What can this possibly mean? Verses 4–5 help us answer the question. In verse 4, Paul insists he has a clear conscience but knows that he is forgetful and fallen. Ultimately, only God's judgment matters. In verse 5, Paul is concerned that people too often judge prematurely, without adequate information.[29] Yet chapter 5 shows that Paul is not averse, in extreme circumstances, to rendering judicial-like verdicts in the church. A persistent, unrepentant sinner who is flaunting his misbehavior under the guise of freedom in Christ must be disciplined by the congregation, Paul insists (5:1–5).

Still, every time the New Testament teaches church discipline, it is always remedial or rehabilitative in intent.[30] Second Corinthians 2:5–11 suggests that the discipline proved effective, that the man has repented, and Paul urges the Corinthians to welcome him back into their fellowship.[31] Jesus teaches

27. W. Bauer et al., eds., *Greek-English Lexicon of the New Testament and Other Early Christian Literature*, 2nd ed. (Chicago: University of Chicago Press, 1979), s.v. "*krinō*," 567–69.

28. See D. A. Carson, "Matthew," in *Expositor's Bible Commentary*, ed. Tremper Longman III and David E. Garland, rev. ed. (Grand Rapids: Zondervan, 2010), 9:221.

29. "Paul does not therefore advocate a thick-skinned indifference to public opinion; his point is a different one, namely, its fallibility, relativity, and limits which make it an unreliable guide on which to depend. Everything must be left with God in the last analysis, and one should give privilege to one's own introspective assessments." Anthony C. Thiselton, *The First Epistle to the Corinthians* (Grand Rapids: Eerdmans, 2000), 341.

30. See esp. Jonathan Leeman, *Church Discipline: How the Church Protects the Name of Jesus* (Wheaton: Crossway, 2012).

31. Some commentators think this is a different man from the disciplined offender of 1 Cor. 5:1–5, but see esp. Colin G. Kruse, "The Offender and the Offense in 2 Corinthians 2:5 and 7:12," *Evangelical Quarterly* 60 (1988): 129–39.

in Matthew 18:15–17 that as a last resort, in order to bring a sinning church member to repentance, the congregation must "treat them as you would a pagan or a tax collector." But Jesus proved surprisingly solicitous toward pagans and tax collectors and other outsiders. At the same time he consistently called them to repentance; he did not treat them like they were already his followers.[32] So it is appropriate for a church to tell a member under discipline that they should not occupy offices, exercise roles, or participate in activities reserved entirely for Christians. But Jesus is not envisioning excommunication, which rarely wins people back but simply alienates them further. He is suggesting a combination of withholding certain privileges while coming alongside and loving the wayward deeply, looking for any possible way to woo them back to God and to facilitate repentance and reinstatement as a Christian in good standing.[33]

The problem for Millennials is that they have seen precious few examples of this being handled well. Indeed, all three of our cohorts have seen too few examples, but since Millennials have lived fewer years than Xers and Boomers, they will on average have seen fewer still. Either churches don't even try to obey biblical teaching about church discipline, turning a blind eye to the most egregious sins of both leaders and members in the name of grace and forgiveness, or they exercise discipline in a heavy-handed way that does not clearly communicate to the offender (or to the congregation) the church's sole desire to win the person back to a godly lifestyle *for his or her own benefit*. Little wonder that too many Millennials want just to avoid even the proper forms of judgment that the Bible calls Christians to exercise. But they must resist the temptation.[34]

Celebrating Individualism

Elisabeth notes that both Xers and Millennials value individualism more than Boomers do. But while Xers often exercise individualism as an act of protest against confinement, Millennials do it as an act of celebration (see chap. 7, "Millennials' Place in the World"). This would appear to be an improvement over the protest motive, but as we have seen with Xers, individualism in the Bible is always trumped by concern for others, especially in groups—the family, the neighborhood, the tribe, the community, the nation, or the church. It

---

32. See further Craig L. Blomberg, *1 Corinthians* (Grand Rapids: Zondervan, 1994), 107–15.
33. See Wilkins, *Matthew*, 619.
34. Hence, in the realm of parenting, the classic little work of James Dobson, *Dare to Discipline*, rev. ed. (Carol Stream, IL: Tyndale House, 1992).

can be healthy and honest when Millennials refuse to speak for anyone but themselves if they are truly expressing just personal opinions. How often did we Boomers try to manipulate our parents and their peers by saying things like, "But everyone's doing it," or "I've got to have x to be considered cool"? Sometimes what we referred to *was* a significant subcultural trend, but often we simply meant, "My three closest friends are doing it and are putting pressure on me to do it!" If Boomers have found status from "big toys" like homes, cars, or boats, and if Xers have found status from "small toys" like designer jeans or trendy handbags, it is significant that Elisabeth does not list in her chapter a comparable kind of toy that Millennials value as a whole. She describes Millennials' lower priority of materialistic pursuits for some subcultures of Millennials or with less focus on a handful of very expensive items, which is both in line with Scripture and holds out promise for improving the church.

On the other hand, when individualism reduces to personal opinion or preference something that is in reality a timeless truth, then Millennials hurt the very convictions for which they claim to stand. For example, it would be absurd to tell someone, "If you want to jump off that high-rise building and take your life, that's your business; I prefer not to commit suicide, at least this year." Life created in God's image is too precious to be treated with such a cavalier attitude, at least from a Christian perspective. But it is equally absurd for a Christian high school student to say to her close friend (who also calls herself a Christian) who has set for herself the goal of sleeping with eighteen different boys by her eighteenth birthday, "Who am I to say you shouldn't do that? It's just my personal preference that I am not going to imitate you in that." With even secular studies showing the long-term difficulties of ever achieving and sustaining emotional intimacy with any partner or friend the more promiscuous one has been, there are good reasons why people should care enough to lay aside their individualism and do as much as they can to prevent such detrimental behavior.[35] And that is completely apart from the standard warnings about STDs and pregnancies, against which no form of contraception is foolproof, much less the biblical teaching against "fornication."[36]

Where individualism overlaps with appreciating each person's uniqueness, it again is valuable from a biblical perspective. We think once more of

35. See, e.g., J. Budziszewski, "Why Hooking Up Is Letting You Down," *Intercollegiate Review*, November 25, 2013, http://www.intercollegiatereview.com/index.php/2013/11/25/why-hooking-up-is-letting-you-down/.

36. To use the language of the KJV. Modern Bible translations sometimes appear not to proscribe premarital sex anywhere, but this stems from the difficulty of translating the Greek *porneia*. This term refers to a wide range of sexual immorality, including but not limited to premarital sex, which is prohibited in Mark 7:21 par.; 1 Cor. 6:13, 18; 2 Cor. 12:21; Gal. 5:19; Eph. 5:3; Col. 3:5; and 1 Thess. 4:3.

Scripture's theology of spiritual gifting. With even identical twins never being exactly alike, human beings are like snowflakes, each one created differently. We hurt each other when we try to remake others in our own image, or any single image, rather than helping one another understand the unique ways in which God has made, wired, and gifted them. Proverbs 22:6 has frequently been misinterpreted, if not even mistranslated. The King James Version is by far the best known: "Train up a child in the way he should go: and when he is old, he will not depart from it." While "the way he should go" most probably refers primarily to teaching children timeless principles of godliness, the Hebrew more literally means "train a youth according to his way," that is, according to a child's unique character, passions, interests, and abilities.[37] So this secondary meaning cannot be excluded. The New Jerusalem Bible sounds a bit colloquial but captures this sense: "Give a lad a training suitable to his character." This kind of Millennial individualism is eminently biblical.

On the other hand, when individualism, perhaps coupled with being "real and honest," becomes an excuse for not seeking increased transformation in godly living, then the Christian who is evaluating trends by biblical teaching will have to demur. A point that applies every bit as much to our earlier comments about judgment is often overlooked: unless someone's physical well-being is under imminent threat, just because Christians see their friends doing something unbiblical doesn't mean it is always their responsibility to point it out on the spot. When one can reasonably accurately predict that a person's response will be only hostile, it may be better to wait for a more "teachable moment." A good friend of mine who pastored a storefront church and coffeehouse, which was open to but not affirming of gay individuals, tells the story of the time two gay men started coming to the church. My friend prayed, "Lord, please don't let them ask me anything about my views on sexual lifestyle until they are ready to hear them." Many people were welcoming, some remained aloof, but fortunately no one scared the two men off. They began to understand the gospel message and speak more and more as if they were becoming believers. Eight or nine months after they first visited, they asked to talk with my friend. "You've never said anything explicitly about it, but we're guessing you don't think a gay lifestyle is consistent with Christianity. Is that right?" Breathing deeply and praying some more, the pastor quietly responded, "That's true." After a long pause, one of the men said, "Yeah, that's the view we think we've been coming to as well."[38] If only there

37. Robert L. Alden, *Proverbs: A Commentary on an Ancient Book of Timeless Advice* (Grand Rapids: Baker Books, 1983), 160–61.
38. Recounted by John Swanger, founding pastor of the Tollgate Coffeehouse and host to Scum of the Earth Church, Denver, Colorado, in the early 2000s.

could be many more such stories to recount! Many Boomers need to learn to wait and pray like my friend did. Many Millennials need to be prepared to answer the question in the same way my friend did when it is finally posed.

Optimism for the Future (and Entitlement versus Expectancy)

If they understood the Bible's overall story line, Christians would be the most optimistic of all people on the planet. If Xers can lead the way in reminding the world of the reality of sin, Millennials have the potential to put Christian eschatology back on center stage. But this time it would not be with the tired old debates about different forms of millennialism, or views of the timing of the rapture, or endless conversations about just how similar or different the church and Israel are. Rather, it would be by reminding the church and the world that the Christian hope is far more glorious than most people realize (see Rev. 21–22).[39] It would stress that Christianity, unlike Eastern religions, is linear rather than cyclical. And unlike the other Western religions that *are* linear, it has full assurance of the culmination in a grand finale for God's people.[40] But more than this, God is working through his people and throughout the world right now, making it a better place than it once was, even with all the evil that still exists. And he has assured his people that they will see a far better world still. The ultimate Christian hope is not that of disembodied heaven but of what Tom Wright has so beautifully called "life *after* life after death"—the new heavens and new earth.[41] Christian communities—as outposts or colonies of the new heavens and new earth, helping advance the "already" of the "already but not yet" kingdom of God on earth—model before a watching world small glimpses of the kind of world God envisions and is in the process of bringing about.

To the extent that this is the kind of change in which Millennials believe, then by all means they should go for it! To the extent that Millennials want to focus attention on the here and now and make a difference in their world while keeping a firm grip on future realities, then so much the better. But if a proper concern for what the church can and should look like in this age, along with the social ministries in which it should be engaged, squeezes out

---

39. Three excellent recent books sharing this emphasis are Dinesh D'Souza, *Life after Death: The Evidence* (Washington, DC: Regnery, 2009); Paula Gooder, *Heaven* (Eugene, OR: Cascade, 2011); and Anthony C. Thiselton, *Life after Death: A New Approach to the Last Things* (Grand Rapids: Eerdmans, 2012).

40. See N. T. Wright, *Surprised by Hope: Rethinking Heaven, the Resurrection, and the Mission of the Church* (New York: HarperOne, 2008).

41. Ibid., 197.

a concern for evangelism and saving lost souls, then, to put it bluntly, all we have done is made the road to hell more comfortable for others. For the last fifty years Ron Sider has championed social justice perhaps more than any evangelical in America when it seemed like that part of the biblical message was getting short shrift. Now, however, he has recently written an open letter to younger evangelicals pleading with them not to jettison concern for people's spiritual salvation, because he senses they have swung the pendulum too far in the opposite direction by focusing solely on social transformation.[42]

Similar contrasts emerge. When Millennials have well-placed expectations about how humans ought to treat one another and God, they may be capturing the sense of the Great Commandment (love of God and neighbor; Matt. 22:37–40) better than other cohorts often have. But when expectancy does indeed turn into entitlement, then they have some growing up to do. Still, all generations today seem to be inflicted by some considerable measure of entitlement, except for times of catastrophe or crisis that rally the populace to give sacrificially of themselves. Paul demonstrates the fascinating ability to forgo all justice for himself in certain situations when it is for the long-term betterment of the church as a whole. But he can turn around and strenuously support justice for others who are oppressed. In the same context of his initial ministry in Philippi, he exorcises the slave girl possessed by a Pythian spirit of fortune telling even though it gets him arrested when her irate owners protest to the city officials. He deliberately chooses not to avoid time in prison by disclosing his Roman citizenship, which would have prevented detention only for himself and Silas. But the next morning, after the providentially timed earthquake that secured his freedom and the jailer's salvation, when the authorities want him to leave town quietly, he does play his trump card. This is no way to have treated a citizen, and the authorities are forced to make a public admission that he has committed no crime, thus ensuring for the coming days the legal well-being of the fledgling church in Philippi.[43] Millennials should likewise move heaven and earth to seek justice for others, especially the most disenfranchised, but be very careful if the sole or main reason for supporting other causes is self-interest.

Commitment versus Lack of Commitment

Despite countless parents who (usually selfishly) nag at their daughters about when they will get married and, if married, when they will start to have

---

42. Ron Sider, "An Open Letter to This Generation, Pt. 1," *Relevant*, March 14, 2011, http://www.relevantmagazine.com/god/deeper-walk/features/24972-an-open-letter-to-this-generation-pt-1.

43. David G. Peterson, *The Acts of the Apostles* (Grand Rapids: Eerdmans, 2009), 471–74.

children, I applaud Millennials' decisions overall to postpone marriage and childbearing. If their general maturity has been delayed, then these decisions make good sense. Their marriages will stand a better chance of lasting, and their parenting skills can only be better if a little more time elapses. Calls for young adults to marry and have children even earlier than their preceding cohorts may be well-intended, but if a couple is emotionally and spiritually immature, early marriage and parenting becomes a recipe for disaster.[44] That the divorce rate is finally starting to go down a little, concurrent with the average age of first marriages being at an all-time high in living memory, suggests that Millennials, as a whole, have made some good decisions in these areas. But if the main reason certain people postpone marriage is that they are simply fulfilling their sexual desires with others outside wedlock, then those decisions displease the Lord.

Millennials' commitment to balance work and family/personal time, even though this translates into less commitment to the workplace, can be healthy from a Christian perspective. Jesus put it plainly, "Watch out! Be on your guard against all kinds of greed; life does not consist in an abundance of possessions" (Luke 12:15).[45] But where, as with Xers, a recurring unwillingness to commit to relationships stems from the fear that something better could always be lurking around the corner, a lack of trust in God's sovereignty and providential guidance is present, whether or not it is recognized. God does not predetermine one and only one perfect spouse, job, home, set of friends, church, school, or club for us, leaving us to play a lifelong guessing game with him as to whether we have found them or not! Short of direct, supernatural communication with us, he calls on us to make responsible decisions in keeping with his revealed will in Scripture about moral living and then to keep the commitments we make.[46] In Acts 15:28, after the complex and contested apostolic council in Jerusalem where the role of the law in Christian salvation was discussed, the best James and his colleagues could say to the churches was, "It seemed good to the Holy Spirit and to us"![47] When Paul and his coworkers one chapter later are seeking God's will as to where they should turn after

---

44. E.g., Al Mohler, "The Case for (Early) Marriage," August 3, 2009, http://www.albert mohler.com/2009/08/03/the-case-for-early-marriage/.

45. Or perhaps "superfluity of possessions." The meaning of *perisseuein* is "to overflow," hence, to have that which is not being used and should therefore better be in others' hands. See Christopher M. Hays, *Luke's Wealth Ethics: A Study in Their Coherence and Character* (Tübingen: Mohr Siebeck, 2010), 126n182.

46. See esp. Garry Friesen with J. Robin Maxson, *Decision Making and the Will of God*, rev. ed. (Colorado Springs: Multnomah, 2004).

47. Commentators stress that by adding reference to the Spirit for the first time in the context of this council, James adds an element of authority not explicitly present earlier in the passage,

revisiting cities evangelized on Paul's first missionary journey, the Spirit of the Lord prevents them from going to various locations (16:5–8). We would dearly love to know how, but Luke chose not to tell us. What is important is that they did not sit back and wait for special revelation from the Lord; they knew their mission, and so they pressed on and let circumstances stop them if necessary.[48] Eventually it became clear where they were supposed to minister (vv. 9–10).

Or consider a quite different area of seeking God's will. I have made a commitment to my wife "until death do us part." I cannot control her actions if, by some scenario that is virtually impossible for me to imagine, she would choose to leave me after thirty-five years. But I do have control over my own actions. No amount of supposed personal happiness gives me permission, as a believer, to renege on my promise. Indeed, almost any area of life depends on promises (or contracts, covenants, or laws) being kept in some substantial measure. When they are not kept, society and social order break down. For anyone, Christian or otherwise, who cherishes democracy, keeping promises and commitments even at the expense of personal happiness should be one of their very highest values.[49]

Genuine Affirmation versus False Self-Esteem

I don't recall consciously doing much as a parent to build self-esteem in my daughters as they were growing up. They were both very talented in a variety of ways, so there were plenty of opportunities for me to genuinely praise them. I rarely pushed them into activities they weren't interested in, or for which they felt very inadequate, unless there was a compelling reason (e.g., if it would be a required subject for several more years in school). I never praised them or gave them a prize or trophy for something they did not deserve. But I was still honestly surprised when each of them, already in grade school, came home on different occasions ranting about the stupidity of some policy or practice that rewarded all students alike for very diverse levels of performance in some task. The competitive spirit seems fairly innate in most human beings, even if

---

but the expression still remains surprisingly mild, esp. also in light of the closing of the letter in v. 29: "you will do well to avoid these things."

48. See further Gene L. Green, "Finding the Will of God: Historical and Modern Perspectives—Acts 16:1–30," in *Mission in Acts: Ancient Narratives in Contemporary Context*, ed. Robert L. Gallagher and Paul Hertig (Maryknoll, NY: Orbis, 2004), 209–20.

49. Numbers 23:19 defines promise keeping as part of the very character of God. Therefore, as we are increasingly remade in his image, it should characterize believers' lives as well. Num. 30:6 and 8 therefore warn against rash promises that one does not keep.

it manifests itself differently, and they understood that it simply wasn't fair to reward students for shoddy work and half-hearted efforts.

I fear that a generation of public school policies designed to mainstream students and instill self-esteem in every child has too often overdone things. Even children who don't perform well know they don't deserve accolades, so self-esteem is hardly instilled by inappropriate affirmation. Christians from my parents' generation have often told me stories about growing up in schools or churches in which not enough praise was given even to children who did well or tried hard, so I have no doubt that a mid-course correction was needed. My sense is that Boomers, as a whole, had better experiences in public schools but not necessarily in churches or church schools. Today, too many public schools seem to have swung the pendulum too far in an opposite direction, while evangelical churches may be achieving a better balance than in past eras.[50]

At the same time, I have heard of liberal Protestant churches, led by Baby Boomers, refusing to sing "Amazing Grace" because of the line John Newton penned about being a "wretch." Perhaps their self-esteem has been so poor throughout their lives that they cannot cope with what is in fact a profound theological truth. But the Millennials and Xers at my church, hardly a bastion of social conservatism, welcome singing lines like "There is a fountain filled with blood drawn from Immanuel's veins," "sin has left its crimson stain; he washed it white as snow," and "saved a wretch like me." From many of their horrible pasts, they know the truth. They don't need someone to lie to them and tell them they have always been basically good people just corrupted by society; they know better than that. What they need is not self-esteem but a healthy dose of "God-esteem"—understanding how deeply God loves them and values them despite their wretchedness. And he loves them too much to let them stay where they are, wallowing in their sins; he wants to remake them into the holy, loving image-bearers they were created to be. This is the message that permeates both testaments of the Bible. Without this understanding of the human person, it is difficult to see how churches or individuals can properly be called Christian.[51]

If Millennials are going to be successful parents, they will have to rid themselves of the notion that "only positive reinforcement will be used to modify or correct behavior" (see "A Sense of Self in Comparison to Others" in chap. 7). The Bible is replete with teaching about how loving parents discipline their

50. Kay Hymowitz ("What the Experts Are Saying Now," *Wall Street Journal*, August 5, 2009) discusses the growing evidence that shows the general failure of secular self-esteem movements in schools.

51. See esp. James R. Beck and Bruce Demarest, *The Human Person in Psychology and Theology: A Biblical Anthropology for the Twenty-First Century* (Grand Rapids: Kregel, 2005).

children, just as God disciplines his spiritual children (see esp. Heb. 12:5–11).[52] Of course, one can do one's best to maximize positive reinforcement, but when children are in one of those moods in which they are bound and determined to do something harmful to themselves or others, negative consequences often become necessary. A loving parent will want to protect their children with discipline.

Only One Way?

The final topic this chapter will consider is the proper response to religious pluralism. Three broad approaches to the question of the destiny of those who do not follow Jesus as Savior and Lord compete for acceptance. The *restrictivist* argues that one must consciously profess faith in Jesus to be saved. The *universalist* affirms that one day all people who have ever lived will be saved. The *pluralist* believes there are multiple ways to salvation, but that not everyone will be saved. Each of these main categories can be further subdivided. Some restrictivists assume that only those who have heard the gospel from some other person or from a written document can truly trust in Christ; others highlight how Jesus may reveal himself through an angel, a special appearance of himself, a dream, or the promptings of the Holy Spirit apart from these more common forms of communication. Some universalists believe in purgatory or a finite hell, so that unbelievers do suffer for their sins, just not eternally; others envision a second chance at salvation after death (based on one interpretation of 1 Pet. 3:18–22 and 4:6); still others believe everyone is forgiven on judgment day by a loving and merciful God because "all roads lead to heaven." Pluralists can envision people coming to faith through two or more different religions or ideologies. Or they may stress that it is only on the basis of Christ's death that anyone is saved, but that doesn't mean everyone who is saved must have heard of Christ. They may come to saving faith in spite of their religion, but not through it. This latter view is sometimes separated off from pluralism and called inclusivism.[53]

A good way to gain clarity on this debate is to consider the Bible's teaching on the fate of people before the time of Jesus. Clearly, many ancient Israelites were brought into right relationship with God without ever having heard in advance any of the details of Jesus's life. Indeed, they did not even know who

52. On which, see esp. N. Clayton Croy, *Endurance in Suffering: Hebrews 12:1–13 in Its Rhetorical, Religious, and Philosophical Context* (Cambridge: Cambridge University Press, 1998).

53. See further Gabriel Fackre, Ronald H. Nash, and John Sanders, *What about Those Who Have Never Heard? Three Views on the Destiny of the Unevangelized* (Downers Grove, IL: InterVarsity, 1995).

their Messiah would be, despite great curiosity (1 Pet. 1:10–12). The further back in time from the first century one proceeds, the less well defined their messianic hope itself was. Ancient Jews were made righteous by their faith in God's provisions for the forgiveness of their sins (see Gen. 15:6; Hab. 2:4). They trusted in God as best they understood him from what he had revealed of himself to them.[54]

Was a Jew living, say, in rural Spain in January of AD 30, who was right with God through trusting in his promises and seeking to follow the law as a lifestyle of faithfulness, suddenly no longer right with God in June of that same year just because the "new covenant age" had now begun after Jesus's death and resurrection? That would seem extraordinarily perverse. But then perhaps "BC" means "before Christ through the gospel comes to any community or individual." Sir Norman Anderson, a leading evangelical scholar of world religions in the 1970s and 1980s, wrote of grace as the watershed that separated true Christianity from false forms of the religion as well as from all other world religions and worldviews. Every other ideology and -ism depends to a significant degree on human performance—"works righteousness," to use the theological expression. If anyone outside Christianity should trust in God, however he has revealed himself to him or her, Anderson would affirm that they might well be acceptable to him.[55] Romans 2:14–16 talks about the gentile who does not have the law doing by nature what the law requires and being in some instance excused by God on judgment day.[56]

The obvious objection to this line of reasoning proceeds as follows. Does this then mean that it is possible for someone to be saved outside the knowledge of Christ, subsequently hear the gospel, and reject it? If that were possible, then we should never commend Christianity to anyone, lest we lead someone who was right with God to be alienated from him! The most straightforward reply to this objection would be to affirm that all who hear a credible retelling of the gospel in the context of a loving ministry and who reject it thereby

54. See further James M. Hamilton Jr., *God's Glory in Salvation through Judgment: A Biblical Theology* (Wheaton: Crossway, 2010), 67–353.

55. Sir Norman Anderson, ed., *The World's Religions*, rev. ed. (Grand Rapids: Eerdmans, 1976), 134.

56. Three main options compete for acceptance in the interpretation of this passage: (1) the hypothetical view—that if one could perfectly keep whatever divine laws one has been given, one would acquire salvation; but no one ever does; (2) the gentile-Christian interpretation that takes "by nature" to modify "do not have by law" rather than "do"; and (3) the view we have sketched out here. For a defense of (1), see Douglas J. Moo, *The Epistle to the Romans* (Grand Rapids: Eerdmans, 1996), 144–57; for (2), see C. E. B. Cranfield, *A Critical and Exegetical Commentary on the Epistle to the Romans* (Edinburgh: T&T Clark, 1975), 1:155–63; for (3), James D. G. Dunn, *Romans 1–8* (Dallas: Word, 1988), 94–107. It would seem that position (3) has the fewest problems attached to it.

demonstrate that they were never previously saved. Otherwise they would have recognized the gospel as ringing true to what they already believed, and they would have accepted it.[57] These convictions could be viewed as embracing a limited form of pluralism or inclusivism. Alternately, they could be thought to embody an expanded form of restrictivism.

On either classification, there are still other variations of this perspective on the question of the destiny of the unevangelized. Many Calvinists simply believe that God has elected some but not all humans to salvation; so if it is possible for anyone to be saved without consciously trusting in Jesus, it will be whoever his elect are, whether or not they have explicitly heard about Jesus. Many Wesleyan-Arminians argue that God's omniscience allows him to know ahead of time how every person who has ever lived *would have responded* to the gospel had they been given the opportunity, and he judges them on the basis of that response. A handful of otherwise orthodox Christians down through the centuries have interpreted 1 Peter 3:18–22 in conjunction with 4:6 as meaning that people get a chance after death to respond to the gospel if they have not already availed themselves of that opportunity in this life.[58]

A fascinating perspective known as "middle knowledge" attempts to mediate between classic Calvinism and classic Arminianism. Middle knowledge postulates that God's omniscience is so great that it extends to God's ability to know in advance *not only* the free, future decisions of all those beings he has created in his image for relationship with him *but also* all the free, future decisions of all possibly created beings. As long as the number of people God has created remains finite, there will always be more possibly created beings that God hasn't in fact created. So the Calvinist emphasis on God's sovereignty and free grace is maintained because God has chosen to actualize a finite subset of the infinite set of possibly created beings, knowing that some will reject him. But the Arminian emphasis on God responding to human choice and free will is likewise preserved.[59] Middle knowledge, in turn, can be held by those who hold to libertarian free will (the ability to choose the contrary of one's deepest desires) as well as to those who hold to compatibilist free will (the ability, at times, to choose only one's deepest desires).[60] But that debate need not detain us here.

---

57. E.g., Don Richardson, *Eternity in Their Hearts*, rev. ed. (Ventura, CA: Regal, 1984).

58. For a full history of the variety of approaches to the topic throughout Christian history, see John Sanders, *No Other Name: An Investigation into the Destiny of the Unevangelized* (Grand Rapids: Eerdmans, 1992).

59. See esp. William L. Craig, *The Only Wise God: The Compatibility of Divine Foreknowledge and Human Freedom* (Eugene, OR: Wipf & Stock, 2000).

60. For the former, see ibid. For the latter, see Terrance L. Tiessen, *Providence and Prayer: How Does God Work in the World?* (Downers Grove, IL: InterVarsity, 2000).

To the extent that they educate themselves about such matters, then, Millennials are uniquely poised to enter the conversations about the destiny of the unevangelized. There are numerous options besides pure restrictivism throughout the history of Christianity. And *pure* restrictivism has not been nearly as common throughout church history as many modern believers sometimes claim. Individuals, and especially Millennials, need to know the history of evangelical Christian thinking in these arenas, lest they dismiss Christianity altogether for believing that it teaches something it doesn't. John 14:6 most definitely teaches that Jesus is "the Way, the Truth and the Life; no one comes to the Father but by me." All who are ever saved are put in a restored relationship with God and come to Christ through what he accomplished on the cross. But the Bible says nothing about whether they have to hear of that atoning sacrifice.[61]

The context of John 14:6 further reinforces this understanding of the text. Jesus is reflecting with his disciples on the debate he has already stirred up repeatedly in the fourth Gospel (especially in chaps. 5–9). Can one claim to be a faithful Jew, serving God as Father, and reject the revelation and person of Jesus? Unambiguously, the Christian claim is that one cannot.[62] First John 2:23 puts it succinctly: "No one who denies the Son has the Father; whoever acknowledges the Son has the Father also." But it would make no sense for Jesus to be claiming that every faithful Israelite who lived prior to his coming was damned because they had not explicitly followed Jesus.

The key to Acts 4:12 is understanding the significance of a "name" in the ancient Mediterranean world. Names were often believed to convey something about the reality of an individual. So a "name" became shorthand for a person's "power" or "authority." Acts 4:7 makes this plain. The Sanhedrin asks Peter by what power or name he has healed a lame beggar (3:6–8). Verse 12 itself falls into two halves, forming a classic instance of synonymous parallelism: "Salvation is found in no one else, for there is no other name under heaven given to mankind by which we must be saved." No other power or person produces salvation except Jesus, but Peter cannot mean that people

---

61. Rodney A. Whitacre comments, "This verse does not address ways in which Jesus brings people to the Father, but what it does say is that no one who ends up sharing God's life will do so apart from Jesus, the unique Son of God who *is*, not just who conveys, truth and life." *John* (Downers Grove, IL: InterVarsity, 1999), 352.

62. Contra the increasingly popular two-covenants approach that argues ethnic Jews can still be saved by faithfulness to Torah apart from Christ. See further Craig L. Blomberg, "Freedom from the Law Only for Gentiles? A Non-Supersessionist Alternative to Mark Kinzer's 'Postmissionary Messianic Judaism,'" in *New Testament Theology in Light of the Church's Mission: Essays in Honor of I. Howard Marshall*, ed. Grant R. Osborne, Ray van Neste, and Jon Laansma (Eugene, OR: Wipf & Stock, 2011), 41–56.

must have literally heard the *name* "Jesus," or he would be damning every one of his own race, tribe, and religion who had preceded him![63]

If all this is true, what do we do with Romans 10:14? There Paul is appealing for people to spread the news about Jesus. He raises the rhetorical questions, "How, then, can they call on the one they have not believed in? And how can they believe in the one of whom they have not heard? And how can they hear without someone preaching to them?" Whatever one understands of the destiny of the unevangelized, it cannot be used as a disincentive for evangelism. In his famous Mars Hill speech in Athens, Paul explains the purpose of general or natural revelation as provoking humans to "seek [the Lord] and perhaps reach out for him and find him, though he is not far from any one of us" (Acts 17:27). The verbs "reach out" and "find" are in the optative mood, rarely used in the Greek of the New Testament. They must, therefore, have been deliberately chosen to reflect the high degree of uncertainty over whether many people could indeed find God this way.[64] Even if some can—and we are not told whether this is actually possible—we can't necessarily know who has done so, so we must share our faith with any who will listen. Presumably anyone who rejects a faithful and loving presentation of the gospel thereby demonstrates that they had not previously found the true and living God. And if there are any who were already forgiven, they, like everyone else who converts, will accept Christ explicitly and have the greater revelation and assurance that the new covenant of the New Testament brings.

Millennials, then, may be right to reject classic forms of restrictivism. But critical thinking about which forms of pluralism or inclusivism might be consistent with Scripture seems rare. It is not even clear whether the position just articulated should be considered a very limited form of pluralism/inclusivism or a somewhat expanded form of restrictivism. After all, even many classic restrictivists, if asked, would say that they believe babies and small children prior to an age of accountability are saved. They would usually extend that

---

63. F. F. Bruce captures the correct balance: "The name of Jesus, by which the cripple had been empowered to spring to his feet and walk, was the name with which Israel's salvation (and, as was to appear later, the salvation of the world) was inextricably bound up. The course and duty of wisdom for the rulers was therefore clear; if they refused it and persisted in their present attitude, they would bring destruction on their nation as well as on themselves.

"The founders of the great world-religions are not to be disparaged by followers of the Christian way. But of none of them can it be said that there is no saving health in anyone else; to one alone belongs the title: the Saviour of the world." *The Book of the Acts*, rev. ed. (Grand Rapids: Eerdmans, 1988), 94.

64. On the optative mood in the Greek of the New Testament, see esp. Daniel B. Wallace, *Greek Grammar beyond the Basics* (Grand Rapids: Zondervan, 1996), 480–84.

concept further to those who are profoundly mentally disabled.[65] So they are not really restricting salvation just to those who have consciously put their trust in Jesus. But it is good that these questions are being openly discussed. When I was a young adult and asked about the destiny of the unevangelized, all I ever heard was Genesis 18:25: "Will not the Judge of all the earth do right?" Undoubtedly he will, but is that all we can say?

On the other hand, many Millennials seem to be opting for more extensive pluralist or even universalist views, which, whether they realize it or not, really make explicitly Christian faith superfluous. Too often I have heard them talk about "community" as the primary or sole reason for attending church rather than corporate worship of the living God with instruction and accountability by duly authorized leadership. Boomers and Xers, to be sure, too often grew up in congregations that had too little genuine Christian community, but Millennials should not swing the pendulum to the opposite extreme and reject the main reasons for gathering together as believers![66]

Conclusion

Millennials' optimism, their respect for good parents and other leaders, their preference for tolerance over legalism and for diversity over prejudice all bode well. However they acquire it, if they do gain a balanced and healthy form of self-esteem, they may go far. Individualism as celebration often requires some community, so this too is an improvement over the Xers' individualism as protest. But there are limits to tolerance and diversity that must be maintained, and self-esteem must not replace serving others. When expectancy leads to entitlement, the classic characteristics of mature people waiting patiently for the Lord to provide in his perfect timing are too easily lost. An ability to understand why God allows suffering and to respond positively to it often disappears also.

Put otherwise, a passion for changing the world, recognizing their inexperience, better relationships with older generations, and technological acumen all bode well for Millennials to make a significant difference in the world in general and in Christian circles in particular. Inability to delay gratification, however, can prove a huge impediment. The entitlement mentality, where it genuinely exists, leads to a record frequency of the dissolution of relationships with others and with God. Doctrinally, Millennials may be the least

65. See, e.g., Ronald H. Nash, *When a Baby Dies* (Grand Rapids: Zondervan, 1999).
66. Still very helpful is David Watson, *I Believe in the Church* (Grand Rapids: Eerdmans, 1979). See also Mark Dever, *The Church: The Gospel Made Visible* (Nashville: B&H, 2012).

equipped of any generation in evangelical history to preserve historic Christian teaching about the principles of the faith that *do* matter.[67] The recognition of their need for community, however, is an encouraging development, especially when it can be fostered with the help of those from other generations who have experienced how to create and sustain it. When critical thinking and spiritual empathy can be inculcated, the ease with which Millennials can access information and interact with it at home and abroad, not least through social media, offers them a great chance to impact the world with positive Christian values.

67. See Mark Driscoll, *A Call to Resurgence: Will Christianity Have a Funeral or a Future?* (Carol Stream, IL: Tyndale House, 2013), 121.

9

Priorities for Ministry with Millennials

Getting in the Game

Teamwork, teamwork, teamwork! When I (Elisabeth) was thinking of a metaphor for this generation, nothing seemed more fitting than that of being on a team. From their infancy Millennials have been participating in teams, small groups, play-dates, and a variety of other collective social activities. While they, as individuals, may not like group work anymore than older cohorts, they have a lot of experience being a part of teams. Even the way they were parented was a collective activity! Millennials have been included, consulted, and collaborated with in nearly every decision of their lives, and it would benefit ministry leaders to include them in the discussion of what is needed to engage them in ministry today.[1]

In any team sport there are common concepts that everyone must be aware of in order to proceed. Engaging Millennials in ministry is no different. In this

---

1. See Jim Schmotzer, "The Next 'Next Generation': Born after 1980, the Optimistic and Community-Oriented Millennials Are Your Up-and-Coming Church Leaders," *Leadership* 25, no. 3 (June 2004): 65–67.

endeavor we have coaches, the players on the team, the opponents, the fans, and the game strategy. This chapter will unpack each of these key elements and their practical application within ministry to and with Millennials.

The People Involved with the Game

First off, let's make one thing clear: calling this a "game" is in no way meant to minimize or trivialize the mission at hand. It is instead meant to be a term that provides a context to which many people can relate. In many ways, this is a battle or a war for the hearts, minds, and souls of a young but powerful generation; each participant is crucial, and each play of the game is critical.

The Players on the Team

Clearly, Millennials are the players on our team in this scenario. Born between 1982 and 2001, this group of expectant, postmodern, technologically savvy, and multiculturally aware people steps onto the field with perspectives, skills, and resources unknown in previous generations. They come with a desire to be coached, along with a desire to work together as a team. Lone rangers may exist, but by and large this group of players believes that the good of the group will in turn be for the good of the individual—and vice versa. The players each come onto the field with a unique role and skill set, and must also understand the role of the other players in order for the team to work effectively. With that being said, each team member still needs and desires individual affirmation, encouragement, and coaching.

The Coaches

For this team, the coach may take on many forms, but what is important is that the coach is personally invested in who their players are collectively as well as individually. The coach is anyone who has more lived experience in a particular area and is willing to share what they have learned. In light of that, this game must involve a team of coaches, as no one person can be the expert at everything. Therefore, in this game, the coaching team may be composed of a combination of pastors, parents, bosses, teachers, older friends (whether chronologically or experientially), mentors, and lay ministry leaders. The coaching team has a big-picture perspective coupled with the ability to train, encourage, and empower the players on an individual level. As with any good coach, this team's coaches understand that the players are the ones on the field, and the coaches provide opportunities for team members to offer input, feedback, and field-condition reports.[2] At the same time, it is important for the coaches to maintain an understanding of the big picture and the long haul, casting a vision to help the players understand how each play contributes to the larger objective. The coaches in this game are not the people who simply bark commands or insist that the players do things their way. Instead, the coaches work *with* the players to cultivate, inspire, and develop the skills necessary for the team to be successful on the field.[3]

The Opponents

In this game, opponents take on multiple forms. The most obvious opponent is the broader culture that overtly and covertly goes up against the gospel. This opponent has changed over the past few decades and has new strategies and maneuvers that previous generations of players never had to go up against. It is important for coaches to hear from their players about the conditions they have experienced on the field, and what they have encountered from their opponents. For coaches to assume that the opponents today are the same as when they were young, and therefore assume that the tactics needed to counter such opponents can be the same as before, is to set the Millennial team up for failure.[4]

The less obvious and yet equally dangerous opponent is the church itself. In this game, the church can be just as detrimental and hindering as any secular opponent can be, and actually has the potential to do more damage if handled incorrectly.[5] In this case the "opponent" takes the form of a bad coach who either leads their team to destruction, or gets ignored and resented by their players due to their unrealistic expectations or outdated playbook. This is seen in churches and ministries that assume that the programs and approaches that worked in decades past will be equally effective on this new field. It is also seen in coaches who treat their players as pawns that are unable

2. See J. R. Kerr, "Open Source Activists: Forget about Implementing the Church's Vision, They Want to Help Create It," *Leadership* 30, no. 3 (June 2009): 35–38.

3. See Sam S. Rainer III, "Next Generation Needs: Leading Millennials Requires Exercising a Different Type of Authority," *Leadership* 32, no. 3 (June 2011): 49.

4. This objective can be met simply by having an intentional conversation with a Millennial for the sole purpose of hearing and learning about the norms, rules, and expectations that they perceive in their environment. This is not a time to object or correct, or a time to offer solutions or advice, but simply a time to listen and learn.

5. See David Kinnaman, *You Lost Me: Why Young Christians Are Leaving the Church . . . and Rethinking Faith* (Grand Rapids: Baker Books, 2011); and David Kinnaman and Gabe Lyons, *unChristian: What a New Generation Really Thinks about Christianity . . . and Why It Matters* (Grand Rapids: Baker Books, 2007), for narrative examples of how the church has contributed to Millennials' disinterest and disassociation with Christianity.

to understand how to play the game. When the church and coaches become the opponent, the players are likely to lose interest in the game, walk off the field, and be resentful of anyone and anything that reminds them of the game.

The Fans

The often forgotten but critical participant in any game is the fan. Fans offer support, encouragement, praise, and affirmation to all those involved in the game. They have more of an observer role, but they can make or break the morale of those directly involved in the game. In this game, the fans are those who are a part of our churches and communities who may not be directly involved in the lives of Millennials but who contribute to the atmosphere, climate, and general environment in which Millennials find themselves. Whether you are directly involved in coaching Millennials or not, you have a choice whether you will be a fan or an opponent. True fans will understand the importance of crafting church and parachurch ministries that equip Millennials to engage the world they find themselves in, whether or not that ministry directly impacts the fans themselves.[6]

Strategy

Before we dive into strategy, we need to take some time to better clarify the game that is actually being played: Is it evangelism? Discipleship? Apologetics? What are we playing here? The game we are playing is focused on long-term effects and success, not on short-term growth or numbers. The long game calls for patience, determination, and an intricate playbook that prepares players to weather changing and challenging conditions. The game is not summarized by better cognitive apologetics, more social justice, or larger ministries; instead, the game comes down to the facilitation of faith development in order to enable Millennials to engage the doubts, questions, and world around them with effectiveness, relevance, and personal conviction.

Ministry through the Lens of Faith Development

James Fowler, in his book *Stages of Faith*, discusses what he considers to be universal stages of faith development, regardless of faith conviction or belief.[7]

---

6. See further Thom S. Rainer, *The Millennials: Connecting to America's Largest Generation* (Nashville: B&H, 2011); and Naomi Schaefer Riles, *Got Religion? How Churches, Mosques, and Synagogues Can Bring Young People Back* (West Conshohocken, PA: Templeton, 2014).

7. James W. Fowler, *Stages of Faith: The Psychology of Human Development and the Quest for Meaning* (New York: Harper, 1981).

There are six stages (and one pre-stage) in Fowler's model. The pre-stage and two earliest stages take place in childhood, and the sixth stage is rarely attained. Therefore, we will look at stages three through five, as they are the most pertinent and relevant to Millennial strategy. To give some context, stage one and stage two of Fowler's model generally take place prior to adolescence and prior to the development of abstract thought. (The pre-stage takes place during the first year of life and is similar to Erikson's psychosocial stage of "trust versus mistrust" in which the individual begins to develop a foundation upon which later faith development will build.[8]) Stage one, labeled "intuitive-projective" faith, is when a person begins to develop values through the use of stories; imagination and fantasy contribute to one's picture of the world. Stage two, labeled "mythic-literal" faith, is when a person begins to use concrete reasoning to understand faith concepts; individuals are able to begin making personal connections between themselves and the larger stories within their faith system.

Fowler labels stage three as "synthetic-conventional" faith and explains it as the stage that most people enter in adolescence. It is also the stage in which many people choose to remain their whole life.[9] People in stage three often place authority for their faith outside themselves, such as in a particular leader or group, and base their faith on the beliefs of the group.[10] "The Stage 3 individual's faith system is conventional, in that it is seen as being everybody's faith system or the faith system of the entire community. And it is synthetic in that it is nonanalytical; it comes as a sort of unified, global wholeness."[11]

Those in stage three may feel as if they have analyzed their faith to a degree, but often their questions remain inside the acceptable boxes of that faith community. For example, a high school or college student engrossed in a debate between Calvinism and Arminianism is still wrestling within the bounds of orthodox Christianity. Fowler argues, and I would agree, that many of our American churches strive to keep people in stage three because they are easier to control, direct, and lead; but they lack a depth of critical thought and ownership in their faith.[12] In this stage, questions are rarely for the purpose of individually distinguishing one's own values or beliefs, and are instead used to help an individual better understand what is acceptable within a particular faith community. More generally, this can most easily be seen in questions such as, "What do Christians believe about . . . ?" versus "What do I believe about . . . ?" The problem with this goal is that the larger

---

8. Erik Erikson, *Identity, Youth and Crisis* (New York: Norton, 1968).
9. Fowler, *Stages of Faith,* 161.
10. Ibid., 154.
11. Ibid., 167.
12. Ibid., 164.

culture places value on the critical thinking and tensions that arise in the next stage, stage four.

According to Fowler stage four, "individuative-reflective" faith, is the stage in which people start to question outside the box, engage the gray areas of faith, and interrupt the "reliance on external sources of authority."[13] Ironically, the bridge from stage three into stage four is often what appears to be a crisis of faith, in which a person begins to shift from an external sense of authority to an internal one. For many churches, this transition between stages, and even the arrival into stage four, is scary. It can appear as if the person in stage four is "backsliding" in their faith, when in reality they are attempting to go deeper and move forward by owning greater dimensions of their faith. The questions and struggles during stage four are attempts to more fully understand and own one's faith through critical reflection. Fowler explains, "The movement from Stage 3 to Stage 4 Individuative-Reflective faith is particularly critical for it is in this transition that the late adolescent or adult must begin to take seriously the burden of responsibility for his or her own commitments, lifestyle, beliefs and attitudes."[14]

In stage four, the individual begins to question the meaning and purpose behind religious symbols, practices, and conventions, often taking years to critically examine their own identity and ideology.[15] Stage-four faith is what an individualistic and postmodern society tends to elevate and respect because it moves the individual into a more self-reflective and self-constructed understanding of the world. This is in stark contrast to many churches and ministries who elevate a stage-three faith, which is less messy. If Millennials are to successfully engage the broader culture, churches and ministries would do well to learn how to come alongside individuals (regardless of age) who are embarking on a season of life in stage four rather than continually strive to keep people in stage three.

Stage five is the last generally attainable stage that Fowler discusses.[16] "Conjunctive faith" is rarely attainable before mid-life due to other developmental accomplishments that are needed to facilitate this level of faith. People in this stage are able to hold seemingly contradictory truths in tandem, to embrace

13. Ibid., 179.
14. Ibid., 182.
15. Ibid., 181–82.
16. Fowler also has a stage six, "universalizing faith," but states that very few people actually reach this level of development, and therefore it will not be discussed in this chapter. It can, though does not necessarily, lead to universalism, which would be heterodox from an evangelical perspective. It is instead conceptualized more as faith that is lived out sacrificially as one approaches life selflessly in a desire to wholly live out their faith convictions (e.g., Mother Theresa, Martin Luther King Jr.).

the mysteries of faith, and engage the beauty and value of faith narratives and symbols. Fowler states, "Stage 5, as a way of seeing, of knowing, or committing, moves beyond the dichotomizing logic of Stage 4's 'either/or.' It sees both (or many) sides of an issue simultaneously. . . . It attends to the pattern of inter-relatedness in things, trying to avoid force-fitting to its own prior mind set."[17]

Those in stage five are less bound by theological boxes, but not for a lack of clear theological conviction. Stage five brings someone out of the rocky terrain that was felt in stage four and into a space where pieces again seem to come together. This coming together is not as tenuous as in stage four or as externally determined as in stage three. To someone in stage four, a person in stage five may seem as if they do not wrestle or grasp the tensions that exist in faith; in reality, someone in stage five has found a way to hold those tensions in tandem, accepting that "truth is more multidimensional and organically interdependent than most theories or accounts of truth can grasp."[18]

In many American schools, children are implicitly taught that stage three is akin to peer pressure, stage four is akin to critical thinking, and stage five is akin to finding yourself. The game that we must be willing and able to coach is how to equip Millennials to navigate the developmental journey through stage three in order to engage stage four and thrive in stage five. If it is true that the gospel is powerful and that Christ is sovereign above all, then our faith should be strong enough to withstand the questions of stage four and beautifully complex enough to flourish in stage five. As a church, as coaches and as fans, we must be willing to help facilitate the growth of our players in developing their faith.[19]

In light of our end-game strategy and Fowler's stages of faith, I propose three objectives for churches and ministries desiring to effectively facilitate ministry to and with Millennials. These objectives build on the idea that ministry to and with Millennials is a cross-cultural endeavor, and it will leave many of us Xers and Boomers feeling out of place or uncomfortable, as it is not what we have needed in our own faith journey. But cross-cultural ministry requires laying down our own preferences for the good of those to whom we are ministering and trying to reach.

17. Ibid., 185.
18. Ibid., 186. For a review of literature and a critique of Fowler's stages, see Stephen Parker, "Research in Fowler's Faith Development Theory: A Review Article," *Review of Religious Research* 61, vol. 3 (2010): 233–52.
19. A potential challenge to many coaches and fans is to develop their own faith beyond stage three. It is quite possible that a sixty-year-old may still be in stage three because he or she perceived the road into stage four as too risky or daunting. Although this discussion is focused on Millennials' faith development, it should be a call to all of us to intentionally and proactively seek the growth and development of our own faith, regardless of our age or stage.

Objective 1: Re-envision the Church's Mission

Most evangelical Christians would agree that, at least in part, the mission of the church is to "go into all the world and preach the gospel" (Mark 16:15). For decades evangelistic efforts have been focused on this, using tools such as the Four Spiritual Laws, the Bridge illustration, Evangelism Explosion, or the Roman Road, to name a few.[20] Conversion has often been the focus, and "bringing people to Christ" is what has generally been meant by evangelism and outreach. But the language of the Great Commission calls us one step further and captures more fully the nature of this strategic play: "Therefore, go and *make disciples*" (Matt. 28:19a). A disciple is not simply a convert but one who accepts and is convinced of a particular set of beliefs, and in that adherence seeks to share that belief with others.[21] If we are simply looking for people to accept and remain in a stage-three faith, then conversion is our end goal. But as we strategically look to develop individuals with stage-four and stage-five faith, discipleship is key.

Undeniably, conversion or regeneration is a foundational step in a relationship with Jesus Christ, but too often this is where ministry stops. Or it assumes that once you "accept Jesus as your Lord and Savior," you will naturally grow in your understanding of who he is and what it means to follow him if you simply participate in the programs and activities that your church offers (such as weekly worship and an occasional Bible study or Sunday school class). This mentality can again keep people in stage three, unless those activities and studies are designed to help people raise the important questions new Christians should keep asking.

The mission of the church, in short, needs to focus on *discipleship*—the cultivation and development of a personal understanding and engaged following of Jesus Christ. This is where we need good coaches! If our strategy is focused on discipleship, we will not neglect evangelism and conversion, as they are necessary parts of the journey of discipleship (sanctification). But if we focus only on these initial steps, we will neglect what is needed for the sanctification journey. Discipleship begins pre-conversion and continues on

20. Whether or not Campus Crusade for Christ (now called "Cru"), the Navigators, or other churches and parachurch organizations have developed succinct and scripturally grounded ways of presenting the gospel, a new tool more tailored to Millennials should highlight these ideas, which focus more on the kingdom of God and mission, and which go beyond conversion: "designed for good, damaged by evil, restored for better, and sent together to heal." See Andy Crouch and James Choung, "From Four Laws to Four Circles: James Choung Has Found a Way to Tell the Old, Old Story to a New Generation," *Christianity Today* 52, no. 7 (July 2008): 30–33.

21. See esp. Michael J. Wilkins, *Following the Master: A Biblical Theology of Discipleship* (Grand Rapids: Zondervan, 1992).

throughout one's lifetime; this is what ministry to and with Millennials must be about.[22]

DEEP, DANGEROUS, AND RISKY

In my chapter on ministry to Xers, I describe the theology professor who once said something along the lines of, "The saying 'Jesus loves you and has a wonderful plan for your life' is one of the biggest bait-and-switches in Christian history." Avoiding this problem proves equally crucial for ministry among Millennials. In a culture where everything from Nike to Coca-Cola promises to make your life better, what makes a "seeker-sensitive" presentation of the gospel any different?[23] For decades we have walked a fine line of being ashamed of the gospel by only presenting the warm and fuzzy parts and being too afraid to present it as the dangerous, risky, and life-altering message that it is. Millennials have products of all kinds promising to make their life better; what they lack is something bigger than themselves that gives their lives meaning, purpose, and significance. Our strategy in discipleship (and evangelism) is to remember the radical nature and power of the gospel and to not be afraid to communicate that to this generation. In a world where everything is centered on them, their souls cry out for something bigger, something greater, something that gives purpose and meaning that extends beyond this life.[24]

What scares many people (consciously or unconsciously) is that when we embrace the idea that the gospel is not simply something that makes our lives "better" and more comfortable, we must then confront our theology of suffering. If God's "wonderful plan" for my life isn't a plan to rescue me from all heartache, trials, and pain, then I must wrestle with what I believe about sin, evil, suffering, and all that is painful in life. Connected to this is

22. See esp. Richard R. Dunn and Jana L. Sundene, *Shaping the Journey of Emerging Adults: Life-Giving Rhythms for Spiritual Transformation* (Downers Grove, IL: InterVarsity, 2012). See also Scot McKnight, "The Gospel for iGens: Reared on Self-Esteem and Impervious to Guilt, the Next Generation Needs Good News That Can Break through Their Defenses," *Leadership* 30, no. 3 (June 2009): 20–24.

23. For both plight and solutions, see esp. Skye Jethani, *The Divine Commodity: Discovering a Faith beyond Consumer Christianity* (Grand Rapids: Zondervan, 2009). See also Fran Blomberg, "Living Hopefully in a World of Instant Gratification," *Journal of European Baptist Studies* 3 (2012): 26–38.

24. In the counseling arena, I have seen more and more of my Millennial students drawn to Adlerian theory and existential theory to explain their counseling framework. In both of these theories, an emphasis is placed on goals, freedom with responsibility, and one's place within the larger system or human story. See Jon Carlson and Michael P. Manciacci, eds., *Alfred Adler Revisited* (New York: Routledge, 2012) for a review of Adlerian Theory. See Viktor E. Frankl, *Man's Search for Meaning* (New York: Simon & Schuster, 1984) for an introduction to existential psychotherapy.

Millennials' concern for social justice; they look at the death, starvation, and injustices in the world and question loudly how a good God could allow such atrocities. Coaches in this game must be able to thoroughly and deeply engage these questions and respond with candor, empathy, and scripturally grounded theology—which requires those of us who are coaches to have wrestled with these questions ourselves.[25] This does not require that we swing the pendulum to a doomsday perspective on life or promote the idea that those who suffer are more spiritual, but it does ask us to engage uncomfortable topics of suffering, pain, and social inequality on at least a stage-four faith-development level because shallow, concrete, black-and-white responses will not sit well with Millennials.

LAUNCHING EXILES

Finally, our strategy to re-envision the church's mission must include training and launching Millennials to be "exiles" in a foreign land.[26] Kinnaman defines exiles as those who are on

> a faith journey in which a person feels stuck between the comfortable, predictable world of church and the "real world" they feel called to influence. Often there is a disconnect between their calling or professional interests and their understanding of the Christian faith. . . . Exiles are most common during periods of profound cultural, spiritual, and technological change.[27]

I absolutely love Kinnaman's use of this metaphor, as he draws parallels between Millennials and the Israelite exiles who had to learn how to maintain their faith *and* gain an audience with the king while exiled in Babylon (see especially the book of Daniel). The parallels to today are profound: Millennials find themselves in their own Babylon, a "foreign land" in which Christian faith is no longer the norm and where cultural beliefs, values, and worldviews at times directly contradict biblical truths. But like Daniel and his friends in Babylon, they find themselves in positions of power, influence, and opportunity in a culture that is foreign to the generations that came before them. Daniel and his friends had to discern the difference between what it meant to

25. C. S. Lewis, *The Problem of Pain* (London: G. Bles, 1940) remains a classic. Philip Yancey has several excellent resources, the most recent of which is *The Question That Never Goes Away: What Is God Up To or Not in a World of Such Tragedy and Pain?* (Grand Rapids: Zondervan, 2013). See also D. A. Carson, *How Long, O Lord? Reflections on Suffering and Evil*, rev. ed. (Grand Rapids: Baker Academic, 2006).

26. For a description of the three types of Millennials he sees leaving the church, see Kinnaman, *You Lost Me*, 75, 246.

27. Ibid., 245–46.

be Israelites in Israel, where the culture supported their diet, worship style, moral convictions, and the like, versus what it meant to be God-followers in a culture that was against them (whether actively or passively) at every turn.

Simultaneously, Millennials feel exiled *from* the Christian community— pushed out because they are misunderstood and therefore unsupported. Kinnaman clarifies that "many of today's exiles, while they are not *political* exiles in the Old Testament sense, feel isolated and alienated from the Christian community—caught between the church as it is and what they believe it is called to be."[28] In this game, it is not an effective strategy to continue to train Millennials to answer the theological or social questions of their parents' generation; we must instead equip them to be exiles, able to survive and thrive in a culture where they are the minority, and able to discern what is a foundational tenet of their faith and what is simply a traditional or cultural expression of their faith. We, as coaches, must listen intently and believe them as they describe a new world (not just a changing world). We must be willing to reflect upon our own convictions, boiling them down to core tenets of faith and letting go of personal and cultural expressions and preferences. To an exile, an effective ministry plan does not focus on how many people they can bring to church service, small group, or some other church-based program. Instead, as exiles, an effective ministry plan looks a lot more like strategizing how *they* can permeate the larger culture, how *they* enter into the social and political spaces of their Babylon, and how *they* can be prepared and equipped to live as foreigners while maintaining a strong faith. Practically, this may look like creating spaces in which Millennials can meet with other Christian professionals in their field and collaboratively brainstorm and share stories about how they reflect their faith in their work.

The church, and the coaches of Millennials, should no longer be training its people to simply be better church members. They should instead begin training them to be launched outside the safety and comfort of an insular community and into the Babylon that surrounds them.[29] The church still has its role as the safe-house, the training ground, and the place where our exiles can return to for resources, encouragement, support, affirmation, and discipleship. The

28. Ibid., 77. See also Christian Smith with Patricia Snell, *Souls in Transition: The Religious and Spiritual Lives of Emerging Adults* (Oxford: Oxford University Press, 2009).

29. The Barna Group identifies five reasons why Millennials *stay* in church. Two of those reasons involve helping Millennials better engage their culture—one through the development of "cultural discernment" and the other through "vocational discipleship" in which they gain insight and tools for connecting their career to their calling. See Barna Group, "Five Reasons Millennials Stay Connected to Church," *Barna: Millennials*, September 17, 2013, https://www.barna.org/barna-update/millennials/635-5-reasons-millennials-stay-connected-to-church#.U0c Z4vldWSo.

mission of the church and its coaches is now defensive, playing the game on the opponents' turf. A church in our area recently described their work with Millennials as focusing on helping them "find a role in our community before you find a role in the church." This church understands the new mission. As American culture dramatically shifts and changes, we must be willing to re-envision what the mission of the church actually is in this current context. We undoubtedly need people of all ages whose call and ministry is to build up the local church, but as Millennials find themselves in their own Babylon, we must be willing to re-envision the church as the launching pad, the training ground, and the support team of those who are going out into Babylon to gain an audience with the king. Practically speaking, this requires a church or ministry to identify their mission and their audience, knowing they cannot be all things to all people. It asks leaders to then strategically shape curriculum and activity schedules around the identified mission, always keeping in mind the reality of the Babylon in which Millennials spend the majority of their time.

To bring us back to the first point within this strategy, discipleship and not simply evangelism is critical in order for exiles to not lose their faith as they are launched into Babylon. My mother has said, "My job as a parent is not to raise *children*. Instead, my job is to help launch self-sufficient adults," and her wisdom is applicable here. The rationale for this distinction is that if your focus is in raising *children*, you will forever see them as children, limiting the scope and vision of what they can grow into being. The same is true for spiritual parenting (or coaching): we must train with the end goal of launching spiritually mature individuals (with stage-four and ultimately stage-five faith), who are well-grounded, passionate, and empowered, and who can make a difference in their Babylon. If we focus simply on evangelism or conversion, we are only "raising children" and will ultimately lose the end game.

Objective 2: Engage Their Doubt

The next key play in our game strategy is actually a call to engage the doubt that Millennials have regarding faith in general and Christianity in particular. The key word in this strategy is "engage." It does not mean to disregard, dispute, refute, or argue against but instead to listen, dialogue, wrestle with, and attend to. The educational system that most Millennials were brought up in taught them to question everything, to dissect, to analyze, and to be skeptical of everything they were taught by someone who claimed to have authority. Ironically, this critical approach was not necessarily imposed on those claiming a personal opinion or perspective, as relativism allows for each person to understand "truth" in their own way.[30] But once you step into the role of being an authority or claim that what you have to say is universally right or true, you will inspire great skepticism, doubt, and disbelief. After all, from a relativistic worldview, claiming to have a corner on truth is nothing but judgmental, closed-minded, intolerant, and disrespectful.[31]

Going back to Fowler's stages of faith, doubt is a critical component of faith development and a key player in moving someone from stage three into stage four (recall Mark 9:24). Coaches need to remember that "doubt is not always faith's opposite,"[32] and "people who experience doubts [don't] simply lack the proper evidence or depth of conviction. But doubt is a far more nuanced and slippery experience that involves personality, lack of fulfillment, notions about certainty, relational alienation, and even mental health."[33]

In light of this, apologetics is still relevant and important, but it must also be redesigned to focus on the relational and experiential elements that contribute to doubt, not simply the intellectual ones. It is important in our game's strategy to remember that doubt can actually enable someone to more fully understand, grasp, and step into their faith *if* they are given the right resources and relationships. For a generation that is highly relational and concerned with how any espoused doctrine will directly relate to a specific person they know (or have heard of), coaches and churches must be able to see questions and doubts as an opportunity for Millennials to more fully engage their faith, rather than a sign of rebellion, disbelief, or disinterest in the gospel.[34]

In education we talk a lot about Bloom's taxonomy—the hierarchy of learning goals that lays out the progression from lower-level learning to higher-level learning.[35] The most basic level is simple remembering or memorization. At

30. I intentionally use the phrase "critical approach" instead of "critical thinking" as the traditional understanding of "critical thinking" involves a very systematic and skillful approach to analyzing the way one thinks about a particular subject or problem. See http://www.critical thinking.org/pages/our-concept-of-critical-thinking/411 for more information. It could be argued that critical *thinking* skills are severely lacking for Millennials. This is generally true for those raised in more mainstream public school settings who were taught to take a critical or skeptical *approach* to information, as well as for those in homeschool or private Christian settings who were taught not to question (or be critical) of anyone in authority.

31. Kinnaman, *You Lost Me,* 185–98.

32. Ibid., 186.

33. Ibid., 186–87.

34. See further Ronald J. Nydam, "The Relational Theology of Generation Y," *Calvin Theological Journal* 41, no. 2 (November 2006): 321–30. See also Thom S. Rainer, "Six Ways Millennials Are Shaping the Church," *Thom S. Rainer Blog,* December 11, 2013, http://thomrainer .com/2013/12/11/six-ways-millennials-are-shaping-the-church/.

35. Lorin W. Anderson and David R. Krathwohl, eds., *A Taxonomy for Learning, Teaching, and Assessing: A Revision of Bloom's Taxonomy of Educational Objectives* (New York: Pearson, Allyn & Bacon, 2000).

this level there doesn't need to be any comprehension or understanding; it's simply knowledge. As we move up through the different learning domains, we encounter the following learning goals: comprehending, applying, analyzing, evaluating, and creating. Too often, in attempts to keep people in stage three of faith development, churches and coaches focus on the first two levels of memorizing and comprehending. But doubt is not engaged or assuaged by simply being able to regurgitate a "right" answer. Instead, we must create relationships and spaces in which Millennials feel comfortable asking questions that take them into the learning domains of applying, analyzing, evaluating, and creating. In these domains coaches must be comfortable with gray areas, messy lives, complicated answers, and criticism, as the "old ways" no longer fit or hold relevance for a new generation. If the gospel is as powerful, applicable, and universal as we claim it to be, then we need to trust that it can withstand the questions and the doubts of this generation. By being unwilling to engage someone's questions and doubts, we are saying more about the weakness of our own faith than we are about theirs, and we are communicating (quite loudly) that we ourselves doubt the buoyancy and resiliency of the gospel. Instead, the doubts and questions that Millennials have should encourage us, inspire us, and call us to delve more deeply into our own faith as we become willing to wrestle and truly *engage* in order to grow.

Practically speaking, Millennials' doubt is not primarily engaged through intellectual discussions or apologetic debates. Instead the process is just that: a process. In keeping with the cultural norms and values of this generation, doubt must be engaged, in relationship and over time. What is old has become new again, as Millennials look to the power of story and narrative to find and make meaning in life. Much like the ancient Israelites, who told stories of God's faithfulness in order to teach the next generation about who he is, Millennials seek out and value the stories that coaches and peers can share.[36] What is so beautiful about true stories is that people can relate to them, they are imperfect and incomplete, and they are multifaceted when they are told honestly and authentically. As with ministry among Xers, authenticity is the key word in this approach.

As we also saw in discussing ministry with Xers, in Christian circles someone often gives a "testimony" *after* a difficult or painful situation has been resolved in a positive way. This gives the impression that there is no story to tell unless it's a "pretty" story with a happy ending. This is not authenticity or transparency in the eyes of Millennials. Millennials crave vulnerability, openness, and transparency from their coaches—a willingness to tell a story that is not yet complete,

36. See Barna Group, "Five Reasons Millennials Stay Connected to Church."

that still has questions, uncertainty, and mystery to it. When their coaches tell real-time, messy, and incomplete stories, Millennials will feel greater freedom to share their doubt. Who wants to admit they are struggling or questioning their faith to someone who only demonstrates an impervious, unreflective, doubtless faith? While it was recommended within our discussion of ministry to Xers that these more honest stories be shared in a larger group setting, Millennials will respond more positively to a one-on-one disclosure. For a coach to trust a Millennial enough to share their story over coffee or dinner speaks powerfully to a Millennial. A story shared with intentionality and individual attention is often experienced as more trustworthy than something said from a stage.

Now, with that being said, it can't be all narrative and stories. Creating a space in which Millennials feel safe enough to voice their doubt requires coaches to be authentic with their own stories while also being able to intellectually engage the discussion. Just because relationship is of high value doesn't mean that intellectual integrity is not. My time in the Navigators captured this balance well for me, and theirs is the model I often look to when envisioning this balance of authentic story with intellectual rigor.[37] I chose to get involved with the Navigators because of their reputation for Scripture memory and deep theological foundations *along with* their emphasis on discipleship and what they called "relational evangelism."[38] In this context, staff members mentored students on a weekly basis, sharing life, meals, prayer requests, personal struggles, and successes. The mentor was not aloof or a removed expert but instead a fellow brother or sister in Christ who happened to be further along in the journey. With that, the mentor was still responsible for providing guidance and some direction, but there was a humble attitude of mutual respect and teachability. Mentors shared their spiritual journeys with their mentorees while simultaneously teaching their mentorees how to study Scripture, wrestle with deeper theological concepts, and apply their learning to their real lives.[39]

---

37. I am sure other campus and parachurch ministries have also done this well, but my personal experience was with the Navigators on the University of Northern Iowa campus in the early 2000s.

38. Relational evangelism builds interpersonal relationships with people who, although different in faith system, would be people you'd naturally be friends with or find yourself around. Your purpose in the relationship is to actually become friends, and *then* out of the context of that friendship you may earn the right to communicate the gospel. There is no hidden agenda of "getting them saved," but there is a prayerful intentionality and openness to sharing the gospel as it naturally arises in conversation and relationship. See John Bowen, *Evangelism for Normal People: Good News for Those Looking for a Fresh Approach* (Minneapolis: Fortress, 2002).

39. Not surprisingly, the Navigators have an excellent book on the topic: Daniel Egeler, *Mentoring Millennials: Shaping the Next Generation* (Colorado Springs: NavPress, 2003).

The development of this type of relationship takes *time*. Safe relationships, particularly for this generational cohort, take time to build as trust is not proven simply by one's title but through experience with that person. It takes longer to share stories than it does to share information, and when the cultural foundation is far less evangelized than it was even twenty years ago, the start of the race is further back than previous cohorts have experienced. No effective coach would ever send a team out to play a game when they haven't practiced or without the proper skills training—the same is true in this scenario. It is unfair and disrespectful to expect a Millennial to step into a relationship and share their doubts without first building a rapport and trust with their coach. And, just like with athletes, each person needs more (or less) time in training depending on their natural abilities, lived experiences, motivation, and injuries.

Doubt for Millennials is not purely a lack of intellectual understanding, but it additionally involves feelings of a lack of fulfillment, rejection, fear, insecurity, and more. Therefore relational space must be created in which doubts can be expressed without the fear of rejection, disapproval, or condescension. This can be done through mentoring relationships or through small group relationships. The key is that churches and coaches do not get so caught up in designing a new program but instead put energy into intentionally developing individuals. What is needed is structure in which there are clear goals, resources, and clearly defined relationships between the Millennials and their coach or coaches. The difference between a structured relationship and a program is that a program has a step-by-step process that most participants follow. A structured relationship has jointly defined goals, but the processes by which those goals are accomplished vary from relationship to relationship.[40] This, again, requires coaches who are themselves at stage five in their faith development, able to step out of black-and-white thinking and not afraid to engage the doubts of those they coach. Doubt can actually foster faith when allowed to be aired in a safe and understanding relationship.

Objective 3: Re-envision Ministry

The natural outflow of re-envisioning the church's mission and engaging the doubts of Millennials is to re-envision what ministry means and looks like. This is not to say that ministry practices of the past *were* ineffective or in some way bad; rather, it is to say that some of those practices *are becoming* ineffective and irrelevant to this generation. It is time that coaches begin

---

40. For many of these points, see Patricia Hendricks, *Hungry Souls, Holy Companions: Mentoring a New Generation of Christians* (Harrisburg, PA: Morehouse, 2006).

to reexamine what is simply cultural habit and preference in the way we do ministry and what is actually scripturally required. If our revised mission is to make disciples, not just converts, then ministry needs to be structured toward this end goal.

NUMBERS VERSUS DEPTH

In his book *Cultivate*, Jeff Myers compares the process of discipleship to that of a gardener tending to crops. In this, the gardener cannot rush growth but plants, nourishes, waters, prunes, and tends to the plant in such a way that *over time* it comes to bear fruit. Myers says that "people grow better through cultivation rather than through mass production," which underscores one of the foundational ways in which ministry needs to be re-envisioned: we must redirect our focus from how many people we can get through our church doors, and instead focus on how we can cultivate the deep faith of a few.[41] In true American fashion, ministry models, for decades, have been based on the idea that bigger is better. Reaching as many people as possible with the gospel is a good goal; but if we look to Jesus's ministry as our model, we see that most of Jesus's time was spent investing in twelve men, eleven of whom would then go out and have an exponential impact on the world.[42] We must keep this model in mind as we cultivate in Millennials the ability to go out into their own Babylon and exponentially increase the influence of the gospel. Similar to Jesus's ministry, cultivating Millennials requires time, intentionality, and roots that run deep so that Millennials may not be swayed as they go out on their own. The challenge is for coaches to step away from the deeply engrained idea that a "successful" ministry is a large ministry, and reorient to the idea that a successful ministry is one that launches Millennials into Babylon as mature, grounded, and fruitful followers of Jesus.

RELATIONSHIP, NOT RELIGION

Faith in Jesus is a relationship, not a religion, and Millennials will not care how much you know until they know how much you care. (How's that for one massively cliché-filled sentence?) The core concept of relationship being at the heart of ministry must be attended to. A generation that is more affectively (emotionally) than cognitively motivated, that desires connectedness with individuality, and that has related to authority figures through the lens of friendship, brings these lived experiences with them into any ministry or

41. Jeff Myers, *Cultivate: Forming the Emerging Generation through Life-on-Life Mentoring* (Dayton, TN: Passing the Baton International, 2010), 32.

42. A point stressed throughout Robert E. Coleman's classic *The Master Plan of Evangelism* (Old Tappan, NJ: Fleming H. Revell, 1963).

church context. As we re-envision what ministry is to look like, relationships must be at the center—and relationships take time to build.

The gospel is all about relationships—relationships being made right between the omnipotent, sovereign God of the universe and people. We have already talked about how solely emphasizing the love of God, and so diluting the power, danger, and grandness of the gospel into simple warm-fuzzies, is unlikely to capture the hearts of this generation. Christian Smith's longitudinal study has characterized the main religion of American Christian Millennials as "moralistic therapeutic deism"—belief in a distant, creator God whose purpose is to keep us happy as we live morally good lives.[43] But this is not the religion of Scripture! On the other hand, swinging the pendulum to the other extreme of "turn or burn" is even more unlikely to be an effective strategy in this game. Instead, the focus should be on the fullness of what it means to be in relationship with another person, complete with depth, complexity, simplicity, and reciprocity. Unique in their collectiveness, Millennials often express that part of what makes the gospel so unappealing to them is its exclusivity. They experience the church as intolerant and unaccepting of those "who don't meet their standards" and "prefer finding areas of common ground rather than emphasizing differences that may lead to conflict."[44] This is where our strategy—not our doctrine—must be willing to adapt.

To many Millennials, the church has defined itself by what it is against, who it is against, and what it will not stand for. For a generation that values inclusion, tolerance, and fairness (over rightness), the church must approach its relationship with Millennials from a different perspective than that of separateness, exclusivity, and superiority.[45] This is tricky, as the gospel *is* exclusive, it *is* intolerant, and it *is not* fair (Matt. 7:14; 12:30; Eph. 2:8–9). And yes, the gospel is also offensive as it flies in the face of all the sin that sits in the heart of each and every one of us. But in being "shrewd as snakes and as innocent as doves" (Matt. 10:16), we are not the ones who are to be offensive, exclusive, intolerant, or unfair as communicators of the gospel. Millennials remind us that we should have empathy, compassion, and passion for those who do not have a relationship with Jesus because we are the ones who most fully understand and have experienced the grace, inclusiveness, and purposefulness that the gospel has brought into our lives. While the gospel itself may be offensive, we as its communicators should not be.

43. Christian Smith, *Soul Searching: The Religious and Spiritual Lives of American Teenagers* (Oxford: Oxford University Press, 2005), 118–71.
44. Kinnaman, *You Lost Me*, 171–72.
45. Ibid., 173.

Rather than approaching those outside the church from a position of differ-ence and disagreement, we should connect in our shared humanness and desire to be loved, accepted, and given meaning. It is in this that re-envisioning min-istry involves the use of restorative relationships. Much like Donald Miller's story in *Blue Like Jazz*, we in the church need to collectively recognize that we owe the world (and specific individuals in our lives) an apology—not an apol-ogy for the gospel, but an apology for how *we* have communicated the gospel in a way that is disrespectful, condescending, legalistic, and self-righteous.[46]

Part of what it looks like to re-envision ministry in this way is to come face to face with the patience, grace, and process that God has brought you through in your faith journey (whether pre- or post-conversion). As coaches and ministry leaders, we must redirect our focus from an "us versus them" mentality of evangelism and discipleship and instead recognize that we, apart from Christ, are no different than anyone else. Additionally, I think often of what our Navigators' staff shared with us when I was in college. They were talking about relational evangelism (that idea that we must build relationships and earn the right to share the gospel if it is to be understood) and shared that it took the average American *experiencing* the gospel seven times (in different contexts and/or from different people) before they were willing to believe it. Additionally, they said this number went up to nearly fourteen times when looking at relational evangelism in Europe, due to its post-Christian culture. Now, fifteen years later and culturally much further down the postmodern trail, I cannot help but wonder what that number would be for Americans today. What if, as we re-envision ministry, we begin to envision ourselves as a link in a chain—a chain that could be anywhere from three to fifty links in length, with each link equally important because it moves the player we are coaching one step closer to a relationship with Jesus? In this analogy I, as the coach, am still not ashamed of the gospel and am prepared to give an account for the hope that I have (Rom 1:16; 1 Pet. 3:15), but I relinquish the pressure and the pride that says I must be the one to "seal the deal."[47] My faith is not dependent on how many people I get to "pray the prayer," and I am not in competition with other coaches to "win" more people to Christ.

When I think about restorative relationships, I think about a dear friend of mine whom I have known for quite a few years. We met because we were in the same profession and shared an office. "Susan" (not her real name) and I are as different as can be. From our sexual orientation to our religious beliefs

46. Donald Miller, *Blue Like Jazz: Nonreligious Thoughts on Christian Spirituality* (Nash-ville: Thomas Nelson, 2003).

47. For inspirational vision-casting with this goal, see Carol Howard Merritt, *Reframing Hope: Vital Ministry in a New Generation* (Herndon, VA: Alban Institute, 2010).

to our physical appearance, we are a study in contrasts. For two years Susan and I shared an office and talked about relationships with significant others, childhood memories, research interests, and everything else that friends and coworkers talk about. But not once did we have a direct conversation about the fact that Susan was a lesbian—and a "neo-pagan lesbian atheist" at that, to use her self-given label. Regularly I wrestled with and prayed about whether I needed to address this topic, to share with her what I believed about God's design for sexuality. But as I listened to her stories, I heard something profound: Susan desperately wanted a relationship with God, but her experiences with people who professed to know Jesus only left her confused and deeply wounded. Her family had shamed her and condemned her in the name of Jesus, but it was a Protestant campus pastor who was the first person to offer her a safe place to "come out" and identify herself as a lesbian (something she says she knew but struggled to admit for nearly ten years prior). For Susan, the very group of people ("Christians") who hurt her the most deeply also offered her the most acceptance, and in that I knew my influence on her life was not to come through words but through action and experience. So, I kept praying, and one day she brought up the subject saying, "So, we've had enough theological conversations that I'm guessing I know what you think about homosexuality, but we've never talked about it. Do we need to talk about it?" My response was, "Do you want to talk about it? I'm comfortable either way, but it's up to you." She replied, "Nah, I know you probably disagree with it, but you've loved me so well I don't care. So, I'm good if you're good." In those two years, I got to verbally lay out the plan of salvation and the gospel message at least three times to Susan, but I also got to show it to her in hospital visits, helping her move, sitting with her after an incredibly painful breakup, and enjoying conversation over dinner on a regular basis. It is not my job to convince Susan of the rationality of the gospel. She knows the Bible and the plan of salvation, but she needs to experience it through redemptive relationships that relate to her out of empathy, understanding, and grace before it can be something she embraces for herself.

Intergenerational Relationships

Millennials are the only generation we've looked at who haven't outright rejected the influence of parents and other authority figures. They were raised with their parents as their friends in more egalitarian environments, and they bring the expectation of equality into other contexts as well. Where Baby Boomers often assume that younger adults wouldn't want their input (because they didn't want their parents' input), Millennials are hungry for it. There is still a time, place, and desire to be with people at the same stage of life, but

Millennials are hungry for intergenerational connections—to be invited into the sacred space of another person's life and journey, to observe, to learn, and to share. As we re-envision ministry, we must include intergenerational spaces.[48]

In many arenas the church has rejected the culture's norms or patterns and so can seem outdated or out of touch with the larger world. But one worldly trend coaches have latched onto, particularly in larger churches, is the push to organize congregants by age or stage of life. We have taken an educational model of putting kindergarteners with kindergarteners, and fifth graders with fifth graders, and applied it to our ministries. While there can be great benefit and need for this type of segmentation, it can also be incredibly detrimental to everyone's spiritual growth. How can the church live out the command for the older to teach the younger (Titus 2:2–5)—which is *not* about grownups teaching children—and for each part of the body to be valued (1 Cor. 12:14–26) if we don't get to know one another, interact with one another, and share across generational lines?[49]

When I moved to a new state for seminary, I was twenty-one, done with college, single, and had a very clear vision for where I was going. I remember vividly visiting a church (that I ultimately made my church home) of about twelve hundred people. I walked up to the information desk to find out about Sunday school classes or small group options. The kind woman behind the counter had a sheet with all the groups on it, complete with descriptions that started with demographics. She started by asking how old I was, and since I was twenty-one, suggested I attend the college group. I politely explained that I wasn't in college, had been involved in collegiate ministry leadership prior to this move, and didn't feel like I fit in that group anymore. I asked about other options. Well, since I wasn't married, I couldn't really go to the young marrieds' class, and the next group beyond that was for people with young children. As she looked down her list, her brow got more and more furrowed. Finally, she landed on a Sunday class literally labeled "TBD" that basically had no description. I said, "I'll take it," and I went to check it out—I simply appreciated the fact that this group wasn't going to box me in or exclude me simply because of a demographic descriptor. This group ended up being amazing! We were all the misfits or the ones who did not want to be categorized by a single demographic variable. We ranged in age from nineteen to forty-five, some were single, some were married, some had kids, some didn't, some had been Christians since childhood, and others

48. Kara Eckmann Powell, Marshall Shelley, and Brandon O'Brien, "Is the Era of Age Segregation Over?," *Leadership* 30, no. 3 (June 2009): 43–47.

49. See, e.g., Ross Parsley, *Messy Church: A Multigenerational Mission for God's Family*, rev. ed. (Colorado Springs: David C. Cook, 2012).

were just coming to explore this Christianity thing, some were in school, and some were successful businesspeople. What united us was that we loved Jesus (or wanted to know more about him), and we wanted to do life together. Period. The class met every Sunday during the first service and then broke into more demographically oriented, small groups during the week, but even then the lines were blurry. Small churches are in a beautiful place of having to function this way—there aren't enough people in each demographic to break down into smaller groups! But even in medium to large congregations, we need to find ways to bridge the gaps and create spaces where people from different generations (and other demographic groups) get to learn from and with one another.[50]

In some churches this takes on the form of a formal mentoring program in which men and women of older generations volunteer their time to intentionally share life with someone younger than themselves. Many churches are comfortable offering this type of structure to their high school students because they are still seen as children. But we need this same type of opportunity for adults *of all ages*. To think that once we graduate high school or college, or once we get married, we are capable of navigating our spiritual and personal growth on our own is at best naive and at worst arrogant and self-righteous. For a culture that is so technologically connected, we are incredibly isolated relationally. David Kinnaman addresses this absence in churches of older generations speaking into the lives of Millennials while they were growing up. He reports that only 39 percent of Protestants and 28 percent of Catholics "had a close personal friend who was an adult at church or parish," and only 17 percent of Protestants and 12 percent of Catholics report that they "had an adult mentor at church, other than the pastor or church staff."[51]

To continue our analogy of the game, effective coaches must know their players intimately—they must spend considerable amounts of time with them, learning how they move, what their skills are, where their vulnerabilities lie, and how they contribute to the overall performance of the team. Whether it is called coaching, mentoring, or apprenticeship (my preferred description), the foundational structure of ministry to and with Millennials needs to be built on intergenerational relationships that are focused on long-term development and maturity.

50. See, e.g., Gilbert R. Rendle, *The Multigenerational Congregation: Meeting the Leadership Challenge* (Lanham, MD: Rowman & Littlefield, 2001); and Jackson W. Carroll and Wade Clark Roof, *Bridging Divided Worlds: Generational Cultures in Congregations* (San Francisco: Jossey-Bass, 2002).
51. Kinnaman, *You Lost Me*, 119.

Apprenticeship

I love the imagery that comes to my mind when I hear the word "apprentice"—some of you may picture Donald Trump and a reality-based television show, but that's not anywhere close to what I see. I, for some reason, am taken back to a blacksmith's shop in which the older, established master blacksmith has taken in a young man who desires to learn the trade. Together they share space for months and years as the master blacksmith teaches his young apprentice the ins and outs of their trade. They work so closely together that the young apprentice learns to read the master's mood and to anticipate how he would respond in any given situation. The master apprentice diligently learns about the young apprentice and where he has strengths, skill, and aptitude. It is the master blacksmith's responsibility to affirm, train, and correct, all with the long-term goal of handing off his business to the young apprentice one day. Apprenticeship has as its goal the handing off of one's role, position, and ministry.[52]

The quaint blacksmith shop is a lovely image, but what does it look like today to rediscover this art of apprenticeship? In light of the charge to move away from programs but maintain structure, I offer six guidelines for engaging in an apprenticeship relationship with a Millennial in which the focus is the cultivation of their long-term growth, maturity, and progression in faith development.

Be intentional. It's really difficult to passively pass on a skill. As someone once said, "Children are wonderful observers and horrible interpreters." Sure, those who come after you will observe what you do and who you are, but without your intentional input, they are left to discern and decode your meaning, purposes, and approaches on their own. To apprentice well, coaches must intentionally seek out and invite a Millennial into an apprenticeship relationship. Once the relationship is clearly established, then intentionality involves the deliberate cultivation of the character, traits, skills, and maturity that you and your Millennial have *collaboratively* identified.[53] This could easily be done with Sunday school classes; in-home small groups that are organized around geographic location; activity groups built around common interests such as cooking, hiking, or car restoration; or church-wide community service projects (like a "day to serve") that connect individuals based on shared passion or ministry interest.

---

52. Almost by definition, the kind of apprenticeship or mentoring that is needed is not that which can be marketed as happening in a short period of time. Contrast, e.g., Gary W. Moon, *Apprenticeship with Jesus: Learning to Live Like the Master—A 30-Day Experience* (Grand Rapids: Baker Books, 2009).

53. For specific dos and don'ts in starting conversations in the apprenticeship relationship, see Myers, *Cultivate*, 82–85.

Be authentic. Perfection is not the goal of the master or coach in the apprenticeship process. You cannot teach what you do not know, and your protégé will both respect and appreciate you more for being honest about your limitations. On the flip side, own what you do know, what you have experienced, and what you have learned—not in an arrogant way, but in a way that communicates and reflects your own struggles, challenges, successes, and journey. I have heard it said that humility is not thinking less of yourself but thinking *rightly* of yourself in light of the cross—do not sell short the work of the gospel in your own life under the guise of humility. Furthermore, authenticity means sharing your testimony before everything has all worked out; it means inviting your protégé into your home and not apologizing for the mess or the fight that your kids got in after school; it means apologizing without defensiveness when you misspeak, overreact, or are incorrect. Authenticity in the apprenticeship process is about being honest with who you are, where you are, and how you got there. It is a willingness to be known and understood—not as you wish to be, but as you currently are in the here and now.

Be teachable. In an apprenticeship relationship the protégé is primarily learning from the master. There will be times when the protégé has a skill, has come to an understanding, or has had an experience that the master has not. In this space, whether big or small, it is critical that the master be willing to learn from the protégé. Whether it is a tutorial on the latest social network fad or a theological realization, the reality is that your protégé will know things you don't, and that you both will benefit from what *they* contribute to the relationship, not just from what you bring. When apprenticing Millennials, you must enter with an attitude of humility and strength—humility rooted in the awareness of your own need for grace, process, patience, and God's goodness, and strength grounded in an understanding of who it is God has made you to be. You cannot teach what you do not know, cannot do, or do not embody. But that does not mean you have to have complete knowledge, a perfect skill set, or flawless character in any area.

Serve with relationship in mind. Millennials have been raised to value community service and social action. Rather than assuming that apprenticeship can happen only while sitting in a coffee shop having deep conversations or in your home around your kitchen table, consider creative activities that speak to the social sensibilities of many Millennials. For example, both my church and our employer do what they call a "Day to Serve" each fall—my church on a Sunday, and our employer on a weekday. On that day we cancel services or close our offices and cancel classes, and everyone disperses to predetermined sites across our community that are in need of help. Sometimes this involves painting a building, sometimes it is doing yard work for an elderly neighbor, sometimes it is delivering food for a "Meals on Wheels" type organization—the options go on and on. The specific activity itself doesn't matter as much as the opportunity to do something together for the good of someone else. On one hand, it can be very tempting to get a group of your peers and friends together and take over one particular site. On the other hand, this is a great opportunity to intentionally mix up your social group and join with Millennials in creating an intergenerational group that goes out to serve together. Another practical idea may be to find out where your protégé regularly volunteers and ask to go with them occasionally. Whether or not you have great interest in that particular charity or organization is not the point; the point is to serve alongside your protégé for the purpose of building relationship.

When possible, go to them. For too many decades the church has stood in the culture saying, "We're right here! If you want to know about Jesus, come to us!" In order to effectively apprentice Millennials, we need to go to them whenever possible, to step into their world and to experience the Babylon in which they exist. As much as they need to learn from us, we need to understand as much as possible about the context in which they are needing to use the skills we have to impart. I am aware of a church that was looking to better develop their young adult ministry. They consistently had a small handful of twenty-somethings who attended their weekly Bible study at the church. They could not seem to grow, and participants were reluctant to invite others despite regularly sharing about spiritual conversations they were having with friends and coworkers. So, the Baby Boomer leader asked his protégés what held them back from inviting friends to the group. Resoundingly, they said that it was because there was no way that their friends would enter a church. Demonstrating intentionality and teachability, the leader asked the group what they thought would make the group more appealing to those who did not yet know Jesus or who were reluctant to come to church. Collaboratively they decided to move their weekly meetings from the church building to a local pub and to focus the group on "life's tough questions." The leader and the core group of participants knew that the goal of the group was to foster spiritual growth in the participants, and to do so by grounding their conversations and answers to life's tough questions in Scripture. The participants were then eager and willing to invite friends to the group. They never hid the fact that the group was part of their church, but they emphasized the casual, relational, and safe environment that the group provided and that they met at a pub. Within three weeks the group had grown from approximately five to nearly twenty regular attenders. Because of the safe environment cultivated by the leader's authenticity, teachability, and intentionality, the group was able to cover more topics of significant moral, spiritual, and scriptural depth than any curriculum or lesson plan would have allowed. I'm not saying Bible studies should always be held in bars; but if our mission is to reach and disciple Millennials, then how we do that should be about what *they* need and not about what makes us comfortable.[54]

Focus on the how *and the* why, *not the* what. As we become more willing to engage Millennials in a collaborative process of apprenticeship, we as the masters or coaches need to be willing to approach things differently than we have in the past. If Boomers are designers and Xers are adapters, Millennials are inventors (see "Innovation and Freedom" in chap. 4); they have an amazing ability to think outside the box and come up with new and creative ways of doing things. Let them! You, as the master or coach, still have a responsibility to help them sort through the implications of their new idea or creation, but you should focus on *why* they want to approach ministry or discipleship in a particular way and *how* they are going to go about it rather than getting hung up on *what* they want to do. Go back to our example of a Bible study in a pub—if we are focusing on the *what*, we may be very concerned with the idea that these young people want to have a Bible study in a *bar*! But if we focus on the *why* and the *how*, we see that the motivation is rooted in an understanding of the culture and the target audience, and that the endeavor does not lack structure. Too often churches and ministries become concerned with the fact that "we've never done it that way before," and therefore they cannot see or appreciate that by not changing the *how*, they may actually be hindering or paralyzing the ministry they want.

Conclusion

The very nature of this game and of this cohort makes it more difficult to provide specific examples of "how to." So much of approaching ministry with Millennials comes down to (1) inviting them into the ministry creation and development process and (2) building intentional, authentic, and transparent relationships with them over time. This, by its very nature, cannot be scripted; it must be pursued with prayer, vision, purpose, and flexibility. Engaging the Millennial generation in ministry is not for the faint of heart, the passive, or those unwilling to embark on a new adventure. Ministry to and with Millennials must not be about what makes Boomers and Xers feel comfortable or validated; instead it must be about the game that Millennials are engaged in, on their turf, with the rules of their culture. Those of us in older cohorts

---

54. Meeting in homes, at coffee shops, or at an ice cream parlor rather than on church grounds has often had similar results.

have the privilege and opportunity to invest in this younger cohort in ways that will strengthen our faith, ground them in theirs, and equip them for exponential influence as they reach their culture.

The world that Millennials live in and will continue to engage is very different from the world that Xers and Boomers grew up in. Not only has the game been moved to where Christians have lost the home-field advantage, but the rules of the game have changed. We have gone from flag football to tackle, and as coaches and fans, we must take an active part in helping our Millennial players learn the rules and navigate the new game on new turf.

Conclusion

We hope you have benefited from your tour of the three largest adult generations alive today in the Western, and especially North American, world. We have suggested that understanding generational differences resembles a knowledge of cross-cultural differences. While plenty of other factors go into making each person a unique individual, one that churches and Christian organizations have been slow to reflect on carefully enough is the identity that someone retains by virtue of being a Baby Boomer, a Gen-Xer, or a Millennial. If we want to maximize our effectiveness in reaching people for Christ, discipling them, involving them in our ministries, and/or sending them on for further service elsewhere, we need to take these distinctives into account, just as we pay attention to their ethnicity, gender, birth order, spiritual gifting, and a variety of other factors.

To this end, we divided our book into three main parts, one for each of these three generations. Within each part, we wrote three chapters. The first built on Elisabeth's psychological research and combined that with a wide variety of related studies to sketch a portrait of a typical member of the cohort. The second drew on Craig's expertise as a biblical scholar abreast of his field to suggest strengths and weaknesses of the cohort when evaluated by means of Scripture's teaching. The third involved both of us making suggestions for optimal Christian ministry with and to the generation at hand. We included numerous concrete illustrations so that these chapters would combine the theoretical and the practical, the abstract and the concrete.

Baby Boomers

Baby Boomers, born between 1946 and 1964, have had several decades of major influence in society and today represent the majority of leaders in the government, the private sector, and the church. Overall, they are confident, assertive, optimistic, and at times iconoclastic. They burst onto the scene as young adults, defining themselves over against "the establishment" (sometimes defined as anyone over thirty)! The term "generation gap" was coined to describe the tension and distance they felt from their parents and other older authorities in their lives. In the 2010s most of them form what is today's "establishment" and, at least compared with the cohorts that have come after them, retain more of their parents' hierarchical thinking and behavior than they might always care to acknowledge. As the oldest of them begin to retire, they face some major crises. They are less prepared financially to retire than the generations that immediately preceded them were, and they can look forward to a longer life span and a longer portion of it in good health than their predecessors as well. As a result, many are in denial that major life changes soon await them. Many keep postponing having to face what they should do when their bodies force them to slow down. Some talk and act as if they are virtually immortal. A higher percentage of them participate in organized religion, especially Christianity, than Gen-Xers or Millennials, but the percentage is not as high as it has been for those who lived earlier (and perhaps entirely) in the twentieth century. Boomers have had a strong work ethic, wrapped their identities up closely with their work, proved highly patriotic even to the point of confusing God and country at times, fought for civil rights for minorities and women with a fair measure of success, and trusted in and seen the power of a large group functioning collectively as a force for change in society. They have seen the most amount of technological change in their (obviously longer) life spans. They have been highly materialistic, thinking that the person who dies with the most "toys" (and for them, we are talking big and expensive "toys") wins. Yet they have watched the authorities in their lives go from being largely trustworthy to somewhat more unreliable, seen their employers and the stock market leave them in the lurch, and divorced their spouses and created broken and dysfunctional families at a record pace.

When we assess the Baby Boomers by biblical criteria, we see numerous strengths in this cohort. Boomers' leadership styles have often mirrored scriptural models, even if at times without quite the emphasis on servanthood that we find in the Bible. Boomers have often demonstrated stellar loyalty and commitment to their ideals, values, work, and society. They have harnessed technology to create an interconnected globalized world that their parents could scarcely have dreamed of. Transportation and communication of the gospel and of resources to meet people's physical and spiritual needs have never been easier thanks to their efforts. Nevertheless, they at times rebelled against previous generations unnecessarily. They occasionally elevated faithfulness to country above fidelity to God. They did not always keep their promises to their spouses and, as we have seen, have not always been the best of parents in other respects as well. And they are comparatively unprepared for retirement and death, and especially for standing before God to account for their life choices, including valuing comfort above conscience.

As a result, ministry with and to Boomers had better ramp up reflection and teaching on preparing for an eternity either with Christ and the company of all the redeemed of all time in untainted happiness or apart from God and all things good in unending regret. Even before they pass away, Boomers will have to make hard choices about access to finite amounts of health care and technology, and about downsizing their property and shrinking their world. Stewardship needs to become a higher priority, including but not limited to giving to churches and other Christian organizations. Mentoring members of younger cohorts will prove crucial if Boomers are to leave the best possible legacy and pass on the wisdom they have amassed. They will have to shift their identity increasingly from their work to their Lord, from jobs to churches. Many will be able to utilize their spiritual gifts just as actively as before, and in some cases more so. But they may not be able to count on getting paid (or paid as much) for doing so. Good mentoring methods and a passion for training the younger generations will need to be inculcated. They will benefit from and bless others as they participate in increasingly intergenerational ministry. And they will need to resist the perennial temptation to assume that the methods from their younger years will always be the best ones (if they even were back then!) and instead encourage younger friends and acquaintances to experiment with new models where they show at least some reasonable potential for being effective. Continued orientation toward the future is unhealthy if it prevents Boomers from slowing down when they need to, but not if it keeps them from dwelling on the past and regularly perceiving the present as a decline from the glory days of yesteryear.

Generation X

Gen-Xers were born during the years spanning 1965 to 1981. They experienced nothing of the post–World War II, pre-Vietnam, and pre-Watergate optimism in their youth that Boomers did. By the time they reached wage-earning years, the country's financial optimism had also waned. They never had heroes who didn't fall, and they suffered the consequences of the freedoms Boomers fought for, especially in the areas of sex and the family. AIDS ended the supposedly limitless nature of the sexual revolution, and a record number of Xers grew up in broken homes. Instead of dreaming about changing the world, they set their sights on smaller, seemingly more realistic, local change. Instead of being "loud, proud, and in charge," they worked quietly behind the scenes, waiting for their chances to lead—and many are still waiting. Xers imbibed the rebellion against absolutes of some of their parents but without having the memory of the norms that they were rejecting. They find it harder to make choices and commitments because of that relativism, never knowing whether better options might be around the corner. They are far less inclined to be involved in organized religion than the cohorts preceding them were, but they may well talk about less-defined forms of spirituality that they value. They will conform to norms with which they disagree for the sake of self-preservation, all the while declaring on the inside that they are not really conforming but rather waiting for permission to disclose their independent and more creative streak. Equality for all people and fairness in all undertakings form important Xer values, and personal identity comes only partially from one's job or career. On the job, they do not expect to be micro-managed, especially not to the extent that Boomers were comfortable with. Rather they expect to be given the freedom to complete their tasks however they think is best (on time and with appropriate accountability at the end of the day, to be sure). They are not nearly as motivated by dreams of financial wealth and power, but they can be just as trendy and cliquish around their own (smaller, less expensive) "toys." They are the first generation to be born into a world with consistent access to safe and largely reliable birth control with abortion as a legal backup. They approach the idea of having children with far more apprehension, hesitation, and concern than previous generations, fearful of repeating the poor parenting models they witnessed in their childhoods. On the other hand, environmental concerns and activities have skyrocketed and remain priorities for many Xers.

Evaluated biblically, Xers have strengths and weaknesses just like Boomers do. Their recognition of the fallenness of every human being and their unwillingness to put others on pedestals represent a very biblical assessment of our natures, even if not every Xer would recognize these human flaws as what Christians call "sin." Their recovery of the systemic and structural nature of evil and their concern for the environment and creation care fits well with the Bible's acknowledgment that all creation groans, longing (metaphorically) for its redemption, as a result of the effects of sin. Their suspicion about institutions, including those of organized religion, matches the prophets' frequent frustration with ancient Israel and Jesus's confrontation with the pervasive legalism and/or compromise exhibited by the Jewish leaders of his day. The desire for transparency and authenticity over anything that smacks of showmanship or artificiality, especially in church life, is particularly laudable. On the other hand, Xers' unwillingness to commit lest something better come along represents a self-serving rather than other-serving attitude that conflicts with biblical principles. Worse still is when commitments are made and then broken simply because people prefer happiness over holiness.

The skepticism, relativism, and postmodernism that Xers have grown up with serve them poorly when they fall back on these worldviews and deny what Christianity affirms—that there is a single metanarrative that explains the universe as we know it now and know it to have been in the past. It spans the entire period of time from creation to new creation, and because of its unique emphasis on grace offers humanity a better hope than any other competing religion or ideology. In still other areas, Xer characteristics make for a mixed bag. Community on the local level is important, but not if it means ignoring the global altogether. Recognizing that there is much more to life than work is extremely healthy until it becomes an excuse for laziness or inaction. Social justice is crucial but has no eternal value unless it is accompanied by evangelism. All of life need not be about jobs or ministries, but all must intentionally fit in with kingdom values in some shape or form. One does not have to be a churchgoer to be a Christian, but intentionally turning one's back on all churches is almost never healthy and usually disobedient to God.

Priorities in ministering to and with Xers begin with giving them a chance to lead. They are reaching the stage where they have paid their dues, to use a Boomer value, and it is covert selfishness and arrogance for Boomers to just keep hanging on without giving others opportunities to serve and be trained and mentored. Reaching Xers for Christ and the church requires a realization of how embedded they are in a postmodern worldview. This can be a strength when it comes to hearing individual narratives, especially when believers share their "testimonies" before they have it all "together" but are on good trajectories toward wholeness. It can be a weakness when it prevents people from even considering the possibility of there being a metanarrative, at which point it may be worth highlighting that the claim that there are no absolutes is itself an absolute claim. The position cannot be correct because it is logically incoherent. But it also breaks down experientially, for even the most hardened Xer usually finds an appeal to relativism unsatisfactory if used by other people to justify their harming the Xer. More significant than either of these tacks is the relational approach. We build friends not for the sake of gaining an opportunity to share Jesus but because all people are created in God's image and are of sufficient worth and dignity to make friendship building with them an inherent good. But we naturally share with friends what we most value, so if we are authentic and transparent, we will tell them at some point about how much Jesus means to us. We will avoid distinctively Christian lingo in favor of speaking in ordinary English about issues that affect both believers and unbelievers, but we will share our Christian take on reality in this language as well. Like inviting a person further and further into the more intimate rooms of one's house, one builds a relationship slowly and discusses what is appropriate at each new level of intimacy. In Christian circles, we will be open to the new, creative, and artistic. We will not cling to tradition for tradition's sake, especially if it no longer serves its original purpose. We will pay special attention to traditional, homogeneously grouped ministries, both because Xers don't always want community just with people like themselves but also because it often leaves too many people out who don't fit the conventional categories. We will not continue to promulgate controversial beliefs and practices simply on the grounds that the Bible teaches them (or is against them), but we will support our convictions with the best rationales we can offer.

Millennials

Millennials were born between 1982 and 2001. Most of their parents were Boomers. Because Boomers on the whole longed for a better relationship with their parents, including less top-down parenting, they have often overreacted by trying to make their children more like friends than like the next generation needing to be trained. As a result, Millennials often really love their parents and don't try to create a generation gap. But they have not always been brought up with adequate discipline, with consistent instruction in centuries-old, cross-cultural truths about what produces growth into healthy adulthood.

Millennials have been affirmed by parents, schools, and educational TV, and told in essence they can do and become anything they want. Some have an attitude of entitlement; many are at least expectant and optimistic about the future. As Millennials come of age, however, they discover the harsher realities of the working world. Employers do not give raises irrespective of performance the way schools gave continuation ceremonies to mark a child's passing from one grade to the next. For a host of reasons, including the lack of opportunity in the workforce even for competent Millennials, adolescence is being increasingly delayed, even up to age thirty. Millennials are likewise marrying and having children noticeably later than in previous generations.

Even in Christian circles, Millennials have difficulty affirming absolute truth because nothing in the rest of society has prepared them for it. More than any other cohort, they report their feelings and convictions as strictly their own and not necessarily anyone else's. Growing up entirely in the internet age, they are aware of how available information is but also how they can find a contradictory claim to virtually any assertion by someone potentially worthy of respect. Millennials are more self-focused, look for tribes of like-minded friends, but insist on tolerance of all kinds of viewpoints and lifestyles. While cherishing individuality and freedom, they also require affirmation more than previous cohorts and expect feedback of all kinds to their work. So far, though, work is less central for them than for past generations. The same is true for organized religion in general and Christianity in particular, with important exceptions. Where there is a renewed interest in church, it is often for the more liturgical forms from which many Boomers fled.

Like the Boomers and Xers, Millennials exhibit both strengths and weaknesses when measured by biblical criteria. They have appropriately valued families of origin in ways that neither Boomers nor Xers adequately did. Given half a chance, they will respect the authorities in their life. It is not their fault that older generations didn't always give them enough of a "kick in the pants" to go along with their nurture and love. Nor is it their fault that social conditions often prevent them from maturing beyond adolescence as early as people used to. To the extent that they refuse to discriminate against others, avoiding the racism, sexism, or ethnocentrism of older cohorts, they model biblical teaching well. To the extent that their appreciation of diversity mirrors the Scripture's teaching on the diversity of spiritual gifts and not trying to remake each other into our own image, they should be commended. But when tolerance and diversity extend to what the Bible calls sin, problems emerge. Even then, they recognize that harsh or confrontational approaches rarely win sinners over from the errors of their ways these days. But if they decide simply to "live and let live" without ever building the relationships that allow for the serious conversations about behavior that Scripture deems harmful (even if the effects are not immediately obvious), then they have abdicated important, God-given responsibilities. If the future is as bright as God promises, an optimistic, expectant spirit is a positive, but it becomes a negative when it turns into entitlement or narcissism. When they cherish and give praise for genuinely good accomplishments, they are more in sync with the Bible than the Boomers' view that no news is good news and that feedback is only warranted if it is negative. When that praise extends to things that do not merit it, then they undercut the ability to give or receive meaningful acclaim for the things that are worthy of acclaim. The exclusivism of the gospel was a scandal in the very relativistic, pluralistic world of first-century Rome, as Judaism had been before it. Those who would be faithful to Jesus as their

Lord today will have to come to grips with that scandal. But Millennials can help us be sure that it is the scandal of the cross and not of more peripheral items that cause people to reject Christ if they choose to do so.

"Intergenerational ministry" may need to be the first and last term to stress with respect to the Millennial generation. The era of the effectiveness of homogeneous groupings characterizing virtually every phase of church life is quickly passing; will church leaders make note and adjust accordingly? Will Xer and Boomer leaders give the mentoring and affirmation needed to cultivate the gifting of Millennials, including them in leadership teams and decision-making groups to maximize the impact of their organizations? Instead of bemoaning the fact that twenty-five-year-olds remind them of their peers when they were seventeen, will they adjust and use all of the appropriate training methods for people at that younger stage of faith development so that the Millennials grow into all that God wants them to be, even if it takes eight more years than it used to? The chances are good that the Millennials will live eight years longer anyway! Will people in every age of influence work toward stage-four and stage-five levels of faith development, recognizing that older cohorts may have matured in other respects more quickly but still lack adequate maturity in faith development that younger people can attain earlier? Can churches re-envision their mandate according to the Great Commission in its entirety so that ministry extends from "the womb to the tomb"? Will they understand that ministry is not primarily about getting people to cross the threshold of faith and then expecting them to mature on their own or according to some uniform program? Will they prepare Millennials for being exiles in their own lands, as Christians in other parts of the world have often already learned how to be? Will we all address the hardest questions of our day and age, recognizing the answers are not always clear-cut? Will we leave space for people to express healthy doubts but also recognize that two thousand years of church history have produced remarkably satisfying answers to just about every "big-picture" question there is? Will we take the time to familiarize ourselves with those answers and not think we always have to reinvent the wheel?

Looking to the Future

As with any broad-brush survey, it would be easy to react to our book the way students in colleges and grad schools respond the first week of a new term with "syllabus shock." No ministry can do everything we have suggested, and some of our recommendations may not even be appropriate in certain contexts. No one can make all the necessary changes overnight, even where it would be good for them to change. A better analogy here rather than the American higher educational system, which tends to spell out every reading assignment in every class in precise detail, would be the British university model. There, students are intentionally given reading lists far longer than anyone could hope to complete—much less master—in a given semester. The idea is for the students to familiarize themselves with a representative sampling of the reading, making specific choices according to their particular interests, passions, and specializations. Our book has not been particularly a "how-to" manual but rather a manifesto for reflection on key areas in generational life that deeply impact Christian life, individually and corporately. Even if you choose only one topic that we have discussed and do something meaningful with it, we believe you will be the richer for it. Many people will most likely recognize several areas in which they are already adopting or adapting the principles we have articulated. But hopefully they will also discover one or more areas they haven't thought as much about and can turn some of their attention to those arenas.

Unlike some doomsayers, we are optimistic about the future of the church. Jesus himself promised to build it so that even the powers of death and hell could not defeat it. It will come and go in different forms in different places, and parts of the world in which it is strong or weak will vary over time. We offer our observations and suggestions out of the conviction that utilizing a cross section of them will, with the Lord's help and through the power of the Spirit, optimize the growth and impact of Christ's church and his kingdom in our day and age. We welcome your responses and pray that God will be pleased with our work and use it for his glory.

Scripture Index

Subject Index

Aamodt, Sandra, 158n41
abandonment, 36
abortion, 55, 134n62, 170, 206
absentee parenting, 100
absolutes, 88–89, 107, 118, 124–26, 138, 141,
    159, 181
academia, 97
accountability, 5
activism, 5, 11, 77, 140
Acton, Lord John, 118
Adam, 28, 115, 116, 120, 134
addiction, 31
Adlerian theory, 233n24
adolescence, 204, 258
adultery, 36
adulthood, 158, 175, 204
advertising, 68
advocacy, 140
affirmation, 51–52, 177, 216–18
"affluenza," 62
ageism, 67–69, 205
age of accountability, 222
aging, 60
agnosticism, 133
Alpha Course, 151n28
"already-and-not-yet," 120, 213
altruism, 117–18
Alzheimer's disease, 73
"Amazing Grace," 217
ambition, 189
American culture, 1
American military, 45, 172
American society, xvn5

amillennialism, 76
Anderson, Norman, 219
angst, 83
antagonism, 178
anti-institutionalism, 120
anxiety, 121–22n30, 186–87, 190
apologetics, 237
apology, 243
apostasy, 72
apprenticeship, 46, 154, 247–50
Arminianism, 72, 116, 220, 229
atheism, 133
authenticity, 106, 133, 143–44, 145, 149, 238,
    248
authority, 11, 155, 179, 191
    distrust of, 23
    expectations of, 12–13
autonomy, 124

Baby Boomers (1946–1964), xv, xvii, 253–55
    in church, 22–24
    church life of, 67–70
    in community, 10–13
    at home, 19–22
    place in the world, 2–6
    values of, 6–9, 34–41
    at work, 13–18
bait-and-switch, 147
Bakker, Jim, 87
Barna Group, 235n29
Barney (TV show), 170
Bauckham, Richard, 140n7
beauty, 160